COLONIAL DEBTS

RADICAL AMÉRICAS A SERIES EDITED BY
BRUNO BOSTEELS AND GEORGE CICCARIELLO-MAHER

COLONIAL DEBTS

THE CASE OF PUERTO RICO ROCÍO ZAMBRANA

DUKE UNIVERSITY PRESS
DURHAM AND LONDON 2021

Printed in the United States of America on acid-free paper ∞
Designed by Aimee C. Harrison
Typeset in Warnock Pro and ITC Franklin Gothic
by Westchester Publishing Services

LIBRARY OF CONGRESS CATALOGING-IN-PUBLICATION DATA
Names: Zambrana, Rocío, author.
Title: Colonial debts : the case of Puerto Rico / Rocío Zambrana.
Other titles: Radical Américas.
Description: Durham : Duke University Press, 2021. | Series: Radical
Américas | Includes bibliographical references and index.
Identifiers: LCCN 2020040152 (print) | LCCN 2020040153 (ebook)
ISBN 9781478010722 (hardcover)
ISBN 9781478011835 (paperback)
ISBN 9781478013198 (ebook)
Subjects: LCSH: Debts, Public—Puerto Rico. | Budget deficits—Puerto
Rico. | Fiscal policy—Puerto Rico. | Postcolonialism—Economic
aspects—Puerto Rico. | Puerto Rico—Economic conditions—1952– |
Puerto Rico—Economic policy. | United States—Economic policy.
Classification: LCC HJ8543 .Z36 2021 (print) | LCC HJ8543 (ebook) | DDC
336.3/4097295—dc23
LC record available at https://lccn.loc.gov/2020040152
LC ebook record available at https://lccn.loc.gov/2020040153

ISBN 9781478091714 (ebook/other)

Cover art: BEMBA PR, *Isla Cancelada*, 2018. Courtesy of the artists.

This book is freely available in an open access edition thanks to TOME
(**Toward an Open Monograph Ecosystem**)—a collaboration of the
Association of American Universities, the Association of University
Presses, and the Association of Research Libraries—and the generous
support of Emory University and the Andrew W. Mellon Foundation.
Learn more at the TOME website, available at: **openmonographs.org**.

For Gabriela

CONTENTS

ACKNOWLEDGMENTS

EVERYTHING IN THIS BOOK WAS MADE POSSIBLE by Anayra Santory-Jorge's philosophical mentorship and friendship. As my first philosophy professor at the University of Puerto Rico, Mayagüez, she taught me what philosophy could do if it was taken beyond its disciplinary boundaries and institutional constraints. I am deeply indebted to the reflections we have shared throughout the past twenty years. Ronald Mendoza de Jesús and María del Rosario Acosta were indispensable interlocutors as I wrote this book. Without their philosophical and political love and friendship this book would not have been written. Our conversations made my thinking richer and my writing sharper. Yarimar Bonilla became a vital interlocutor as I produced various drafts of the book. I thank her energy, support, and friendship. I am deeply grateful for Shariana Ferrer-Núñez's political and intellectual insight, inspiration, and friendship. I saw Ariadna Godreau-Aubert speak in fall 2016 and continue to find invaluable keys in her writing.

Nelson Maldonado-Torres gave important feedback and offered support at various junctures. I am also grateful.

I have been gifted with interlocutors far and wide. In and from Puerto Rico and at the University of Puerto Rico, I am indebted to conversations and exchanges with Ryan Mann-Hamilton, Giovanni Roberto, Sofía Gallisá Muriente, Sarah Molinari, Pedro Lebrón, Marisol LeBrón, Aurora Santiago-Ortiz, Jorell Meléndez-Badillo, Luis Othoniel Rosa, Nicole Cecilia Delgado, Raquel Salas Rivera, Miguel Rodríguez-Casellas, Juan Carlos "Juanqui" Rivera-Ramos, Alejandro Quinteros, Marina Moscoso, José Atiles-Osoria, Miriam Muñiz-Varela, Mabel Rodríguez-Centeno, Cesar Pérez-Lizasuain, Beatriz Llenín-Figueroa, Patricia Noboa-Ortega, Adriana Garriga-López, Gustavo García-López, Erika Fontánez-Torres, Zaire Dinzey-Flores, Mariana del Alba López, Luis Alberto Zambrana, Bernat Tort, Eva Prados, Deepak Lamba-Nieves, Federico Cintrón Moscoso, Federico Cintrón Fillao, Carlos Rojas-Osorio, Marta Torres, Dialitza Colón, among others, including Frank Gaud with whom I shared conversations over a 16-year period. Students in my Pensamiento y Feminismo Descolonial seminar at the University of Puerto Rico in fall 2018, especially Aliana Coello and Ruth Figueroa, were important dialogue partners as well. I presented early versions of chapters at the Seminario de Filosofía Ludwig Schajowicz at the University of Puerto Rico, Río Piedras, and at an event organized by Corporación Cultural Educativa y de Estudios Interdisciplinarios (CEDEI). I was honored to share reflections developed in this book at la Colectiva Feminista en Construcción's Escuela Feminista Radical (ESFRA) in May 2020.

At the University of Oregon, I am grateful for Bonnie Mann, Scott Pratt, Beata Stawarska, Camisha Russell, and Erin Mckenna's support and enthusiasm, and for conversations about debt, Hurricane María, and Puerto Rico with Alaí Reyes-Santos, Cecilia Enjuto-Rangel, and Mayra Bottaro. I thank the Center for the Study of Women in Society's Women of Color Project, especially Michelle McKinley, Sangita Gopal, Gabriela Martínez, and Lynn Fujiwara, for feedback on and support of the project. Anita Chari's love, friendship, and intelligence, as well as Michael Allan's and Sergio Rigolleto's, sustained me throughout the transitions that writing this book entailed. I thank Óscar Ralda, Eli Portella, Rosa O'Connor Acevedo, and students in my Women of Color Feminisms seminar and in my courses on Marx, for probing questions. I am indebted to Juan Sebastián Ospina for indispensable work on the manuscript and engaging conversation about its contents. I thank my new colleagues at Emory for enthusiasm about the book and Jason Walsh for help preparing the manuscript to go into production.

ACKNOWLEDGMENTS

I spent winter 2018 at Northwestern University. I thank Jorge Coronado, Penny Deustcher, Alejandra Uslengh, Peter Fenves, Marlon Millner, Eli Lichtenstein, and students in my courses on decolonial thought and on debt for thoughtful conversations. I am deeply grateful for conversations with Ramón Rivera-Servera, Zorimar Rivera-Montes, and Arnaldo Rodríguez-Bagué that began at an event at Northwestern. During my time in Chicago, conversations with Alejandra Azuero Quijano were important. I thank Andy Clarno for generating rich dialogue by organizing "Hurricane María and the Crisis of Colonialism," at University of Illinois, Chicago. I presented various versions of this work at the New School for Social Research. I am grateful, as always, for Jay Bernstein, Dick Bernstein, Nancy Fraser, Cinzia Arruza, and Chiara Botticci's questions and support. I am indebted to REC Latinoamérica, in particular Alejandro Cortés and Jaime Santamaría, for engaging conversations. I thank Santiago Castro Gómez for his insightful comments on early drafts of parts of the book, to Ochy Curiel for incisive questions at REC's first congress on Latin American and Caribbean Thought, and to Agustín Laó-Montes for his interest. Conversations with Celenis Rodríguez Moreno while I was preparing the book to go into production made key arguments of the book clearer and sharper. I am forever grateful for our encounter. I thank Natalia Brizuela, Samera Esmir, Wendy Brown, and Judith Butler for incisive questions and comments during a visit to Berkeley. I am indebted to conversations with Verónica Gago and Luci Cavallero. I shared various spaces with Pedro DiPietro and Yala Kisukidi while I presented this work and am thankful for the opportunity to learn from them.

I began to write this book in 2016 after a detour: from Foucault, power, and US colonial rule in Puerto Rico, a project I began around 2000 at the University of Puerto Rico, Mayagüez, to Hegel, Marx, and critical theory as I unwittingly became a diasporic subject in New York, then Oregon, and now Atlanta. Writing this book was a return when actual prospects of return narrowed by the day. The first writing on Puerto Rico since the 2000 BA thesis was done around 2012. I began to write the book itself in fall 2016, while on sabbatical at the University of Puerto Rico, Río Piedras. That summer, Supreme Court cases had announced the death of the Estado Libre Asociado (ELA) and the US Congress passed the Puerto Rico Oversight, Management, and Economic Stability Act (PROMESA) instituting a Fiscal Control Board that arguably returned Puerto Rico to a form of pre-ELA colonialism. I finished a first draft in 2017, just as Hurricane María marked us all in deep and deeply different ways. Revisions to the second draft of the book were completed in the aftermath of #RickyRenuncia. In writing about events unfolding, I attempted to document and understand, centering the voices of those acting and writing in Puerto Rico. In that process, I have been gifted somewhat of a return. The love of my family has been essential in this process. They welcome me time and again as I go back and forth from Puerto Rico and the United States. Nadya Marie García, my mother, models love—unyielding, complex, forever present. My sister, Elimari Zambrana, extends memory and laughter. Giancarlo Burgos, my nephew, is full of kindness. Gabriela Mercado, my niece, has been my friend, my daughter, my sister. I am sustained by her love. This book is for her.

I am grateful for George Ciccariello-Maher and Bruno Bosteels's excitement about the manuscript. I thank Courtney Berger for her interest and enthusiasm as well as her editorial insight. At Emory, I am grateful to Sarah McKee for her interest in publishing the book in Open Access through TOME, and to Emory University and the Andrew W. Mellon Foundation for generous financial support. I thank referees for invaluable feedback. The opening sections of chapter 3 and the conclusion, as well as parts of the last section of chapter 1, are translations of my columns for *8ogrados*, "Rendir cuentas, pasarle la cuenta," "Vida póstuma," and "Feminicidio e institucionalidad." Material from the first section of chapter 4, Pasarse Políticamente, first appeared in "Pasarse Políticamente—Interrupting Neoliberal Temporalities in Puerto Rico," in María del Rosario Acosta and Gustavo Quintero's *Collective Temporalities and the Construction of the Future*, a special issue of *Diacritics*. The last section of the conclusion, Organizing Pessimism, appeared in "Deudas coloniales/Colonial Debts," in Sara Nadal-Melisó's *Una Proposición modesta: Puerto Rico a prueba/A Modest Proposal: Puerto Rico's Crucible*. Funding for *Colonial Debts* during 2016–17 was made possible by the Ford Foundation.

INTRODUCTION COLONIAL DEBTS

"coats are not exchanged for coats"

let us take two commodities such as
50 years of work and one debt
accumulated over 50 years.

as proprietor of the first
you decide to take it to caribe hilton banking
where *i offer my life to pay this debt*.

but they explain that *it's not enough*

> just as the debt and the fifty years of work have use-values that
> are *qualitatively different,* so are the two forms of labor that
> produce them: that of the investor and that of the colonized.
> your life is not enough. you will have to pay with the labor of your
> children and your children's children.

let's say you tell them *i never had any because*
i never wanted to make heirs of those who
barely know the difference
between milk and coquito.

but they explain that even if you don't have a lineage
your neighbors, the dog that plunders your trash,
doña sophia with her luminous rosary,
your abuela that barely leaves the house to go to the pharmacy,
angelía that still awaits your book,
luis that finally has a job but still has debts to pay,
that guy who mugged you for ten bucks
will inherit.

imagine
that you come back with your neighbors,
with your abuela, with the dog
that sometimes searches your trash,
with angelía, with luis, and say
here are my heirs.
do you accept our payment?
will you terminate our debt?
will you erase our names from the system?

but they say
where are the rivers?
el río guajataca, el río camuy,

el río cibuco,   el río bayamón,

el río puerto nuevo,   el río grande de loíza,

el río herrera,   el río mameyes,

el río sabana,   el río fajardo,

el río daguao,   el río santiago,

el río blanco,   el río humacao,

el río seco,   el río maunabo,

etc. etc. etc.

they will be your heirs.
—RAQUEL SALAS RIVERA, *lo terciario / the tertiary*

IN JULY 2019, two weeks of protest ousted Governor Ricardo "Ricky" Rosselló. On July 12, the Centro de Periodismo Investigativo (Center for Investigative Reporting) released 889 pages of a Telegram thread in which Rosselló interacted with his closest advisors.[1] The publication of the messages came days after the FBI arrested top government officials, including the Secretary of Education charged with mishandling $15.5 million during a two-year tenure in which 438 schools were closed. Not all eleven men Rosselló affectionately called "brothers" on the Telegram chat were government officials. The brothers discussed public policy and corporate interests as well as public perception in the media and social media. They traded misogynist, homophobic, transphobic, racist, classist "jokes," expletives, and memes. They discussed suppressing information regarding hurricane relief and recovery. They made light of the deaths of Hurricane María. The chat revealed overall apathy for ordinary Puerto Ricans navigating economic downturn and steep austerity measures for over a decade.

For two weeks, people took to the streets. Overcoming political divisions, indignation was expressed with astounding diversity and celebrated creativity: marches, motorized caravans, *cacerolazos* (on the street and in the home), combative dance (from *perreo* to salsa), renamed streets (physically and on Google Maps).[2] These, among other forms of protest, were met with the unconstitutional clearing of the streets of Old San Juan at 11 p.m., with tear gas, with a police force reinforced by the Fuerza de Choque (Tactical Operations Unit) and correctional officers.[3] Rosselló resigned late evening July 24. Indignation, indeed rage, *rabia*, interrupted an impunity evident in the chat. *La generación que no se deja* (the generation that won't take it) made clear that *la era de conformarnos con el menos malo* (the era of settling for the lesser evil) was over. Protestors subverted the brothers' misogynist, homophobic, racist, and classist tropes and expletives: *los criminales usan corbata* (criminals wear ties), *siempre putxs/patxs, nunca pillx* (always a "whore"/queer, never a robber).[4] The success of #RickyRenuncia transitioned to already developing *asambleas de pueblo* (town assemblies). The asambleas might be seen as a form of prefigurative politics, modeling political participation yet to come.[5] As Yarimar Bonilla put it in field notes shared on Facebook, "Assemblies are not imagined as [an] event but as communities: they have Facebook pages and demands. They are emerging as new political constituencies."[6] The assemblies as well as the protests can be seen as building on the "silent coup" (*toma silenciosa de poder*), as

I.1 & I.2 San Juan, Puerto Rico, July 2019. Photo from Luis Othoniel Rosa's Facebook page.

I.3 & I.4
San Juan,
Puerto Rico,
July 2019. Photo
from Luis
Othoniel Rosa's
Facebook page.

I.5 San Juan, Puerto Rico, July 2019. Photo from Luis Othoniel Rosa's Facebook page.

I.6 Caguas, Puerto Rico. Asamblea de Pueblo (town assembly), August 3, 2019. Photo by Rocío Zambrana.

Bonilla puts it elsewhere, that varieties of *autogestión*, "autonomous organizing" or "mutual aid," have performed in the wake of María.[7]

On September 20, 2017, Category 4 Hurricane María made landfall in Puerto Rico.[8] Debilitated by Hurricane Irma two weeks prior, Puerto Rico's infrastructure collapsed. The electrical grid, water distribution and filtration systems, and the telecommunications network were severely compromised. Throughout the months that followed, the humanitarian crisis unfolding given the effects of a decade of austerity measures intensified. To different degrees, Puerto Ricans faced difficult mobility or outright isolation due to debris, collapsed bridges and roads, and flooding. They faced limited communication in addition to water, gas, and food shortages. People sought water in superfund sites.[9] Calls made to 911 reporting domestic violence tripled.[10] Members of the trans community faced discrimination at refuge centers and lost access to hormone replacement therapy (HRT) for months.[11] Eleven months after María, it was reported that the last family without electricity regained service.[12] Many homes never received tarps from the Federal Emergency Management Agency (FEMA), compounding damages from subsequent rains and flooding. Many FEMA and insurance claims remain outstanding, given misinformation, language barriers, and lack of property titles required by federal law, despite the fact that there is no requirement to hold a title and register property in Puerto Rico.[13]

Federal and local government response was plagued by mismanagement, inefficiency, and corruption. The Jones Act, which regulates maritime commerce, was suspended for only ten days, hindering relief efforts considerably.[14] Throughout 2018, shipping containers, *vagones*, filled with expired provisions were found in abandoned lots, thousands of water bottles were left to rot on an airport tarmac, dead bodies were revealed to have been stacked in shipping containers if not buried in backyards.[15] It is estimated that 4,645 people died as a result of the hurricane, exceeding the official death count raised in August 2018 from 64 at first to 1,427 and then to 2,975.[16] An epidemic of leptospirosis occurred in the aftermath of María, despite denials from government officials.[17] Around 200,000 people left the territory in the wake of María, with an estimated 130,000 relocating permanently.[18] The president of the United States famously hurled paper towels at a crowd of survivors in the immediate aftermath, purportedly gesturing aid distribution, and stated that the US budget was "thrown out of whack" by the devastation. These gestures were the beginning of various attacks on Puerto Rico on Twitter. María clarified not only a humanitarian crisis underway, given a decade of austerity. It brought to light the depths

I.7 Humacao, Puerto Rico, September 27, 2017. Photo from *Metro Puerto Rico*.

I.8 Ceiba, Puerto Rico. 23,040,000 bottles of water found on tarmac, *El Vocero*, September 18, 2018. Photo from *El Vocero*.

of an unequal distribution of precariousness along race/gender/class lines in the territory. The Telegram chat, however, laid bare a well-functioning necropolitical state. It disproved the view that the debt crisis and mishandled hurricane relief and recovery index an absent state.

In February 2018, the now destitute Ricky Rosselló announced that Puerto Rico is "open for business."[19] The "aspiration" for rebuilding Puerto Rico was to be a "blank canvas for innovation."[20] Seeking to attract investors eager to take advantage of opportunities offered by a collapsed infrastructure, the governor stressed the benefits of the ambiguities of the territorial status.[21] As an unincorporated territory of the United States, political and economic rights and regulations in effect in states are lacking in Puerto Rico. Rosselló also highlighted the advantages of Puerto Rico's political economy under US colonial rule. Tax-exempt foreign investment has been the pillar of economic development for this unincorporated territory since 1917.[22] In addition to exemptions on corporate investment and bonds, Act 20/22 of 2012 offers wealthy individuals from the United States tax haven conditions in real estate. Rosselló further underscored the flexibility made possible by austerity measures. The 2017 labor reform reduced benefits and sick leave, increased probationary periods, facilitated layoffs, and lowered wages. A then pending education reform, health care revisions, and reduced allocations to municipalities and the public university system were framed as "right sizing" efforts favorable for investment.[23]

Rather than an expression of disaster capitalism, Rosselló's response indexes the relation of colonialism and coloniality distinctive to the case of Puerto Rico.[24] Minimally, colonialism refers to a form of juridico-political control. Aníbal Quijano's decolonial framework offers the notion of "coloniality of power," *colonialidad del poder*, which refers to a race/gender/class hierarchy posited by a colonial history but that exceeds colonialism as a juridico-political relation.[25] The concept of coloniality names the "afterlife," to borrow Saidiya Hartman's term, of the colonial project of capitalist modernity in postcolonial contexts.[26] It names the race/gender/class hierarchy installed by this project but that continues, rearticulated, in altered historical and material conditions. As an unincorporated territory of the United States, as a colony of the United States, the case of Puerto Rico presses us to consider the continuation of the colonial condition in its afterlife. The actualization of race/gender as the central technology of modernity/coloniality is guided by the operation of capital in its specificity, in the present juncture, neoliberal financialized capitalism. Ariadna Godreau-Aubert puts it best in a set of passages that I return to various times throughout this book: "The colony is what happens [*transcurre*] in 'repeated acts of capture.'"[27] "Indebted life," she adds, "is the continuation of colonial life."

Puerto Rico currently holds $74 billion of bond debt and $49 billion in unfunded pension obligations. Puerto Rico's $123 billion debt is the largest municipal debt in US history. In May 2017, Puerto Rico filed for bankruptcy under Title III of PROMESA.[28] This 2016 federal law instituted a

Fiscal Control Board. *La Junta*, as the board is known in the territory, is tasked with achieving fiscal responsibility and regaining access to capital markets. Debt restructuring is coupled with austerity, privatization, and other modes of dispossession in the board's efforts to ensure that creditors are repaid, that Puerto Rico's good standing is regained. The US-appointed board can override local government decisions that conflict with its aims, despite the fact that Puerto Rico has no voting representation in Congress and cannot cast a presidential vote. If filing for bankruptcy delegates some power to US District Court Judge Laura Taylor Swain, it nevertheless underscores the fact that the US Congress remains the seat of juridico-political sovereignty despite the creation of the Estado Libre Asociado in 1952. Restructuring deals for the Urgent Interest Fund Corporation (Corporación del Fondo de Interés Apremiante, COFINA) and Puerto Rico Electric Power Authority (Autoridad de Energía Eléctrica, PREPA) but also the bankruptcy plan unveiled in September 2019 not only mortgaged Puerto Rico's future. They have traded with life itself, raising utility costs, intensifying regressive taxation, and lowering or eliminating pensions. The deals and plan have been formulated and reached without an audit, despite a legal and political movement demanding an independent audit, particularly a citizen audit, since at least 2015.

Debt functions as a form of coloniality, I argue in the chapters that follow. In the Americas, as we will see in chapter 3, the independence debt France and its allies levied on Haiti in response to the successful slave revolt that founded the first black republic in the hemisphere is the first case of debt as an apparatus that continues the colonial condition.[29] In contemporary Puerto Rico, the focus of this book, debt actualizes, updates, reinstalls the colonial condition. However, it does so in ways that run deeper than the imposition of a Fiscal Control Board. It does more than further erode the purported sovereignty established by the Estado Libre Asociado, revealed to be none most recently by the 2016 US Supreme Court's *Puerto Rico v. Sanchez Valle* ruling. Debt functions as an apparatus of capture, predation, extraction in neoliberal financialized capitalism, according to Maurizio Lazzarato. It is a key apparatus for the creation and extraction of value in financialized capitalism, yet one that requires states for its actualization. As an apparatus of capture, I add, the operation of debt involves expulsion, dispossession, and precarization through which race/gender/class hierarchies are deepened, intensified, posited anew. Debt lands, *aterriza*, as Verónica Gago and Luci Cavallero suggest, on bodies and populations. Debt's operation, its landing, I add, should be understood more precisely as a form of coloni-

†

ESTADO LIBRE ASOCIADO

(ELA)

1952-2016

"NI PAN, NI TIERRA, NI LIBERTAD"

Agradecemos al país que, de alguna u otra forma, soportó 64 años de limbo político. Que el espíritu de la autodeterminación ilumine cada uno de nuestros corazones e infunda, asimismo, valor para encarar lo que parece imposible. Descansa en paz.

Proyecto ELA I-ELA/No la ki/día: Albdo Burn /X 9/0

I.9 Satirical obituary for ELA. "'Neither bread, nor land, nor liberty.' We are grateful to the country that has in one way or another withstood 64 years of political limbo. May the spirit of self-determination illuminate each of our hearts and give us courage to do the impossible. RIP." *Primera hora*, (daily newspaper), July 24, 2016. Translation by Adriana Garriga-López.

ality. It actualizes, adapts, reinscribes race/gender/class posited by the history of colonial violence that produced the modern capitalist world. Debt does so responding to altered material and historical conditions, building on rather than annihilating difference, incommensurability, heterogeneity in the very reproduction of life—in labor, authority, subjectivity. Debt, then, is key to the rearticulation/reinstallation of colonial life in the current economic-political juncture. In the case of Puerto Rico, the afterlife of the colonial world posits the colonial condition, the territorial status, anew. It does so by actualizing the work of race/gender/class evident in the unequal distribution of precariousness, dispossession, and violence in the territory.

This book aims to understand the operation of coloniality in the colony, centering the political economy that guides their relation in the present. This book also explores multiple attempts to interrupt this operation, considering variations of decolonial praxis in the territory. Two conceptual perspectives guide these aims. They are approximations to the language of "operation" and "interruption" central to the discussions that follow. The term *operation* seeks to name the effectivity—the work, the productivity—of an apparatus, norm, political-economic rationality, mode of perceiving and sensing but also desiring that articulate the world of capital/coloniality.[30] These do so in the very material organization of existence, of binding existence in certain ways rather than others. They do so within the very reproduction of life, including the body, sensation, frameworks of sense but also land, the city, the ocean, the other.[31] Far from abstract, these are fundamentally concrete, heterogeneous, and simultaneous, as we will see. The operation of debt as an apparatus of capture, predation, dispossession, and expulsion, for example, is only clarified by the ways it lands on racialized/gendered bodies and populations. For this reason, we cannot speak of debt abstractly. We cannot speak of the creditor-debtor relation universally. We can offer a feminist reading of debt, as we will also see, but in the case of Puerto Rico it will require specifying debt's intensification of a racial hierarchy posited by the territory's multiple colonial histories.

"Interruption," on the other hand, seeks to name attempts to turn coloniality inoperative.[32] The variations of protest I examine draw from material conditions at specific political-economic junctures, seeking to seize the power to bind in order to articulate those conditions anew. That binding life anew, that organizing life in its very reproduction anew, that rearticulation of sensibility itself anew requires unbinding the world posited by capital/coloniality. As Frantz Fanon argues, "Decolonization, which sets out to change the order of the world, is clearly an agenda for total disorder."[33] These protests employ tactics of subversion, inversion, refusal, and rescue/occupation aimed at interrupting the operation of debt.[34] Specifically, they seek to turn the work of productivity, propriety, and private property central to the reproduction of capital/coloniality inoperative. They do so by inhabiting the strictures of debt, especially the injunction to repay and the positions of power it generates in the creditor-debtor relation. They also subvert or refuse the deferral involved in binding subjects and populations to determined conditions. Acts of subversion or refusal can aid the effectivity of coloniality/capital, to be sure. They can intensify rather than dismantle race/gender/class hierarchies within and through contexts of contestation, opposition, protest. Subversion or refusal that targets the work of race/gender/class even in a fraught political terrain, in contrast, interrupts, aiming to short-circuit their productivity here and now. The results are inevitably complex, as subversion and refusal entail forms of complicity that admit of simple cooption. The point is that complicity is often tactical, hence at the ready to respond to neoliberal cooptation.

The language of operation and interruption stem from two conceptual perspectives that emerge from the current predicament, as mentioned above. First, while I consider the current economic-political downturn as the relation of colonialism and coloniality in the territory, it is important to underscore that the notion of coloniality does not track the legacy of the colonial violence that produced the modern capitalist world. The claim is stronger. Coloniality names the operation of contemporary capitalism's organization of existence by reproducing modalities of colonial violence that installed the modern capitalist world centuries ago. Hartman's notion of the afterlife of slavery, also rendered as the afterlife of property, is helpful here. It specifies the persistence of slavery in the present in the fact that "black lives are still imperiled and devalued by a racial calculus and a political arithmetic that were entrenched centuries ago."[35] She writes that "[t]his is the afterlife of slavery—skewed life chances, limited access to health and education, premature death, incarceration, and impoverishment." Elsewhere she adds that the afterlife of property is "the detritus of lives with which we have yet to attend, a past that has yet to be done, and the ongoing state of emergency in which black life remains in peril."[36] The afterlife of slavery/property is not a legacy, then, if by legacy we understand the result of something past or passed on. It is rather an operating rationality and sensibility organizing the very reproduction of life through the attrition of life in the present. In the case of Puerto Rico, in the life of the colonized, skewed life chances and spectacular forms of violence are both also part of the ordinary. Both index the productivity of colonial violence in the present. The present *is* the past, then, in altered material-historical conditions.

I do not want to suggest that Hartman's exposition of the continuation of a racial calculus that imperils black lives in the United States today is simply transferable to the case of Puerto Rico, however. This would run the risk of rendering invisible different histories in need of exposition, although I insist that centering the afterlife of slavery and hence the antiblack violence that structures race/gender/class hierarchies in Puerto Rico today is crucial.[37] I want to expand on this key moment in Hartman to understand the backward positing of the work of coloniality in the colony. Nelson Maldonado-Torres argues that coloniality represents a "veritable metaphysical catastrophe." Coloniality posits a world to the measure of colonial violence at the level of power, being, knowledge, and sensing. The technology of race/gender produces ideas of the human and nonhuman in the organization of labor, in the production of subjectivity and knowledge, in the articulation of political authority. It functions by establishing populations racialized as nonwhite as subject to ubiquitous violence in such articulation of existence. The race/gender norm, as María Lugones puts it, works as a tool to "damn" the colonized by establishing a lack of proximity to humanity.[38] I discuss these concepts in detail in the chapters that follow. The point here is that coloniality operates as a backward positing. The metaphysical catastrophe that coloniality represents, Maldonado-Torres writes, is "informed by and helped to advance the demographic catastrophes of indigenous genocide in the Americas and the middle passage, as well as racial slavery, among other forms of massacre and systematic dehumanization in the early modern world."[39] The productivity, the ongoing effectivity or work, of the infrastructures of sense put in place by catastrophes of demographic nature, I argue, represent the actualization and thereby reinstallation of the colonial project of capitalist modernity at the metaphysical level. They represent the positing of the world to the measure of colonial violence anew, in light of altered material and historical conditions. In the case of Puerto Rico, coloniality posits the colony anew. As a form of coloniality, debt posits the colony anew—within and through the strictures of financialized neoliberal capitalism. The present *is* the past.

Second, and for this reason, decoloniality is a matter of turning the present into the past. It entails disorder, to recall Fanon. It entails "practical and metaphysical revolt," as Maldonado-Torres suggests. Rather than liberation or freedom, however, I argue that decoloniality is a praxis that seeks to unbind the world of capital/coloniality, intervening in material conditions to dislocate modes of power, being, knowing, and sensing. Notions of liberation or freedom must also be unbound from the image of the capitalist/ colonial world. Hence, I focus on variations of material praxis that attend to present material conditions. Many of these practices deploy the language of freedom, sovereignty, and solidarity, but the content of those terms is prefigured, rather than stated, by the reorganization of life itself. The content is articulated in and by a material praxis that alters the relation to land, the city, the coast, the ocean, the body, the other. Such approximation is suggested through subversion, thus in complex proximity with that which it aims to dismantle. This is why such praxis is easily coopted, even complicit with capital/coloniality despite the fact that it seeks to disorder that very world.[40] Land rescue/occupation, defiant refusal, queer laziness, as we will see, are exemplary of attempts to unbind and bind anew, disarticulate and rearticulate anew, turn inoperative and initiate new forms of doing, being, sensing—all in all, relating. The point here, to recall Hartman, is "the detritus of lives with which we have yet to attend, a past that has yet to be done." Decoloniality is a material praxis that attends to the ongoing productivity of the demographic catastrophes that installed the modern capitalist world, thereby interrupting the reinstallation of the metaphysical catastrophe that coloniality represents.

Subversive interruption can be seen as a form of historical reckoning, I thus argue in the chapters that follow. Interruption turns inoperative the work of coloniality in the present juncture by inhabiting and subverting the strictures of debt. Decoloniality is a material praxis that turns coloniality inoperative by short-circuiting its strictures. Interruption is subversive, rather than reifying, when it targets the reproduction of a race/gender/class hierarchy through the asymmetry debt generates in the creditor-debtor relation, through the deferral debt requires to exercise control. A debt is a bind. In this context, it is a promise to repay that binds parties to a future purportedly irrespective of changing conditions. Unpayable debts, unpaid debts, function as markers of culpability—a broken promise, a failure to meet oneself in the future. Culpability legitimates the injunction to repay, installing modes of subjection through subjectivation that actualize, update, rearticulate race/gender/class in the colony. Culpability and the injunction to repay makes possible, however, indexing material conditions that led to the promise and its fulfillment or failure. Financial debts leave a trace, then. They admit an audit. They are subject to accounting, to account giving. Subversion and refusal of repayment seek to turn the work of culpability inoperative by capturing account giving. They invert collection itself, capturing accountability. They do so, moving from financial debts to historical debts. This move is not an exit from the histories that install specific material conditions. On the contrary. It has the power to interrupt the work of historical, indeed colonial, debts by capturing financial debts that posit the former anew. Audits can function accordingly, as a political tool of accountability rather than as a mechanism by which access to financial markets is regained.

In the case of Puerto Rico, to move from financial to historical debts is to address colonial debts. This shift makes possible more than linking financial debts to government corruption or, more generally, the political economy of Puerto Rico under US colonial rule. It makes possible specifying the work of debt as a form of coloniality, linking current financial debts with the reinstallation of a race/gender/class hierarchy in the colony. Moving from financial debts to historical debts makes possible elucidating not only the effects but the effectivity of austerity, for example, through race/gender/class. I suggest that subversive interruption can therefore be seen as spaces-times of confrontation with the colony as well as coloniality. Some of the cases I examine, in particular concerning the subversion of private property, can even be said to turn decoloniality into a form of reparation. They do so, however, beyond the juridical paradigm of reparative justice. They invert the position of the creditor and the debtor, inverting who owes what to whom by taking back what is owed. They seek to posit life beyond the strictures of private property, challenging private property itself. They aim to generate infrastructures for a life yet to come from within material conditions here and now. They affirm that we, in fact, are all heirs taking back rather than paying back.

ROADMAP

The conceptual perspectives described above are developed in detail throughout the chapters that follow. I offer them as provisional approximations in light of my engagement with the intellectual-practical production in Puerto Rico about Puerto Rico at the center of the book. Concepts emerge from a specific historical, economic, political juncture, whether that is made explicit or not. Whether they elucidate other contexts is not a matter philosophy or theory ought to try to settle, but rather for those who are compelled or repelled by them to address. Puerto Rico is not a case study of the concepts developed in the chapters that follow, then. It is not a mere "example." Neither is the specificity of Puerto Rico's current predicament universalizable, although this is not to say that Puerto Rico is marked by singularity. On the contrary. The chapters that follow seek points of contact with as well as divergence from other histories of the production of and opposition to the world of capital/coloniality. They invite engagement with other histories within and beyond Puerto Rico.

"Neoliberal Coloniality," chapter 1, examines Maurizio Lazzarato's work on debt as an apparatus of capture and as a mode of subjection through subjectivation in postfinancial crisis neoliberal capitalism. It moves from Lazzarato's account of the "making of the indebted man" (*la fabbrica dell'uomo indebitato*) to Ariadna Godreau-Aubert's notes toward a "pedagogy of the indebted woman" (*una pedagogía de las endeudadas*). For Lazzarato, debt intensifies core features of the neoliberal project by reterritorializing value creation and the capture of value in apparatuses deemed as "destructive": the technocratic state's use of taxation and austerity and its modes of subjection in the figure of the "indebted man." Verónica Gago, Luci Cavallero, and Rita Segato's work presses us to rewrite Lazzarato's account of the work of debt, specifying the way debt "lands [*aterriza*] in diverse territories, economies, bodies, and conflicts," to quote Gago and Cavallero. I extend this analysis, arguing that debt should be understood as a form of coloniality. Aníbal Quijano's notion of the coloniality of power and Nelson Maldonado-Torres's Fanonian rendition of coloniality as a metaphysical catastrophe are key here. I examine Godreau-Aubert's exposition of the relation between debt, austerity, and coloniality in Puerto Rico. The cartography of debt that a pedagogy of the indebted woman makes possible maps the necropolitical effects of austerity, specifically in relation to women, with particular attention to black women, in the racial feminization of poverty and in femicide. It thereby maps the work of coloniality in the indebted colony.

Colonial Exceptionality, chapter 2, examines José Atiles-Osoria's notion of a "colonial state of exception," which seeks to illuminate Puerto Rico's juridico-political status and the conditions of capture it generates. Atiles-Osoria draws from this discussion to develop the notion "neoliberal colonialism," which explains the installation of neoliberal rationality through the increase in use of declarations of states of emergency in the administration of the colony. I argue that the analytics of exceptionality does not track the relation between colonialism and coloniality through its material conditions and effects. Miriam Muñiz-Varela and Anayra Santory-Jorge's conceptions of an "economy of the catastrophe" and "catastrophe by attrition," in contrast, center material conditions and effects that exceed the decision of a sovereign. Their work elucidates the "slow death" of neoliberal coloniality, as Lauren Berlant's notion suggests, though Muñiz-Varela stresses the spectacular forms of violence that make up the ordinary in the indebted colony. I discuss Marisol LeBrón's work here as well, specifically in relation to the forms of "punitive governance" central to the economy of the catastrophe that Muñiz-Varela clarifies. I pay attention to how debt lands on black masculinity and masculinity racialized as nonwhite in this context. These discussions transform Berlant's notion of the "environment" of slow death in financialized capitalism into the "weather," more specifically, the "climate" of indebted life in the colony. The latter draws from Yarimar Bonilla's engagement with Christina Sharpe's work. I argue that the environment as climate, rather than political-juridical control, is the site of colonial exceptionality. It exhibits a state of emergency that is not the exception but the rule.

"Historical Reckoning," chapter 3, explores the subversive potential of the reversibility of debt made possible by its strictures. David Graeber's account of the social logic of debt as a combination of equality and hierarchy is insightful. It makes clear that debt operates by installing asymmetry and deferral. I engage two critical theories of debt that draw from

Marx to elucidate debt as a site of subversion and social rearticulation. I examine two core assumptions that require attention in this context. Debt discloses irreducible social bonds *or* it indexes the material and historical conditions that produce a sociality reconfigured by debt. Debt is either a site of restitution of a fundamental interdependence *or* a site of reckoning with the potential to dismantle material and historical conditions that produced debt in the first place. Turning to Godreau-Aubert's work on debt and coloniality in Puerto Rico once more, I argue that debt is a site of subversive interruption that involves moving from financial debts to historical debts. This move remains an exposition of material conditions, however. Subversive interruption seizes the power to bind that instituted historical debts reproduced in financial debts. Historical reckoning is subversive if it interrupts modes of binding of a debt economy *and* the race/gender/class hierarchy that it reinstalls. I discuss debates concerning a debt audit in this context as well as interventions by la Colectiva Feminista en Construcción, a political project that follows the tradition of black feminism in the struggle against heteropatriarchy, antiblack violence, and capitalism, exemplary of historical reckoning.[41]

"Subversive Interruption," chapter 4, explores the aesthetic/epistemic strictures of hopeful protest through a reflection on the political power of failure. Guillermo Rebollo-Gil's notion of *pasarse políticamente*, to politically cross the line, specifies failed protest as the power of refusal as well as subversion of norms through which coloniality operates. The norm of productivity is central in this context. Productivity links race and gender in light of the specific economic, political, and historical juncture. Pasarse políticamente clarifies the inadvertent or explicit subversion or refusal of productivity that goes beyond normative measure. I begin with Rebollo-Gil's account of the 2010–11 student strike at the University of Puerto Rico. This discussion maps the aesthetic/epistemic terrain in which opposition to austerity, the Fiscal Control Board, and government corruption has been pursued in the colony. I then examine the operation of the norm of productivity within the distinctively neoliberal work ethic that Miguel Rodríguez-Casellas calls *echarpalantismo* (forward-facing resilience). Mabel Rodríguez-Centeno's extension of Rodríguez-Casellas's critique of echarpalantismo in what she calls *vagancia queer* (queer laziness) clarifies strictures of the subversive interruption of productivity.[42] In this context, I explore the subversive potential of the July 2019 protests that ousted Rosselló in challenging the aesthetic/epistemic coordinates of protest.

"Decoloniality as Reparations," the conclusion to the book, discusses Maldonado-Torres's distinction between decolonization and decoloniality, building on my suggestion that Quijano's concept of coloniality of power should be understood in light of Hartman's notion of the afterlife of slavery/ property. I argue that decoloniality is a material praxis that turns the present into the past and explore the material praxis of land "rescue" (*rescate*) or "occupation" (*ocupación*) that seeks to unbind the world of capital taking back what is owed. Through a reading of Fanon's engagement with the question of reparations, I argue that these can be seen as reparations beyond a juridical paradigm. In Puerto Rico, this material praxis challenges private property, seeking to build power in common by rescuing the common(s). It attempts to turn inoperative the reinstallation of the colony/coloniality through new rounds of enclosure in the context of the debt crisis and the aftermath of Hurricane María. Liliana Cotto-Morales, Érika Fontánez-Torres, Miriam Muñiz-Varela, and Marina Moscoso's works are key here. They assess the long-standing praxis in Puerto Rico of interrupting the colonial lives of property through taking back land (*toma de terrenos*)—the countryside, the coast, the city. A new round of land rescue/occupation underway takes back what Muñiz-Varela calls the "taken island." The territory is an occupied land through the multiple rounds of colonial/capitalist capture that comprise its history. It is taken *and* rescued/occupied anew in and through the current economic juncture. I end with a reflection on the notion of pessimism as the site of hope.

Neoliberal Coloniality   1

Una deuda es una condición de lugar. Cuando son otros los que nos endeudan, a pesar de nosotras, esa condición de lugar es también una manera de despojarnos del cuerpo aun que lo llevemos puesto.

A debt is a condition of place. When it is others who place us in debt, in spite of us [women], that place is also a way to get rid of the body even when wearing it.—ARIADNA GODREAU-AUBERT, *Las Propias*

IN THE FOREWORD TO HER BOOK *Las Propias: Apuntes para una pedagogía de las endeudadas,* Ariadna Godreau-Aubert writes that "to be in debt," *estar en deuda,* is to "have something and, at the same time, to be dispossessed of something."[1] Debt is a social, economic, political relation. It is at once material and "affective." As a relation, debt is irreducibly spatial and temporal. It is a state of being—something to traverse, undergo, surpass. Yet that is to say that it is a place, a location. It has spatial-temporal coordinates. It generates—indeed *is*—an environment. To be indebted, however, is to be "temporarily or permanently" "nowhere," according to Godreau-Aubert. Debts are not accrued in a void.[2] A debt is not a promise, even when it bears the mark of obligation.[3] To be in debt is to inhabit a space and time of capture, dispossession, expulsion, exploitation.

In a chapter entitled "Nosotras que no nos debemos a nadie: Las Propias en tiempos de austeridad y deuda pública," Godreau-Aubert returns to the spatial-temporal description of debt with which she opens the book. She indexes the space and time of debt to the case of Puerto Rico.[4] To speak of debt from the colony, *desde la colonia*, is to speak of and from a place that has been "surpassed" (*superado*), she says. It is to speak from a place that "appears" "nowhere." That is to say: debt structures space and time itself. "The colony," she writes, "takes place [*transcurre*] in 'repeated acts of capture.'"[5] In the case of Puerto Rico, "[t]he colony is that which appears nowhere, that which has been surpassed in discourse and practice: that which is substituted by the 'post-colonial.' The colony is that which is abandoned by everyone [*todas y todos*], except by those who keep finding how to exploit it."[6]

In an article that distills the main arguments of his two books on debt, *The Making of the Indebted Man* and *Governing by Debt*, Maurizio Lazzarato writes: "The financial crisis, transformed into a sovereign debt crisis, has imposed new modalities of governmentality as well as new subjective figures, since it has determined, on the one side, the governors' deployment of a 'technical government' and, on the other side, the transformation of the governed into the indebted man who atones for his error through taxation."[7] Debt functions as an apparatus of "capture," "predation," and "extraction," intensifying a neoliberalism reconfigured by the financial crisis.[8] Debt intensifies the neoliberal project on two counts. Neoliberalism turns the state into an apparatus of capture that serves the rich, corporations, and creditors through tax cuts, tax exemption, and the creation of tax havens.[9] Debt expands this shift by externalizing the debt of banks, firms, and the state itself. It intensifies this shift by burdening individuals who must take on debt to meet basic needs such as housing, health care, and education and who must bear the burden of public debt through regressive taxation and austerity. Additionally, subjectivation within debt economies draws from the value of personal responsibility central to neoliberal ideology. Neoliberal subjectivity is no longer a matter of *homo economicus* as entrepreneur, however. It is a matter of assuming and repaying debt accrued in consumption and shifted onto populations through regressive taxation and austerity. The entrepreneurial subject is necessarily an indebted subject. Indebtedness, however, is a form of abject subjectivity. The "indebted man" is a *failed* neoliberal subject, a failed enterprise. He is bound to the fate of capital through his failures.

In Puerto Rico, an unincorporated territory of the United States, the debt crisis binds subjects and populations by establishing that they are failed economic agents parasitic on federal "handouts." Yet, in Puerto Rico, indebtedness is not only the fate of failed neoliberal subjects. It is the fate of failed colonial subjects, who affirmed cultural autonomy while purportedly reaping the benefits of US economic prosperity with the creation of the Estado Libre Asociado (ELA) in 1952. As an apparatus of capture, debt is a form of coloniality (*colonialidad*), to recall Aníbal Quijano's term.[10] Minimally, colonialism refers to a form of juridico-political subordination. Coloniality, in contrast, refers to a race/gender/class hierarchy produced by a colonial history, but one that exceeds colonialism as a juridico-political project. To speak of coloniality in the colony, from the colony, to recall Godreau-Aubert once more, is to locate oneself within the no-place of colonial debts allegedly surpassed by the creation of the ELA. It is to track the effectivity, the work, of coloniality within the spatial-temporal coordinates of the fiscally distressed colony. This means, however, that it is to track the unequal distribution of precariousness and violence in the indebted colony along race/gender/class lines.[11] That debt reinstalls Puerto Rico's colonial status by actualizing, updating, race/gender/class in altered material and historical conditions becomes clear when one considers the necropolitical effects of austerity implemented in response to the crisis.[12]

In contrast to Lazzarato, who offers an account of the "making of the indebted man" (*la fabbrica dell'uomo indebitato*), Godreau-Aubert offers notes toward a "pedagogy of the indebted woman" (*una pedagogía de las endeudadas*). Such a pedagogy elucidates the relation between debt, austerity, and coloniality. The "cartography of debt" that this pedagogy allows maps the production of a doubly abject subject central to the work of neoliberal coloniality. Nelson Maldonado-Torres draws from Quijano's coloniality of power, specifying that coloniality is the articulation of existence in light of a race/gender hierarchy that marks bodies and populations as disposable.[13] As an apparatus of economic capture, predation, and extraction, debt actualizes and intensifies the work of race/gender/class, positing bodies and populations as disposable. Debt allows the deployment of austerity as an injunction to pay, marking culpability. The injunction to pay actualizes, indeed updates, the work of race/gender/class, intensifying its effectivity in the unequal distribution of precariousness, dispossession, violence. Debt and austerity disproportionately impact women, especially black women, in the territory, renewing a racial order in altered material and historical conditions. As Godreau-Aubert writes, "Blame in this country, or in any other, is never an orphan. She is poor, black, and a woman."[14] Precarity and violence stem not from the colonial condition, then, but from an ongoing coloniality that adapts race/gender/class according to capital's changing needs. Debt continues the no-place of life in the colony, the spatial-temporal coordinates of colonial life. Debt captures the body, the space and time, of the indebted "even when wearing it" (*aun que lo llevemos puesto*).

This chapter develops the concept of neoliberal coloniality by considering its manifestation in indebted life in the colony. The first section, Neoliberal Governmentality, tracks Lazzarato's Deleuzian transformation of Michel Foucault's account of neoliberal governmentality, emphasizing his exposition of the actualization of finance in a debt economy. Debt intensifies core features of the neoliberal project by reterritorializing value creation and the capture of value in apparatuses of power that can be deemed as "destructive," specifically, the technocratic state's deployment of taxation and austerity along with its modes of subjectivation. I transform Lazzarato's account through Verónica Gago and Luci Cavallero's feminist reading of debt, centering the specificity with which the apparatus of debt "lands [*aterriza*] in diverse territories, economies, bodies, and conflicts."[15] The second section, Neoliberal Coloniality, moves from neoliberal governmentality to neoliberal coloniality by considering Quijano's conception of the coloniality of power and Maldonado-Torres's Fanonian rendition of coloniality in the notion of "metaphysical catastrophe." This discussion explicates the work of debt as an apparatus that actualizes, updates, reinstalls a race/gender/class hierarchy. It clarifies that the production of abject subjectivity, the failed neoliberal and colonial subject, works as an injunction to pay by marking racialized/gendered populations as disposable. Key here is Rita Segato's work. The third and final section, A Cartography of Debt, examines Godreau-Aubert's account of the indebted woman in Puerto Rico. The cartography of debt that a pedagogy of the indebted woman makes possible maps at least two modalities of gender violence subtended by antiblack violence. The deepening of the racial feminization of poverty and an increase of femicide in the indebted colony are exemplary of the necropolitical effects of neoliberal coloniality.[16]

NEOLIBERAL GOVERNMENTALITY

Throughout his books and articles on debt, Lazzarato argues that the neoliberal project "comes to fruition" in debt economies and, especially, in debt crises. Debt crises are central to the reconfiguration of neoliberalism by the 2007–8 financial crisis. Debt intensifies the success *and* the failure of the two main features of neoliberalism.[17] Neoliberalism is understood here as a set of economic policies that, from the 1970s onward, sought to shift the cost of social reproduction from the state to populations. These policies promote privatization and subcontracting of public services, taxation, and expenditure that favor enterprise and the rich, and the deregulation of the financial sector. First, Lazzarato maintains, sovereign (or public) debt crises represent the full inversion of the Keynesian state.[18] The state retains its central role in redistributing wealth, yet the "direction of redistribution has been inverted."[19] While neoliberalism turns the state into an apparatus of capture that serves the rich, corporations, and creditors, debt represents the success of the attempt to shift the cost of social reproduction from the state to populations. Yet debt expands and intensifies this shift. It expands the shift by externalizing not only the cost of social reproduction but also private and public debt: the debt of banks, firms, and the state itself.[20] It intensifies the shift by burdening individuals who must take on debt to meet basic needs such as housing, education, and health care but must also assume public debt through regressive taxation and austerity.[21]

Second, key to neoliberalism is the affirmation of personal responsibility.[22] Debt crises represent, at once, the fulfillment *and* failure of the value of personal responsibility. The state is an inverted "welfare" state whereby wealth is transferred from "non-owners" to "owners," Lazzarato argues.[23] In a post-Fordist context, the distinction between nonowner and owner is structured in terms of the "credit dynamic," which binds debtors to the logic of capital through a neutralization of possibility.[24] A new form of subjectivity, the "indebted man," is thus central to a neoliberalism reconfigured by the financial crisis. Especially after the financial crisis, neoliberal subjectivity is no longer a matter of homo economicus as entrepreneur, no longer a matter of responsibility for oneself as an enterprise. It is a matter of assuming and repaying debt—debt accrued in consumption and debt shifted onto populations by the state.[25] On the one hand, the entrepreneurial subject is necessarily an indebted subject. He can only function as "human capital" by taking on debt.[26] On the other hand, indebtedness articulates a form of abject subjectivity. The indebted man is a failed enterprise. In debt crises, indebtedness is tantamount to culpability. The subject of debt is the subject of guilt.[27] As culpable, subjects and populations are bound to the logic of capital through their purported failures.

In his books on debt, especially in *Governing by Debt*, Lazzarato pursues a Deleuzian transformation of Foucault's treatment of neoliberalism. Key here is the notion of political rationality. This notion illuminates the relation between liberalism and the state and the way in which that relation configures the relation between the economy and the political beyond the state. Following Gilles Deleuze, Lazzarato maintains that liberalism and neoliberalism are specific forms of state capitalism.[28] The economy requires political articulation irrevocably tied to the state. What interests me in this context, however, is Lazzarato's rewriting of Foucault's conception of political rationality. With this transformation, Lazzarato accounts for the actualization of finance and thus the operation of debt through destructive and regressive features. This discussion is crucial for specifying the work of debt, its effectivity, as an apparatus of capture, predation, and extraction. Ultimately, this discussion will allow me to speak of debt as a form of coloniality with necropolitical effects. To do so, greater specificity on modalities of reterritorialization at the heart of the actualization of finance is needed.

Foucault's concept of governmentality tracks the political rationality underpinning technologies of power.[29] Rather than measure a certain "regime of rationality" against the value of reason, Foucault explains, "I would prefer to analyze it according to two axes: on the one hand, that of codification/prescription (how it forms an ensemble of rules, procedures, means to an end, etc.), and on the other, that of true or false formulations (how it determines a domain of objects about which it is possible to articulate true or false propositions)."[30] A rationality, then, concerns "the development of a series of knowledges," although this claim bears ontological weight.[31] It not only carves out a discursive field that articulates concepts, rules, procedures, goals, imperatives, modes of justification, modes of intervention, and so on. It also carves out a domain of objects to which these refer. The point here is to track the ways in which specific rationalities inscribe themselves in institutions, practices, regulations. Foucault's analysis of neoliberalism accordingly tracks the relation between an ensemble of institutions, procedures, calculations, tactics *and* political economy as a form of knowledge. Within neoliberalism, the market functions as a "site of veridiction."[32] The market "must tell the truth [*dire le vrai*]" in relation to governmental practice, since it produces a domain of objects and hence a specific mode of intervention.[33]

The institution of a domain of objects is also the production of a specific type of subjectivity and set of populations. The concept of governmentality thus also tracks the relation between forms of power and modes of subjectivation whereby technologies of rule interlock with technologies of the self.[34] Governmentality, according to Foucault, is a matter of "the conduct of conduct."[35] Foucault recalls us to the fact that up until the eighteenth century, "government" is used in political but also religious, pedagogical, medical, and philosophical contexts.[36] It referred not only to a political relation, but also to the problem of self-control, management of the household, direction of the soul, and so on. The notion of government in question thus ranges from "governing the self" to "governing others." The modes of subjectivation distinctive of liberal and neoliberal governmentality take heed from the market. They incite rather than subjugate or command. While liberalism's notion of homo economicus is tied to a conception of freedom of exchange, neoliberalism's notion is tied to a conception of enterprise, specifically, self-management.[37]

In "The Birth of Biopolitics," the relation between apparatuses of government and a political rationality allows Foucault "to show how the modern sovereign state and the modern autonomous individual co-determine each other's emergence."[38] Crucial here is the conception of the state that follows from Foucault's insistence on examining technologies of power and subjectivation rather than the "institution." The state, Foucault explains, "is nothing else but the mobile effect of a regime of multiple governmentalities."[39] It has no heart, Foucault says, in the sense of having an "interior." It is "nothing else but the effect, the profile, the mobile shape of a perpetual statification (*étatisation*) or statifications." Although the state has no heart, it is the effect of a perpetual statification guided by the market as a site of veridiction.[40] As an effect, the state is organized in light of a goal or aim determined by "the market."

Foucault explains neoliberalism's transformation of classical liberalism by tracking its distinct organizing principle, which shapes the relation between the state and the economy. Exchange is liberalism's principle, which establishes freedom of exchange as the core of liberalism. In contrast, competition is neoliberalism's principle, which establishes enterprise as the core of the neoliberal project. Exchange and competition not only guide the modes of intervention of the state but also bring into being a domain of objects, a type of subjects, and a form of "society." Neoliberalism's transformation of liberalism is thus not merely an inversion of the relation between the state and the market, but the transformation of political rationality that binds them.[41] The state no longer merely carves out a space for the market to function, placing its authority behind private property.[42] Rather, it actively constitutes the market. It does so by extending an economic rationality to the social domain, tying the rationality of government to the action of individuals. Instead of ensuring the freedom of exchange, it promotes a "constructed freedom" with its view of the self as an enterprise. It produces subjects responsible for self-management, hence responsible for modes of self-control that make possible economic success.

Lazzarato follows Foucault's analysis of governmentality, tracking the form of government and modes of subjectivation distinctive of a neoliberalism reconfigured by the dynamic of credit and as a debt economy. He tracks the political rationality underpinning a neoliberalism first reconfigured by the hegemony of finance, then in light of the economy of debt crises. The logic, the rationality, of finance is self-valorizing money.[43] Recall that in *Capital*, Marx argues that despite interest-bearing capital being the most "irrational form of capital," a "misrepresentation and objectification of the relations of production," it is the starkest expression of the nature of capital as "value in motion."[44] The overall circulation process of capital, that is, the circulation of value that *is* capital, is composed of valorization, realization, distribution, and the renovation of money as capital. As David Harvey explains, valorization is a matter of the creation and extraction of surplus value in production.[45] Realization is a matter of the transformation of value "back into the money form" through the exchange of commodities in a market. Distribution is a matter of disbursement of value and surplus value "among various claimants." Finally, there is a return to valorization through "capturing" some of the money in circulation in order to convert it into money capital.

In "interest-bearing capital," these relations are in their "most superficial and fetishized form," Marx argues, because "self-valorizing value," "money that produces more money," is treated "without the process that mediates the two extremes."[46] Marx explores the relation between commercial and finance capital, for example, to point out the radical abstraction at work in the credit dynamic. This allows him to further explicate the relation between production and circulation.[47] Credit plays an organizing role in production, more precisely, finance capital in commercial capital. Credit assists production, financing the production process itself.[48] Lazzarato draws on Marx but is interested in elucidating a post-Fordist context through the reconfiguration of the relation between finance and production by financial and monetary "axiomatics."[49] "With money, the dynamics of capital contains within itself its own end," Lazzarato writes, "yet it is only with the cycle of finance capital (M-M') that the immanence of capital's functions coincide with its concept."[50] In a post-Fordist context, finance not only "captures value."[51] It is the "principal producer of value." It not only appropriates capital flows, but "configures them for the sake of its own valorization."[52] Key here is the actualization of finance.

Lazzarato draws from Deleuze's "axiomatics" to theorize the actualization of finance as a "dual movement": a movement of abstraction or "deterritorialization" and concrete realization or "reterritorialization."[53] This dual movement accounts for the institutional reconfiguration implied by the hegemony of finance, where in the very management of money and capital flows is turned into the central site of value creation. This reconfiguration installs debt as a central apparatus of capture within the neoliberal version of finance capital. Financialization first requires a process of abstraction: "freeing up" value creation from the confines of territory, sovereignty, and nation, as well as from the qualification of production and hence labor.[54] It seeks to assure "only functions and relations between non-qualified flows."[55] Financialization is thus a matter of "decoding" in which "economic codes (full employment), social codes (the social state), and political codes (political parties) that governed social relations in Fordism" are "destroyed."[56] It is a matter of mobility (liquidity), of a displacement of limits.[57] Financialization not only shifts capital from one country to the next, one sector to another.[58] It frees up the very movement of abstraction distinctive of capital, the "permanent disequilibrium, its systematic search for asymmetries and inequalities, [which are] the conditions of its valorization."[59] Decoding is a process of destruction through disarticulation.

The actualization of finance requires a "reterritorialization," however. It requires concrete institutional articulation through which value can be captured. Finance nestles what it liberates in other apparatuses of power.[60] Reterritorialization is also a movement of destruction, then, given the specific ways in which such apparatuses "land," to recall Verónica Gago and Luci Cavallero's term. In a financial and postfinancial crisis context, reterritorialization exploits "regressive" features of capital expansion.[61] Debt appears not as assisting the creation of value. Rather, unpayable debt itself appears as a site of value creation and extraction.[62] Now, axioms "define principles."[63] They shape economic policy and thus forms of governmentality. While axioms are "declared" by financial and transnational institutions, states are central to their deployment.[64] Axioms are imperatives: "Repay creditors, increase taxes, cut welfare services, streamline state budgets, etc." They articulate a technocratic state guided by crisis management.[65] Within debt crises, actualization operates with fewer axioms: "Reimburse creditors, drastically reduce wages and social services, and privatize the welfare state."[66] The technocratic state functions through "simplifications, unilateral decision-making, and authoritarian decree."[67]

Lazzarato argues that the capture apparatus of taxation monetized the debt crisis.[68] He establishes its central role in concretely capturing value (reterritorialization) within the financial crisis. "By determining who must pay (certainly not those responsible for the crisis) and where the money must go (to the creditors and the banks responsible for the crisis)," he writes, "taxation ensures the wholly *political* reproduction of an 'economy' which by itself would be incapable of functioning according to the fundamental political divisions that constitute it (creditors/debtors, capital/labor, etc.)."[69] The crucial point is the link between taxation and austerity. Taxation is the "barometer" of austerity policies. Debt itself functions as an apparatus of capture through taxation: regressive taxation for populations, reduced taxation and tax exemption for the rich, creditors, and corporations. It binds subjects and populations through austerity: reduced or altogether eliminated essential services such as education or health care. Taxation is the apparatus by which wealth is captured in relation to current revenues within the credit dynamic, while austerity serves as an "injunction to pay."[70] Taxation and austerity are realizations of the technocratic state in its purported aim to manage fiscal crisis.

Forms of subjection through subjectivation are crucial to the work of debt as an apparatus of capture. While in *Governing by Debt* Lazzarato focuses on the deterritorialization of psychic and bodily subjectivity through Deleuze's notion of the "dividual," in *The Making of the Indebted Man*, he explores in greater depth the reterritorialization of the credit dynamic in the figure of the "indebted man."[71] The latter is most relevant. This discussion elucidates the link between debt and guilt central to a debt economy. It clarifies the moralization of debt as the production of guilty subjects and populations who must pay. It explicates the transformation of neoliberal subjectivity in a regressive key. Although we will have to complicate Lazzarato's account, moving from the indebted man to the indebted woman, this discussion makes possible an exposition of the specific ways in which debt operates concretely: exploiting difference, intensifying hierarchies, producing distinct modalities of violence.

As an injunction to pay, austerity requires the production of a culpable, and not merely a responsible, subject. The indebted man is a "regressive figure."[72] He failed to live up to the promise of neoliberal subjectivity: self-responsibility, self-management, indeed the self as enterprise. Unpayable debts restrict the promise of creativity, innovation, flexibility that self-management made possible in the first place. They capture the future, possibility itself. The indebted man is a failed enterprise, then.[73] He failed to capitalize on his investments, indeed on the "assistance" of credit/debt itself. Far from autonomous, unencumbered, sovereign, unpayable debt establishes him as radically dependent, fundamentally bound. His failure is thereby individualized. It does not index a system of social labor. It points to an irresponsible individual who was unable to "take on and confront risk" in generative ways.[74] His are not only faulty choices but also corrupt behaviors. Unpayable debt thus indexes an undisciplined, corrupt individual. This is an abject subject, responsible for the failures of the neoliberal project. As an injunction to pay, austerity is an opportunity for expiation. The indebted man must sacrifice himself, bear the cost of social reproduction through austerity. He is also subject to regressive taxation while the rich, creditors, corporations access tax exemptions.

Debt binds, captures, and extracts establishing culpability, then. Unpayable debt forecloses the future, yet as a mode of political control. By "training the governed to 'promise' (to honor their debt)," Lazzarato argues, capitalism exercises "control over the future."[75] Debt allows calculation, the establishment of equivalences between current and future behavior.[76] It is an economic apparatus but also a "security-state technique of government" aimed at managing the uncertainty of time.[77] In *Governing by Debt*, Lazzarato proposes refusal as a mode of interrupting such foreclosure. He argues for the refusal of work beyond as well as according to the rules of "human capital": as "consumer, communicator, user, or unemployed person."[78] He adds that such refusal must expand to "normalized gender identities" and "a range of techniques of governmentality, those of valorization and those of subjection/enslavement." Such refusal will need to be rethought beyond the strictures of exploitation, indeed as nestled in the dynamics of dispossession, expulsion, expropriation. The refusal to pay, the subversion of repayment, the seizing of the power to bind, the appropriation of the commons, I will argue throughout this book, are modes of interruption that aim to turn the effectivity of debt inoperative beyond the dynamics of exploitation.

The claim that debt functions as an apparatus of capture in neoliberal financialized capitalism by binding taxation and austerity is key to an analysis of the case of Puerto Rico, as we will see throughout this book. Economic "development" based on tax exemption for corporations and tax-exempt financing has been central to the political economy installed by the colonial relation under US rule since the dawn of the twentieth century.[79] The neoliberal rearticulation of this colonial political economy binds taxation and austerity with necropolitical effects. Taxation and austerity not only depend on but deepen the production of a regressive figure, an abject subject, that actualizes the technology of race/gender that grounds the colonial relation in the first place. The apparatus of debt "lands" in a way that capitalizes on and thereby exacerbates the relation of colonialism and coloniality in Puerto Rico, where unincorporation facilitates the reproduction of a race/gender/class hierarchy that itself organizes the political-juridical status. Debt thereby functions not only as an apparatus of capture but also as a form of coloniality. Through austerity, debt extends its reach to those not even "worthy" of debt; those not legible as "productive" members of "society"; those who are subject to predatory lending given their position in a race/gender/class hierarchy; those who seek debt in informal economies, so on.[80]

It is thus crucial to complicate Lazzarato's account, underscoring the necessity of specifying the distinct ways in which debt lands. In *Una Lectura feminista de la deuda*, Verónica Gago and Luci Cavallero reject Lazzarato's account of the indebted man on the grounds that it posits a "universal subjectivity distinctive of the creditor-debtor relation."[81] Lazzarato fails to take into account two "fundamental aspects" of the operation of debt within the neoliberal context: gender and the potential for disobedience internal to the work of debt itself.[82] For Gago and Cavallero, these two aspects are linked. Especially though not exclusively in Latin America, the feminist response to the violence of neoliberalism, specifically in relation to the modalities of violence distinctive of debt, is evidence of such a link. More than a political fact, however, a feminist elucidation of the work of debt does not admit circumventing the specificity of its operation. It cannot ignore the different modalities of violence that it produces as well as the forms of disobedience that it makes possible. In examining the productivity of debt on feminized bodies and in relation to a history of gendered exploitation where women bear the burden of social reproduction, it becomes clear that the work of unpayable debt is not universalizable.

The operation and effects of debt differ along gender lines. Gago and Cavallero argue that debt operates in distinct ways due to "(1) particular modes of moralization directed at women and feminized bodies; (2) differential modes of exploitation given the relations of subordination involved; (3) a specific relationship with debt given the tasks of reproduction; (4) a singular impact with respect to sexist [*machista*] violence with which debt is articulated; (5) fundamental variations on possible returns involved in financial obligation in the case of feminized bodies."[83] As we will see throughout this book, debt does not reduce but rather exploits difference, asymmetry, hierarchy. It does so in distinct ways in "domestic," "popular" (or mostly unwaged), and "waged" economies.[84] A feminist reading of debt, they thus argue, elucidates its work on women and feminized bodies not only in relation to the financialization of basic services. Gago and Cavallero show that it also clarifies debt's relation to dependence on pesticides in farming practices, to mass incarceration and the economies inside and outside prisons, to what is incurred when abortion is clandestine, to unbridled consumption, to the recruitment of labor at any price within legal as well as illegal economies, to dispossession through housing crises, to the ubiquity of domestic violence and femicide exacerbated when women are not able to exit the home.[85]

Quoting activists in Argentina, Gago and Cavallero note that debt is that which "does not allow us to say no when we want to say no."[86] Debt forecloses the future, but it does so by "binding women to violent relations, to sustaining broken links given financial obligation." It "blocks economic autonomy," but it does so ambivalently. Debt allows movement. It does not merely fix. However, in movement or fixity, debt exploits a future possibility to work, it installs conditions that must be accepted.[87] It assists exploitation. Specifying modalities of exploitation, as we will see, requires indexing race as a vector of difference in the expression of the ambivalence of debt.[88] Now, recall that Gago and Cavallero argue that internal to the very work of debt are possibilities for its disobedience. To disobey debt, one must "narrate" debt, give it body, establish its ubiquity, link its distinct modalities, make visible its commonality across differences. To narrate debt is to challenge the violence of financial abstraction. Disobeying debt hence requires eliminating its "power of abstraction."[89] It must do so, however, within and not despite its ambivalence. To narrate debt, they underscore, is to resist the view that women traversed by this apparatus are "either victims or entrepreneurs."

It is important to amend Lazzarato's account of neoliberalism emphasizing this ambivalence. In *Neoliberalism from Below*, Gago discusses the "baroque economies" that emerge in the neoliberal context in Latin America. One key feature of Gago's account is Foucault's rendition of what she describes as a "nonantagonistic pair" at the heart of self-management: singularization and universalization. The "increasingly complex notion" of an individual is here coupled with a "standard mode of collective functioning, which operates on the level of the population simultaneously demanding and reducing the continuous singularization of each person."[90] Neoliberal subjectivity bears the burden of social reproduction under the guise of self-responsibility, but it thereby becomes the site of "sovereignty."[91] Sovereignty here is not the liberal unencumbered self, but a relationship to oneself in terms of "control, organization, and production of a territory that is the body itself, as a set of norms for its defense and enrichment."[92] Control over the body as territory is coextensive with subjection to the body-territory of a population. Such dynamic, Gago explains in her book with Cavallero, is one key "limit" that capitalism requires for its operation.[93] It is therefore one key site of its subversion.

Gago insists that neoliberalism does not merely produce precarity, altogether neutralizing the subjects and populations on which its apparatuses land. A view from Latin America suggests a subversion, indeed seizure, of the modes of calculation at the center of neoliberal rationality. Calculation is key. It is not a matter of reduction implied by commodification. It is a matter of a subverted self-management. We must abandon the moralization of utilitarian anti-capitalist interventions, indeed abandon moralistic rejections of calculation, she argues. Neoliberalism from below allows a view of the "monstrosity" of the imperative to assume responsibility for conditions that "are not guaranteed" but that admit modes of collective articulation when navigating or subverting these conditions. What is produced, Gago says, is a "relation of promiscuity" whereby "adaptation to the rule of control (or to normalization, the logic of security) [is also] production beyond measure, surplus, excess."[94] "This excess," she stresses, "is not waste." Self-management is turned into nonacceptance. Calculation here means "stealing, working, making neighborly bonds, and migrating to live. It does not accept dying or seeing life reduced to a minimum of possibilities."[95] Self-management turns into "undertaking, getting by, saving yourself."

Baroque economies "mix logics and rationalities that tend to be portrayed (in economic and political theories) as incompatible."[96] They draw from resistance and survival in the colonial period and are "another name for the 'mottleying' (*abigarramiento*) of times and logics of operations."[97] "In Latin America," Gago writes, "the baroque persists as a set of interlaced modes of doing, thinking, perceiving, fighting, and working; as that which supposes the superimposition of nonreconciled terms in permanent re-creation."[98] Neoliberalism from below betrays a baroque articulation in the "strategic composition of microentrepreneurial elements, with formulas of popular progress, that compose a political subjectivity capable of negotiating and disputing state resources," effectively overlapping traditional and nontraditional contractual formats.[99] Neither victims nor entrepreneurs, then, given the modes of subversion available within neoliberal rationality that exceeds its very logic. Such possibilities, such excesses, are internal to its operation in this postcolonial context. These are powerful concepts, but they will need to be amended, given the strictures of the case of Puerto Rico. Lacking here is an exposition of the productivity of coloniality in and through baroque economies, in and through the ambivalence distinctive of their neoliberal expression, in a colonial context.[100] Furthermore, it is necessary to center race and, in the case of Puerto Rico, antiblack violence as key for understanding the production and productivity of gender, shifting thereby our conception of a feminist reading of debt.

NEOLIBERAL COLONIALITY

Nancy Fraser maintains that Marx offers a two-tiered account of capital in *Capital*.[101] While the "front story" is a matter of exploitation, which centers the dynamic of value creation and capture in production, the "backstory" is a matter of expropriation, which centers the history of "conquest, enslavement, robbery, murder, in short, force" that makes exploitation possible in the first place.[102] The originary accumulation of capital entails a history of the creation of the worker through a process of "becoming free," Marx argues with irony. Workers are free "*from*, unencumbered by, any means of production of their own" and free *to* sell their labor power.[103] Marx acknowledges that this process is traceable not only to the enclosure of the English commons but also to the "discovery of gold and silver in America, the extirpation, enslavement and entombment in mines of the indigenous population of that continent, the beginnings of the conquest and plunder of India, and the conversion of Africa into a preserve for the commercial hunting of blackskins."[104] The political relation that subtends exploitation, the owner/nonowner distinction, is installed through a history not merely of expropriation but of radical violent dispossession.[105]

Marx's irony, however, addresses the qualified "freedom" of the worker— of wage work. He writes that workers are "free workers, in the double sense that they neither form part of the means of production themselves, as would be the case with slaves, serfs, etc., nor do they own the means of production, as would be the case with self-employed peasant proprietors."[106] Paradigmatically, in being considered part of the means of production, the enslaved is subject to modalities of violence of a radically different kind to those established by the contract.[107] We must move beyond Fraser and recall Marx's note that "the veiled slavery of the wage laborers in Europe needed the unqualified slavery of the New World as its pedestal."[108] The creation of the worker through a process of dispossession that posits the laborer as a commodity in a market, as subject to the strictures of wage labor in a production process structured by the contract, is bound to turning other bodies "fungible," in Saidiya Hartman's term.[109] Fungibility indexes the simultaneous disposability and indispensability of captured and enslaved Africans, and the normative and affective economy made possible by the economy of slavery.[110] Distinct from the strictures of wage labor, "the dispossessed body of the enslaved is the surrogate for the master's body since it guarantees his disembodied universality and acts as the sign of his power and domination."[111] In the context of emancipation, she argues, this relation is retained rather than eliminated in the "rights of man and citizens" and in wage labor. Hartman rewrites Marx's quip on freedom accordingly. With the notion of "burdened individuality," she notes the double bind of freedom as "freed from slavery and free of resources, emancipated and subordinated, self-possessed and indebted, equal and inferior, liberated and encumbered, sovereign and dominated, citizen and subject."[112]

Centering the dynamic of dispossession indicates not only capitalism's need to posit limits that it will transgress, hence the necessity of its logic of predation, extraction, expulsion, dispossession.[113] Capitalism fundamentally requires the articulation of existence in light of the production of alterity and otherness, positing asymmetries that make possible economic expansion and that necessitate political control.[114] Such alterity and otherness is instituted concretely, generating rather than collapsing an irreducible heterogeneity in modes of organizing existence. More precision is needed, then, since capitalism does not merely operate through this dynamic. It operates through technologies of alterity and othering: race, and, along racial lines, gender, sexuality, class. It organizes existence in its heterogeneity through modalities of reterritorialization that ongoingly necessitate updating, adapting, actualizing the technology of race/gender/class. This is what Aníbal Quijano calls the "coloniality of power"(la colonialidad del poder).

Quijano argues that capitalism is a matrix or pattern (patrón) of domination/exploitation/conflict articulated around the axis of work that integrates all other historically known modes of organizing labor.[115] Capitalism is articulated, indeed installed, with the conquest and colonization of the Americas, the invention of the Americas, "disintegrating all previous patterns of power and absorbing and redefining those structural elements and fragments that were useful or necessary, and successfully imposed to date over all possible alternative patterns."[116] This means, however, that capitalism requires incommensurable yet simultaneous modes of organizing production, circulation, but also dispossession, enclosure, extraction. Wage labor coexists with slavery, indentured servitude, debt peonage, small commodity production. These discontinuous, indeed conflicting, modes of organizing labor respond to a "dominant logic" buttressed by the organization of authority and processes of subjection and subjectivation along with its forms of knowledge and knowledge production, imagination, and sensibility. An account of capitalism hence accounts for the production of a global matrix of colonial power. A "historical-structural heterogeneity" (*heterogeneidad histórico-estructural del poder*) is its mark.[117]

Race, according to Quijano, is the central technology through which capitalism is articulated and installed in conquest, colonialism, and independence as well as updated and reinstalled ongoingly—in altering conditions throughout time. The notion of coloniality of power is key to this account. It is instructive to consider it more closely. Power, according to Quijano, is the attempt to gain control over basic areas of human existence. "As we know it historically, on a social scale," Quijano writes:

> power is a space and net of social relations of exploitation/domination/conflict articulated basically in function of and centered around the dispute over the control of the following areas of social existence: (1) work and its products; (2) given the former's dependence on it, "nature" and its resources for production; sex, its products, and the reproduction of the species; (3) subjectivity and its products, material and intersubjective, which include knowledge; (4) authority and its instruments, in particular, of coercion in order to secure the reproduction of this matrix of social relations and to regulate its changes.[118]

Coloniality, in turn, is the form of domination distinctive of the global capitalist order installed by conquest and colonization. It refers to (a) the classification of the world's population by racializing the relation between the colonizer and the colonized; (b) the configuration of a new system of exploitation that articulates under one matrix or pattern, capitalism, all forms of control of labor—wage labor, slavery, indentured servitude, small commodity production; (c) Eurocentrism as a new mode of production and control of subjectivity; and (d) the nation-state as a system of collective authority that excludes populations racialized as inferior.[119] Whereas power articulates economic, epistemic, and political relations in historically specific ways, coloniality organizes existence ongoingly in light of the aims of capital by updating a system of racial classification born from indigenous genocide, the Middle Passage, and racial slavery. Eurocentrism is central to processes of subjectivation, knowledge production, imagination, and sensibility that continuously shore up such a system. The coloniality of power and modernity/rationality institute the coordinates of existence of the capitalist world.

For Quijano, labor, race, and gender are central "axes of articulation" around which capitalism develops, with which capitalism is anchored, and from which capitalism derives its authority.[120] Now, labor and gender are central axes, given that they are purportedly tied to "social survival" and the "biological reproduction of the species." Although labor is a central axis, since it "implies control over the labor force, its resources and products, including nature and institutionalized as property," distinct modes of labor and their modes of domination are produced in light of the technology of race. Control of "sex" and its products ("pleasure and offspring") is for the sake of "property." "Gender," he argues, was always central to the reproduction of the species, hence social reproduction. Race, in contrast, was incorporated into the ends of labor with the invention of the Americas, inflecting the control of, he says, "sex." A system of racial classification based on the distinction European/American instituted racial categories such as "Indian," "white," "black," and "mestizo," he argues, central to both labor and gender. Labor, however, is a "central and permanent" relation in which domination makes exploitation possible but differentially articulated in light of the newly created racial categories. Race and labor are tightly bound, then, since racial identities are not only produced. They also function to distribute who is exploitable versus who is fungible—who has access to wage labor, who is subject to slavery. "Sexual exploitation" is "discontinuous" with domination, purportedly, since it is essential for the "reproduction of the species."[121] Thus, race sustains the colonial project that organizes labor and inflects gender in light of the aims of capitalism.[122] The naturalization of race, race understood as a "biological" category, is the key technology of capitalist power, producing modalities of violence central to a functioning capitalist system.

María Lugones challenges the asymmetry in Quijano's treatment of race and gender.[123] She points out that Quijano's biological understanding of sex is already gendered: a construction of sexual difference as dimorphic and heterosexual as well as patriarchy as productive of a gender hierarchy central to colonial power. Quijano's conception of gender is based on claims about the reproduction of the species, missing that the global pattern of colonial power is in effect a "colonial/modern gender system." Drawing from Paula Gunn Allen and Oyéronké Oyewùmi's work, she argues that he fails to consider that a dimorphic and heterosexual understanding of sex was not only imposed on indigenous populations, but that such imposition is an essential aspect of the colonial project that he otherwise carefully tracks. While Allen's work elucidates how biological dimorphism was central to the productivity of race, Oyewùmi's work clarifies the transformation of social relations under a patriarchal system by the colonial project. The coloniality of gender, then, elucidates that race organizes not only labor but also sex/gender, installing the very category of woman as bound to bourgeois whiteness. This gender norm—"Woman"—produces alterity as well as otherness in positing racialized bodies, sexualities, and forms of relationality that cannot embody the norm, as Celenis Rodríguez Moreno argues.[124] As such, these bodies and populations are subject to forms of labor, authority, violence beyond those articulated by the race/gender norm.[125] For Lugones, then, there is a "light/visible" and "dark/hidden" side of the colonial/modern gender system. For Rodríguez Moreno, the colonial/modern gender system produces "obscure versions" of the gender norm that subtend it. The coloniality of gender actualizes or updates how the race/gender norm posits "incomplete subjects/partially human" in an ongoing manner.[126] It actualizes the content of incompleteness/partiality in reference to a race/gender norm replenished in light of altered material and historical conditions.

Rita Segato rejects the basis for Lugones's critique, though she develops an account of the coloniality of gender as well. The claim that gender is a production of the modern colonial project, she argues, is anthropologically unsound. She finds historiographic and ethnographic evidence of the existence of recognizable structures of difference, "which contain hierarchies of prestige along masculinity and femininity and are represented by figures that can be understood as men and women."[127] We might call these "preintervention" (colonial) distinctions "dual," whereas we might understand those articulated by modernity/coloniality as "binary."[128] The dual is a "variant of the multiple" while the binary posits the "other" in order to reduce it to the same.[129] The crucial point for Segato is that patriarchy was not installed by the modern colonial project, but the latter "captured" and reconfigured it. "[G]ender relations proper to the colonial matrix," she writes, "capture preceding forms of patriarchy which, although existent and hierarchical, did not obey the same structure, and they transform them into a much more lethal form of patriarchy, such as the modern."[130]

I am interested in this aspect of Segato's account. Her understanding of coloniality as the capture, actualization, and intensification of a hierarchy helps establish the work of debt as a form of coloniality. Let us set aside, then, questions about precolonial expressions of gender/sex. Let us set aside as well Quijano's own treatment of labor, race, and gender. Let us keep, however, Quijano's view that these are "axes of articulation," arguing with Lugones that race/gender is the central technology in the articulation of labor differentially. Let us hold on to the thought that race/gender produces distinct modalities of dispossession and violence. Race/gender organizes labor but also normativities, institutionalities, subjectivities, modes of embodiment thus modes of knowing and sensing as well as their ongoing actualizations in the reproduction of the capitalist colonial world. Race/gender is for this reason central to the inscription of territories, economies, and bodies in which apparatuses of capitalist capture, predation, and extraction land. Debt lands not merely exacerbating a history of racial/gender violence, then. It reinscribes it, actualizes or updates it, rearticulates its differences and intensities. Race/gender reinstalls the global capitalist order according to the latter's changing needs heterogeneously but continuously. Debt operates as a form of coloniality, accordingly, since it does more than capture value, land, the body, sensation itself. It captures, extracts, predates not merely "along" race/gender/class lines. It actualizes race/gender, initiating new or altered modalities of dispossession and violence. Yet it thereby also indexes sites and modes of interruption, disobedience, refusal.

With the process of conquest and colonization, Segato argues, a "turn" that "exacerbates" the "originary" hierarchical pattern—one that she describes as a "low intensity patriarchy" (*patriarcado de baja intensidad*)—occurs.[131] A gender multiplicity that admits of a "feminine/masculine" hierarchy is reduced to a binary. This mutation of gender is accompanied by a transformation of the "field and meaning" of sexuality now pervaded by "harm and cruelty": "not only the appropriation of bodies, their annexation *qua territories*, but also their damnation."[132] The hierarchy is "more lethal," since the body now appears as territory within the logic of capitalist capture. In the context of neoliberal capitalism, what Segato calls the "apocalyptic phase of capital," territoriality is exercised on women's bodies.[133] Examining femicide in Ciudad Juárez in the context of the North American Free Trade Agreement (NAFTA), she argues that this mutation of capitalism can be said to return us to a logic of conquest instead of a sublimated coloniality.[134] Bodies are marked as women by being marked as territory in an updated economy of capture organized in light of the racial norm. Neoliberal trade agreements land not only through the labor of women, women from the global South, women at the border, migrant women. They actualize race/gender in a way that intensifies their effectivity to the degree that a specific modality of violence emerges. The "expressive violence" turns women's bodies into the site through which impunity is constructed and communicated emerges. I come back to this point and discuss the link between debt and femicide below.

Coloniality operates by marking bodies and populations as disposable. Lazzarato argues that, in the context of debt crises, the biopolitical power to "make live and let die" means "if you can pay, you can live, and if you cannot pay, you can die, insofar as your exposure to death, to the risks of social death (impoverishment, misery, exploitation, domination, inequalities) and political death (exclusion, rejection), increase."[135] Segato similarly argues that the "abyss" between those who own the resources of the planet and those who do not is precisely the power to decide to make live or let die.[136] This is not merely the decision of a sovereign, as we will see in chapter 2. Neoliberal financialized capitalism trades on its necropolitical effects. Life is "subjugated to the power of death," as Achille Mbembe puts it, through a political economy that depends on political and juridical institutions for its actualization.[137] The point is that this political economy creates and extracts value from death itself.[138] Precarization, expulsion, and death itself are key for the actualization of finance through multiple apparatuses. To make live or let die or to fully subjugate life to the power of death by extracting value from precarization, expulsion, death itself generates distinct modalities of violence.

These modalities of violence are the continuation of colonial violence, which produced a norm of humanity bound to bourgeois whiteness. Maldonado-Torres's Fanonian concept of "metaphysical catastrophe" is insightful here. It rewrites Quijano's notion of coloniality of power, specifying the installation of a human/nonhuman distinction that subtends the continuation of the colonial condition. Maldonado-Torres argues that coloniality is a "veritable *catastrophe*," a "down-turn." It emerges from yet also advances catastrophes of a "demographic" nature that compose colonial violence in the early modern world: indigenous genocide, the middle passage, racial slavery.[139] Coloniality is a *metaphysical* catastrophe, however, since it is the "production" of a world not "according to practices or beliefs, but to degrees of being, human."[140] Coloniality is the organization of existence, the meaning and relation of "thinking and being," including "temporality and spatiality," to the image of humanity bound to a racial order.[141]

We have seen that coloniality is the ongoing productivity of race/gender, updating modalities of violence initiated by the installation of the capitalist modern project in altered material and historical conditions. The coloniality of power organizes labor and its modalities of violence, but it produces subjectivity and knowledge as well, including imagination, desire, and sense. Modernity/rationality shapes not only views of history (linearity, maturity), temporality (futurity), and universality inscribed in institutions such as the state. It shapes sensibility itself, trafficking with categories of intelligibility that capture the imagination, the body, memory, and sensation. A race/gender system of classification not only posits and actualizes a hierarchy, then. It turns unintelligible or coopts by rendering intelligible visions of the world, forms of knowing, sensing, experiencing, and relating as well as memory that exceed modernity/rationality. Race/gender organizes labor, authority, subjectivity in terms of proximity or distance to humanity, a humanity bound to bourgeois whiteness.

The concept of metaphysical catastrophe develops further Maldonado-Torres's notion of the coloniality of being. The coloniality of being tracks the "misanthropic skepticism" that establishes degrees of humanity through the technology of race/gender. One must trace the birth of the modern capitalist colonial world to the "slave-trading system out of Africa" initiated by the Portuguese in 1441, as Sylvia Wynter notes.[142] Quijano stresses the Valladolid debate, wherein the legal and moral status of the conquest was debated in light of the humanity of indigenous people, as key to binding humanity, rationality, and bourgeois whiteness. Enrique Dussel develops the thought, arguing that the Cartesian *ego cogito*, the founding gesture of modern rationality through the question of certainty, was built on the *ego conquiro*, the historical ground of modernity.[143] Modern rationality depends on a structure of conquest that institutes alterity only to destroy it. Certainty is only thereby guaranteed. Maldonado-Torres rewrites Dussel's suggestion, arguing that the Cartesian "I think therefore I am" should be rewritten in an ontological key as "I think (others do not think, or do not think properly), therefore I am (others are-not, lack being, should not exist or are dispensable)."[144]

Misanthropic skepticism is not a matter of epistemic or juridical doubt. It names the production of a world through a distinction between being human and "not being human" that stems, according to Maldonado-Torres, from turning the exceptional conditions of war into ubiquitous features of the experience of the colonized. "While in war there is murder and rape," he writes, "in the hell of the colonial world murder and rape become day-to-day occurrences and menaces."[145] Through the naturalization of colonial violence the colonized are seen as "inherently servants," "their bodies come to form part of an economy of sexual abuse, exploitation, and control."[146] It is important to note that ubiquitous violence operates differentially, tracking distinct histories hence distinct logics of colonial capture, commodification, disposession. For Maldonado-Torres, the point is that for the colonized the ubiquity of violence ongoingly normalizes "questioning one's humanity."[147] The colonized "exist in the mode of not-being there, which hints at the nearness of death, at the company of death." The colonized is "either invisible or excessively visible."

I come back to Maldonado-Torres's discussion in the conclusion to this book. Here, I seek to retain the critique of political economy central to Quijano's work. The normalization of war should be understood rather as the naturalization of dispossession, expulsion, precarization. To be sure, Maldonado-Torres notes that the colonized "are meant to be bodies without land, people without resources, and subjects without the capacity for autonomy and self-determination whose constant desire is to be other than themselves."[148] "Like colonialism," he adds, "coloniality involves the expropriation of land and resources" and its continuation within "the market and modern nation-states."[149] Building on this discussion and recalling Segato's work, I suggest that coloniality updates and intensifies the work of race/gender through a reterritorialization that involves establishing the disposability of bodies and populations in altered historical and material conditions. Debt actualizes race/gender in positing anew certain bodies and populations as disposable, amenable to more than political control but rather violence, expulsion, precarity, outright death. Debt marks disposability by establishing culpability, I want to suggest accordingly. Culpable subjects are abject subjects. They threaten identity, system, and order, but they thereby function as economic opportunities: to be appropriated, put on reserve, expulsed, exploited, or altogether eliminated.

Disposability as abjection is key to the account of subjection through subjectivation that links debt and guilt. The apparatuses of capitalist capture, such as debt, land on bodies and populations producing space and time, body and sense, to the measure of colonial violence. They inscribe race/gender/class by producing abject subjects—the indebted man, the indebted woman. These subjects are not disposable in general. They are marked as such by race/gender/class. They are marked as other in excess of the race/gender norm that binds productivity, propriety, and whiteness. They are marked by given concrete capitalist/colonial ends. Subjects are not killable in general, but killable because they are perceived as "dangerous," as we will see in chapter 2, or as "defiant," "excessive," as we will see below.

Subjects are not dispossessed in general, but subject to the extirpation of material conditions for life in austerity given their "irresponsibility" or "laziness" or "corrupt" behavior. Subjects are not exploitable or displaceable in general, but because they are posited as responsible for social reproduction by "nature." In each case, the operation of race/gender is updated, adapted, reinstalled. Each is a site in which coloniality operates. A cartography of debt maps these instances in their specificity.

A CARTOGRAPHY OF DEBT

In *Las Propias*, Godreau-Aubert speaks of debt from the colony, *desde la colonia*. The colony, recall, takes place, happens (*transcurre*), in repeated acts of capture. "Indebted life," she writes, "is the continuation of colonial life."[150] In the case of Puerto Rico, the colony is that which appears nowhere, that which is "substituted by the 'post-colonial.'" To speak from the colony of Puerto Rico is to speak from a place "abandoned by everyone, except by those who keep finding how to exploit it."[151] It is to speak from a no-place (*no-lugar*). To be in debt (*estar en deuda*) is to be located in a space and time of capture, dispossession, expropriation. A cartography of debt locates, *ubica*, bodies and populations in the no-place of debt. It maps *being placed* in the no-place of debt, being *occupied* by debt. It locates "colonial power."[152] It tracks the productivity of coloniality. This cartography maps where debt lands, the way it updates and reinstalls race/gender/class, the modalities of violence such actualization produces. This mapping, however, is done "knowing that we do not owe ourselves to anyone."[153]

A debt is a condition of place, Godreau-Aubert argues. "When it is others who place us in debt, in spite of us," she writes, "that place is also a way to get rid of the body even when wearing it."[154] Godreau-Aubert's conception of the body, *cuerpa*, is crucial. In a footnote, she writes that with the term *cuerpa* she understands the "nominal, material, spiritual, and political entity from which we situate ourselves when we identify as women or at the margins of the coordinates, traditionally demarcated, for bodies, genders, and sexes."[155] She adds, "a body [*una cuerpa*] is also a degenerate/degendered [*una degenerada*] that occupies or is occupied by."[156] The latter is key. Una cuerpa is not merely the material/symbolic site of "women," cis and trans. It is the site of occupation that produces race/class, binding the category of woman to bourgeois whiteness. But it is therefore also a site of the subversion or refusal of material and symbolic/normative occupation itself, as we will see. In Puerto Rico, the body-territory of women is a place for the adaptation and reinstallation of the relation between colonialism and coloniality.[157] In contemporary Puerto Rico, what is "announced" in the body-territory, more precisely, body-colony of women is the continuation of colonial life through debt. But it is also the site of taking back, refusal, subversion.

Austerity, to recall, functions as an injunction to pay. It binds debt and guilt, turning debtors into culpable subjects that must pay. Unpayable debt indexes an irresponsible individual unable to thrive on human capital. Such failure is also of a population that must bear the burden of the cost of social reproduction, especially in times of economic downturn. The indebted man is an abject subject, but an account of the effects of such injunction on women reveals that the nature of this abjection cannot be universalized. In Puerto Rico, these differences multiply. Unpayable debt is not only the fate of failed neoliberal subjects—men or women. It indexes the fate of failed colonial subjects who affirmed a qualified autonomy for the purported benefits of US economic prosperity with the creation of the Estado Libre Asociado. Debt binds establishing the failure of economic agents parasitic on federal "handouts," recalling a history of racial justification for juridical-political subordination and control, as we will see in chapter 2. In the colony, culpability explicitly actualizes race/gender/class.

In the colony, the abject is the failed neoliberal but also failed colonial subject. As such, abjection marks a site of economic opportunity—some thing, some one to be captured, put on reserve, expulsed, or altogether eliminated. Abjection is the mark of a body or a population that admits of modes of control, violence, expulsion. It marks the body of the "degenerate/degendered" that is "occupied by." Disposability generates a problem of visibility. It generates "hypervisibility" in the Fanonian sense. To be seen is not to appear. It is rather to be reduced to an object indexed by race/gender/class. The colonial subject, the failed colonial subject, only appears racialized/gendered as nonwhite, though not all colonial subjects appear likewise. In the colony, antiblack violence organizes the racial hierarchy that structures the colonial relation beyond juridical-political control. Debt intensifies this hypervisibility when it updates, adapts, race/gender/class in altered material conditions. This hypervisibility sustains the modalities of violence that austerity produces. Godreau-Aubert's work maps the work of coloniality in the racialized feminization of poverty. Segato's work and interventions by la Colectiva Feminista en Construcción name the operation of coloniality in femicide. These are the necropolitical effects of debt's reterritorialization—its landing—on women.

The work of debt can be mapped through the "pornography of austerity," Godreau-Aubert maintains.[158] This pornography "uses" the body of the indebted woman to "anchor uncertainty." It thereby serves as the "injunction" (*exigencia*) to pay. The pornography of austerity has two elements: the "colonial condition" and "footage of poverty and numbers."[159] The former tracks indebted life as the continuation of colonial life. The latter tracks the production of culpability, establishing amenability for technocratic control. The colonial condition makes debt invisible as an apparatus of capture. It makes debt illegible as a form of coloniality. With austerity, however, such invisibility gains "pornographic" visibility. Godreau-Aubert focuses on the double invisibility that results from Puerto Rico's juridico-political lack of sovereignty. While the United Nations adopted principles on sovereign debt restructuring processes, these address sovereign nation-states.[160] Puerto Rico was removed from the United Nations list of non-self-governing territories in 1953. International forums that purport to monitor the effects of debt repayment are out of reach. Such invisibility is also expressed in the institution of a Fiscal Control Board through PROMESA, as we will see in chapter 2. The board is tasked with achieving "fiscal responsibility" and "access to capital markets," irrespective of social costs.

The double invisibility of Puerto Rico's colonial condition gains pornographic visibility in austerity. It is exposed in the reduction of the lived experience of the indebted woman to "photos and numbers," to the journalistic picture and the statistic amenable to technocratic control.[161] This reduction *exposes* "induced poverty," a poverty that must be understood as "vulgar" *because* it is "induced." The hypervisibility gained in photos and numbers makes possible mapping the work of coloniality. Godreau-Aubert maps debt's landing on women, especially black women in the territory, accordingly.[162] She discusses two examples. First, a 2016 *New York Times* article that portrays Puerto Rico as a "showcase of the surreal" in which "patriots" shop at Walmart and 12 percent unemployment is coupled with "unwillingness" to harvest coffee.[163] The photos that accompany the article portray "principally women: resting, sitting, hungry, unoccupied, never working."[164] This is an "imaginary of debt" that "insists on its legitimacy insofar as it feminizes the face of the bully, 'happiness,' the culpable."[165] Poverty is situated in a refusal to work—a defiant refusal. Women are at the same time hungry, resting, happy. They become the image, indeed the face, of a colonial condition maintained *by* these women. These women are purportedly complicit with the colonial relation by depending on federal "handouts"—welfare.[166] This dependence couples hunger and happiness.

1.1 *Source:* "A Surreal Life on the Precipice," *The New York Times,* August 6, 2016.

1.2 Perla Bowl, San Juan, Puerto Rico. Skateboarding bowl and pool built in 2006 in La Perla community by artist Chemi Rosado-Seijo with Roberto "Boly" Cortés and neighbors of La Perla community, July 23, 2017. *Source:* Bowl La Perla Facebook page.

These women are culpable of their own fate. Hypervisibility indexes a culpable subject, material conditions for life itself to be cut in austerity.

Second, poverty is measured in numbers. In austerity, the lived experience made invisible by the statistic gains hypervisibility. In various writings, Godreau-Aubert invites the reader to consider that a box of tampons costs around $7 without tax.[167] With PROMESA's austerity plan, minimum wage could be reduced to $4.25 an hour for workers under the age of twenty-five.[168] Given federal cuts in the Nutritional Assistance Program, a family might have access to as little as $36 in cash (from $60).[169] The statistic gains pornographic visibility in the stain, in the calculus involved at the bodily level of hygiene. Culpability and responsibility produced by disgust. The "vulgarity" of an induced poverty turned into the "vulgarity" of the person who bleeds—a cis woman, a trans man, a nonbinary person unemployed, on welfare, but also the teacher or nurse who must supplement what is lacking in a crumbling infrastructure with their own body. Photos and numbers feed the "controlling image" of the "welfare queen" in Puerto Rico.[170]

In a chapter entitled "Esa tipa es una yal; el chiste, la pobreza, y la negritud sin retorno," Godreau-Aubert discusses the production of female blackness in Puerto Rico in the criminalization of poverty.[171] Black women are posited as "maintained body" (*cuerpa mantenida*), body on welfare. In "Degradando a la 'yal': Racialización y violencia antinegra en Puerto Rico," Katsí Yarí Rodríguez-Velázquez explains that "la yal" is a stereotype of poor racialized women living in *caseríos* or public housing.[172] La yal is "poor, lazy, indecent, hyper-fertile."[173] She is unproductive, "irresponsible," "unhealthy," suspicious, "availed." In her landmark work, Zaire Dinzey-Flores shows that public housing is key for the production of race in Puerto Rico, specifically through the criminalization of poverty.[174] The latter draws from a long history of antiblackness tied to slavery and made invisible through an ideology of *lo criollo* that has dominated discussions of race in Puerto Rico.[175] As la Colectiva Feminista en Construcción writes:

> In the colony of Puerto Rico, the racial state operates with diverse logics. The criollo imaginary reproduces racial narratives of a mixture that does not recognize the anti-Black violence that it entailed. It is hidden as well, behind the mixture of races, the confinement of Black bodies/territories to the marginalized, the expropriable and the criminalized. Just as is hidden the fixing of mestizo bodies/territories with white aspirationism in different dimensions: from the aesthetic to the economic. Likewise, behind the mixture of races, is hidden the devaluation of the

work carried out by visibly Black people and how their bodies are turned disposable in the face of physical, economic and environmental violence perpetrated by the racial state.[176]

Since the 1990s, as Dinzey-Flores shows and as we will see in chapter 2, crime-fighting policies in the context of the rise of a drug economy are vital to the production of a racial hierarchy based on antiblackness.[177] State violence against drug-related violence within public housing, coupled with state-sanctioned private housing in gated communities owned by mostly middle- and upper-class white Puerto Ricans, spatially as well as ideologically posited black and brown men as "dangerous, violent, poor."[178] Public housing, however, is mostly inhabited by women, thereby seen as living in the site of drug and crime.[179]

Godreau-Aubert argues that when one says "yal," one is indexing the "geographic coordinates of the country": public housing, *el barrio*, the street (*la calle*).[180] Yet that is to say that one is indexing the "unmeasured intervention of the police and the media."[181] She writes: "to receive social assistance locates these women in a diffuse space in between the private and the public, a space that seems to be open to judgment and active intervention by those-who-are-not-a-yal. If feminist geographies begin with the body—*la cuerpa*—the first space of poor black women in the country [*el país*] is that of an occupied zone [*zona ocupada*]."[182] The term *yal* indexes "the outside [*el afuera*]," Godreau-Aubert notes. La yal is a limit that the race/gender/class norm posits to capture, exploit, displace, or altogether eliminate. More precisely, la yal is the other that the race/gender norm that binds "woman" to whiteness, work, propriety requires for its functioning. To map the geographic coordinates of the country, then, is to track the operation and actualization of whiteness, its ongoing need to shore itself up by producing modalities of antiblack violence. As Rodríguez-Velázquez argues, the yal must thus be understood in the impossibility but also in the *refusal* to embody the race/class norm that establishes propriety in terms of white bourgeois ethics/aesthetics, cisheteronormativity and the nuclear family, and the "advanced, civilized, on the way to progress."[183]

Debt and austerity intensify a second modality of violence: femicide. In 2018, twenty-four women were killed by husbands, partners, or ex-partners.[184] One hundred and eighty of reported cases of domestic violence were perpetrated by police officers. Approximately 2,554 sexual assault forensic exams remain unprocessed to this day. Although the numbers are alarming, they are part of a pattern of gender violence where, for example, twenty-five women were killed by their intimate partners in 2011. From 2018 to 2019, sexual violence increased by 7 percent.[185] In Puerto Rico, only 2 percent of cases of rape and sexual violence are reported; only 7 percent of those are investigated and clarified. Edda López-Serrano states that these numbers are akin to the sexual violence within a state of war.[186] Violence in the immediate aftermath of Hurricanes Irma and María disproportionately impacted cis and trans women, especially poor women, the elderly, girls, and immigrants—specifically Dominican immigrants.[187] Emergency 911 calls related to domestic violence tripled.[188] Lacking money due to lack of work, many women struggled to access food and basic resources. Trans women reported that they were particularly vulnerable, given a collapsed electrical grid and discrimination at refuge centers.[189]

On November 23, 2018, la Colectiva Feminista en Construcción performed a sit-in, Plantón Feminista, in front of la Fortaleza, the official residence of the governor of Puerto Rico.[190] With the sit-in, la Colectiva brought an Executive Order to Declare a State of Emergency regarding gender violence to then-governor Ricardo Rosselló. The sit-in lasted for three days. No government official interacted with la Colectiva, though there was confrontation with the Tactical Operations Unit of the police, la Fuerza de Choque, on November 25, the International Day for the Elimination of Violence against Women. Shariana Ferrer-Núñez, cofounder, explains that la Colectiva's intervention sought to connect information about gender violence circulating in the media and addressed by feminist organizations, making visible the systemic nature of intimate partner killings, unprocessed sexual assault forensic exams, and cases of domestic violence. La Colectiva thereby sought to hold the state accountable for gaps in resources, education, and other modes of addressing gender violence and femicide. As Eva Prados emphasizes, the impact of austerity is clear in resource allocation to address gender violence, from the dismantling of education with gender perspective, impunity to government and law enforcement officials with records of domestic and sexual violence, to governmental and nongovernmental campaigns and prevention efforts.[191]

La Colectiva's use of the category of femicide is key.[192] They employ the category in a confrontation with the state, aiming to capture the norms of the state by calling for a declaration of a state of emergency. El Plantón subverts the state's main mechanism for installing neoliberal rationality in the colony, namely, declarations of states of emergency, as we will see in detail in chapter 2. Here, the declaration aims to interrupt impunity. Segato's work is decisive at this juncture. She develops the notion of "expressive violence" to specify the work of femicide, distinguishing expressive from "instrumental violence."[193] Instrumental violence pursues a specific aim while expressive violence articulates determined and comprehensible relationships between bodies, particularly around the hierarchies of a territory. This modality of violence is expressive in producing implicit rules and regulations through which legal and nonlegal power circulates, as Gago puts it.[194] Segato maintains that gender violence writes a message on the woman's body and, I add, on bodies that challenge the white bourgeois cisheteronormative order. That message has to do with impunity. She does not argue that impunity is the cause of femicide. On the contrary, femicide (re)produces impunity. This impunity is not merely an institutional problem—something to be measured and, through structures of accountability, ameliorated. It is transversal, producing sensibility itself.

Expressive violence is part of a "pedagogy of cruelty." "Every act of violence, as a discursive gesture," Segato writes, "bears a signature."[195] The necropolitical operation of coloniality is clarified in femicide's display of "vertical" power.[196] This is a modality of power—the power of patriarchy, of capital—"spectacularized."[197] Important here is not the subject that signs—a toxic, violent masculinity, patriarchy itself.[198] Crucial here is the "message to peers" that expresses itself in impunity, an impunity that manifests itself when the neighbor as well as the state remain silent in the face of gender violence. It is here that we find the subject that signs. Dispersed, although at the same time precise. This is the horizontality of gender violence, according to Segato, one that cannot be separated from the vertical deployment of sexist violence (*violencia machista*). Such horizontality manifests a cruelty at the level of the sensible, a sensibility trained to the "not-binding," *el no-vincular*.[199]

Godreau-Aubert speaks of a "pedagogy of the indebted woman" as an act of "healing." It names what has already been announced in the body of women: that indebted life is "dehumanizing," "illegitimate."[200] Like Gago and Cavallero, she argues that such a pedagogy narrates indebted life in the colony, resisting its abstraction. It resists the broken, fragmentation of debt. A cartography of debt "tells" (*dice*)—names, narrates—indebted life in the colony "in pieces," *en pedacitos*.[201] To tell the "broken time" of debt, she writes in a footnote, is not a marginal note about "social fragmentation."[202] To write about crime in Puerto Rico, she adds, is not a note on "street violence" (*violencia callejera*). It requires breaking with a discourse that "condemns imperialism and at the same time buttresses the murderous, patriarchal violence of banking." She elaborates what it might mean to tell or narrate indebted life in pieces: like finding a corpse. It has the weight of "supreme loss." To realize "one of your own" is culpable is even worse.[203] What is found is the corpse of a postcolonial in its afterlife.

The colony is no-place, except for those who keep finding how to exploit it. The colony "is never a safe space: for women, it is hostile territory, qualified [*matizado*] by the increase of gender violence, precarity, the criminalization of protest, the impunity of a public official who has raped women and of a church that prays for him and his family. The island is no-home [*La isla es un no-hogar*]," Godreau-Aubert writes.[204] The no-place of debt is nevertheless the location from which to interrupt the colony, the operation of coloniality. Activists in Puerto Rico have deployed a variety of tactics locating themselves within the strictures of debt in order to subvert it. Refusal, nonpayment, subversion, rescue/occupation and other forms of interruption, as we will see, exploit the asymmetry of the injunction to pay. The subjects of guilt are not merely subjected to debt. They interrupt the work of debt through a defiant affirmation of nonpayment, moreover, through a reversal of culpability. We will need to move from an economic to a historical understanding of debt, however, from debts to capital to historical, indeed colonial, debts to be settled in order to consider the power of these modes of interruption. In the case of Puerto Rico, such a move first requires shifting from an account of colonial exceptionality to an exposition of the slow death of neoliberal coloniality.

Colonial Exceptionality 2

El desastre es la colonia.
The disaster is the colony.
—JORNADA: SE ACABARON LAS PROMESAS

La invasión no es un evento, es una estructura.
The invasion is not an event, it is a structure.
—ANAYRA SANTORY-JORGE, "Lo prometido es deuda"

The tradition of the oppressed famously teaches us that the "state of
emergency" in which we live is not the exception but the rule.
—WALTER BENJAMIN, "On the Concept of History"

IN JANUARY OF 1899, the United States made official exchange rates for
the multiple currencies circulating in the newly acquired colony of Puerto
Rico. The Puerto Rican peso was deemed to be worth 60 cents. James Dietz
explains that the devaluation of the Puerto Rican peso facilitated the pur-
chase of land by American sugar corporations, and it created conditions for
predatory lending by the American Colonial Bank.[1] The latter, in turn, fed
the former. Small landowners would come to default on their loans or sell
their lands to sugar corporations when faced with the prospect of default.
The reduction of wealth and the creation of conditions for the continued

capture of wealth and land can be understood as the first act of capture by the new colonial regime.[2]

With the Treaty of Paris of 1898 that ended the Spanish-American War, Spain ceded Puerto Rico to the United States.[3] Congress ratified the Treaty on April 11, 1899, setting in motion more than a century of juridico-political control inseparable albeit distinguishable from economic capture. The Foraker Act of 1900, the Insular Cases of 1901–1922, the Jones Act of 1917 and 1920, Law 600 of 1950, the Supreme Court's *Puerto Rico v. Sanchez Valle* ruling in 2016, and PROMESA of 2016 articulate the strictures of Puerto Rico's status as an unincorporated territory of the United States. These laws and court decisions concretely shape conditions for capture, predation, and extraction discussed in chapter 1. Examining Puerto Rico's juridico-political status is thus a necessary starting point for assessing the debt crisis.

José Atiles-Osoria argues that the concept of "state of exception" illuminates Puerto Rico's juridico-political status and the conditions of capture that it generates.[4] He develops the notion "colonial state of exception," which is at once juridical and ontopolitical.[5] Law, politics, and economy intersect in the creation of an unincorporated territory, producing a colonial social, economic, and political reality.[6] Although Atiles-Osoria does not fully account for the correlation economy-exceptionality, he draws from his discussion of unincorporation to develop the notion "neoliberal colonialism."[7] The latter sheds light on the way in which neoliberal rationality was installed as the dominant logic of colonial exceptionality.[8] Neoliberal colonialism tracks the increase in use of declarations of states of emergency in the administration of the colony, reconfiguring conditions of capture made possible by Puerto Rico's juridico-political predicament.

While neoliberal colonialism illuminates key features of colonial exceptionality, the analytics of exceptionality do not account for the "slow death" of neoliberal coloniality. It does not track the relation between colonialism and coloniality through its material conditions and effects, focusing instead on exceptional measures made possible by the political-juridical apparatus. I turn to Miriam Muñiz-Varela and Anayra Santory-Jorge's conceptions of an "economy of the catastrophe" and "catastrophe by attrition" to center material conditions and effects that exceed the decision of a sovereign.[9] Lauren Berlant's notion of slow death and her critique of exceptionality are insightful here.[10] To speak of "crises," "declarations of emergency," the "event," the "sovereign who decides," indeed the "state of exception," she argues, is to speak of the intensification of an environment in which the reproduction of life involves the attrition of life. As Muñiz-Varela makes clear, the political economy of Puerto Rico has always been the "destruction of general conditions of life" in its purported attempt to articulate those very conditions. In contrast to Berlant, Muñiz-Varela illuminates the normalization of spectacular violence as part of the ordinary in the no-place of life in the indebted colony.

This chapter is composed of three sections. The first section, Colonial State of Exception, examines Atiles-Osoria's notion of a colonial state of exception in light of his critique of Charles Venator-Santiago's work on exceptionality in Puerto Rico.[11] While Atiles-Osoria underscores the administrative use of declarations of states of emergency, Venator-Santiago stresses the production of liminal juridical spaces that create conditions for economic capture. In line with Venator-Santiago, the second section, Colonial Exceptionality, moves from Atiles-Osoria's notion of neoliberal colonialism to Muñiz-Varela's exposition of an economy of the catastrophe. The latter maps modalities of violence distinctive of post-Fordist Puerto Rico. Marisol LeBrón's work is helpful here.[12] She discusses what she calls "punitive governance" in this political-economic economy. State measures against drug-related crime not only increase but also cause a violence that is both "spectacular and quotidian." I pay attention to the production of racialized masculinity that binds criminality and blackness in this context. Such production indexes the actualization of race/gender/class through exceptional measures. The last section, Slow Death of Neoliberal Coloniality, examines the slow death of neoliberal coloniality in the indebted colony through an engagement with Muñiz-Varela, Santory-Jorge, and Yarimar Bonilla. It rewrites Berlant's critique of the analytics of exceptionality and her conception of slow death. The environment of indebted life in the colony admits of spectacular forms of violence as part of the ordinary. Bonilla's reference to Christina Sharpe is crucial here as well. The no-place of indebted life in the colony is more precisely understood as the "climate" generated and sustained by the logic of disposability distinctive of coloniality. This, I maintain, is the site of colonial exceptionality: a state of emergency that is not the exception but the rule.

COLONIAL STATE OF EXCEPTION

Atiles-Osoria and Venator-Santiago transform Giorgio Agamben's notion of the state of exception to examine Puerto Rico's status as an unincorporated territory of the United States. Agamben draws from Carl Schmitt's understanding of the sovereign as "he who decides on the state of exception."[13] For Schmitt, the state of exception designates the suspension of the law in times of war, civil unrest, or, more generally, political threat. Agamben understands exceptionality more broadly, attempting to track the creation of a juridical void crucial to the maintenance of the status quo. Exceptionality thus refers to a space in which the force of law exists without the law, a space in which the "rule maintains itself in relation to the exception in the form of suspension."[14] The possibility of suspending the law is internal to "liberal, democratic states," since it is a measure for addressing crises or situations that exceed normality.[15]

Atiles-Osoria and Venator-Santiago seek to develop Agamben's understanding of the liminal logic of exceptionality. Agamben describes the state of exception as "neither external nor internal to the juridical order, and the problem of defining it concerns precisely a threshold, or a zone of indifference, where inside and outside do not exclude each other but rather blur with each other."[16] The state of exception is the creation of a juridical void of "being-outside, and yet belonging," as Venator-Santiago puts it.[17] Or, as Atiles-Osoria puts it, "the exercise of sovereign power is the inclusive-exclusion or the inclusion that excludes."[18] Here we begin to see a difference in emphasis. Venator-Santiago underscores the space of anomie instituted by the sovereign, whereas Atiles-Osoria is interested in the sovereign who decides. This difference is decisive. Rather than the seat of sovereignty, as we will see, focus on the material conditions and effects of the liminal logic of exceptionality should be centered. The point here is that the liminality distinctive of the state of exception is well suited for assessing Puerto Rico's status as an unincorporated territory that "belongs to" but is "not a part of" the United States.[19]

Atiles-Osoria launches important criticisms of Agamben's genealogy of the state of exception. Agamben traces it to the Roman *iustitium*, discussing its deployment in the global North.[20] Atiles-Osoria notes the Eurocentrism of this genealogy, pointing out Agamben's failure to consider non-Western experiences decisive for its development.[21] Atiles-Osoria's critique of Agamben's treatment of the state of exception in the United States is most relevant. Agamben considers the suspension of habeas corpus during the Civil War as well as exceptional measures during the First World War, the Great Depression, the Second World War, and the War on Terror.[22] Yet he forgoes reflection on US imperial practice as an important precedent for or extension of the creation of spaces of anomie. Exemplary here is the 2008 Supreme Court ruling on *Boumediene v. Bush*, which established the Insular Cases as the legitimating jurisprudence for the detention camps in Guantanamo Bay, Cuba.[23]

Although critical of Venator-Santiago, Atiles-Osoria draws from his work. Venator-Santiago documents the creation of anomalous legal spaces, stressing the significance of the generation of *narratives of space* for the United States' nation-building agenda.[24] The doctrine of territorial incorporation is crucial for the acquisition and administration of "'borderland' territories," those situated in liminal constitutional spaces.[25] The United States' project of nation-state building has many simultaneous starting points. However, three juridico-political and socio-historical experiences are crucial, according to Venator-Santiago. The territorial conquest of indigenous populations establishes the foundational character of a settler colonial project; court decisions that created a zone of indifference between the international and the domestic; doctrines that sought to retain the union within the Civil War are key.[26] Only the third explicitly deploys a declaration of a state of emergency. Venator-Santiago focuses on the first two, centering the strictures of these spaces of anomie.

Venator-Santiago's account is based on a distinction between what he sees as the United States' colonial, imperialist, and postcolonial traditions of expansionism.[27] While the nineteenth-century colonial project sought to annex new territories that would be subsequently organized into new states and were thus treated as parts of the United States for constitutional purposes, the imperialist project was based on the occupation of territories ruled as possessions and situated outside the United States for constitutional purposes regardless of their geographic location.[28] Between 1898 and 1901, the United States developed a new tradition of expansionism, which allowed it to "annex new territories without binding Congress to colonize them into states of the Union."[29] Territories acquired within this postcolonial tradition were ascribed a borderland status for constitutional purposes. All three traditions build on a race/gender system of classification based on the federal government's treatment of indigenous populations.[30] The subordination of nonwhite populations is inherent to the creation of such spaces of anomie, given the eminently settler colonial character of US expansionism.

Four colonial and imperial experiences, Venator-Santiago argues, frame the juridico-political perspective at work in the Spanish-American War. First, the Northwest Ordinance of 1787 provided the juridico-political justification for a spatial conception of government and the nation's outward expansion. The Indian Boundary Line of 1816 epitomizes this spatialization.

The ordinance established a process of settlement that would place territories in a "temporary status of development."[31] Those residing within these territories were subject to a different set of laws.[32] This was a deeply racializing/gendering process, which rearticulated preindependence and postindependence representations of indigenous people as "savages."[33] The ordinance drew on debates that instituted a distinction between "civilized/ friend" and "savage/enemy." It also established equivalence between maturity and "manhood" for purposes of annexation.[34]

Second, Venator-Santiago discusses the creation of the anomalous status "Domestic Dependent Nation" within the Marshall Trilogy. These cases established indigenous nations as domestic for federal and international concerns but not for constitutional purposes.[35] They secured the property rights of white expansionists, seeking to legitimize the capture of indigenous lands. Third, he considers the treatment of black people in light of US territorial law.[36] Already in the ordinance there was a demarcation between slave and free territories while at the same time affirming the powers of state-funded "fugitive slave bounty hunters."[37] After the Civil War and Reconstruction, these spatial narratives were replaced by spatial constructions in Jim Crow laws.[38] Fourth, Venator-Santiago discusses the experience of "imported workers" in the so-called Guano Islands during the nineteenth century. The Guano Islands Act protected those who "discovered" the islands and the economic interests at hand but did not extend constitutional rights or guarantees to workers.[39]

Puerto Rico is central to the articulation of the third tradition of expansionism, which appropriated territories without creating a path to annexation.[40] Key here is the creation of a distinction between incorporated and unincorporated territories in 1901. Recall that Spain ceded Puerto Rico to the United States in 1898. The Supreme Court considered Puerto Rico under the Territorial Clause. The clause explicitly treats territories as property.[41] It establishes the power of Congress over new territories. This entailed a repudiation of Dred Scott principles, "which subordinated congressional powers to the Constitution." A military government administered the territory until the Foraker Act came into effect in 1900. Narratives of American expansionism informed the military administration of the territory. Occupation was seen as a civilizing mission. "Savages" unfit for self-government populated Spanish colonies.[42] Circumventing naturalization of a non–Anglo Saxon population, the United States granted protection to Spanish subjects and created a Puerto Rican national status.[43] Though not sovereignty, Puerto Rico had gained autonomy from Spain a year before the occupation.

The Foraker Act established colonial administration under a civil government until the ratification of a Puerto Rican Constitution in 1952. It neither contained a Bill of Rights nor extended the US Bill of Rights to the territory.[44] It also defined key economic structures.[45] Puerto Rico was incorporated into the US monetary system, devaluating the Puerto Rican peso. Puerto Rico could not negotiate commercial treaties with other nations; neither could it determine its taxes and duties. The act established strictures of free trade between Puerto Rico and the United States, imposing duties on Puerto Rican commodities entering the United States. It established the collection of taxes as well, which created a condition of taxation without representation. As Dietz explains, as a result of the Foraker Act, Puerto Rican producers were not only competing with the fastest-developing capitalist nation without the possibility of elaborating means of protecting local industry and commerce.[46] The law established conditions of exploitation by its more powerful neighbor by designing modes of capture intrinsic to the territorial status.[47]

Puerto Rico's status as an unincorporated territory was clarified by key Supreme Court decisions within the Insular Cases.[48] These cases considered whether the Constitution "follows the flag." They "constructed a pattern of exclusive inclusion," as Atiles-Osoria puts it, "founding the axiological paradigm of the relations of exception" that still defines the relation between the United States and Puerto Rico.[49] *Downes v. Bidwell* (1901) is perhaps the most important case. It concerned collection of duties and taxes but raised questions about the constitutionality of the Foraker Act. Justice Brown wrote the court's opinion. Citing congressional powers established by the Territorial Clause, the case affirmed the act's constitutionality.[50] It maintained that the Constitution's Uniformity Clause does not apply to Puerto Rico, since it is a "territory appurtenant and *belonging to* the United States, but not a *part of* the United States."[51] Puerto Rico was deemed a foreign country for constitutional purposes, yet under the sovereignty of the United States. Justice White further legitimized the construction of this liminal space by drawing a distinction between incorporated and unincorporated territories. Congress was granted the power to decide whether a territory would be considered incorporated or unincorporated.[52] The Bill of Rights and constitutional limitations would apply to incorporated territories, while only fundamental restrictions on government power would apply to unincorporated territories. An unincorporated territory was not on the path to statehood. It could be kept in colonial subordination indefinitely.

Venator-Santiago highlights narratives of space central to the institution of liminal juridical spaces. These narratives generate political-economic strictures specific to these borderland spaces. Venator-Santiago stresses that attention to these narratives clarifies rights and protections as well as lack of rights and protections for citizens and noncitizens in occupied territories.[53] Atiles-Osoria argues that Venator-Santiago's analysis is overly legalistic, forgoing an account of exceptionality's ontopolitical status.[54] Rather than regulating, the creation of a liminal space produces a political, economic, and social reality. Examining such productivity is crucial. The Foraker Act is the first law of exception in Puerto Rico. It produces territoriality but also colonial subjectivity at the turn of the century.[55] Congress is posited as the seat of sovereignty.

This operation is repeated in subsequent laws that redefine the political, economic, and social reality of Puerto Rico through the liminal character of unincorporation. The Jones Act of 1917 extended US citizenship to Puerto Ricans while forgoing a path to annexation. In addition to blocking political participation and representation in the United States for citizens residing in the territory, US citizenship blocked the possibility of economic and political participation in Puerto Rico for those who decided to opt out.[56] The Jones Act of 1920, which regulates maritime commerce in US waters and between US ports, deepened the conditions of capture instituted by the Foraker Act.[57] The Jones Act established that goods transported must be carried on ships built, flagged, and crewed by the United States. The cabotage laws—still in effect—raise the cost of commodities for Puerto Rico considerably.

Law 600 of 1950 consolidated colonial exceptionality. Congress allowed Puerto Rico to draw up a Constitution while leaving its territorial status intact.[58] The Estado Libre Asociado (ELA) was established in 1952 after a contested referendum in 1951 yielded a favorable vote.[59] Congress required the exclusion of Section 20, which established employment and adequate standards of living as rights to be guaranteed through economic development. Congress also required the addition of a disposition where no "future amendments to the constitution could alter the relation with the United States."[60] The ELA came into effect once these changes were made. Although the terms of the territorial status remained intact, the ELA purportedly represented a "compact" with the United States.[61] The latter was cited for Puerto Rico's elimination from the United Nation's list of non-self-governing territories in 1953. As recently as June 2016, however, it became undeniable that no such symmetry had been achieved, no process of decolonization had occurred. The Supreme Court's decision in *Puerto Rico v. San-chez Valle*, a double jeopardy case, made clear that the seat of sovereignty remains with Congress.[62]

While Atiles-Osoria's account is insightful, I move away from his emphasis on sovereignty. His insistence on the ontological status of exceptionality is important. It is necessary to stress that unincorporation produces an economic, political, and social reality. However, the effectivity of coloniality exceeds a decision by the colonial juridico-political apparatus even if such decision installs its strictures. Atiles-Osoria locates sovereignty too narrowly, then. Now, Atiles-Osoria does not develop his account in relation to the "status question," which has been the center of debates about decolonization in Puerto Rico for over a century.[63] Understanding sovereignty nevertheless narrowly leads us to these debates, shifting attention to the question of annexation or independence. Yet neither annexation nor independence by necessity neutralizes the work of coloniality. Specifying the effectivity rather than source of the productivity of coloniality before entering those debates is, in my view, key.

COLONIAL EXCEPTIONALITY

Consider key features of the political economy articulated by Puerto Rico's status as an unincorporated territory of the United States. Rafael Bernabe explains that Puerto Rico's economy has been "shaped by the priorities of US capital" since 1900.[64] US corporations have not only owned but also determined the main sectors of the territory's economy: the sugar plantation before the Second World War; light manufacturing from the 1940s to the 1970s; and intensive manufacturing, especially pharmaceuticals, from the 1980s to the present.[65] This orientation has resulted in an economy based on unilateral specialization geared toward exportation. This, in turn, has created the need to import the great majority of what is consumed in Puerto Rico, including food. Today, 85 percent of what is consumed is imported.

In this political economy, profits generated in the territory necessarily "escape" predominantly to the United States.[66] "At present," Bernabe writes, "it is estimated that more than 35 billion dollars leave the island every year, in the form of dividends and other payments to external investors. This is around 35 percent of Puerto Rico's gross domestic product. This figure includes both profits generated in Puerto Rico as well as declared there for tax avoidance purposes."[67] The flight of profit generates unemployment in Puerto Rico, since capital is not reinvested in the territory. Unemployment has been a permanent fixture of Puerto Rico's economy, even in times of postwar expansion, when Puerto Rico was presented as a showcase for the success of democracy and capitalism in the Caribbean. Unemployment has been offset by mass migration to the United States since the early twentieth century.[68] Throughout the last decades, unemployment hovers around 13 percent, though in 1985 it reached 21.8 percent.[69] Only 40 percent of the population is part of the workforce; 60 percent is neither working nor searching for work. Decline in unemployment signals a shrinking population, especially after Hurricane María. The debt crisis has led to migration patterns that exceed the Great Migration.[70] Between 2011 and 2013, for example, Puerto Rico's population decreased by fifty thousand people annually. Two hundred thousand Puerto Ricans migrated in the months following María, with 130,000 relocating permanently.[71] Around 45 percent of the population and 55 percent of children live below the federal poverty line.[72] Economic development, impoverishment, and expulsion are two sides of the same coin even in times of purported economic thriving.[73]

Bernabe underscores that Puerto Rico's territorial status has generated conditions of capture through *taxation*.[74] Puerto Rico's political economy is based on a strategy of foreign investment through tax exemption since the Jones Act of 1917, which instituted triple tax exemption on bonds. However, as José I. Fusté notes, a congressional report argued in favor of developing infrastructure in Puerto Rico and other territories through triple tax exemption on bonds in 1906.[75] Muñiz-Varela highlights Section 931 then 936 of the Internal Revenue Code, which offered federal tax exemption on profits generated by US corporations in the territory since 1920.[76] Before the establishment of the ELA in 1952 and with Manos a la Obra (Operation Bootstrap) specifically through capital subsidies from 1947 onward, the central "axis" of Puerto Rico's "economic discourse" was "to be a tax haven."[77] Most relevant for our purposes is Section 936, in effect since 1976 and progressively eliminated from 1996 to 2006. It gave US corporations exemption on income earned whether from production or interest on local bank deposits, thereby promoting the flight of profit and the disparity in taxation between corporations (9 percent) and the general population (33 percent).[78] The elimination of Section 936 sent the territory into recession.[79] Rather than revisit taxation laws to address the flight of capital, the government responded by issuing more debt and increasing regressive taxation.[80] A sales tax in effect since 2006, for example, is currently at 11.5 percent.[81]

As we will see, Act 20/22 of 2012 continues the pattern of tax exemption in the realm of real estate, driving displacement, dispossession, and expulsion.

Atiles-Osoria draws from his analysis of the colonial state of exception to develop the notion of neoliberal colonialism. Neoliberal rationality was installed through an "internal state of exception"—by local elites.[82] The 2006 declaration of fiscal crisis and the ensuing government shutdown initiated an intensification of the use of declarations of states of emergency for economic administration.[83] Subsequent administrations further intensified these efforts. Seeking to secure good standing in the eyes of credit agencies, in 2009 the government declared a state of fiscal emergency. This declaration allowed the government to pass Law 7, which implemented austerity measures that included steep government worker layoffs, a reduction of the University of Puerto Rico's budget, and heightened privatization.[84] In 2010 an energy crisis was also declared. Aiming to purportedly reduce the use of fossil fuels, the newly created Energy Affairs Administration generated a set of profit-driven projects and contracts for local elites. The measures excluded citizen participation, which resisted these projects on ecological grounds.[85]

Recent administrations have relied on emergency-exceptionality most heavily. In 2014, Puerto Rico's credit ratings faltered, leading to a declaration of emergency that established fiscal recovery as a government priority. That year, Law 71 articulated a local bankruptcy process. The federal court, then the US Supreme Court, rejected this attempt in a 2016 ruling, citing a 1984 decision to exclude Puerto Rico from chapter 9.[86] The local government's response was more austerity.[87] In 2015, a report on Puerto Rico's fiscal crisis by former International Monetary Fund (IMF) functionary Anne Krueger determined that Puerto Rico's debt was unpayable, an assessment echoed by then-governor Alejandro García Padilla. In light of this assessment, a series of laws were passed that further dismantled democratic participation, consolidated technocratic power, and reinforced narratives of fiscal responsibility as a public priority.[88] These uses of emergency-exceptionality prepared the ground for the Puerto Rico Oversight, Management, and Economic Stability Act (PROMESA), yet they are also necessary for the latter's operation. In June 2019, Governor Ricardo Rosselló employed Law 5 of 2017, extending the state of fiscal emergency to the end of the year.[89] Law 5 was amended by Law 46 in July 2017, which amended the Internal Revenue Code and expanded the extension period for declarations of states of emergency. One key rationale for Laws 5 and 46 is the ability to meet the demands of PROMESA and thereby facilitate the work of the Fiscal Control Board.

PROMESA is a US federal law passed in 2016. Through PROMESA, the US Congress instituted a Fiscal Control Board known in the territory as la Junta. The board comprises seven unelected members to oversee a debt restructuring process.[90] The seven members, six men and one woman, were appointed by then-president Barack Obama. Because Puerto Rico has no voting representation in Congress and does not cast a presidential vote, the institution of the Fiscal Control Board represents the collapse of a purported democracy in the colony. PROMESA overrides any law or regulation understood to be incompatible with debt repayment. Conflicts of interest have been noted in the case of various board members.[91] Lack of access to information and transparency are main features of the evisceration of democracy. A citizen debt audit is a key demand within citizen, student, and worker resistance to the Fiscal Control Board, as we will see in chapter 3.[92] In May 2017, Puerto Rico filed for bankruptcy under Title III of PROMESA, placing its fate in the hands of US District Court Judge Laura Taylor Swain. Litigation not only with creditors but also between Puerto Rico's government, legislature, and the board continues to articulate the strictures of exceptionality in the indebted colony.[93] More than two hundred lawyers, consultants, and other contractors compose the workforce of the board, spending at least 80 million in Puerto Rico taxpayer dollars by August 2018.[94]

Atiles-Osoria's notion of neoliberal colonialism sheds light on the continuation of the colonial condition through the institution of the Fiscal Control Board. It centers the role of local elites. This is an important perspective. However, local elite management of the colonial condition through political positions and government contracts represents a reinstallment of a race/gender/class hierarchy within the territory by the political economy of the colony. Atiles-Osoria argues that given the complicity with neoliberal-colonial control, we should "abandon" the law.[95] Yet illuminating the nature of such juridico-political operation and imagining modes of interruption, which might be better served by subverting rather than abandoning the law, requires examining its material conditions and effects.[96] Given its focus on the juridical-political apparatus, "neoliberal colonialism" is limited. The institution of a Fiscal Control Board intensifies the operations of colonial power through debt, but it does so by drawing on forms of capture made possible by Puerto Rico's liminality. The board is tasked with achieving fiscal responsibility and access to capital markets irrespective of social costs.

It pursues tax and austerity measures that rearticulate the structures of capture already in place.

Muñiz-Varela's work is key here. In *Adiós a la economía*, she discusses the economic crisis as part of the regulation of accumulation in a post-Fordist context driven by financialization. She highlights the significance of the use of declarations of state of emergency and the increase of policing systems, though she stresses that these are operations of coloniality in this political economy.[97] In this context, the role of the state and the legal apparatus are subordinate to coloniality, even when they are necessary for the actualization of finance in and through the colonial condition.[98] The modern category of sovereignty and the investment in locating its seat is abandoned, then, given the dispersed nature of coloniality.[99] If the case of Puerto Rico can "serve as an example" of the operations of neoliberal financialized capitalism, Muñiz-Varela writes, it is because the "coloniality of power has little to do with the quota of autonomy that states exhibit."[100] "It is precisely coloniality," she continues, "that maintains what has been and is the 'truly existing development.'"

Muñiz-Varela situates the political economy of Puerto Rico within the increased hegemony of finance throughout the twentieth century, mapping the transformation of notions of economic development in the unincorporated territory.[101] Puerto Rico is not an "anomaly," the Caribbean miracle declared in the mid-twentieth century. Rather, economic downturn, thriving informal economies, violence, corruption, and precarization establish it as a "mirror" of the transformations of capital. Neoliberal financialized capitalism is a perpetual originary accumulation not "content with exploitation."[102] Its "movement," Muñiz-Varela writes, is the "destruction of the general conditions of life." This is an *economy of the catastrophe* in which the creation and the capture of value is bound to violence and decay in everyday life. "A death vector," she adds, "and a drive to terror impose themselves today as part of the speculation and power of capital."[103] Society must not be defended, but destroyed. Accumulation is tied to regulation and control with necropolitical effects.

Muñiz-Varela's crucial insight, however, is a move from necropolitical to necroeconomic effects. In her book and in other essays, she argues that we must move from biopolitics to bioeconomy, from necropolitics to necroeconomy. Rather than the management of populations in the state's control over life, hence over death, it is through the commodification of life itself that modes of control embedded in and beyond the juridico-political apparatus operate.[104] This is key for understanding not the control of life and hence death through the regulation of a population, but the destruction of life in the very reproduction of life. In a post-Fordist context, nothing and no one is "unproductive." In *Adiós a la economía*, she writes: "the marginal, the unemployed, the illegal, the informal, the disabled, the incarcerated, the loose [*al garete*], the autonomous, but also the sick, the half-alive or half-dead all contribute [*abonan*] to abundance."[105] In a recent essay on the current debt crisis, she reiterates the point: "The times today called post-political, could be understood . . . as the dominion of bioeconomy, which makes life a monetary value, ranging from pharmaco/biotechnology and technogenetics to different forms of indebtedness. Although curiously and paradoxically [it] coexists and promotes forms of necroeconomy, which also links debt with depredation, impoverishment, expropriation and the abandonment of life. Puerto Rico has a hefty record of these varied forms of commodified life, even at the extremes of abandonment and death."[106] Bernabe and Atiles-Osoria underscore the impact of the elimination of Section 936 when explicating the debt crisis. Muñiz-Varela explores this impact as well, helpfully situating it within Puerto Rico's transition to a postindustrial context with and after the elimination of oil import quotas and the OPEC oil embargo in 1973. The oil crisis launched a new form of accumulation in Puerto Rico. In 1976, the US Congress increased federal transfers, especially nutritional support, and enacted Section 936. The disappearance of nine Puerto Rican banks from 1973 to 1983 is relevant here as well. It initiated the now hegemony of Puerto Rico's Banco Popular. More importantly, it installed American banks as the center of financial capital in the territory, "turning Puerto Rico into a center of international financialized capitalism and a bridge for the transfer of earnings to the United States."[107] It is in this context that debt begins to subsidize the state itself.

Contraction in waged work, increase in public and private debt, fluctuation in federal transfers, and continued patterns of unbridled consumption established in decades of supposed economic prosperity are the coordinates of economic downturn through economic "development" thereafter, Muñiz-Varela explains.[108] The identification of work ethic with propriety and the "American way of life" are crucial to modalities of regulation and control at work in each. The elimination of Section 936 did not end Puerto Rico's status as a tax haven, reinstalled first with Clause 30-A and today with Act 20/22, for example. It nevertheless provided a "discursive shift" in notions of economic development in an increasingly financialized economy. The events of 1973 and then 1976 generate a context in which Puerto Rico's informal economy grows.[109] This informal economy did more, however, than absorb the "surplus population" in a postindustrial context. A thriving drug economy became an economic motor comparable with the 936.[110] In 1997, the flight of capital made possible by the drug economy was $16.0 billion, matching the estimated $16.5 billion made possible by the 936.[111]

Muñiz-Varela draws attention to the discursive shift in ideas of development in a post-936 world.[112] The political economy of Puerto Rico is explicitly understood as requiring forms of regulation and control that manage the human and nonhuman "waste," "excess," and "surplus" it generates.[113] Citizenship, for example, has always been "surplus-waste citizenship," a form of managing "an incomplete salaried society." Yet in a post-936 world there is an imperative to manage an unsalaried population tied to consumption, dependent yet free to move.[114] The collapse of the figure of the worker and the American dream is shifted onto "unproductive lives."[115] The crucial point here is that this shift guides modes of "ordering" (*poner en orden*) populations posited as culpable for economic downturn, the rise of an informal economy, and crime.[116] Muñiz-Varela discusses the impact of this discursive shift on women, racialized single mothers who defy "work, family, security and law."[117] The thriving informal economy drives condemnation of a purported abandonment of work, family, and law.[118] As we saw in chapter 1, these women are posited as culpable in great part through the spatial articulation of race that links poverty and crime to public housing.

Recall that Muñiz-Varela underscores the significance of regulation and control in the use of declarations of states of emergency and the increase of policing systems in the economic context she reconstructs. LeBrón's notion of "punitive governance" is here insightful. Both Muñiz-Varela and LeBrón elucidate not only the ubiquity of violence tied to a shifting political economy in Puerto Rico, one that thrives on the destruction of general conditions of life. They also, crucially, consider its normalization. In her work, LeBrón recounts the production of "common sense" around outright violence, incarceration, and premature death of abject populations. She considers the production of racialized masculinities by policing initiatives to intervene in drug-related violence. This discussion adds to Muñiz-Varela's analysis, where ubiquitous violence ranges from the spectacular to the ordinary. The point is that the spectacular is part of the ordinary in the slow death of neoliberal coloniality. This violence cannot be accounted for in light of the analytics of exceptionality that Atiles-Osoria develops, though it involves modes of regulation and control tied to the state and the legal apparatus.

In *Policing Life and Death*, LeBrón traces the rise of punitive governance to Mano Dura contra el Crimen (Iron Fist against Crime). Mano Dura is an anticrime measure that, through 1993 to 2000, deployed police and military forces in public housing and low-income spaces.[119] Governor Pedro Rosselló ran on a campaign of Mano Dura in 1992, pledging to institute legal reforms and new law enforcement policies, "including allocating more funds to the police department and doubling the size of the force, limiting the constitutional right to bail, federalizing crimes involving firearms (thereby making them eligible for the death penalty), and even activating the Puerto Rican National Guard."[120] Rosselló's rhetoric within and beyond his campaign turned citizens into victims of crime while building on ideas of poverty as disorder. His administration represents a crucial turning point in the criminalization of poverty in the territory. In 1993, soon after his election, Rosselló signed an executive order activating the National Guard to intervene in drug-related crime, LeBrón notes, consolidating the notion of the criminal as the enemy of the state.[121] As LeBrón clarifies, "although mano dura was short-lived, lasting from approximately 1993 to 2000, for many Puerto Ricans with whom I spoke, it marked a turning point when the state increasingly relied on punitive power to demonstrate its capacity and maintain social control."[122]

Mano Dura is exemplary of "punitive governance," LeBrón argues. Punitive governance refers to the ways in which "the Puerto Rican state . . . reassert[s] itself in the lives of Puerto Ricans through technologies of punishment such as policing and incarceration, as well as the violence (state sanctioned and other) they often provoke."[123] LeBrón draws from Stuart Hall, who argues that, during economic crisis, "panic over crime and violence can 'serve as the articulator of the crisis, as its ideological conductor.'"[124] The state responded to the informal economy that grew into an economic driver in ways that posited populations living in poverty—especially, those living in public housing—as "criminal," "dangerous." Conversely, these measures posited middle- and upper-class Puerto Ricans living in gated communities as threatened, in need of "security." These spatial distinctions not only install a racial hierarchy. They are actualizations of race/gender/class, as we began to see in chapter 1 with Zaire Dinzey-Flores's work. These spatial distinctions link blackness, poverty, and crime while binding whiteness, upward mobility or affluency, and work ethic. The state, itself implicated in illicit or illegal activities, "turned to punitive governance to suture the ruptures of colonial capitalism."[125]

2.1 150 police agents took over Lopez Nussa Housing Project in Ponce, May 31, 2002. Photo by Gary Gutierrez.

Mano Dura deployed punitive logics and practices that are "spectacular and quotidian."[126] Today, Puerto Rico's murder rate is four times that of the United States, the *New York Times* reports, roughly twenty murders per hundred thousand people.[127] The Associated Press reports that in the first weeks of 2019, at least thirty people were killed. In 1994, 995 homicides were recorded. This was the highest in the history of the territory at the time.[128] Administrations previous to Pedro Rossello's, specifically Rafael Hernandez Colón's, had already acknowledged that police intervention in the drug economy exacerbated its violence. In addition to police violence itself, shifting territories generated battles internal to this economy.[129] Incarceration only embedded this violence in prisons, though 60 percent of individuals incarcerated on drug-related offense are users.[130] As in the United States, black men and individuals from low-income communities are overrepresented in Puerto Rico's prisons. In Puerto Rico as well, profits from incarceration and security-related services are substantive.[131] Mano Dura's explicit use of force in police intervention and deterrence turned drug-related homicide, shootings, and raids into the ordinary.

The crucial point is that punitive governance "marks" how life and death are "understood and experienced" in Puerto Rico.[132] Mano Dura operated through an unequal distribution of risk, harm, and death.[133] The deaths of those involved in economies related to drug trafficking were "naturalized," LeBrón writes, "as expected outcomes of police work and a necessary component of a crime prevention and deterrence strategy."[134] The state thus advanced policies that "'let' alleged dealers and criminals die." Given Mano Dura's spatial inscription of danger/security, the naturalization of violence and death is more precisely the naturalization of premature death of black and brown men now associated with the narcoeconomy, despite the fact that this economy's main agents lived neither in poverty nor in public housing. The policing of black and brown "youths," LeBrón notes, generated a form of "hypervisibility" that obfuscates the role of the state not only in exacerbating but also provoking such violence with its mode of intervention.[135] A tacit acceptance of the harm and death of this population was thereby installed. The association of blackness, poverty, and crime, despite racial identification of individuals living in public housing, established these spaces and people as targets not only of regulation and containment but of outright violence and death now perceived as normal.

Common sensibility articulated within the context of Mano Dura and its aftermath, then, binds poverty, blackness, and crime. It posited black masculinity as "dangerous." In chapter 1, I argued that the spatial racial, specifically antiblack, feminization of poverty is linked to the production of black and nonwhite masculinity. Here we see the inverse. The hypervisibility of black masculinity in police intervention and deterrence established men as the only victims of police violence. Yet mostly women head households in these targeted spaces. Moreover, as LeBrón also notes, the hypervisibility of racialized masculinity makes invisible the forms of sexual violence that women experienced in National Guard and police raids as well as in other violent measures implemented within Mano Dura. To be sure, as LeBrón also points out, racially and economically marginalized men were subject to unparalleled scrutiny and violence by law enforcement and fellow citizens.[136] Yet such scrutiny impacts the racialization of women posited not only as natural bearers of social reproduction but also as targets of surveillance and state sexual violence.

The state of emergency is not the exception but the rule, then. The juridico-political apparatus is necessary for the actualization of an economy of the catastrophe, and the use of declarations of emergency certainly establish its significance. However, the effectivity as well as effects of any measure are the site of the features of colonial exceptionality, hence of the reproduction of the colony. An exposition of colonial exceptionality should thus pay heed to the effectivity of coloniality rather than the installation of its conditions. Tracking material conditions and effects of an economy of the catastrophe calls for an account of the environment generated by neoliberal coloniality: the spectacular and quotidian violence that composes the ordinary in the no-place of life in the indebted colony. Berlant's critique of an analytics of exceptionality and her notion of slow death are insightful here. They help articulate the work of colonial exceptionality as the attrition of life within the building of life, as the destruction of general conditions of life within the very reproduction of life. We will have to complicate Berlant's analysis, nevertheless. She polarizes exceptionality and ordinariness, disallowing an exposition of the ordinariness of the spectacular distinctive of colonial exceptionality in Puerto Rico. This requires moving from the environment to the climate, as explicated by Christina Sharpe, of neoliberal coloniality.

SLOW DEATH OF NEOLIBERAL COLONIALITY

In her recent work, Muñiz-Varela describes Puerto Rico as a "taken island."[137] Financialization intensifies an ongoing expropriation through the "axiomatic of property in the mortgage" and the "apparatus of the capture of life through debt," specifically debt restructuring deals. While declarations of a state of emergency from 2008 onward confiscate through privatization, layoffs, dismantling of labor rights, and pension reform, tax exemption remains the central apparatus of capture. Debt continues to be accrued through triple exempt bonds; regressive taxation continues to subvent part of the debt; Act 20/22 reboots tax haven conditions in the realm of real estate. This, Muñiz-Varela points out, is added to the $3 billion granted annually to corporate capital in approximately 70 tax exemptions.[138] A "shy" 4 percent tax was imposed on the "old world pharmaceutical enclave." The intensification of the capture of the future, the body, land, and public wealth through taxation comes into focus.

First, the island is "taken and sold" through the axiomatic of property in the mortgage.[139] Once a refuge for corporations and a successful narco-economy, the debt crisis turns the territory into a site for the "new owners of global 'real estate.'"[140] Crucial here is Act 20/22 of 2012. Consistent with the political economy of the colony since 1917, it installs Puerto Rico's tax haven status in the realm of real estate. It would purportedly attract foreign investment and create jobs by providing tax breaks for wealthy elites from the United States residing in Puerto Rico for at least half a year. The piece of legislation exempts new residents from paying federal and local taxes, capital gains tax, and taxes on passive income until the year 2035, regardless of whether they generate employment or invest in the local economy, as Yarimar Bonilla and Marisol LeBrón explain.[141] It is the only place in the United States where such income is not taxed. Note, however, that the 2008 mortgage crisis decreased the value of property in Puerto Rico by 40 percent, initiating a new round of displacement and expulsion through foreclosures and the acquisition of devalued or foreclosed property. A housing crisis is unfolding with an estimated 250,260 homes currently at risk.[142] Between January and February of 2019, banks seized 459 homes, of which 60 percent of those have been abandoned by their owners, Muñiz-Varela notes. An average of fourteen families lose their homes every day. Relevant here as well are the Opportunity Zones installed by Donald Trump's tax reform. These are investment areas eligible for tax benefits. The incentives purport to promote "economic development" in "depressed areas." In the United States, Joel Cintrón Arbasetti reports, local governments designated 25 percent of the territories they qualify. In contrast, an exception from Congress allowed for the designation of 98 percent of the territory as an Opportunity Zone. It is not clear how municipalities or communities navigating the impact of large-scale investments will benefit from such purported stimulus.

Second, debt restructuring is successfully inversely redistributing wealth, to speak with Lazzarato. Muñiz-Varela discusses the Urgent Interest Fund Corporation (Corporación del Fondo de Interés Apremiante, COFINA) deal, but the Puerto Rico Electric Power Authority (PREPA) deal is also relevant. A public corporation, COFINA was formed in 2006 to issue bonds to refinance the extra-constitutional debt.[143] The source of repayment for these bonds is the sales tax presently at 11.5 percent. The February 2019 restructuring deal establishes that, for the next forty years, a handful of investors will receive 53 percent of Puerto Rico's sales tax revenues. PREPA also reached a restructuring deal in 2019.[144] Investors will exchange their bonds at 67.5 cents on the dollar for new Tranche A bonds and 10 cents on the dollar for new Tranche B bonds.[145] The latter would be contingent on full payment of Tranche A bonds and future electricity demand on the territory. PREPA will pay off the new bonds through a special charge levied on its customers starting at approximately 1.000 cent per kilowatt hour prior to the deal's closing, increasing to some 2.768 cents per kilowatt hour upon closing and gradually increasing to approximately 4.552 cents per kilowatt hour during the expected forty-year lifespan of the bonds.

As Muñiz-Varela puts it, the debt is paid with life—very concretely, sales tax, foreclosure, utility costs.

In "Destruir un país es un asunto de hombres," Anayra Santory-Jorge argues that we should understand Puerto Rico's debt crisis as a "catastrophe by attrition."[146] She draws from Rob Nixon's notion of "slow violence."[147] Nixon builds on Berlant's conception of slow death in order to name a form of violence that "occurs gradually and out of sight, a violence of delayed destruction that it disperses across time and space, an attritional violence that is typically not viewed as violence at all."[148] Rather than "immediate in time," "explosive and spectacular in space," slow violence is "incremental and accretive." Its repercussions are felt in different "temporal scales."[149] Slow violence, then, is not neatly bounded in time or space. For this reason, it faces "representational, narrative, and strategic challenges."[150] It is not readily graspable, chipping away at life in the everyday.[151] Santory-Jorge extends the meaning of the term, arguing that slow violence names a dissimulated quotidian reality disclosed in the event. Hurricane María, as we will see, revealed institutional collapse and precarious conditions in the territory already underway. These conditions are dissimulated in the everyday effects of austerity. Populations paying the debt with life endure catastrophe by attrition.

In *Cruel Optimism*, Berlant argues that the "genre of crisis can distort something structural and ongoing within ordinariness into something that seems shocking and exceptional."[152] It is a "heightening interpretive genre," which turns an "ongoing condition" into an "intensified situation."[153] The extensive is turned into the intensive, the structural and the ordinary into the shocking and the exceptional. Rather than exceptional, crises correspond to a "logic of adjustment."[154] Such logic is at work when navigating what is "overwhelming" across space and time. The exceptional marks shifts in something ongoing, yet it obfuscates an unfolding already present.[155] Slow death refers to the "physical wearing out of a population in a way that points to its deterioration as a defining condition of its experience and historical existence."[156] It names an experience that is "simultaneously at an extreme and in a zone of ordinariness, where life building and the attrition of human life are indistinguishable."[157] Neoliberal financialized capitalism, she adds, does not produce waste, but slow death—the attrition of subjects and populations through the determination of value.[158]

I will come back to Berlant's critique of crisis, which she more precisely develops as a critique of exceptionality. I will come back to her distinction between the production of waste and slow death as well. For the moment,

I want to suggest that operation of colonial power, of colonial exceptionality, should be understood as the *coextensive* unfolding of the extreme and the ordinary in the *coextensive* reproduction of life building and the attrition of human life. What appears as a crisis, hence as requiring exceptional measures, is the rearticulation of processes that make up the ordinary to greater degrees for some populations.[159] It is a reinstallment of terms that have already been endured extensively by those populations, though they appear in need of exceptional measures in a moment of generalized intensification. These junctures are occasions for instituting or deploying new modalities of capture. The point, however, is that such rearticulation is only clarified by attending to ongoing structures that make it possible in the first place. It is only clarified by mapping ongoing material effects of those structures.

Berlant argues that notions of sovereignty and the event are central to crisis as an interpretive genre. In this context, sovereignty is a matter of "events of decision-making."[160] Whether individual or state sovereignty, at work here is a notion of agential "control." This obscures the work and effectivity of agency, however. Sovereignty should thus be doubly rethought. Practical sovereignty, she writes, is a "shape made by mediating conditions of zoning, labor, consumption, and governmentality, as well as unconscious and explicit desires not to be an inflated ego deploying power and manifesting intention."[161] Mediating social and material conditions are the site of practical sovereignty. Activity that is not life building, forward intending, control seeking should be thought of as agency. The former leads to a displacement of the centrality of the event and toward a consideration of an "environment." The latter leads to a consideration of "management" as a form of agency in the context where life building and the attrition of human life are not only coextensive but also indistinguishable.

The event is an analytic of the immediate—intensities, impact.[162] An environment, by contrast, "denotes a scene in which structural conditions are suffused through a variety of mediations, such as predictable repetitions and other spatial practices."[163] These might go under the radar, she says. They might simply not take the form of an event. An environment "can absorb how time ordinarily passes, how forgettable most events are."[164] In an environment, an event is an "episode," "occasions that frame experience while not changing much of anything." The crucial point is that slow death "prospers" in the spaces-times that compose the ordinary. Crisis, emergency, the event attempt to make an environmental phenomenon "appear," calling for a decision, for an intervention. Yet this is not the stricture of slow death. Slow death, the "structurally induced attrition of persons keyed to their membership in certain populations," is "neither a state of exception nor the opposite, mere banality, but a domain where an upsetting scene of the living is revealed to be interwoven with ordinary life after all."[165] A coextensive death and living on might appear as an event, but it does not unfold as an event.

An environment constructs a space and time of agency that defies notions of sovereignty as control. An environment is the "domain of living on" in which "diverse temporalities" and "horizons of the taken-for-granted" are lived *through*.[166] Slow death, then, renders subjectivity as the site of intention inadequate. Sovereign subjectivity assumes that agency is a matter of "self-extension," embedded in a project of seeking to "lock in the will-have-been of future anteriority."[167] Viewed in light of sovereign subjectivity, any "lack of self-cultivating attention can easily become recast as irresponsibility, shallowness, refusal, or incapacity."[168] The subject in the environment in which slow death thrives does not manage its condition with heroic gestures. However, this individual does not lack agency. The subject of capital's attrition seeks "survival" in forms of perceived passivity. Agency here is a matter of "maintenance," of "self-continuity." Rather than "impassivity," "alienation," "coolness," "detachment," or "distraction," activity is "directed toward making a less-bad experience."[169]

I want to rework key elements of Berlant's discussion in light of Muñiz-Varela's and LeBrón's. Berlant contrasts slow death with the production of waste. She argues that neoliberalism embeds a logic of attrition in the very reproduction of life. It does not merely discard and expulse. In the case of Puerto Rico, life building and the attrition of human life are indistinguishable in a political economy that produces waste, the disposable, the abject as a feature of life building and where spectacular violence is a ubiquitous feature of modes of economic and political unfolding. The zone of ordinariness is composed of the normalization of violence, though in vastly different degrees across race/gender/class lines. Modes of living on appear as impassivity, laziness, dependence, neutralized or criminalized defiance. These are more than modes of reproducing life nonheroically, simply living on. As I will argue in chapter 4, they are also modes of interruption rather than mere management. Slow violence is attritional, not spectacular, according to Nixon. Yet in the case of Puerto Rico, spectacular violence composes the zone of ordinariness and follows a logic of attrition. It is tied to the reproduction of life in conditions of expropriation, dispossession, expulsion. It is key for the reinstallment of a race/gender/class hierarchy at the center of an economy of the catastrophe, more precisely, for the actualization of race/gender/class. Violence is ubiquitous and spectacular yet at the same time dissimulated, gone unnoticed, normalized. It might appear, though it is not grasped. Despite these differences, I argue that spectacular violence and abjection are "slow," then, because they are not grasped as the effectivity of neoliberal coloniality. They go unnoticed, they are normalized, embedded in the everyday.

Santory-Jorge begins her essay recalling that, in January 1899, the United States made official exchange rates for the Puerto Rican peso.[170] In April 1900, Congress passed the Foraker Act, authorizing the Treasury to exchange pesos for dollars until July of that year.[171] At the end of the period, the Puerto Rican peso would hold no value. Debts incurred in pesos would become debts to be paid in dollars. Santory-Jorge also recalls that on August 8, 1899, Hurricane San Ciriaco devastated Puerto Rico. On September 18, 1899, the *New York Times* published "Suffering in Puerto Rico: Hurricanes Deprived Lower Classes of all Means of Livelihood."[172] The article distinguishes between those who suffered damages to their property and those who, "bordering on absolute poverty," were faced with threatened starvation. The storm "affected the two classes very differently," given the economic and political context in which it landed. San Ciriaco hit in a moment of "standstill." A new political economy was being articulated by a new colonial power. At a standstill, "the merchants of Puerto Rico had been patiently waiting for the United States to give them relief." In the context of the hurricane, both classes waited for relief efforts, albeit managing radically different conditions.[173]

On September 20, 2017, four months after Puerto Rico filed for bankruptcy under Title III of promesa, María made landfall. María revealed an already collapsed infrastructure. It revealed the impact of austerity, the necropolitical/necroeconomic effects of the debt crisis. A year earlier, a three-day blackout announced a faltering electrical grid. Reports that 99.5 percent of the territory's drinking water was in violation of the Safe Drinking Water Act had already surfaced.[174] A study by Harvard published in the *New England Journal of Medicine* estimates that approximately 4,645 people died prematurely "as a result of the slow institutional collapse that María accelerated."[175] "The disaster is not natural," "El desastre no es natural," was a central slogan within a protest organized by la Colectiva Feminista en Construcción days after the hurricane.[176] The disaster is the unequal distribution of precariousness along race/gender/class disclosed by the hurricane's impact. It is the consequence of an economy of

2.2 Hurricane María. Yabucoa, Puerto Rico, September 26, 2017. *Source:* Associated Press.

the catastrophe intensified but not produced by measures implemented in response to an unpayable debt, heightened in the context of disaster relief. Santory-Jorge moves to speak about risk, underscoring the "collective irresponsibility" and the further erosion of democracy evident in risks taken by a government—specifically, "men"—that accrued an unpayable debt without the consent of those who would pay with life itself. Any such risk, like any such decision, should be assessed in light of the account of the environment of which María was an event.

Yarimar Bonilla describes the temporality of disaster in the wake of María.[177] She explores the way in which the aftermath of the hurricane "operated as a moment of temporal rupture."[178] In describing the wait (weight) of disaster, she maps the environment of an economy of the catastrophe intensified in hurricane relief. Bonilla argues that a "temporal mode that we can call emergency" characterized Puerto Rico post-María.[179] This mode is a heightened awareness, a quickening of pace, a need to move, save, fix, repair. However, this temporal mode was met with "a crushing wall of inaction."[180] She writes:

> For weeks on end there was no school, no work, no power, no lights, no phones, no internet, no television, no public services. With hospitals closed or able to attend to only the most critically ill, sick patients were

sent home unable to receive things such as cancer treatments or dialysis. Without electricity, funeral homes were unable to embalm the dead. Although given the impassable roads, many are said to have buried the dead in their own backyards. For weeks on end, roads remained blocked; food, water, and gasoline were scarce, and cell towers were down rendering most phones inoperable.

The wait of disaster, a temporal mode of "standstill" where Puerto Rico seemed trapped in a stalled present," set in.[181] The present no longer gave way to a future. It "linger[ed] longer than it should."[182] Those who had savings and were able to participate in the hurricane economy waited in line for hours for food, gas, cash. Many had not worked since Hurricane Irma weeks before, so had no money waiting to be withdrawn. The state's abandonment filled the present. Bonilla continues:

> Government trucks did not turn up to clear the debris—instead, neighbors had to clear their own paths with machetes. Tankers of drinking water didn't appear—so residents headed to the river with buckets, or built their own make-shift infrastructure out of PVC pipes connected directly to mountain springs. They drank rain water or opened up wells that were later revealed to be toxic. Food was not delivered for weeks— so community kitchens sprung up, sometimes feeding a single block, sometimes feeding half the town. For weeks on end there were no aid workers, no helicopters, no military hospitals, no distribution centers— the state simply left its citizens waiting. When government aid finally arrived it came as a slow and insufficient trickle, with none of the "shock and awe" that many had come to associate with the "most powerful military in the world." Some meal boxes distributed held offered only a can of sausages, a bag of skittles, a roll of paper towels—this is not the imagined bounty of empire.[183]

The wait of disaster does more than disclose abandonment, decay, precarization. It is a point in which the extensive turns into the intensive, where the logic of attrition is experienced, felt, all at once. Bonilla notes that "emergency is not expected to be an enduring state" and points out that this is what Christina Sharpe calls "the weather."[184] I discuss Sharpe in the conclusion to this book. There, I build on her account of Saidiya Hartman's notion of the "afterlife of slavery" to specify coloniality as the afterlife of colonialism that reinstalls the colony in the case of Puerto Rico. Here, the turn from environment to weather, specifically climate, is insightful.

It captures what, as we saw in chapter 1, Ariadna Godreau-Aubert calls the no-place of life in the indebted colony. Climate names the spectacular as part of the ordinary, mapping the coordinates that bodies and populations marked as disposable navigate in multiple intensities. María laid bare the logic of attrition at work in austerity, but it heightened the spectacular forms of violence also distinctive of the economy of the catastrophe. In the wake of María, for example, calls related to domestic violence tripled, trans women reported being particularly vulnerable to violence and discrimination, suicide increased.[185]

Sharpe builds on Hartman's notion of the afterlife of slavery to elucidate the ubiquity of antiblack violence. This violence is at once attritional and spectacular. Mass incarceration, police killings of black men and women, majority killing of black trans women are coextensive with redlining, a racially coded GI bill, predatory lending, racial bias and discrimination. As Hartman writes in *Lose Your Mother*, "This is the afterlife of slavery—skewed life chances, limited access to health and education, premature death, incarceration, and impoverishment."[186] In *In the Wake*, Sharpe writes, "The weather is the totality of our environments; the weather is the total climate; and that climate is antiblack."[187] Sharpe makes a distinction between the singular and the singularity of slavery in the United States. The event is understood as singular even in its duration throughout time. Yet this obfuscates the strictures that produce and sustain it as it changes in new material conditions. Slavery, she argues, is often understood as a singular event. However, it should be understood as a "singularity—a weather event or phenomenon likely to occur around a particular time, or date, or set of circumstances."[188] Slavery is thus most properly understood when we think of the weather as pervasive in terms of "climate." Climate is precisely where antiblack violence is located. Climate is the "atmospheric condition of time and place" that maintains black lives "imperiled" and "devalued."[189]

In the case of Puerto Rico, weather as climate names the logic of disposability at work in the dispersed, pervasive operation of coloniality. It names the productivity of the economy of the catastrophe distinctive of coloniality in a neoliberal financialized context, not merely the decision of those who install the colony time and again through decisions embedded in the politico-juridical apparatus. There is a racial calculus involved, to be sure, where *élites criollas* realize the conditions that imperil and devalue black and nonwhite lives. However, weather as climate indexes the coordinates, hence the strictures, that compose the environment of colonial exceptionality. Such environment sustains an attritional violence that includes the spectacular. It is likely to become graspable in the event, not merely hypervisible in its unfolding. But it can also become hypervisible in the event itself—for example, through the axiomatic of property and the apparatus of the capture of life that is debt in the wake of a hurricane. An account of the slow death of neoliberal coloniality allows us to map an attrition that is as spectacular as it is unperceived. It is not eventful, even when spectacular. It structures the ordinary. Its visibility also turns on a hypervisibility, remains the site of invisibility through normalization, through the production of a common sense that tacitly accepts it. Even when intensified in an event—María, any occasion for a declaration of a state of emergency, so on—the point is to locate its effectivity in its extension.

The wait of disaster is only one modality of the temporality of the slow death of neoliberal coloniality. Muñiz-Varela speaks of the temporal logic of carceral waiting, which is not merely the wait of a sentence to be completed, parole granted.[190] It is also the wait of violence and inhuman conditions within prisons.[191] We must also speak of the wait of gender violence, for example, of intimate partner killings increased in times of austerity and in the aftermath of the hurricane. It is the wait of a necropolitical state that does little to eradicate gender violence. It is the wait of trans women and men who navigated discrimination at refuge centers as well as loss of access to HRT for months, compounding heighted precarity with lost access to health care and misgendering.[192] We should also speak of the wait of drug-related crime and of police intervention and deterrence that exacerbates it. This would in turn require that we track the wait of spatial racialization and modes of surveillance and public scrutiny of those who live in public housing or barrios versus those who live in gated communities. We might consider as well the wait of bureaucracy, of access to essential services, basic resources.[193] We might speak of the temporality of displacement, whether in the form of rising evictions or the disarticulation of a community that results from school closures or mass migration to the United States.[194] Closures entail the wait of transportation to other neighborhoods or municipalities to access education. Closures entail the further deferral of political participation, since schools serve as voting centers. Closures drive mass migration—expulsion. These are the spatio-temporal coordinates of the no-place of indebted life in Puerto Rico. They are some of the coordinates of the slow death of neoliberal coloniality within the indebted colony pre- and post-María.

Walter Benjamin wrote that the "tradition of the oppressed famously teaches us that the 'state of emergency' in which we live is not the exception but the rule." For the oppressed, the state of emergency is the ordinary, the everyday. The no-place of indebted life in the colony is a space-time structured by the destruction of life within the very reproduction of life. It is an environment but, more precisely, a climate in which bodies and populations navigate the impact of a political economy that thrives on a logic of disposability. Declarations of emergency and exceptional measures intensify the slow death of neoliberal coloniality, but they disclose the norm. They build on conditions already in place, already at work. Declarations of states of emergency, decisions in the face of emergency, are already too late. They are not the site of agency, whether we are speaking of the management of the ordinary or the exercise of colonial power. Punctual intervention has the power to rearticulate conditions to differing degrees, yet it draws from the strictures that I have argued are the site of colonial exceptionality.

The extensive nature of an economy of the catastrophe, the slow death of neoliberal coloniality, presses us to move from an economic to a historical understanding of debt. A critique of debt must reckon with historical debts that not only produce financial debts but also are debts consummated in financial debt. Historical reckoning, however, requires reversing the purported powerlessness of the indebted through practices that subvert repayment. These practices do not seek forgiveness or reconciliation. They seize the power to bind that instituted historical debts consummated in financial debts in the first place. Seizing the power to bind entails appropriating more than the power to decide. It requires dismantling the structures of neoliberal coloniality sustained by colonial exceptionality.

Historical Reckoning   3

Que paguen los culpables.
Let the guilty pay.
—ANONYMOUS

Nos deben a NOSOTRAS.
They owe US [women].
—COLECTIVA FEMINISTA EN CONSTRUCCIÓN

Es hora de cobrar todo lo que NOS DEBEN.
It is time to collect everything WE ARE OWED.
—JORNADA SE ACABARON LAS PROMESAS

IN 1789, Saint-Domingue was the most lucrative colony in the Americas, supplying two-thirds of the overseas trade of France.[1] Its exports to France exceeded total exports of all thirteen American colonies to Great Britain.[2] St. Domingue was also the greatest individual market for the European slave trade, as C. L. R. James explains.[3] Between 1697 and 1804, 800,000 captured Africans were shipped to and enslaved in St. Domingue's plantations.[4] Anthony Phillips notes that a complete turnover in the slave population occurred every twenty years, given the death rate that resulted from particularly cruel conditions.[5] In 1791, the enslaved defeated local whites and soldiers of the French monarchy, a Spanish invasion, a British expedition, and a French expedition. Each expedition was composed of approximately sixty thousand men.[6] In 1803, Napoleon Bonaparte's expedition was defeated, marking the single successful slave revolt in history. In 1804, the Republic of Haiti, the first black republic in the Americas, was established.[7]

In 1825, France and Britain demanded reparations for former slave owners in exchange for official recognition of the nation-state of Haiti.[8] With a flotilla of French warships surrounding the young republic, Jean-Pierre Boyer signed Charles X's Royal Ordinance.[9] French diplomatic recognition of Haiti was granted in exchange for a 50 percent tariff reduction on French imports and 150 million francs indemnity payable in five annual installments. Reparations would compensate planters for "lost property": land and slaves. The amount exceeded estimates of the "losses" by 50 million francs. Haiti borrowed the 30 million francs due on December 1825 from France itself, considerably increasing what is referred to as the "independence debt."

The independence debt operated as an apparatus of economic capture and political control.[10] The only successful slave rebellion in history was neutralized through debt. The population of Haiti today continues to resist subjection to the interests of capital managed by states and international institutions such as the IMF. In 2003, Jean-Bertrand Aristide declared that France, not Haiti, is the debtor.[11] Haiti would sue France over that "long-ago heist." He argued that because the debt accrued was based on the threat of reenslavement at a time when the international community regarded slavery as an evil, as Naomi Klein explains, the contract was invalid.[12] No such lawsuit took place. Aristide was, in fact, removed from power. During his visit to Puerto Rico in December 2018, Camille Chalmers noted that the struggle for the restitution of $24 billion, the amount estimated to have been paid over a century, continues in Haiti.[13]

How we are oriented, where we are located, when we speak of debt, Shariana Ferrer-Núñez rightly underscores, is crucial.[14] The case of Haiti is exemplary of the operation of debt as an apparatus of capture and predation, but also as a form of coloniality. The concept of coloniality names the afterlife of the colonial project of capitalist modernity in post colonial contexts. It clarifies the race/gender/class hierarchy installed by this project but that continues, rearticulated, in different historical and material conditions. In Puerto Rico, one must track the relation of colonialism and coloniality. This relation varies given the operation of capital. "The colony," Ariadna Godreau-Aubert writes, recall, "is what happens [*transcurre*] in 'repeated acts of capture.'"[15] "Indebted life," recall as well, "is the continuation of colonial-life."[16]

Debt captures time and space, body and social bond. It generates a "no-place," as Godreau-Aubert says. Debt, I add, captures value through *deferral*. It captures, it is a form of predation, by taking advantage of a temporal gap. It operates through *diversion*. Debt exercises control through the generation of *asymmetries*: the creditor, the debtor. It links to a certain future. That is to say, it has the capacity to deprive us of the future itself.[17] It can strip us of the body itself "even when wearing it."[18] Haiti is exemplary, furthermore, of the *reversibility* of debt. Debt is not reversible because it can return us to a previous state of affairs. It is reversible because it is possible to invert the positions it generates, the power it exercises. The deferral, the diversion, that debt produces in order to exercise its power can open spaces-times of reckoning, of giving accounts, of holding accountable.

Maurizio Lazzarato argues that debt is an apparatus of capture and a mode of subjectivation, thereby linking debt and guilt, as we have seen. Austerity works as an injunction to pay, establishing populations not only as responsible but also as guilty. The production of the indebted through guilt, I add, updates race/gender/class, reinstalls a race/gender/class hierarchy. It is here that we can locate the continuation of colonial life, the operation of coloniality. Debt captures, but it does so by augmenting blame. Payment is not its end. It generates precarity, identifying thereby economic opportunities. But it therefore leaves a trace, revealing more than financial transactions. Financial debt indexes historical debts, I want to suggest. In the case of Puerto Rico, it indexes colonial debts.

Debts are reversible, not merely cancelable. Minimally, an audit—a citizen audit—establishes whether a debt is illegal, illegitimate, odious. It does so for the sake of cancellation. Such intervention interrupts the necropolitical effectivity of debt: the impacts of austerity on already precarious populations given their position in a race/gender/class hierarchy articulated by capital. An audit would point out the agents of capital by their first and last name—banks, law firms, politicians. Their decisions nourish some while stripping others of the body itself. An audit would moreover shed light on the political economy that makes interventions by the agents of capital possible in the first place. However, debt admits of much more, I want to suggest. It makes possible giving accounts, holding accountable, reversing who is creditor and who is debtor, who is the one who has to pay.

The reversibility of debt enables subversive interruption. When activists in the unincorporated territory of Puerto Rico demand that "the guilty pay," that "they owe us," and that "it's time to pay," they locate themselves within the asymmetry distinctive of debt to subvert it. This is a taking, a seizing, of the normativities of debt itself, moving from economic to historical debts—that is, colonial debts. They challenge the perception of the indebted as neutralized, without power, merely bound to economic/historical/colonial debts. They not only invert who is creditor and who is debtor. They affirm dismantling the political economy that sustains the colonial condition through an ongoing coloniality. They seek to dismantle race/gender/class hierarchies in their multiplicities, intensities, differences. They seek to interrupt the actualization of race/gender/class. They go beyond cancellation, therefore, nevertheless recognizing its urgency.

In previous chapters, I have discussed the logic of capture and predation of a debt economy in the context of financialized neoliberal capitalism. In this chapter, I explore the logic of reckoning generated within debt itself given its asymmetry and deferral. I do so through an engagement with two critical theories of debt that, drawing from Marx, understand debt as a site of subversion and social rearticulation.[19] We find two core assumptions that require attention. Indebtedness *either* discloses irreducible social bonds that follow from interdependence *or* it indexes the material and historical conditions productive of a sociality reconfigured by debt. Indebtedness is *either* a site of restitution of a fundamental interdependence *or* a site of reckoning with the potential to dismantle material and historical conditions that produced debt in the first place. While the first version relies on a theory of recognition, the second considers indebtedness as a thoroughgoing historical phenomenon. Defending a historical rather than moral critique of debt is necessary when specifying the nature and possibilities of debt. Rejecting accounts that seek a moral ground for a critique of debt allows an assessment of its subversive possibilities, which depend on interrupting the work of the race/gender/class norm vital to coloniality.

The first section, Debt, considers David Graeber's account of the social logic of debt as a combination of equality and hierarchy.[20] Graeber's exposition makes clear that debt installs and operates through asymmetry and deferral. This discussion allows me to specify the reversibility of debt. The second and third sections, Recognition and History, respectively, examine two versions of a critique of debt that highlight logics of restitution or reckoning generated by debt itself. First, I examine Federica Gregoratto's engagement with Marx's 1844 "Comments on James Mill." For Gregoratto, Marx develops a conception of recognition that elucidates how debt exploits and thereby distorts interdependence. Second, I examine Richard Dienst's discussion of Marx's *Capital*, where debt indexes a history of material conflict. In *Capital*, debt is the ongoing "enclosure of the body that capital takes for granted."[21] The last section, Reckoning, develops Dienst's account in a different direction. Returning to Godreau-Aubert's work on debt and coloniality in Puerto Rico, I argue that indebtedness is a potential site of subversive interruption that involves moving from financial debts to historical, indeed colonial, debts. I suggest that subversive interruption should be understood as a mode of historical reckoning. I assess claims for a debt audit in this context and move to a discussion of two interventions by la Colectiva Feminista en Construcción exemplary of historical reckoning. The Feminist Embargo is key here.

DEBT

Debt is a social relation. It has received cosmological, theological, and economic articulation for centuries.[22] Yet, at its core, debt is a form of social binding, hence a social bond.[23] Ostensibly, debt is a promise to repay. It is a social bond that binds an individual or a population to a determined future purportedly irrespective of changing circumstances. Debt is a fundamentally ambivalent relation, then. It is necessarily "bilateral," as Godreau-Aubert puts it, generating a universe of obligations between parties, implying an irreducible relationally.[24] At the same time, it is fundamentally "unilateral," she adds, since repayment institutes an asymmetry between parties.

Godreau-Aubert argues that repayment can generate two distinct types of social logics.[25] It can set in motion logics of capture, punishment, and debasement, but it may also provide an opportunity to reckon with what is owed. More precisely, then, debt is a mode of social power. It can exploit interdependence, but it can also generate a space and time of reckoning with material and historical debts. This ambivalence can be put in temporal terms. Debt can foreclose the future for those bound to past conditions. It can also generate possibilities by reckoning with past binds that foreclose present and future bonds. The debtor's future can be in the hands of the creditor. The creditor's grip can be dissolved through reckoning with a past that is the present.

Graeber frames his study of the long history of debt, *Debt: The First 5,000 Years*, as an exposition of the relation between economies and "human economies," the economy of obligation and actions. Debt is an instance of the economic subsumption of a human economy. Debt is a promise to repay, to recall. It holds moral authority within purportedly strictly economic contexts. The fact that some debts are considered more "sacred" than others, such as the imperative to repay creditors at the expense of a population's basic needs and rights through austerity, betrays an entanglement of morality and economy that requires illumination. To this end, Graeber sketches three "main moral principles" on which economic relations are founded: "communism," "exchange," and "hierarchy."[26] Communism, exchange, and hierarchy represent "rough-and-ready" ways to "map out" social interactions of the type "tit-for-tat," which represents the most rudimentary economic interaction.

Communism, "any human relationship that operates on the principle of 'from each according to their abilities, to each according to their needs,'" is the foundation of all human sociality.[27] Unless the other is considered an enemy, if the need is great enough and the cost reasonable enough, the principle applies. Graeber is not speaking of reciprocity here, but rather of equality. What is equal is the knowledge that the other person would do the same.[28] Communism represents the priority of "immediate and practical questions of who has access to what sort of things and under what conditions."[29] Unlike communism, exchange is based on equivalence. Equivalence is never exact, however.[30] Competition is internal to exchange. Exchange requires that both parties "are keeping accounts."[31] Unlike communism, which has no temporal restriction, relations of exchange can be "canceled out," "either party can call an end to it at any time."[32] This is crucial. Because exchange is an interaction that can be completed, it can also bring to an end the relation between parties. Completing an exchange "frees" individuals from the economic *and* social bond. Equivalence is doubly formal, then. It abstracts from the social relation to the point of ending all relation as well as from the incommensurability between objects and the labor they embody. Hierarchy, in contrast, works on a "logic of precedent."[33] Lines of "superiority and inferiority" follow a logic of precedent, since an expectation is instituted. Hierarchy is the opposite of reciprocity. It lacks social bonds even if lines of superiority are no longer maintained by force. They can be maintained, rather, by habit or custom. Hierarchy is a relation among people that have no social relation, then, whether we are speaking of "plunder" or "selfless charity."

Debt is "always a combination of equality and hierarchy."[34] Debt requires "a relationship between two people who . . . are . . . potential equals."[35] They "are not currently in a state of equality," but "there is some way to set matters straight."[36] Debt is an exchange that has not been brought to completion. During the time that the debt remains unpaid, the logic of hierarchy "takes hold."[37] The logic of exchange makes debt repayment *and* cancellation inherent to the very relation. There is thus no such thing as a debt that cannot be paid or canceled, a relation that cannot be "restored." This is crucial for understanding the moralization of financial debt. Debt is a negative thing because it implies payability. Given this inherent payability, the inability to pay one's own debts signals that one must be culpable, guilty. Culpability is moralized as the inability to meet oneself in the future. The logic of hierarchy preys on the logic of exchange, then. Debt is a combination of equality and hierarchy not only because it is based on an interaction between equals that has yet to come to fruition. It assumes that the debtor can give back what is owed, that the debtor is responsible for their own fate. At the heart of financial debt is thus an atomistic conception of sociality that assumes that "we all start out as individuals who don't owe each other anything."[38]

Financial debt, in sum, represents a colonization of equality by the logic of exchange and intensified by the logic of hierarchy. Now, although Graeber's account of the logic of debt establishes that it is an entwinement between equality and hierarchy, he highlights the logic of exchange as the mediating factor when specifying the nature of the social relation that debt represents. He argues that "debt is just the perversion of a promise . . . by both math and violence."[39] Debt reduces "human cooperation, creativity, devotion, love and trust back into numbers."[40] Markets "drift freely" from their "violent origins" and can produce new forms of social bonds, but they reduce those very bonds to economic calculation. Challenging debt therefore requires resisting economic reduction. Graeber overemphasizes exchange, in my view, downplaying the hierarchy distinctive of debt. This compromises the diagnostic power of his critique of debt.

Emphasizing economic reduction does not capture the ambivalence distinctive of debt.[41] As an entwinement of equality and hierarchy, debt is a social relation the sociality of which has been evacuated. Rather than replaced by instrumental relationality, the bilateral nature of sociality is turned unilateral, expectations of reciprocity foreclosed. Reading Graeber against Graeber, we might say that while equality is mediated by the equalizing logic of exchange, exchange is mediated by the differentiating logic of hierarchy. The logic of hierarchy institutes a "superior/inferior" distinction, as he puts it, that makes possible unilateral relationality in the first place. The point here is not the social ground of any economic interaction—what Graeber discusses under the rubric of moral principles. Rather, the point is the ambivalence generated by the combination of equality and hierarchy that Graeber theorizes. This ambivalence establishes the reversibility of debt, hence the possibilities of subversion within.

Debt exploits the temporal gap opened up by the lack of completion of an exchange. A hierarchy is installed by the deferral of such completion, binding the debtor to a determined future but also to specific conditions. Debt is an economic bond, then, that binds through the very evacuation of sociality through such deferral: for the time being, until the debt is repaid. Debt turns social binds into economic bonds between parties that are not on equal standing: creditor, debtor. During this time, parties are keeping accounts. A debt can be paid or canceled, the hierarchy displaced, but such displacement requires accounting for who has to pay. Precisely because of the temporal gap and the material conditions that set its strictures, the hierarchy can be subverted. Restoring equality, reciprocity, is not merely the consequence of payment or cancellation. It does not necessarily follow from letting go of the bind at hand. It requires giving accounts, holding accountable, establishing who is creditor, who is debtor, who owes what to whom. It requires tracing the history of the hierarchy at hand—its installment, its reproduction, its effectivity, its work.

Highlighting the asymmetry characteristic of debt allows reflection on the logic of restitution or reckoning generated within. This reflection, however, requires examining assumptions about the relation between human economies and a debt economy at work in a critique of debt. Key here is examining the assumption that interrupting modes of capture and control made possible by the hierarchy distinctive of debt requires moral restitution rather than historical reckoning. This assumption is most clearly present in Frederica Gregoratto's essays on a critical theory of debt. She emphasizes the restitution of interdependence appealing to a theory of recognition in early Marx. Any such restitution, I maintain in contrast, should be specified concretely—through an exposition of the material conditions productive of debt in the first place.

RECOGNITION

In "Debt, Power, and the Normativity of Interdependence," Gregoratto argues for a return to Marx's 1844 "Comments on James Mill" to articulate the "normative ground" of a critical theory of debt. Because debt is a matter of an asymmetry, it leads to an account of social power.[42] Critical theories of debt, however, fail to conceptualize debt as a form of social power intersubjectively instituted and sustained. They thereby fail to account for the nature of debt and its subversive possibilities. Specifying the nature of debt requires more than an exposition of the structure of the social relation expressed by debt—the "intersubjective financial bond," as she puts it.[43] It requires an exposition of the distortion of sociality that debt represents.

Gregoratto reads Marx against Lazzarato. Gregoratto focuses on Lazzarato's account of subjectivation, arguing that it lacks a conception of the intersubjective relation that the production of the indebted man requires. Lazzarato discusses debt in light of a "supraindividual" conception of power, assessing the "bundle of practices, strategies, techniques, dispositifs, axioms ('axiomatics')" that "mold" a subject that feels compelled to pay an individual and collective debt.[44] But he does not, she argues, provide an account of the relation between debtor and creditor that mediates the "supraindividual" and the individual.[45] Because Lazzarato forgoes an account of the relationality of debt, he conceives of the creditor as powerful and the debtor as fundamentally powerless. The one-sided nature of Lazzarato's account is due in great part to his allegiance to Nietzsche's conception of debt within his discussion of *Schuld* (guilt) in *On the Genealogy of Morality*.[46] Nietzsche allows Lazzarato to account for the emergence of a type of subject that holds itself culpable, compelled to repay its debt.

Marx's discussion of credit in the "Comments" is helpful, Gregoratto maintains. Recall that the "Comments" are part of Marx's early discussion of alienation (*Entfremdung*).[47] Marx famously argues that, under capitalist conditions, labor is alienated labor. He distinguishes between objectification (*Vergegenständlichung*) and alienation. As embodied, living creatures, human beings necessarily have a metabolic relation to nature. Productive activity, objectification, is hence essential to what it is to be human. The notion of alienation tracks the ways in which the aim of capitalism, the accumulation of profit, distorts the human's relation to (1) the product of labor, (2) productive activity itself, (3) nature, (4) and other human beings. The product of labor appears as autonomous, as a lord over the producer. Productive activity, the source of human realization, is turned against the human through wage labor and dehumanizing working conditions. Nature appears as something to exploit. The life of the species is turned into a means for individual life. Capitalism, in short, distorts the fact that human beings produce as a species and for the species.

Marx begins his "Comments" articulating the nature of money as a form of alienation. The "essence of money," however, is not that "property is alienated in it."[48] Rather, the "*mediating activity* . . . , the *human*, social act by which man's products mutually complement one another, is *estranged* from man and becomes the attribute of money, a *material thing* outside man." Money turns the nature of social bonds against these very bonds, establishing financial relationality as something beyond individuals. Human bonds are mediated by an abstraction, then. They are turned into an abstraction. In credit, however, it seems as if the "power of the alien, material force were broken," the alienation "abolished."[49] Credit, it seems, reestablishes human bonds. Because credit requires trust, it centers the interdependence of creditor and debtor. It makes explicit the relation of recognition that structures sociality.

Yet this is merely an "appearance," Marx argues.[50] He writes:

> *Credit* is the *economic* judgment on the *morality* of a man. In credit, the *man* himself, instead of metal or paper, has become the *mediator* of exchange, not however as a man, but as the *mode of existence of capital* and interest. . . . *Human individuality*, human *morality* itself, has become both an object of commerce and the *material* in which money exists. Instead of money, or paper, it is my own personal existence, my flesh and blood, my social virtue and importance, which constitutes the material, corporeal form of the *spirit of money*. Credit no longer resolves the value of money into money but into human flesh and the human heart.[51]

Credit is the further reduction of social bonds. It turns bonds, indeed individuals themselves, into the medium of exchange. The crucial point here is that credit preys on trust. It uses trust as a medium of exchange. Credit is thus the epitome of capital's rearticulation of social bonds in light of the logic of exchange. It is the pinnacle of the instrumental rationality distinctive of capital. The "alienation, the dehumanization, is all the more *infamous* and *extreme*," Marx concludes, since "under the appearance of man's *trust* in man . . . is the height of *distrust*."[52]

Note that credit is and does much more, according to Marx. Credit is the institution and maintenance of a fundamental asymmetry. It inscribes the economic and political hierarchy distinctive of capital within the very bonds of human sociality. It does so in a "double way," Marx says.[53] The bonds of trust become an opportunity to drive the "antithesis between capitalist and worker" even deeper.[54] Credit is an opportunity for the rich to accumulate wealth while the poor find themselves at the "arbitrary discretion of the rich" who will "confirm or deny [their] entire existence."[55] While credit seems to be based on trust (of repayment), it is in fact an exercise of power because it binds the poor to the rich, the worker to the capitalist. What is more, a "man without credit . . . possesses no trust, no recognition."[56] He is a "social pariah, bad man," adding insult to injury.[57] Credit, therefore debt, turns the poor into a "counterfeit coin," seeking to obtain credit by any means.[58] Finally, credit turns the state into "the plaything of businessmen."[59]

Gregoratto understands debt as an asymmetrical relation, although she does not stress the political asymmetry that Marx tracks. She highlights Marx's account of the reduction of sociality into a means of exchange, arguing that it sheds light on debt's "distortion of that relation of recognition that best defines human nature."[60] To be sure, Marx ends "Comments" with an articulation of interdependence in its idealized form. In "human production," Marx famously writes, each would have "affirmed himself and the other person."[61] Human production would not only be a "manifestation of my life," I would have mediated "another man's essential nature," and I would have served as a "mediator between you and the species."[62] So conceived, Gregoratto maintains, interdependence allows us to track its "disruption" "in production and exchange and in the credit system—as it becomes a power relation."[63] An idealized account of sociality, then, is necessary for a critical theory of debt.

Now, Gregoratto maintains that rather than merely unilateral, power is relational.[64] Power is "exercised by A over B when A is able to put B in a position of dependency. Dependency means that B needs A, and the products of A's activities, in order to satisfy her needs (and desires)."[65] She adds that "power exercised by A over B consists also in . . . subjectivation processes [that] make and govern needs and desires as means for attaching B in a position of dependency."[66] The crucial point is that debt is a form of "domination" when the creditor's power results from "the impossibility for the debtor to counter-balance" it.[67] However, given the relational nature of power, the debtor is not powerless, as Gregoratto argues Lazzarato "hastily" assumes.[68] The direction of power can be "reversed."[69] Such reversal is not an expression of domination when it resists the type of "forgetting" distinctive of alienation, the obfuscation of interdependence that comprises alienation. Such reversal restores rather than exploits interdependence.

Gregoratto's resistance to considering the debtor as powerless is important, yet the premise that understanding the nature of the credit-debt relation requires an account of the "basic social bond and its internal normativity" should be rejected.[70] I am not arguing against interdependence as the ground of sociality or as the ultimate goal of emancipatory or subversive practices. The worry here is about the claim that a moral ground is needed for a critique of debt, one found in an account of interdependence that does not track its own relation to the race/gender/class norm. Gregoratto's assumption that a critical standpoint that articulates an "ethically meaning good" tied to the "realization of the essence of human beings" or the "social grammar of recognition" treats normativity as if it were exempt from the exercise of power distinctive of capital/coloniality.[71] This assumption gives primacy to the restitution of interdependence without first engaging the material and historical conditions not only productive of debt but that *are* debts reflected in or expressed by financial debt. Lacking this materially and historically indexed reckoning, restoring interdependence becomes empty, normalizing, violent. It reinstalls the race/gender/class norm central to the work of coloniality. In *Contract and Contagion*, Angela Mitropoulos cautions against the "inclination toward normative rectification that is more or less violent in its requirements and decidedly transcendental in its vantage point."[72] By not working through hierarchies that are debts, restitution reproduces forms of sociality that are "modes for the legitimate distribution of property and right": "(contractual) exchange conceived as *the* form of relation; of productivity as its premise and promise; and of the subjective homologies of marital, wage, social, and fiduciary contracts."[73] Such reproduction, as I have argued in chapters 1 and 2, shores up the race/gender norm vital to the work of coloniality.

I come back to Mitropoulos below. Here, in contrast to Gregoratto, I suggest that indebtedness reverses its purported powerlessness through practices of subversion that reckon with what is owed. The work, the effectivity, of subversion is a matter of reckoning with concrete race/gender/class asymmetries installed by material, political, historical conditions not only productive of debt, but that *are* debts consummated in financial debt.[74] Any conception of normative sociality deployed in a critique of debt should be elaborated in a second step, through historical reckoning and as a result of a political process of contestation of terms involved in that reckoning. In *Capital*, Richard Dienst argues, Marx treats debt historically, tied to the ongoing logic of dispossession. Drawing from this aspect of Marx's corpus, I suggest, provides the proper framework for articulating the subversive possibilities within debt itself.

HISTORY

In *The Bonds of Debt*, Dienst suggests that debt "articulates the *historicity of life*."[75] Debt is "basic to the experience of social being as a dimension of historicity."[76] These are not abstract claims, however. Dienst discusses debt as a form of sociality central to capitalism. He calls attention to three distinct "moments" in Marx's corpus useful for elaborating the nature of debt:

a philosophical moment, found in the "Comments"; an economic moment, found in *Grundrisse: Foundations of the Critique of Political Economy* and volumes 1 and 2 of *Capital*; and a political "even utopian" moment opened up in volume 3 of *Capital*. The speculative language of Marx's early work, he argues, does not allow us to materially index debt as "constitutive of the social body . . . registered as a material conflict."[77] The economic-political treatment of debt, in contrast, centers debt as the product of such material conflict. Dienst locates Marx's treatment of debt in the accounts of originary accumulation and the reserve army of labor. Marx's suggestion that we find radical prospects in the "most advanced edge[s] of capitalist logic," he also maintains, gains significance in this context.[78] Debt is one of those edges.

In the *Grundrisse*, Dienst writes, "Marx offers a derisory portrait of the capitalist who thinks the worker 'owes an obligation to capital for the fact that he is alive at all.'"[79] Dienst draws from this moment in the *Grundrisse* to track debt in *Capital*, where it is tied to the originary accumulation of capital. As we saw in chapter 1, Marx's account of originary accumulation traces the history of "conquest, enslavement, robbery, murder, in short, force" that accounts for the original accumulation of capital.[80] It describes the history of the creation of the worker through a process of becoming free *from* any means of production in order to become free *to* sell their labor. This process is not only traceable to the enclosure of the English commons, recall. It is bound to conquest, genocide, slavery, colonial violence. It tracks the modalities of violence of dispossession, which exceeds those made possible by the contract. Debt, accordingly, is the result of the creation of "free" subjects released from feudal obligations and slavery.[81] Debt is now an obligation to capital, Dienst maintains, given the worker's release from these modalities of violence. It is a violently enforced obligation, however, where the worker is punished if they fail to comply by the terms of the contract. Thus, in *Capital*, debt appears as the "loss of self-sufficiency."[82] The point is not dependence, but variations of dispossession and created misery.[83]

This origin story allows Marx to highlight that dispossession is necessarily ongoing.[84] As the result of the history and ongoing logic of dispossession, debt is precisely what "capital takes for granted at every level."[85] The binding of the worker to the logic of capital is not only a matter of subjectivation, however. It is a matter of subjection. In *Capital*, Dienst suggests, debt is indexed to a "primary enclosure of the lived body."[86] Enclosure is not only a matter of the capture of land but also of body, activity, and time. For

Dienst, this means that the worker is bound to capital not only by the contract that binds labor and right but also the ever-present threat of impoverishment and misery.[87] This is, of course, an induced misery. An example of the legacy of originary accumulation, Dienst thus argues, is Marx's notion of a reserve army of labor.[88] It articulates capture as the "socialization of misery."[89] The mode of capitalist production, according to Marx, necessarily generates poverty. The notion of a reserve army of labor explains the necessity, to an "increasing extent," of a laboring population that is "superfluous".[90] Such population addresses the changing needs of capital through the creation of a "mass of human material always ready for exploitation."[91]

With this discussion, Marx makes two points. First, an army of laborers serves to consolidate exploitation. The creation of a relative surplus population is the "background against which" the law of supply and demand of labor works.[92] It is a central tool of control over labor in confining the "field of action of this law" to "capital's drive" to exploit and dominate workers.[93] "The over-work of the employed part of the working class," Marx writes, "swells the ranks of its reserve, while, conversely, the greater pressure that the reserve by its competition exerts on the employed workers forces them to submit to over-work and subjects them to the dictates of capital."[94] "Enforced idleness," then, is key to the asymmetry distinctive of capital.[95] Second, Dienst argues, the creation of an unproductive sector submits workers and nonworkers to the logic of debt. Marx clarifies that the worker's superfluousness is a condition to which all workers are subjected. Yet it is expressed more precisely in "floating," "latent," and "stagnant" reserves of unproductive, inactive workers.[96] The floating reserve moves in and out of employment while the latent reserve is thrust out of work by the expansion of capital beyond capitalist sectors.[97] The stagnant reserve, in contrast, is chronically underemployed and falls into poverty. Marx famously writes: "Pauperism is the hospital of the active labor-army and the dead weight of the industrial reserve army. Its production is included in that of the relative surplus population, its necessity is implied by their necessity; along with the surplus population, pauperism forms a condition of capitalist production, and of the capitalist development of wealth. It forms part of the *faux frais* of capitalist production: but capital usually knows how to transfer these from its own shoulders to those of the working class and the petty bourgeoisie."[98] The issue is not merely that idleness and poverty are necessary features of the capitalist mode of production. The point is that "unproductive bodies" can only be "fed by submitting to the law of debt."[99] Debt is the "means by which misery becomes socialized."[100]

Debt actualizes dispossession. In this context, it binds through the socialization of capture within the circuit of wage labor. This form of binding exhibits a logic different from the equalization distinctive of exchange. As we have seen, in his early work, Marx argues that credit distorts sociality in order to "perfect it."[101] Money reduces sociality to an abstraction amenable to the logic of exchange. Under the guise of relational purity, credit consummates this rationalization. It organizes a "hitherto chaotic process." It mobilizes "vast untapped resources" necessary for value creation and the capture of value. As such, credit operates in a fetish-like manner.[102] In *Capital*, in contrast, indebtedness is not a "formal or spiritual position," hence not a matter of the reduction of sociality to the instrumentality of exchange. Debt, in other words, is not a matter of the obligation to express everything in the form of value. It bespeaks an asymmetry that subjects such reduction to an alternative logic. Under capitalist conditions, as Dienst writes, there is "credit without debt for the few (who can wield the power of investment without accountability) and debt without credit for the many (who bear the hazards without exercising choice)."[103]

Dienst points to a third moment in Marx's discussions of not debt per se, but rather credit. In *Capital*, credit is the site of a political, "even utopian," moment, though for different reasons than those offered in the "Comments."[104] Dienst quotes volume 3 of *Capital*, where Marx writes:

The credit system . . . accelerates the material development of the productive forces and the creation of the world market, which it is the historical task of the capitalist mode of production to bring to a certain level of development, as material foundations for the new form of production. At the same time, credit accelerates the violent outbreaks of this contradiction, crises, and with these elements the dissolution of the old mode of production.

The credit system has a dual character immanent in it: on the one hand it develops the motive of capitalist production, enrichment by the exploitation of others' labor, into the purest and most colossal system of gambling and swindling, and restricts ever more the already small number of the exploiters of social wealth; on the other hand, however, it constitutes the form of transition toward a new mode of production.[105]

The fictionality of credit contains transformative potential, according to Dienst. It represents a site of undoing of capital's "strictest bindings" from within capital's actuality.[106] In presenting the immense "productivity as a collective conjuration," credit is able to reveal what has been "accomplished by the whole system of social labor."[107] Yet the fictitious character of credit does more.[108] In "these living acts of the imagination," we can "find a way to recall and reclaim their own creative powers."[109] Credit not only makes visible the fictitious character of value itself. In making visible the imaginary production of a whole system of value—a production with violent grounds and effects—credit makes the reconfiguration of social labor possible.

While Dienst's suggestion does not reproduce the problems that Gregoratto's normative elaboration of credit generate, I nevertheless argue that Marx's discussion of debt in *Capital* is more promising. Dienst's own analysis provides important clues. He writes: "If *credit* is understood as the sweeping gesture with which capital lays claim to the present in the name of the past and the future, debt may be seen as a mark of the nonsynchronous, the stubborn insistence of everything resistant to economic rule. If creating credit *ex nihilo* is a sublime projection of an economic order and system, indebtedness must be the *deferral* or *withdrawal of value*, a way to play for time in order to keep something alive."[110] Unlike the temporal logic of exchange, which binds by reducing the past and future to a present abstraction, the temporal logic of debt binds by resisting such reduction through a deferral, by interrupting the completion of any such exchange. Debt requires a deferral within limits, however, indexed to specific material and historical conditions. If it actualizes dispossession, if it indexes the heterogeneity as well as interdependence of exploitation and dispossession by centering the latter, then debt allows for historical reckoning. It makes possible concrete modes of accounting as well as specific modes of interruption that range over the economic, the political, and the historical.

It is crucial to underscore that the political moment is not a matter of temporality as such. Focusing on temporality would introduce a formality that dispossession and capture refute. It is neither merely a matter of interrupting the consummation of an exchange, thereby resisting the economic reduction of social relations. Merely unmasking the fictitious character of the system of social labor such that another can be imagined and installed in its place is not enough. Although it is that too, interruption here is a matter of reckoning with historical debts inscribed in, indeed expressed by, a race/gender hierarchy that made possible debt's function as an apparatus of capture and predation in the first place. The temporal gap opened up by the deferral necessary for the very work of debt is thereby grasped as a site of interruption.

The nonsynchronous, stubborn resistance to economic rule, the withdrawal of value opens up a space and time of reckoning. Debt appears as a site of subversion. It is possible to invert the positions it generates, the power it exercises. The deferral that debt produces to exercise its power can open spaces-times of reckoning—of giving accounts and holding accountable. Debts are seen in their double actuality then, financial and fundamentally historical, expressing past and present modes of dispossession. Dienst suggests that, understood as the articulation of the historicity of life, indebtedness leads us to "wonder . . . whether our historical situation can be grasped only when we try to take all of our debts into account, and . . . whether all of our ideas of 'history' or 'the world' are not, before all else, debts we take on (or not) in every act of thinking."[111] I seek to amplify this claim, arguing that in indexing debt to past and present modalities of capture, historical reckoning tracks originary and ongoing modes of dispossession, creation of misery, production of abjection. Historical reckoning indexes an ongoing coloniality and, in the case of Puerto Rico, the reproduction of the colonial condition.

While there are significant differences between what I am calling historical reckoning and what Mitropoulos calls genealogy, it is instructive to consider her critique of genealogy at this point. She argues against a genealogical approach, claiming that it fares no better than the normative rectification distinctive of theories of recognition and right. She maintains that genealogy "authenticat[es] power through origin stories and their transmission," establishing a "naturalized foundation."[112] Genealogy purports to "recognize . . . to whom and what we owe our existence."[113] But in so doing, it seeks to establish the "boundary between that which is excessive and that which is proper."[114] Genealogy is thus "a means of discerning the legitimate ordering and transmission of property, money, right, and debt."[115] Origin stories, that is to say, become essential to the logic of the contract that links labor and right. Much like normative restitution, then, what Mitropoulos calls genealogy reproduces the logic of the *oikos*—the productive household. It thereby leaves the race/gender norm central to the reproduction of capital intact. It leaves coloniality intact.

Mitropoulos argues that the task is not to "instill pride—how to reckon debts, origin, and filiation so as to secure recognition and the boundaries by which this is made to appear normal, folded back into the flow of rights, property, and re-/production."[116] Rather, it is to interrogate "lines of indebtedness," to track "plausible infrastructures in the composition of political demands."[117] The task is not to pursue the question of how debts can be "erased."[118] Debt cancellation on its own risks reproducing the social system that led to its accrual in the first place. Instead, it is to track lines of indebtedness by discerning "how debt is defined, whether it takes the form of a financial obligation or some other consideration of relational inter-dependence."[119] This entails interrogating what debt "lets flourish" and what it "obscures."[120] Now, Mitropoulos couples this suggestion with an affirma-tion of the subversive potential of credit. Such interrogation calls for "the transformation of infinite debt into endless credit."[121] Unlike debt, which is fundamentally a matter of binds, bonds, forms of binding, forms of bond-ing, credit is limitless. In fact, what is revealed in usury, Mitropoulos main-tains, is an excess that should be affirmed. The latter counters the gesture of rectification distinctive of critiques of debt.[122] The excess of credit, espe-cially in interest, interrupts a rearticulation of the proper.

There is an important note of caution in Mitropoulos's rejection of genealogy as akin to normative restitution. In rejecting normative restitu-tion, her understanding of credit rather than debt is also appealing. Never-theless, a critique of debt is more promising. Precisely by requiring that we track to whom and what we owe our existence, debt appears as a site of historical reckoning. This is not a matter of establishing a single lineage. Neither is it a matter of reigning in what is excessive to the proper. It is a matter of tracking a history of material dispossession and conflict. Account-ing for historical debts consummated in and expressed by financial debts allows forms of unbinding, disarticulating the world of capital/colonial-ity. The possibility of subverting the purported powerlessness of indebt-edness lies therein. Historical reckoning seeks to dismantle the hierarchy that reproduces colonial violence. For this reason, it cannot initially affirm unqualified excess. It seeks to *seize the power to bind* that instituted the link between property and right and that maintains the logic of the oikos in the first place. Godreau-Aubert elaborates a critique of debt in precisely these terms. La Colectiva Feminista en Construcción's actions subvert the opera-tion of debt in Puerto Rico in precisely these terms.

RECKONING

Recall Graeber's account of debt: Debt is an entwinement of equality and hierarchy mediated by the logic of exchange. A critique of debt requires resisting the reductive power of the equalizing logic of exchange. I have suggested, in contrast, that what is distinctive of debt is the mediating power of the logic of hierarchy. Hierarchy mediates exchange. A critique of debt requires the subversion of the hierarchy distinctive of the obligation to repay.[123] Any such subversion requires that we move from financial to historical debts, however. Critique entails reckoning with historical debts that not only produce financial debt but that are debts consummated in financial debt. Historical reckoning seeks to reverse the purported powerlessness of the indebted through practices that subvert repayment. Subversive practices do not seek forgiveness or reconciliation. They seize the power to bind that instituted historical debts consummated in financial debts in the first place.

Godreau-Aubert's work is decisive here. She argues that repayment can generate two distinct types of social logics. It can set in motion logics of capture, punishment, and debasement. Yet it can also open up a space and time of reckoning.[124] Key here is distinguishing not between hierarchy and exchange, but between a "logic of collection" (*lógica de cobro*) and a "logic of payment" (*lógica de pago*). To collect financial debts entails a dynamic of "persecution," yet it can be subverted into a matter of accountability.[125] Subverting debt requires seizing "structures of collection," turning them into structures of accountability by moving from financial debts to historical indeed colonial debts. Such subversion comes into sharper focus if we abandon the assumption that a critique of debt necessitates restoring structures of reciprocity without first examining the history and operation of specific norms of reciprocity. Subverting structures of collection is an act of power from disempowerment, as we will see, that requires resisting reinstalling the purported legitimate distribution of property and right, productivity and propriety, distinctive of coloniality.

We can distinguish between the logic of collection of capital/the colony and a logic of payment, Godreau-Aubert argues. A logic of collection captures the body, time, coasts, bonds with another, value in all senses. It reproduces punishment, it sustains the production of an abject indebted subject summoned to pay through austerity, dispossession, and expulsion. It domesticates debt itself by directing it toward credit, as Fred Moten and Stefano Harney maintain.[126] It settles in order to regain access to financial markets. This is the charge of the Fiscal Control Board. La Junta is the apparatus that actualizes the interests of capital through debt restructuring. Debts that are settled to generate more credit reinstall structures of collection, initiate new logics of persecution. "Restored credit is restored justice and restorative justice is always the renewed reign of credit," Moten and Harney argue, "a reign of terror, a hail of obligations to be met, measured, meted, endured."[127] Debt restructuring that serves credit restores race/gender normativities that make possible the operation of debt as an apparatus of capture and predation in the first place. "So long as they pair in the monogamous violence of the home, the pension, the government, or the university," Moten and Harney write, "debt can only feed credit, debt can only desire credit. And credit can only expand by means of debt."[128]

In contrast, the logic of payment places us in a material history. It invites us to turn the deferral, the diversion, of debt itself into spaces-times of accounting—*rendición de cuentas*. A logic of collection deployed against those deemed culpable, guilty, responsible for financial debts, the debt to capital, can be subverted into a settling of historical debts, past debts inscribed in present hierarchies. Reckoning, accordingly, is a settling of debts coextensive with a refusal to pay. As activists in Puerto Rico say, *esa deuda no la vamos a pagar*, "we will not pay that debt." Refusal, however, requires dismantling the structures that reproduce the race/gender/class norm, not only the colony. Giving accounts, holding accountable, requires navigating one's location within a race/gender/class hierarchy that complicates complicity with the aims of interruption. Regarding capital and its logic of collection, "We [*nosotras*] do not owe ourselves to anyone," Godreau-Aubert writes.[129] She adds, "I will insist on the distance between promising (owing oneself) and duty."[130] The bonds of debt with another are not like the binds of debt of capital, yet there is no promise that is exempt from critical examination. Those to whom one is *not* owed, referring here to the debt to capital, are precisely those with whom one can settle historical debts by refusing to pay. Those to whom one is *not* owed are those whom one must hold accountable. At the same time, one is accountable to those *with* whom one pursues subversive interruption, *with* whom one refuses to pay the debts of capital. Reckoning dismantles race/gender/class hierarchies transversally.

Reckoning inverts the asymmetry distinctive of debt on various scores, then. It subverts the logic of collection to a matter of giving accounts, holding accountable. Rather than financial debts on their own, reckoning addresses a history of capture and predation of land, body, time through which race/gender/class operates, indeed, shores itself up. It confronts an ongoing coloniality, the production of abject bodies and populations central to dispossession. Reckoning subverts the imperative to repay as well as the individualist impulse in this imperative. It is not an individual in isolation, their particular failures or modes of corruption in isolation, who should give accounts, who should be held accountable. The system of social labor is answerable. Reckoning entails holding specific individuals and institutions responsible, yet it involves tracking the political economy that made possible their interventions in the first place. Collection is thereby turned against itself, redirected to individuals, institutions, and structures that capture and govern through debt.[131] In this way, reckoning subverts the moralization of debt. It turns subjection through subjectivation whereby the indebted is compelled to pay against itself. It subverts the logic of abjection from populations to the system of social labor itself.

Reckoning, in sum, distinguishes between a logic of collection and a logic of payment, between debts to capital and historical debts, between a refusal to pay and assuming historical responsibility. It is subversive when it interrupts the modes of binding distinctive of the logic of capture of a debt economy and the race/gender/class hierarchy that such logic reinstalls. Refusal to pay is thus not asking for forgiveness. It is not a letting go of an obligation. Refusal involves *seizing the power of binding* in order to dismantle the asymmetry at hand. Reflecting on fiscal disobedience in Cameroon, Janet Roitman argues that "seizure" reverses a social order in which dispossession is central to accumulation.[132] Seizure operates as a form of "redistribution" within conditions of dispossession.[133] Associated with the exercise of power from within disempowerment, modalities of seizure do not represent an "opposition between order and disorder."[134] Rather, they represent a "*diversion* that is produced out of the system of exchange itself."[135] Historical reckoning should be conceived accordingly, as a material praxis that seizes the power to bind from within conditions of dispossession. Such praxis exploits the diversion that financial debts install in order to capture, capturing debt itself. It exploits repayment to interrupt coloniality, to turn it inoperative.

Capturing debt itself requires placing financial debts in a material/colonial history, as we have seen. Giving accounts and holding accountable are thus not merely discursive practices. Neither are they merely a matter of monetary compensation. If a political economy that reproduces the colonial condition is left intact, if the race/gender/class hierarchy it installs is left intact, the subversion of debt has been neutralized. If the settling of debts can be said to restore sociality, it is because those to whom one is not owed are confronted with their historical debts. Reckoning does not seek to restore what is excessive to the proper. It does not seek to determine the legitimate distribution of property and the legal, familial, political contracts that subtend it. It seizes the power to bind that affirms these norms and their mere expansion without question. Here we find the need, the urgency, for an audit, cancellation, nonpayment among other efforts that challenge the legitimacy of debt. These are spaces-times of confrontation with historical debts. In the case of Puerto Rico, they are spaces-times of confrontation with colonial debts.

It is instructive to consider demands for a citizen debt audit in Puerto Rico. Law 97 of 2015 created the Commission for the Comprehensive Audit of the Public Credit. The commission was tasked with examining irregularities in the issuing of bonds and the overall accrual of debt but also to establish priorities in public spending. Ricardo Rosselló's government repealed the law in 2017, however, citing PROMESA as the proper mechanism to pursue an audit whether through the Fiscal Control Board or the courts within a bankruptcy process. The governor furthermore argued that the audit would not be necessary given negotiations with creditors.[136] The commission was dismantled even though it published two reports, which indicate that part of the debt is unconstitutional.[137] In response, the Citizen Front for the Debt Audit (Frente Ciudadano para la Auditoría de la Deuda) began fund-raising efforts to pursue an independent audit.[138] El Frente seeks to establish the legality of the debt, reverse the constitutional priority to repay creditors, and pursue just debt restructuring.[139]

José Nicolás Medina-Fuentes, in contrast, argues against an audit.[140] He maintains that there are roughly three perspectives on Puerto Rico's debt. First, a "colonial" perspective holds that creditors must be repaid regardless of life, human rights, and a diminishing population. This position regards mishandling of public funds and corruption as the culprits of the unpayable debt. Second, a "reformist" perspective calls for a just restructuring through a citizen debt audit. This is a conservative position, according to Medina-Fuentes. It diverts attention away from generating an "anti-colonial consensus." In affirming restructuring and repayment, in shifting attention to partisan politics within the territory, it forgoes a critical assessment of the colonial relation that generated conditions for the accrual of an unpayable debt in the first place. Calls for a citizen audit do not call into question Section 210 of PROMESA, which establishes that a territory's public debt is not the responsibility of the federal government. Third, an "anti-colonial" perspective appeals to the category of odious debt within international law. Puerto Rico's lack of sovereignty establishes that the debt is the metropolis'. This third option, which Medina-Fuentes affirms, holds that a citizen audit is a colonial concession.

Medina-Fuentes misses, however, that a citizen audit is conceived as a political rather than economic tool. Instead of affirming the legitimacy of the debt, purportedly betraying indifference to the colonial political economy that made it possible, a citizen audit is conceived as a way of holding accountable. It seeks to name names—corrupt politicians, firms, and banks. Yet it aims to do much more. It seeks to trace the political economy that made possible the accrual of such debt, thereby indexing the colonial history that installed these structures in the first place. As Eva Prados notes, an audit sheds light on illegalities and fraud that can lead to canceling much of the debt, as in the case of Ecuador.[141] Yet rather than reestablish credit and reentry into financial markets, debt cancellation aims to interrupt the necropolitical operation of austerity whether implemented by the state or the Fiscal Control Board.[142] Prado adds that "citizen audits have strengthened social movements by giving them the information and data that demonstrated how unnecessary many economic reforms were with serious impacts for the people."[143] This is key for understanding the political function of the audit, as became clear during the July 2019 protests. The promise of an audit lies in becoming a tool of reckoning that subverts debt itself.

Along with the removal (*destitución*) of governor Ricardo Rosselló and the Fiscal Control Board, the demand for an audit was consistent throughout the protests.[144] The audit is here explicitly conceived as a political tool. The demands *¡Que se vayan todos!* (They all must go!), *¡Vamos por todxs!* (We are going after them all!), *¡Vamos por la Junta!* (We are going after la Junta!) appeared alongside checklists containing names of politicians next to be destitute.[145] Checklists and signs also demanded a citizen audit. The audit is seen here as a form of holding accountable: bringing to light government corruption, aiding the removal of corrupt officials, delivering corrupt officials to the justice system—I will come back to this. A call for the restitution of misused or stolen public funds in this context might also be read in light of the ubiquitous demand that the guilty pay since the installation of the Fiscal Control Board in 2016. Demands for an audit call for more than the restoration of credit. In fact, they call for more than holding accountable those guilty of corruption and those whose economic interests are served by a colonial political economy that thrives through debt and debt restructuring. They call for the interruption of the necropolitical operation of coloniality, targeting the system of social labor by targeting a "government of the rich."

Although organic and self-convened, the July protests were not spontaneous.[146] They drew from a political field of action traced by interventions in resistance to the Fiscal Control Board. These in turn drew from a long tradition of anti-colonial, environmentalist, and feminist struggle in the territory.[147] The form of protests, however, broke with traditional scripts, as we will see in chapter 4. While interventions by Jornada Se Acabaron las Promesas and others are crucial, most relevant to the present discussion are the interventions by la Colectiva Feminista en Construcción. Since especially 2016, la Colectiva has questioned the premise that the state is absent, has argued that it is necropolitical, and has focused on confronting it.[148] La Colectiva's interventions strategically inhabit the asymmetry distinctive of debt, seeking to invert the positions of power it installs. In chapter 1, I discussed the 2018 Plantón. Here, two interventions are key: the 2017 campaign against ex-mayor of Guaynabo Hector O'Neill and the 2019 Feminist Embargo. The first inverts structures of collection into a matter of accountability, shifting the power to bring to justice and the responsibility to break impunity to the streets. The second moves from financial debts to historical debts by inverting the power of banks involved in the debt and housing crises.

The 2017 campaign against Hector O'Neill comprised traditional protests, a confrontation with O'Neill in a restaurant, and a performance.[149] The latter is most relevant. La Colectiva staged performances in the Escambrón beach and in Plaza las Américas under the rubric *Si lo ves, arréstalo* (If you see him, arrest him). O'Neill, then mayor of Guaynabo, was charged with sexual harassment, sexual assault, and corruption.[150] He was eventually suspended from his post and ultimately resigned, though months after then-governor Ricardo Rosselló asked for his resignation. La Colectiva's performance consisted of staging a citizen's arrest of an O'Neill leisurely walking at the beach or in the mall, as he "continued to do so in Guaynabo's city hall" despite charges, protests, and the governor's request.[151] Members of la Colectiva would ask passersby whether they had seen the mayor. They staged a citizen's arrest and incarceration. Four women declared *Si tocan a una, nos tocan a todas* (If they touch one of us, they touch all of us) as they grew closer, closed in on, and finally enclosed one member wearing an O'Neill mask.[152]

The action is complex. It seemingly uncritically affirms a justice system steeped in racial as well as class violence, which la Colectiva, as a political project, specifically fights against.[153] La Colectiva's comments to the press clarify this aspect of the protest, despite lacking an explicit expression of abolitionist commitments.[154] They explained that the performance aimed to shift accountability. The staged arrest sought to interrupt the impunity of a government official with sexual harassment and sexual assault charges, a man in power who would not face the same fate as impoverished or working-class men, especially black men or men racialized as nonwhite, with similar charges.[155] O'Neill should not merely resign, they noted, he should be held accountable transversally. Note that the beach and the mall are spaces of gathering, spaces in which arguably publics potentially emerge even given the mall's individualizing consumerism. More importantly, note as well the

3.1 *Si lo ves, arrestalo.* La Colectiva Feminista en Construcción. Playa Escambrón, Puerto Rico, April 13, 2017. Photo from La Colectiva Feminista en Construcción's Facebook page.

increasing proximity among the women performing the arrest, signaling a "gaining of collective consciousness" that turns "accountability into one forced by collective, popular power."[156] La Colectiva's performance staged a transversal interruption of impunity, then, by shifting responsibility for such interruption to all, especially when official processes have failed.

The Feminist Embargo is most significant. The embargo was part of La Colectiva's actions during the 2019 International Working Women's Day celebrations. The March 8 Coalition of which la Colectiva was part called for a Women's Strike against debt.[157] Composed of organizations and groups in different parts of the territory, the coalition articulated eight claims against the payment of an illegal, illegitimate, odious debt. Public health, education, the autonomy of bodies, work, immigration, public safety, the eradication of sexist violence, and housing were axes from which to refuse payment of a debt that has not been audited. More than the evisceration of transparency and citizen participation central to any democratic process, the lack of an audit allows the debt to operate as a lethal apparatus of capture. As we have seen, austerity deploys the violence of a necropolitical state. The real cost of paying the debt, the coalition stressed, is a dismantled public education and the breaking up of communities that it entails. It is the loss of work itself, not only benefits and pensions. It is sexist violence left unattended. It is the attack on the autonomy of bodies and reproductive rights via Senate Bill PS950. It is an alarming number of foreclosures and evictions. It is contaminated water with toxic coal ash deposited in Peñuelas.

The Feminist Embargo initiated la Colectiva's actions on March 8. With the embargo, they denounced the role of banking in the housing and debt crises.[158] The embargo was composed of a protest that shut down Santander, Banco Popular, Oriental Bank, and First Bank centers in Plaza las Américas. Signs and slogans cited the number of foreclosures processed by these banks, stressing the number of families that lost their homes as a result. Between January and February of 2019, 459 homes were foreclosed by the banks.[159] In May 2019, it was estimated that 250, 260 homes were at risk of foreclosure.[160] La Colectiva pointed out that evictions impact women disproportionately, especially black women and women racialized as non-white. Two-thirds of those who have lost their homes in Puerto Rico are women heads of household. Many of these women were unable to make mortgage or rent payments, given job loss in the context of the recession, bankruptcy, and the aftermath of Hurricane María. Evictions impact women living in public and subsidized housing in large numbers as well.[161] Not only the banks but also the state and the courts are culpable, la Colectiva stressed. Public policy and court decisions install legal normativities that make possible the transfer of wealth that the housing crisis represents, as we saw in chapter 2.

The embargo is a form of reckoning through the subversion of repayment and the inversion of culpability. It put on display who owes what to whom. Albeit for a short time, Santander, Banco Popular, Oriental Bank, and First Bank had to close. The closure inverted, for a moment, who is foreclosed. Signs stressed this reversal of culpability. Rather than those who have not paid their mortgage or rent, banks are culpable. La Colectiva linked the banks' role in the housing crisis, the right to housing, and the norm of private property. Homelessness, migration and its dissolution of communities, and inability to exit domestic violence are intrinsic to the affirmation of private property that subtends the operation of the banks. The demonstration also subverted the role of mediators—law firms, lobbyists, politicians—who function as agents of capital. They are revealed to be dependent on a social system that requires dispossession. As Miguel

3.2 Embargo Feminista. La Colectiva Feminista en Construcción. Plaza las Américas, San Juan, Puerto Rico, March 8, 2019. Photo from la Colectiva Feminista en Construcción's Facebook page.

Rodríguez-Casellas writes, these are the real *cuponeros*.[162] The Feminist Embargo opened up a space and time of reckoning, then. The deferral, the diversion, that debt produces to exercise its power was amplified, opening up a space and time of giving accounts, of holding accountable. Such reckoning addressed not only financial debt but also historical, indeed colonial, debts. It indexed not the historical root of financial debt in the crisis, but the continuation of a history of colonial violence in the housing crisis.

Roitman argues that "moments of transgression are interpreted as such not simply because they confront order with disorder but because they raise the specter of the impossible."[163] The impossible is unlike the excess that Mitropoulos seeks to affirm by conceiving of usury as a site for the subversion of debt. Occupying the space of diversion created by debt itself, subverting determinate material conditions, seizure conjures the impossible—the possibility of moving beyond those conditions. Its effectivity depends on interrupting the limits imposed by debt without in principle affirming an excess equally foldable into the logic of capital. Roitman writes that acts of subversion "both utterly confound and generate novel instances of truth."[164] They appear as disorder, "criminal," violent, yet they index the violence of the "odd pairing of dispossession and accumulation" in debt.[165] Seizure occurs from the "periphery of the periphery," she argues.[166] Precisely because practices that seek to seize the power to bind emerge from the space of diversion of debt itself, because they are subject to modes of hypervisibility distinctive of coloniality, subversive interruption faces deep representational challenges. Modes of interruption are precarious for reasons that exceed the position of the subjects and populations that pursue them. They require the very transformation of the framework of sense to be grasped as forms of reckoning in the first place.

Subversive Interruption

4

Pasarse políticamente.
To cross the line, politically.
—GILLERMO REBOLLO-GIL, *Última llamada*

Político es crear las condiciones
para una serie de corto-circuitos
de la imaginación.

Political is to create the conditions
for a series of short-circuits
of the imagination.
—MIGUEL RODRÍGUEZ-CASELLAS, "De lo Superfluo"

"WHEN WE SPEAK of the right to protest," Ariadna Godreau-Aubert writes, "we are not speaking of the possibility of reconciliation. There can be no doubt. The gap is insurmountable and precisely our fight demands that we denounce it and *open it even further*. The justice system is colonial, patriarchal, slow, and punishing. The fight against la Junta is anti-colonial, feminist, agile, liberatory."[1] In Puerto Rico, acts of subversive interruption not only denounce the gap between law/state/capital *and* a population that must assume layoffs, foreclosures, school closures, tax incentives for the rich, creditors and corporations, regressive taxation for the poor and the working class, PROMESA, the Fiscal Control Board, and so on. *They open the gap even further.*[2] Protest involves "discomfort" (*incomodidad*). To protest is to "dislocate" (*dislocar*). Protests generate discomfort by indexing the slow violence of debt, austerity, coloniality. They have the potential to dislocate by amplifying discomfort, disclosing such violence as induced. Acts of subversive interruption involve the perception of a violence that is ubiquitous.

In *Última llamada*, Gillermo Rebollo-Gil examines variations of protest that dislocate, that generate discomfort. They are all forms of what he calls *pasarse políticamente*—to politically cross the line, to go beyond the limit, to overreach. Pasarse políticamente is to "overturn the limits of political action, to transcend the register of acts and expressions customary and easily accepted by society at large as reasonable forms of protest, to the point of bordering on the ridiculous or the dangerous or the undesirable, in sum, in all that is difficult to accept even within the opposition itself."[3] Rebollo-Gil seeks to call attention to the assumption in Puerto Rico that political dispute, irrespective of "gravity or urgency," should never turn "offensive or violent," "unfriendly or rude."[4] Pasarse políticamente, then, is an interruption of the "violence of quotidian life" that offends. The point is that it should offend because "the objective violence to which it points is extremely offensive."[5] Pasarse políticamente is a precarious form of protest, given the discomfort it generates. It is precarious not only because it indexes the race/gender/class hierarchy on display when acts are deemed unruly, vulgar, violent. It is precarious because, by and large, it fails to appear as an act of protest at all. Rebollo-Gil calls these precarious acts "hopeful" nevertheless. They are hopeful because they require the transformation of the very "framework of sense" (*entramado de entendidos*) to be grasped as forms of protest in the first place.

In chapter 3, I argued that historical reckoning is subversive when it interrupts modes of binding distinctive of the logic of capture of a debt economy *and* the race/gender/class hierarchy that such logic reinstalls. Subversive interruption seizes the power to bind that instituted historical debts reproduced in financial debts. It seizes forms of binding, modalities of bonding, that reproduce the colonial condition through an ongoing coloniality. In this chapter, I explore the aesthetic/epistemic strictures of hopeful protest, in Rebollo-Gil's sense, through a reflection on the political power of *failure*. Pasarse políticamente helps specify failed protest as the power of refusal as well as subversion of norms through which coloniality operates. The norm of productivity is central. Crucial to a work ethic and cisheteronormativity, productivity links race and gender in light of the specific economic/political/historical juncture. It installs that link as a key site of the operation but also interruption of coloniality. Pasarse políticamente, I suggest, names the inadvertent or explicit refusal or subversion of productivity that goes beyond normative measure. Protests *que se pasan*, that cross the line, index the violence of such system of social labor, but they also have the potential to capture modalities of hypervisibility. They have the potential to sidestep or invert the power the latter deploy.

The first section, Pasarse Políticamente, examines Rebollo-Gil's account of the 2010–11 student strike at the University of Puerto Rico (UPR). Rebollo-Gil's discussion of the uptake of the two phases of the strike—the first creative, the second violent—maps the aesthetic/epistemic terrain in which opposition to austerity, the Fiscal Control Board, and government corruption has been pursued. Rebollo-Gil's discussion of the second phase of the strike, the violent strike, as a hopeful failure is key. In this context, he explores protests beyond the university that have the potential to interrupt the framework of sense central to the work of coloniality. The second section, Vagancia Queer, examines the operation of the norm of productivity within the distinctively neoliberal work ethic that Miguel Rodríguez-Casellas calls *echarpalantismo*, which I translate as "forward-facing resilience."[6] I discuss Mabel Rodríguez-Centeno's extension of Rodríguez-Casellas' critique of echarpalantismo in what she calls *vagancia queer* (queer laziness). I argue that vagancia queer clarifies strictures for interrupting productivity. The last section, Perreo Intenso, explores the queer appropriation of *perreo* in the July 2019 protests that ousted Ricardo "Ricky" Rosselló as a mode of anti-capitalist and decolonial interruption. In the context of unprecedented protests deemed creative by local and international media, el perreo intenso on the steps of San Juan's Cathedral offended. However, it indexed the history of colonial violence inscribed in the very steps of the cathedral.

PASARSE POLÍTICAMENTE

The 2010–11 student strike at the University of Puerto Rico responded to then-governor Luis Fortuño's austerity plan.[7] Fortuño's government consolidated neoliberal policies and intensified what César Pérez-Lizasuain calls an "economic state of exception."[8] In 2009, Wall Street credit houses threatened to demote Puerto Rico's credit rating to junk status.[9] Fortuño declared a state of fiscal emergency. Thirty thousand government workers were eventually laid off; bargaining rights and social protections for public employees were suspended; privatization and private contracting were intensified; steep budget cuts to the University of Puerto Rico were announced. The budget reduction, elimination of tuition waivers, and implementation of a tuition increase, as Rima Brusi puts it, "would exacerbate existing inequalities via the reduction of access to higher education."[10] Low-income students and students from working-class families were already underrepresented among the UPR population.[11] A defunded primary and secondary public education system compromises access to public higher education, given the latter's academic admission standards. This raises student debt among low-income students enrolling in private universities.

Recall José Atiles-Osoria's argument, discussed in chapter 2, concerning the colonial state of exception. In Puerto Rico, neoliberal rationality was installed through the administrative use of declarations of states of emergency. With the concept "neoliberal colonialism," Atiles-Osoria names the process by which local elites, from politicians to banks and firms, actualize economic interests that exceed the boundaries of the state. While these interests exceed the metropolis and the territory, they require apparatuses of capture tied to the state: development and implementation of economic policy, most notably. Pérez-Lizasuain builds on this perspective, yet he references Brusi's work. Brusi argues that the University of Puerto Rico functioned as a testing ground for the neoliberal economic order, coupling budget cuts and private contracting with state violence.[12] On October 2009, an estimated 200,000 people participated in a *paro general* (general strike), protesting Fortuño's announcement that seventeen thousand government workers would be laid off. As Marisol LeBrón notes, student opposition to budget cuts in the wake of the paro general was immediately met with police intervention. Students declared a forty-eight-hour strike on April 21, 2010, and an indefinite strike on April 23, when the university administration was unresponsive. Fortuño's administration stationed police at the perimeter of the UPR Río Piedras campus immediately following the announcement of an indefinite strike.[13]

In *Rebelión, no-derecho, y poder estudiantil*, Pérez-Lizasuain argues that the student strike should be understood as a response to the articulation of the neoliberal university as part of the real subsumption of labor necessary for the installation of neoliberalism in the territory. Recall that in *Capital*, Marx makes a distinction between formal and real subsumption that arguably expands the account of originary accumulation that we saw in chapters 1 and 2. Capitalism is installed, Marx maintains, through the subsumption of labor under its process of valorization. "Since work creates value only in a definite useful form," Marx writes, "and since every particular useful form of work requires materials and instruments with specific use-values, . . . labor can only be drained off if capital assumes the shape of the means of production required for the particular labor process in question, and only in this shape can it annex living labor."[14] Subsumption is formal when the subordination of the labor process does not change the real mode of production. Rather, it captures the labor process, nestles it in the cycle of value creation and extraction distinctive of capital. Real subsumption, in contrast, posits the labor process to its "own image." It establishes the labor process itself in light of the aims of the creation and extraction of surplus value. A crucial aspect here is the overcoming of "frictions," as Marx puts it, that arise not only from the nature of the relation of production itself but also from the subsumption process itself.[15] Marx cites removing "all the legal and extra-economic impediments to its freedom of movement in the different spheres of production" as an integral part of the real subsumption of labor.[16]

To say that the university was a testing ground for the installation of neoliberal rationality, one already steeped in a debt economy by 2010, is to say that the budget cuts, the elimination of tuition waivers, and tuition increases were part of shifting the cost of social reproduction to the population. The crucial point, however, is that this is to name a process by which the creation and capture of surplus value is reorganized in light of "human capital."[17] This is not only a rearticulation of an institution, then. It is a reconfiguration of a normative field all the way up to its work ethic, all the way down to its perceptual features. As a testing ground for neoliberal colonialism, the university plays a key role in instituting modes of "regulation and control" through normative appraisal on all of these registers. It is crucial to add that neoliberal colonialism's normative reorganization, one backed by state violence, actualizes, updates, reinstalls race/gender/class. State violence played a key role in such reorganization, but its tactics had been tested, as we saw in chapter 2, on the regulation and control of space that shored up antiblack racism within a rising drug economy. As LeBrón notes, while initially the police remained at the perimeter and respected the university's nonconfrontation policy, the deployment of the police and eventually the Tactical Operations Unit, la Fuerza de Choque, drew from the legacy of Mano Dura discussed in chapter 2.[18] As we will see, what LeBrón calls "proxy violence" is key to understanding the uptake of the form of violence deployed on the student strikers. The distinction between populations that admit state violence and those worthy of state protection betrays the necropolitical operation of coloniality.

Pérez-Lizasuain discusses the normative field that students resisted. More significant, however, is the one that emerged. The strike can be understood as a "zone of contact" (*zona de contacto*), he maintains. A zone of contact is a field of antagonism that contests constituted power, particularly the state.[19] "The zone of contact of UPR student revolt," Pérez-Lizasuain writes, "is the time-space of the state-of-rebellion from which a series of normative practices were instituted by its very performativity, or set of acts, modes, and processes."[20] Most significant, therefore, is the normative field that emerged in the very contestation of the installation of the neoliberal university. This normative field resisted the juridical-political capture of the process itself. What emerged is an "autonomous" normativity, indeed, one at the "margin of the state."[21] These acts, modalities, and practices in turn generated frames of understanding, of sense—*marcos de entendimiento*.[22] Horizontal political organizing was key to the emergence of decentered, nonhierarchical, and participatory normativities. The development and use of an autonomous media and social media contributed to the dissemination of information and greater participation—within and beyond the strikers themselves. These practices, as Iván Chaar López notes, were not only driven by but articulated a state of rebellion that affirmed difference and set out to defend "the common."[23]

Rebollo-Gil discusses the strike in relation to its two phases.[24] From April to June 2010, students occupied ten out of eleven University of Puerto Rico campuses.[25] From December 2010 to March 2011, the police besieged the UPR campus in Río Piedras, breaking the university's nonconfrontation policy. The political horizontalism, creation of an autonomous media, artistic demonstrations that characterized the first phase were deemed the "creative strike."[26] Alliances with the environmental, LGBTQ, and independence movements were consolidated.[27] The strike had the public's support. The second phase responded to the government's attempt to undermine the UPR's internal governance and bargaining agreements with students.[28] A two-day strike was planned for December 7–8, but security guards removed gates at the UPR Río Piedras campus to prevent student occupation. Court, state, and police actions against students were varied, but they included violence toward a parent delivering food, hence an attempt to control resources on campus; criminalization and prosecution of student strikers; legal and discursive strategies that presented students as consumers rather than workers, thereby delegitimizing striking as an appropriate mode of political opposition.[29] Students threw smoke bombs and rocks, wore hoods and masks.[30] The strike was criticized by the public and deemed a "failure."[31]

It is instructive here to consider the 2017 student strike. Although the figure fluctuated, the Fiscal Control Board announced in April 2017 that the UPR system would suffer a $450 million budget cut, which would entail closing campuses and programs, a tuition hike, and the elimination of tuition waivers.[32] *Cerrar para abrir* (close in order to open) was one of the main slogans of the strike. Shutting down operations aimed to create time and space to contest debt repayment, given its impact on public education. From its inception, the demands exceeded the institution that the strike paralyzed. In addition to resisting austerity and the neoliberalization of the university, the strike was articulated around the demand to audit the debt and oppose the precarization of public education in general.[33] The strike drew from the horizontalism of the 2010 strike but protested the Fiscal Control Board. Its claims addressed not only the UPR or Puerto Rico's government but also the Fiscal Control Board itself.

While many saw the strike as the first bastion of resistance to the imposition of la Junta and its austerity measures, others saw it as a failure that culminated in costly property damages to the university and symbolic damages to the resistance. If a strike is already a wrong mode of resistance for students who are not workers, critics argued, striking to resist the Fiscal Control Board was a category mistake.[34] In addition to organizing symposia on neoliberalism, debt, urbanism and democracy at the gates, strikers organized activities that addressed the impact of austerity on the trans community and affirmed feminist and queer sexualities. They also interrupted a meeting of the UPR's Board of Trustees, compelling them to sign a document in support of a debt audit and the rejection of budget cuts. The students were accused of "vandalizing" campuses and overstepping bounds in the actions against the Board of Trustees. Despite the mixed reception, the Fiscal Control Board granted the student movement a meeting.[35]

Rebollo-Gil discusses the 2010–11 strike under the heading *Fracasos*, "Failures."[36] "Collective memory," he says, distinguishes between the strike's two phases not according to occupations. Rather, people remember each phase according to tactics the students employed "above all those used in confrontations with agents of public order."[37] People recall the first phase of the strike, the creative strike, in terms of the autonomous media, horizontal organizing, artistic activities, and ecological interventions such as the organic gardens. They recall the creative strike as the "affectionate contact" between the striking student body and various sectors of society.[38] It was a successful "rational understanding" that, "with its aesthetic," "moved" a country that seemed to be "asleep."[39] The creative strike offered a new image of student strikers, historically seen as unruly—*pelús*—now as innovators of diverse, participatory, nonhierarchical, nonviolent forms of political opposition.[40] Cordiality and courtesy were thereby reified as the only appropriate means of contestation, Rebollo-Gil argues. Aesthetic standards are deployed to assess "attractive or convincing" modes of opposition.[41] The normative field that emerged in the very performativity of the strike, then, is not exempt from moral distinctions concerning appropriate forms of protest. Given the contrast with the second phase of the strike, Rebollo-Gil's account suggests, promising emergent normative fields can remain nestled in scripted propriety.

The second phase was deemed a "failure" because of its scenes of "violence, discontent, frustration, and lack of control."[42] Smoke bombs, damaged property, covered faces sullied the newly "cleansed" image of the student striker.[43] Rebollo-Gil's use of the term *cleansed* is important here. He stresses the aesthetic components of the strike to point to the race/gender/class hierarchy operating not only within the striking body but most significantly in the public uptake. LeBrón's notion of "proxy violence" is key here. With the notion, LeBrón names the UPR and the state's use of racial stereotypes to disarticulate the student movement. In December 2010, university administrators hired the private security firm Capitol Security for approximately $1.5 million.[44] Confrontations with young black men from Loíza and Carolina, predominantly black and impoverished towns, hired to "subdue the students" fed an image of violence, disorder, lack of control.[45] Conversely, it generated sympathy for students deemed under attack by those who "appeared" as "thugs."[46] Giovanni Roberto, a student activist, himself black and from a low-income background, addressed the Capitol Security guards in a speech that went viral. Roberto linked racism and economic inequality to the aims of the strike.[47] The speech built solidarity between strikers and the guards he addressed, although these guards were quickly replaced. Capitol Security argued that the guards had suffered "Stockholm syndrome."[48] Rather than held in captivity by the students, the guards were victims of police violence twice over, LeBrón notes, "First by witnessing and experiencing rampant police brutality in their community, and second through the dehumanizing expectation that they would enact similar violence among others as police proxies."[49]

LeBrón also highlights that many of the *loiceños* that Capitol Security hired reported that they had never visited the Río Piedras campus until they arrived to take down the gates, indeed until they were hired as "violence workers."[50] It is particularly important, then, to note that proxy violence operated not only through race but also class, more specifically around notions of productivity. While student strikers appeared as unworthy of police violence, the guards had suffered such violence with and after Mano Dura as part of their everyday experience. Even when student strikers rejected state violence, LeBrón also notes, insignias that read *Somos estudiantes, no criminals* (We are students, not criminals) and *Luchar para una educación pública de excelencia no es un delito* (Fighting for a quality public education is not a crime) "reinforced the idea that students, unlike 'real' criminals, are undeserving of violence at the hands of the state."[51] The distinction between those who admit of ubiquitous violence and those who do not is inseparable from who is seen as a productive member of society and who is not. As we saw in chapter 2, the spatial production of race—blackness as criminal, as dangerous—through public housing and welfare assistance runs along these precise lines. It, in fact, draws the lines, establishing productivity—work, upward mobility, a white bourgeois aesthetic, the cisheteronormative family—as markers of who requires security rather than policing.

Despite the public's defense of the students against police violence, Rebollo-Gil points out, for some, confronting state violence by throwing smoke bombs and rocks, wearing hoods and masks compromised the normative field and its positive uptake distinctive of the first phase of the strike. In contrast, he questions the view that the second phase was a failure. The second phase was deemed a failure because the students "crossed the line, they overreacted, acted poorly, incurred in practices contrary to the interests of the groups and the ideals they were supposed to represent."[52] He contrasts the second phase of the strike not to the first, but to Occupy Puerto Rico. Among other things, he reflects on instances in which Occupy collaborated with authorities in planning and executing protests.[53] Occupy PR was not a political force in the territory, although it was seen as unruly. Its unruliness was tied to trash left at the campsite. The student strikers, in contrast, did not cooperate with authorities, responding to and thereby amplifying the violence of capital/law/state within and beyond the institution. "[T]hat overdoing, that violent excess," Rebollo-Gil writes, "offensive, wrong, alarming within the context of protest makes possible a clear, dynamic, and risky image of opposition, which in turn serves as a starting point for critical reflection and to make adjustments to our methods and manners as we go."[54] The second strike was thus an "inspiring failure."[55]

In a chapter entitled *Aguafiestas* (Killjoys), Rebollo-Gil examines modes of political opposition in Puerto Rico that defy "traditional scenes" either because the "claims are not easily comprehended by the public" or they are enacted by "subjects that are not recognized as political actors."[56] He begins the chapter by arguing that to protest is "anything that has hope."[57] He argues that, because the subject who protests cannot control the meaning of their act, because it is a matter of the public's uptake, there is a "deficit of meaning when they follow a script that is well known by the public."[58] Even if a protest disturbs the flow of quotidian life, it is not hopeful if it does not interrupt the operative framework of sense (*entramado de entendidos*). "Protests are only hopeful," Rebollo-Gil writes, "when their claims result incomprehensible thus *impossible to address without transforming the framework of sense in a community*."[59] "The repetition of [forms of protest] without major disturbances throughout time," he adds, "can even be proof of the stability of the prevailing order."[60] He goes as far as saying that "traditional protests in Puerto Rico have ceased to be insofar as they lack hope."[61] Despite the power of forms of opposition that generate alternative normative fields, these can remain scripted if they do not challenge sense, perception, affect, forms of knowing that sustain the conditions they oppose in the first place.

Hopeful protests dislocate. That they produce discomfort indicates that they have the capacity to interrupt sensibility itself. The challenge, then, is to grasp acts *as* acts of protest "*especially* when what the subject of protest does seems extreme, or unpleasant or capricious and it is done in an inadequate place, an inadequate time, which could be understood as too much stupidity or irresponsibility on the part of the agent to be catalogued as a clear manifestation of political opposition."[62] The point here exceeds the strike. Moving beyond the university, the precarious nature of such acts is in many cases due to the precarious nature of individuals protesting, individuals whose location within a race/gender/class hierarchy limits their epistemic authority, compels a perceptual, indeed somatic, block.[63] The point is that they are precarious because they defy the framework of sense in effect, yet they thereby have the power to break it. They have potential to turn it inoperative. These acts amplify the violence to which they are responding, but they thereby have the power to contest it. They contest ubiquitous forms of violence from within. They do not necessarily have an aim, since they challenge structural features that exceed an institution in isolation. Precisely because they amplify the conditions to which they respond, they cannot secure their own appearance or normative stability.

Rebollo-Gil discusses three precarious acts of protest beyond the university. Consider the following two. First, a series of 2013 tweets perceived as a threat to then governor Alejandro García Padilla.[64] The tweet vented frustration about withheld tax refunds. Roughly translated and abridged, the tweet reads:

> MR GOVERNOR THE WORST THAT YOU HAVE DONE IS FUCK WITH THE PEOPLE'S MONEY DO NOT KEEP MAKING MISTAKES BECAUSE IT CAN COST YOU YOUR LIFE YOU DRIVE A 300C AND I IN . . . THAT DOES NOT MEAN THAT IT IS NOT BULLET PROOF DO NOT BE TAKING FROM HERE TO PUT OVER THERE . . . TOMORROW WE MARCH AT 1PM . . . MY REFUND OR WE KIDNAP . . . AND WHOEVER COMES TO SETTLE MATTERS WITH ME WILL DIE ATT ME.[65]

The author of the tweet was incarcerated for six months. The tweet was not intended as a mode of political opposition. No political group defended its author. Yet, the incarceration of this individual should make us pause, Rebollo-Gil suggests. In Puerto Rico, those who attempt to address systemic inequality as a public problem are "punished and censured."[66] The tweet should be read in light of the systemic "invisibilization and disappearance of a sector—young, male, predominantly black and poor."[67] The subject that speaks is a subject "traversed" by race/gender/class and, as a result, "marked as a subject of violence." The point is that this subject is allowed to appear *as* a subject of violence if he does not articulate such violence as "the direct result of a social system."[68] The question that we must ask, then, the question that might turn venting on Twitter into an act of political opposition, perhaps even a hopeful act, is as follows: "Exactly how should we expect these young people to articulate their claims if not through the discursive codes that they manage in their quotidian life, in all its crassness? *Seen as such, of course the tweet should offend, because the objective violence to which it points is extremely offensive.*"[69] The man's venting was turned into an act of violence, violence itself individualized. He indexed himself as suspicious, dangerous, violent in indexing the violence of the no-place of indebted life in the colony.

Consider, second, the exit interview of a woman who attended the Tradicional Fiesta de los Días de Reyes in January 2013. In this event, low-income children collect Christmas gifts. That year, the children were asked to draw something in return. The woman was asked to reflect on her day and the present her daughter received. She seemed unhappy with the event, in particular with the gift—*un trapo e' bola*, "a lousy ball."[70] In the media and social media, the woman was said to be "ungrateful and a bad mother, guilty of imparting the wrong values to her daughter."[71] Rebollo-Gil reminds us that the Tradicional Fiesta de los Días de Reyes is part of what is seen as the culture of *mantengo*—welfare. With it, the government attempts to instill the value of work and responsibility, not only gifting educational presents but also turning the gift into payment for something accomplished— the drawing.[72] Rebollo-Gil writes:

> *El trapo e' bola* became the metaphor for a lousy life [*una cotidiani-dad al garete*], a life lived poorly in thousands of homes throughout the island. That is to say, the critique the woman launched to the event was redirected, transformed into an allegation of culpability. It was not a lousy ball, but a lousy mother with a lousy life, offering her child a lousy upbringing, and just who does that lousy woman think she is to complain. In this way, her expression became the principle reason [*razón principalísima*] for not recognizing at all her right to speech.[73]

The woman's complaint was turned into her guilt, poverty individualized. She indexed herself as guilty in indexing the guilt of a political economy that induces poverty.

In both cases, Rebollo-Gil argues, the subjects are killjoys, *aguafiestas*.[74] *Se pasan*, they cross the line, from the get-go. They are an "uncivilized excess." They can only be read as "dead weight." They are scapegoats. As protestors, they inhabit the most vulnerable of positions. They are not students or workers, readable as productive members of society. They do not redeem productivity. They are failed neoliberal *and* colonial subjects. Their protest is "incomprehensible," hence they are punished or silenced. But these are protests perhaps in the most proper sense, Rebollo-Gil argues. They are hopeful. They interrupt everyday life because they "kill the joy of our ideological fiesta."[75] They protest despite obstacles and from the least adequate space: without organization or committees or signs.[76] Nevertheless, they are protesting. In most of these cases, however, the protest did not appear as such.[77] The offensive violence that they put on display is turned against them. They appear not as figures of hope, but as figures of violence. They index systemic violence, yet they index themselves as violent. They are the condition for the disclosure of violence, hence for something else to happen, *and* for violence itself.

"Political," Miguel Rodríguez-Casellas writes, "is to create the conditions for a series of short-circuits of the imagination, in other words, break up groups [*romper bonche*], and begin to visualize other ways of thinking about coexistence, from the things that are essential and that this model of country and territory does not meet, nor has the capacity to attend."[78] Protests are hopeful not because they might achieve a utopian state, but because they might create the conditions for a series of short-circuits of the imagination, perception, sense itself. Failed protests are failed because they have the potential to dislocate norms through which coloniality operates all the way up to an institutional level, all the way down to perceptual and somatic features of experience. This is not an abstract claim, however. Such short-circuit is an interruption of key norms and sensibilities that structure even the most promising of emergent normative fields. It is thus instructive to consider productivity and propriety in light of two precarious forms of protest that have the potential to turn these inoperative: refusal and subversion.

VAGANCIA QUEER

In August 2011, Banco Popular launched the campaign Echar Pa'lante.[79] The campaign, Banco Popular states on its website, is "committed to promoting new projects that open possibilities for the future and the work of our country. Our philosophy is that only with everyone's effort, we will be able to transform a reality that presents great challenges of progress." The campaign was built on two focus areas: (1) education, as the "principle axis of change," and (2) the development of an entrepreneurial sector as the "emergent paradigm and motor of economic development." The campaign is framed as a "banner for overcoming for our socio-economic challenges." It is an "invitation to leave behind all those things that do not let us progress in life (pessimism, indifference, resistance and conformity) and make a change." A key component of the campaign is the Gran Combo's rewriting of one of their most famous songs. The song, an "example of poverty of spirit," is "No Hago Más Na'" (I do nothing more). "No Hago Más Na'" is a "hymn to passivity," the bank states. The Gran Combo's rewriting in the now-renamed "Echar Pa'lante" moves from the original's purported affirmation of a man who enjoys life without working (*que vive del cuento sin trabajar*) to an affirmation of work, indeed of the desire to work (*qué bueno es vivir así, con ganas de trabajar*). In the face of adversity—by 2011, a debt crisis, austerity, and all we have seen they entail—the campaign is an imperative to overcome "hardship" (impoverishment, expulsion) through entrepreneurship. The campaign compels the individual to take on a collective project, *un projecto de país*, through decisively neoliberal means. Education is an investment, as Foucault argued in the *Birth of Biopolitics*. It nurtures human capital. As the motor of economic development, entrepreneurship capitalizes on the individual as human capital. Here, it moves the country forward.

In a 2013 essay, Rodríguez-Casellas launches an important critique of what he termed "echarpalantismo."[80] The term captures the neoliberal work ethic distinctive of this historical, economic, political juncture. Echarpalantismo names the transformation of the classical liberal notion of self-reliance, the imperative to pull-yourself-up-by-the-bootstrap, into the decisively neoliberal affirmation of *forward-facing resilience.* Recall Puerto Rico's transformation of work in the context of Operation Bootstrap. Manos a la Obra (Put Your Hands to Work) replaced an agrarian system predominantly based on the sugar plantation. It installed an economy that privileged external capital through tax exemption, cheap labor, and "trainable" workers. In reality, a land reform and efforts to develop government-owned industries gave way to ownership by a private sector that promised work but only captured profits. While, as we saw in chapter 2, the economic boom was in great part possible by mass migration and generated a continuing pattern of unemployment, Luis Muñoz Marín framed Manos a la Obra stating that "we are trying to pull ourselves up by the bootstrap." Work is here coeval with the promise of modernity through the eradication of poverty, even if it required a neocolonial framework developed in light of the imperatives of capital. By the 1970s, what had been postwar expansion became a postindustrial desert, rising debt, steady unemployment, uneradicated poverty, and the rise of a thriving drug economy. Federal transfers—nutritional support, public housing, etc.—were coupled with a consumer economy. Lack of work, then, has been central to a project of economic development, ideologically based on the link between work and upward mobility that would eventually lead to political self-determination.

With echarpalantismo, Rodríguez-Casellas names the double injunction of "the bank and the party, which stigmatizes the problematizing view of the past while at the same time positing an optimistic framing of the future, where only the most explosive enthusiasm and, in general, an immeasurable sense of well-being and effusive invitation to conquer life fit."[81] Rodríguez-Casellas develops the notion with reference to two widespread (*divulgada*) aspects of this neoliberal injunction. First, echarpalantismo names the attempt to "rearticulate an ethic of the working people" (*una ética del pueblo trabajador*). This is the most ubiquitous aspect of the injunction. It compels individuals to move the country forward through enterprise, indeed the self-as-enterprise. In reality, however, "it is based on the conviction that the Puerto Rican has become lazy and lacking initiative." This passivity is based on the negativity of pessimism, indifference, but also resistance and conformity. Echarpalantismo is thus based on a rejection of the "clouded mood of those who celebrate tragedy at all cost, perpetuate irrational hatred from media platforms and . . . who think from the cold recognition of the dysfunctionalities installed like a hard cyst in the institutionality of the country."[82] The second, less explicit though deeply connected aspect of this injunction is the perception of the past as "closed to analysis, abject refuge of those who do not want the country to grow, historical impediment to new social contracts, new balancing acts that would allegedly give new life to the island about to succumb to its unproductiveness, population loss, and imminent siege of creditors." Critical reflection, analysis, historical context are deemed stifling, a backward turn that sustains a backward condition. "To forget," he concludes, "would seem to be once more the national motto. And every attempt at reflection, at a time when the executive order only looks forward [*mira pa'lante*], is seen as an act of high treason."

Echarpalantismo is no mere discursive phenomenon, a mere campaign launched by a bank that seeks to be perceived as of the people—*banco popular*—but is deeply implicated in the unpayable debt, the housing crisis, and other economic-political operations of capture.[83] Rodríguez-Casellas discusses the articulation of this distinctive work ethic through "fast-tracking" and efficiency characteristic of 1990s neoliberal public policy, contracting, and development in the territory. He explores an "emboldened government management" that "demonized" the "intellectualization" of development it deemed paralysis-inducing. Echarpalantismo is a neoliberal ethic of the working people installed by an emboldened rather than absent state. The efficient deregulation of land, the further suburbanization of the archipelago, the heightened privileging of the car, the multiplication of corporations such as Walmart in the territory, the power asymmetries in the acquisition of permits and contracts were measures of progress.[84] Demonizing the role of public planning itself, Rodríguez-Casellas argues, is indicative of the forward-facing amnesia crucial to this specific version of the neoliberal work ethic.[85] It is the "power asymmetry that exists in Puerto Rico," he writes, "that those who affirm echar pa'lante dissimulate when they pretend to make us believe that we are all in the same egalitarian boat."

Echarpalantismo, accordingly, is not the neoliberal version of the liberal self-reliance or the neoliberal self-management that, as we saw in chapter 1, was turned against the indebted to compel populations to pay through austerity. Echarpalantismo is a version of neoliberal self-as-enterprise in the context of collapse, capture, dispossession. Self-reliance is turned into *resilience*.[86] The entrepreneurial self is turned into the self that overcomes adversity in a postindustrial context, in times of unpayable debt, in the context of austerity, in times of dispossession and expulsion. The fast-tracking efficiency of the 1990s is an injunction to forget not only the material conditions that have been eroded, from schools, to health care, jobs, and housing. It is an imperative to forget the race/gender/class hierarchies that remain intact when individuals and populations persevere, indeed set out to thrive, within such economic/political conditions. Resilience, the "ability to absorb or bounce back from experiences of shock," as Yarimar Bonilla notes, is key to a version of neoliberal subjectivity that overcomes not only collapse but also failure.[87] Forward-facing resilience, accordingly, is an injunction to bounce back from the shocks of economic collapse, ecological degradation, and racist and sexist violence. The ability to overcome adversity is not due to material conditions or social networks. The resilient subject, indeed population, can more than weather; it can thrive in the face of absent material conditions, intensified capture, heightened expulsion.

In 2016, the social media campaign #YoNoMeQuito (I don't give up) affirmed entrepreneurship in the wake of fiscal crisis.[88] It implied that the thousands of Puerto Ricans who migrated to the United States and elsewhere given the crisis had indeed "given up." Those who remined in the territory were committed to a collective project, fighting for their livelihood. However, this affirmation entails political amnesia, since structures of privilege inflect who can stay and who are forced to leave or cannot return. Migration, as we have seen, has been a central part of economic development in the territory. The distinction between who can stay and who must leave is not stable, since privilege/lack of privilege can work in both directions. The point here is that it reifies the very distinction of those who are working for the country's future and those who abandon it, those who are productive members of society and those who are an excess. #YoNoMeQuito suffers from political amnesia, since it forgets the material conditions generating those migratory patterns and the operation of coloniality that they betray. Forward-facing resilience has been especially key in the wake of 2017 Hurricanes Irma and María. #PuertoRicoSeLevanta, "Puerto Rico Rises," made visible forms of *autogestión* that emerged in the context of hurricane recovery and rebuilding: "From clearing roads, setting up community kitchens, delivering aid to forgotten residents, building roofs and even directing traffic and intersections," as Bonilla notes. The hashtag was first used by the Puerto Rican government to inform the public about recovery efforts after Irma, Bonilla continues, but it quickly became a way of affirming governmental efficiency and care despite mismanagement and corruption. Rather than an absent state, however, a necropolitical state was at work in hurricane relief and recovery. The hashtag shifted government responsibility to individuals and communities fending for themselves.

I will come back to the forms of autogestión that are amenable to but aim to resist neoliberal resignification in the conclusion to the book. The point here, however, is tracking the operation of a decisively neoliberal work ethic as overcoming through entrepreneurship. Echar pa'lante, no quitarse, levantarse reify modes of responding to economic collapse based on the conviction that Puerto Ricans have become lazy, that these indebted colonial subjects lack initiative, to recall Rodríguez-Casellas's account. The implication betrays a view of agency as "self-extension," embedded in a project of seeking to "lock in the will-have-been of future anteriority," to recall Berlant's notion of slow violence discussed in chapter 2. Passivity, detachment, refusal are modes of nonagency. They are modes of dependence. They undermine the collective project that entrepreneurship seeks to sustain. Crucial here is the gendered character of echarpalantismo. In the 1990s, "[Pedro] Rosselló," Rodríguez-Casellas writes, "mounted the thesis of the man who acted, of homelands that were made through work rather than dialogue, of commitments met in concrete works, and an entire sexist image [*trasunto macharrán*] of the man-of-action against an effeminate thinking [*afeminamiento ponderador*]." Echar pa'lante is an eminently masculinist view that affirms a collective project through the work, strength, and inventiveness of the resilient man.

Rodríguez-Centeno builds on Rodríguez-Casella's critique of echarpalantismo and develops the notion of vagancia queer.[89] Vagancia queer tracks the masculinist character of echarpalantismo and conceptualizes its interruption in the refusal of a neoliberal work ethic. Rodríguez-Centeno draws from Jack Halberstam's notion of the queer art of failure.[90] Halberstam discusses activities that seem like "indifference or acquiescence as 'hidden' transcripts of resistance to the dominant order."[91] Failure can be understood as an "oppositional tool." It is better described as one among various "weapons of the weak." Weapons of the weak "recategorize what looks like inaction, passivity and lack of resistance."[92] Failure can be understood, accordingly, as "alternatives already embedded" in the operation of power and its field of sense. Halberstam writes: "Heteronormative common sense leads to the equation of success with advancement, capital accumulation, family, ethical conduct and hope. Other subordinate, queer, or counterhegemonic modes of commonsense lead to the association of failure with nonconformity, anti-capitalist practices, nonreproductive lifestyles, negativity, and critique."[93] Failure has the power to interrupt this framework or field of sense, exploiting the "unpredictability of ideology and its indeterminate qualities."[94] Hence, Halberstam concludes, it "must be located within that range of political affects that we call queer." Rodríguez-Centeno draws from this suggestion with full modal strength. That failure must be located within what we understand as queer means that failure is distinctively a space of dislocation of capitalist, modern, masculinist, cisheteronormative sense.[95]

In her essays, Rodríguez-Centeno recounts the criminalization of laziness in the territory throughout its colonial history, indeed before the US invasion in 1898. She traces the ideological function of the "material and moral life" of the territory in its archipelagic character to nineteenth century vagrancy laws.[96] "The recurring 'Puerto Rican laziness,'" she writes, "has historically been seen as an obstacle to progress, giving rise to stigmatizing discourses about alternative economic practices and measures of social control in order to eradicate laziness and get the 'people to work.'" The nineteenth century is exemplary for its complexity. Although slavery was abolished in 1873, mass importation of enslaved Africans came to a close in 1840 generating a "labor supply problem."[97] With the 1849 Reglamento de Jornaleros, the colonial government sought to "force smallholders and landless peasants to become plantation day laborers." This supply of laborers resisted incorporation into the plantation system, preferring subsistence farming and having access to land to "own or squat." This coerced-labor code forced free peasants with access to less than two acres of land to "hire themselves out" as day laborers in sugar plantations and coffee haciendas.[98] A *libreta de jornal* functioned as a record of labor and moral conduct. It tracked movement between municipalities. Being found without the libreta was punishable by eight days of public labor at half pay.[99] Slavery, which continued to be key for the sugar plantation, and the libreta system were both abolished in 1873. Elements of the latter shaped the forms of subjection of *libertos* during emancipation.[100] Laziness, lacking or refusing work, is linked to masculinity through these forms of control. To discipline a population to work is to construct the race/class norm of (white) masculinity.

Gender operates through the "differentiated definition of the legitimate uses of the body," Rodríguez-Centeno writes, "to produce social artifacts called man-virile or woman-feminine." A man who does not work is "not virile because he incurs in illegitimate uses of the body." Rodriguez-Centeno discusses Gran Combo's rewriting of "No Hago Más Na'" in "Echar Pa'lante" with which I began this discussion. She notes that both versions of the song operate in the same way. The original song is not an ode to nonwork. It is a "mockery that seeks to ridicule a man who eats without working, who spends all day inside the domestic space and who is a 'maintained' by his wife and the state (welfare)." The original song aims "to force (virile) bodies to work (whatever and however) and to safeguard normative masculinity (which is of course heterosexual, hardworking and capitalist)."[101] Drawing from Rita Segato's and Sayak Valencia's work, she notes that the song, hence the work ethic it aims to instill, is a "real danger to our bodies and our lives because the insult enhances the lethality of violated masculinities." Productivity indexes the dependent man not as failed, but as a threat to the very order.

Laziness, Rodríguez-Centeno thus argues, "shakes the very architecture of narratives of conquest and progress because it transgresses/subverts the social norms of modernity."[102] It threatens the modernizing function of work, its purported facilitation of moral and material progress, and its link to masculinity.[103] Laziness unsettles being sinful, announcing poverty and backwardness, agitating the social and making progress impossible. Laziness "is a displacement of normative (hetero) masculinity" itself.[104] However, it has the capacity to displace when nestled in the political affect "we call queer," to recall Halberstam. Laziness as such would only further shift labor to women, to other racialized and marginalized subjects and populations. Laziness within the confines of the cisheteronormative order indexes a discursive forgetting of its material effects. Queer laziness, in contrast, aims to name the subversive possibilities of laziness, its capacity to turn inoperative race/gender/class through an aesthetic/epistemic dislocation with material effects. "The body of the lazy person," Rodríguez-Centeno maintains, "is able to strategically twist gender constructions, making visible disputes that betray/destabilize male domination of the sex-gender system via the productive-reproductive system."[105] Laziness is hopeful if it requires the very transformation of sense to be grasped as a form of refusal, as a weapon of the weak in the first place.

Drawing from Monique Wittig, Rodríguez-Centeno argues that "laziness is not to work what woman is to man."[106] Given the gender division of labor, where women have traditionally been relegated to domestic work, to the very reproduction of life, laziness is structurally denied to women. If women's labor is not work, then she cannot inhabit the position of laziness.[107] Hence, "the lazy are not women." Similarly, "laziness is not to work what the homosexual is to the heterosexual because what we recognize as non-hetero (gay/lesbian/trans/inter) is that Other that allows recognition of the heterosexual as measure to 'delimit the space of the allowed' from sexual norms."[108] Although she does not expound on race in this context, her reading of a song by La Sonora Matancera does.[109] The song recounts the story of the Negrito del Batey for whom work is an enemy. He references its institution in original sin as punishment. One might add that laziness is not to work what the black man is to the white man because blackness is that Other that allows whiteness, upward mobility, and work to be linked. The "infamy of no-work," she writes, not only "emasculates" but removes the possibility of an honorable life, an exit from slavery itself, from the colony itself.[110] This is also a matter of Caribbeanness, Rodríguez-Centeno argues, as unruly, impossible to embody the "white homo-economicus."

Rodríguez-Centeno suggests that laziness "is above all a performance that *displaces* man as the natural and universal political subject, laziness is to man its queer Other, the Other of others."[111] Like queerness, laziness names "spaces in which the most varied of dissidences to labor and sexual norms fit, in which identity is a mere strategy, with imprecise limits and redefining itself in a changing way."[112] Vagancia queer, then, is a strategy of refusal that dislocates, displaces the gendered/racial nature of echarpalantismo. Vagancia queer challenges the construction of the dangerous individual living in public housing if it challenges upward mobility as an aesthetic/epistemic project associated with middle-class whiteness. This is not to evacuate the content of queerness. Specifying any nonnormative mode of displacement as queer without grasping the economic, political, and racial experiences of queer populations in Puerto Rico would be a mistake. It is rather to note the possibility of displacing the limits of the neoliberal work ethic through strategic practices that inhabit laziness. Refusal to work is here understood as a refusal of the ethic of work in a neoliberal key. It is to imagine life beyond the binary of victim and entrepreneur, as Verónica Gago and Luci Cavallero would say.

The lazy body *se pasa*, crosses the line. It defies not only its own proper place but also the very project of moving the country forward. It is treasonous, not merely dangerous. It doesn't look to the past. Rather, it refuses the normative field in which the injunction to be resilient functions. In this field of sense, as we will see in the conclusion to the book, the present *is* the past. Grasping the lazy body as a form of refusal, as a dislocation, of forward-facing resilience requires the very transformation of sense. It dislocates by breaking the perceptual, affective, indeed somatic bind between work, masculinity, and progress: productivity as the proper. Queer laziness bears deep representational challenges, then, and for this reason it is hopeful in Rebollo-Gil's sense. Laziness appears as abject, but it has the capacity to unsettle neoliberal overcoming.

PERREO INTENSO

In July 2019, two weeks of protest ousted Ricky Rosselló. As Joel Cintrón Arbasetti writes, Rosselló became governor in 2017, promising a new government: transparent, efficient, open, cooperative with the Fiscal Control Board.[113] He promised to pay the debt, restructure the government, achieve statehood. His government would be led by "facts and evidence." However, Cintrón Arbasetti continues, his administration is better known for a labor reform that further eroded worker's rights, the closing of 438 schools, support for the Fiscal Control Board's austerity measures while inflating high official salaries. His time in office is marked by Hurricane María, which collapsed the country's infrastructure, destroyed 75,000 homes while another 335,000 suffered damages. The mishandling of hurricane relief provisions and funds increased the disaster in which approximately three thousand people died, though the often-quoted number is Harvard's estimate of 4,645. The July 10 FBI arrests of top officials, including Secretary of Education Julia Keleher charged with mismanaging $15.5 million, was followed by the Centro de Periodismo Investigativo's release of 889 pages of a Telegram thread where Rosselló interacted with his closest advisors. Although Sandra Rodríguez Cotto, an independent investigative journalist, released eleven pages of the thread on July 8, the July 12 dissemination of 889 pages was a catalyst for the protests.

Rosselló discussed public policy, corporate interests, and strategized how to control public perception on the Telegram thread with the eleven men he affectionately called "brothers."[114] Not all members of the chat were government officials. The thread was full of misogynist, homophobic, transphobic, racist, classist assertions, "jokes," expletives, and memes. The brothers made light of the deaths of Hurricane María and discussed the suppression of information regarding hurricane relief and recovery.[115] In Raquel Salas Rivera's translations, the brothers, for example:

> Make fun of the women who are protesting because of all the women being killed by domestic violence

make fun of a man wearing a *pava*, a traditional hat worn by poor field workers and farmers; ... of the way poor people from rural areas speak; ... of their poverty saying, "That guayabera shirt costs more than what you make in a month, you might get dirty"; ... of the *libreta de jornal*, a notebook used to keep people enslaved in Puerto Rico after slavery was abolished by keeping track of how many hours they had worked and who they worked for"; ... of them being "old and [not being] able to produce"; ... about the United Food Company coming to the Puerto Rican countryside and tricking people into trusting them by telling them that the company is working for their well-being

play with double entendre to identify themselves as ... cocks ... making up hashtags like #CockIsCulture, #FightingForOurCocks #WeAreAll-Cocks, #CockIttude

say that they have to "kill the story" about the numbers of hurricane-related deaths, as the dead are yet to be counted; discuss a strategy for hiding the numbers of those killed during María and jokingly ask "Don't we have some cadavers we can use to feed the crows?"

comment that "Nothing says patriarchal oppression like Ricky Martin," that "Ricky Martin is so misogynistic that he fucks guys because women are not good enough. Pure patriarchy."[116]

If María laid bare the humanitarian crisis that was already underway given austerity, the governor's words, the brothers' words, laid bare a well-functioning necropolitical state. It dispelled the view that the debt crisis and hurricane relief and recovery disclosed an absent state. Crucial here, however, is that it put impunity on display. It made clear the very structure of impunity, in Rita Segato's sense. It disclosed the pedagogy of cruelty at work in government dealings and in the generation of public policy. A pedagogy that trains sensibility itself into not-binding, *el no-vínculo*, as we saw in chapter 1, here explicitly frames public policy. Misogyny, transphobia, homophobia are installed by outright violence, yet they are sustained by the pact among peers expressed in silence. No member of the chat interrupted the discussion. The brothers not only support, they enhance each other. They sustain the very structures of violence their dealings, comments, laughter index. Rosselló alleged that the offensive texting was his way of blowing off steam—*liberar tensiones.*

Protests began on July 11 when a group convened by la Colectiva Feminista en Construcción gathered at the Luis Muñoz Marín Airport, where

Rosselló arrived from a supposed family vacation. They continued well after Rosselló announced he would resign, uploading a prerecorded video on Facebook late July 24. The protests were largely auto-convened and organic. They were not spontaneous, however.[117] They drew from the feminist transformation of traditional protest discussed in chapter 3 with reference to la Colectiva. Groups resisting the Fiscal Control Board through actions with anarchist bent, such as Jornada Se Acabaron las Promesas, also contributed to the emergence of new forms of protest. The horizontalism of the student strike and the modes of autogestión developed in the wake of María provide an organizational context and praxis crucial to understanding the effective construction of diffuse and diverse collectives. A history of anti-colonial, worker, student, teacher, environmentalist, and queer resistance is also significant.

It is instructive to consider the protests in light of Rebollo-Gil's discussion of the distinction between the creative and violent student strike. The uptake of the proliferation of forms of protest run precisely along these lines—the creative and the offensive, unruly, violent. Although the protests were successful in ousting Rosselló, throughout the protests and in their aftermath, some argued that the protests were a failure. They failed to change a still-corrupt government, installed an unelected governor, emboldened the Fiscal Control Board. Indeed, some argue that the economic interests that la Junta represents were strengthened by the political shifts that the protest initiated.[118] Protests gave way to equally unprecedented town assemblies, *asambleas de pueblo*, that sought to move from protest to proposal. A hard distinction between the type of intervention the protests and the assemblies express, however, implies that protests themselves are a mere negative act, a force of removal (*destitución*) that does not in fact make coloniality/the colonial condition inoperative by constructing new forms of political participation.[119] The question, however, is whether the protests can be understood as an inspiring failure in Rebollo-Gil's sense, whether the effectivity of the protests rests on the possibility that they have the potential to transform the very framework of sense necessary for any proposal that would not leave coloniality intact.

In "(O)ponerse donde sea: Escenarios combativos de la indignación," Yara Maite Colón-Rodríguez and Luz Marie Rodríguez-López document the shift in the very form of protest in the territory throughout July. The sheer diversity and creativity of manifestations establish such transformation.[120] Two things must be noted at the outset. To say that there is a shift in the form of protest itself is to say that there is a shift in the content of the protests. One cannot keep separate form and content. The protests addressed the operation of coloniality, the violence of the race/gender/class hierarchy that reinstalls the colony. They addressed a violence that is ubiquitous yet equally spectacular. This inseparability of form and content, second, is grounded in what is announced in the title of the piece. (*O)ponerse* references at once to opposition and to the role of the body in opposition. To be *puestx pal problema*, for example, is to be willing to put your body on the line. From surveillance and incarceration to becoming a meme, *ponerse*, putting or placing oneself on the line, is a use of the body that admits of public uptake, judgment, manipulation, violence. The body, then, becomes a site of reproduction *or* contestation in relation to the space that it aims to question or resignify. Accordingly, Colón-Rodríguez and Rodríguez-López discuss the role that space played in "strategies of insurgency" in the protests. Bodies, I want to suggest, are "instruments of disobedience," as Colón-Rodríguez and Rodríguez-López put it, with the capacity to reify as much as dislocate the normative field operating within space itself. Such normative field is not merely a matter of public uptake but also of the very history inscribed in the materiality of space indeed place itself.

The July protests ranged from marches, a motorized caravan, biking, kayaking, diving, yoga, dancing, praying, renaming streets both physically and virtually, to graffiti and signs subverting expletives and generating lists of the next to be destitute.[121] Insults and slurs addressed every day to women and the LGBTQ community, *puta* and *pato/pata*, were subverted, indeed affirmed, in signs that read, for example, *siempre putx/patx, nunca corrupta*, "always a 'whore'/queer, never corrupt."[122] Every evening at 8 p.m., the sound of *cacerolazos* filled houses and buildings, merging the sound of opposition in the street, where cacerolazos were ubiquitous, with the sound of opposition in the home. Cintrón Arbassetti's reflections on silence and noise in "La Guerrilla sonora que derrocó a Rosselló, o la protesta como tumulto sónico" are insightful. The silence of the shock of 889 pages of insults turned to indignant noise. The cacerolazos, three thousand motorbikes entering San Juan, music that filled the streets composed a "dispersed and congregated tumult," Cintrón Arbassetti writes, "subverting quotidian objects."[123] He adds:

> The noise of pots [cacerolas] marks the point of tension while breaking the silence of the suburban order. Sirens and the explosion of tear gas grenades is the only noise that the force of a police that executes the monopoly of violence permits itself. A fleeting aerial sound that drowns soon before the roar of motorcycles. Rey Charlie and his motorized cavalry make their entrance up the Norzagaray, down la Calle del Cristo.

The multitude explodes in screams, there are fireworks. The rúm Rúm prá Prá of the engine that turns against the order that conceived it as a sign of progress.[124]

Power remains silent. The street is all noise.[125] The motor, key sign of progress, contests the reigning order. Pans and pots, key signs of food, of the reproduction of life itself, women's invisible labor, opposing the reigning order: austerity, a long history of stifled food sovereignty, the gendered division of social labor. Protest "expands, enters, hurts, adheres," Cintrón Arbassetti adds, quoting Félix Jiménez.[126]

This subversion of power through the subversion of body/space, indeed place, was nationally and internationally deemed "creative."[127] Other forms of protest, however, were deemed offensive. Echoing Argentina's 2001 protests and multiple removals, the slogan ¡Que se vayan todos! (They must all go!) became ¡Vamos por todxs! (We are going after them all!). This turn indicates the power of removal driven by collective rage—nuestra rabia junta (our rage together), read one sign.[128] It points to an ongoing holding accountable to the point of removal that stems from rage, resentment, negative affect, lacking positive proposals that would purportedly ameliorate the state/law/capital.[129] The state's repressive violence—the state's use of pepper spray and unconstitutional evacuation of the streets of Old San Juan at 11 p.m., for example—was met with well-organized self-defense.[130] Yet despite the fact that even mainstream media aired instructions on making "Seattle Solution," a pepper spray antidote, confrontations with regular police, la Fuerza de Choque, and correctional officers deployed to reinforce police, were by and large disparaged as compromising the creative, nonviolent, diverse, productive nature of the protests.[131] A long history of repression of anti-colonial movements in the territory, to be sure, is relevant in this context.[132] The May 1, 2017, National Strike is most relevant.[133] Thousands marched toward the financial district protesting the debt crisis and the installation of the Fiscal Control Board. A group of protestors threw objects at banks and private establishments, breaking glass windows. Confrontation with the police led to the arrest of seventeen people, including Nina Droz, who was charged with attempting to set fire to a building owned by Banco Popular. She served a thirty-seven-month sentence in a federal prison. Hoods, masks, breaking private property, overall confrontations with the police are routinely encountered with state repression. They are also faced with public scrutiny as sullying creative, peaceful, productive protest. Indexing the violence of finance capital and private property index the protestors as violent.

4.1 Jornada Se Acabaron las Promesas. San Juan, Puerto Rico. Paro Nacional (National Strike), May 1, 2017. Photo from Jornada Se Acabaron las Promesas's Facebook page.

It is instructive to consider, however, el perreo intenso at the footsteps of San Juan's Cathedral. It is exemplary of offensive protest through the affirmation of shamelessness, pleasure, and nonproductivity. *El perreo intenso* came to be known as *perreo combativo* as well, thanks to a tweet by Tommy Torres, Ileán Pérez writes in "Poner el cuerpo."[134] Rosselló posted a prerecorded video with his resignation on Facebook on the evening of July 24. The video was to be released at 11 p.m., but problems with the upload meant that it aired close to midnight. There were various calls for perreo in the streets of old San Juan that evening, including one by Guayoteo, a party collective. The LGBTQ community convened el perreo intenso on the footsteps of *la Catedral*. Earlier in the day, they had staged a *grajeada combativa*, combative make-out, in this space as well. Videos of el perreo intenso went viral.[135] Guayoteo posted a statement distancing themselves from the protest at the cathedral, clarifying that they had acquired the city's permission and that the other group made them "look bad." The archbishop of San Juan tweeted: "We repudiate the disrespect for the Cathedral of San Juan because the cathedral represents the transcendent values of our Puerto Rican culture. And although we are aware that it is a protest against the Governor of Puerto Rico, which should have already resigned, we cannot allow disrespect for our national and religious symbols."[136] A week later, "acts

4.2 Still from video *Perreo combativo* (2019) by Karla Claudio-Betancourt; video still edited by Elena Cardona.

of reparation" on the part of the religious community sought to cleanse the supposedly defiled cathedral.

Unlike Rebollo-Gil's examples beyond the student strike, like the breaking of the windows of Banco Popular, el perreo intenso was a decisively political act, given the space it occupied, the context it referenced, and the history it indexed. We must recall that perreo, dance associated with *reggaetón*, was at the center of the 2002 Anti-Pornography Campaign in Puerto Rico. Multiple Senate hearings articulated a discourse of "disreputability, respectability, and honor" in this context.[137] These processes are inseparable from the long history of disciplining populations into "decency" that installed the race/gender/class norm, as Petra Rivera-Rideau argues referencing Eileen Findlay's landmark work on the imposition of decency in Puerto Rico.[138] Reggaetón developed in *barrios* and *caseríos* during the 1980s and 1990s and was criminalized in the context of Mano Dura, as Mayra Santos Febres and Raquel Z. Rivera have documented.[139] In 1995, the Drugs and Vice Control Bureau of the Police Department of Puerto Rico raided six record stores in San Juan. Public debate about the "violence" and "vulgarity" of reggaetón and perreo in great part responded to the success of religious groups in linking race, poverty, indecency, drugs and sexual "deviance."[140] Raids impacted the LGBTQ community and sex workers as well.[141] As Rivera puts it, "underground's self-identification with ghetto hardness and lawlessness was an attempt at vindicating urban marginality."[142]

For the state/religious right, such affirmation was a form of "cultural contagion," where the margins posed a normative threat to be contained.[143]

El perreo intenso on the evening of July 24 can be seen as a queer appropriation of reggaetón (and trap), an affirmation of despised sexualities and nonreproductive pleasure. In "Paro Nacional, perreo, y Antonio Pantojas," Yoryie Irrizarry writes: "There, on those steps, all together (*todes juntes*), LGBTQ+ and hetero, *maricones*, *buchas*, and *femmes*, trans and cis, and nonbinary, young and not so young, released their bodies, delivering them in playful abandonment, to the rhythm, to pleasure (*goce*). Sweating and *perreando*, *hasta abajo*. That happened there on the steps of one of the institutions that has persecuted us the most, that has continuously tried to control our bodies (*nuestres cuerpes*) not only from its pulpits, but also by lobbying against the elimination of sodomy laws, laws that assign clothing according to genitalia, arbitrary guardians of concepts such as 'decency' and 'values' that are constantly used against poor people, against young people, against women, and against queer people."[144] The ongoing alliance between religious fundamentalism and the state within the debt crisis intensifies the erosion of LGBTQ and gestating bodies' reproductive rights.[145] El perreo intenso indexed and subverted a history of antiblack violence as well.[146] In response to the religious indignation about the supposed defilement of the cathedral, Yolanda Arroyo-Pizzaro noted the cathedral's history. The cathedral was built in 1521. It is one of the oldest buildings in San Juan and the oldest cathedral in the United States and its territories. It houses the tomb of Juan Ponce de León. Within its walls and on its steps, enslaved people were bought and sold, women were persecuted.[147] El perreo intenso indexed, then, the continuation of a history of violence recorded on those very walls and steps.

Perrear on the steps of the cathedral, I want to suggest, interrupts the construction of the body-territory, of the body-colony: the racialized/gendered body as something to contain, bound, control, extract, police. It affirmed the use of the body in "illegitimate" ways *sin vergüenza*, shamelessly, not merely as an expression of pride. Lawrence La Fountain's discussion of queer *sinvergüencería* is insightful here. He argues that "to be a sinvergüenza is to have no shame: to disobey, break the law, disrespect authority (the family, the church, the state), and in a perverse and curious way to be proud of one's transgression, or at the very least lack a feeling of guilt."[148] That lack of guilt, that defiant excess, that affirmation of impropriety and indecency has the potential to turn inoperative the race/gender/class norm. As many pointed out, Pedro Rosselló, Ricky Rosselló's father, implemented Mano Dura. Ricky resigned while people were *perreando* on the steps of the cathedral.[149] El perreo intenso, combativo offended in its queerness, in its irreverence. That irreverence short-circuits the field of sense that blocks the perception of the violence recorded on the walls and steps of the cathedral. El perreo intenso thereby linked colonial violence with an ongoing coloniality. "For me el perreo intenso and combativo," Irrizarry writes, "was one of the most powerful political acts that has been witnessed, after the national strike. Perrear on the steps of the cathedral could very well be the equivalent of burning the American flag. The one colonizes countries, the other colonizes *cuerpos y cuerpas* (bodies), both colonize our minds."[150]

Like smoke bombs, hoods, shattered glass and thrown rocks, bodies perreando on the steps of the cathedral se pasan. They cross the line. They appear as a political act of defiance through defilement. It is not creative. It is distasteful, rude, unruly, indecent, in need of reparation. El perreo intenso can be seen as a subversive interruption that dislocates the "transcendent values of our Puerto Rican culture," in the words of the archbishop. It is not a political act that installs new parties, proposes new agendas. It appropriates a practice that has long named a site of repression *and* resistance defiantly, sin vergüenza. It affirms queer and women's sexuality, the latter often complicated in the hypersexualized and misogynistic lyrics of reggaetón. *El boom del pueblo* is not to be credited with ousting the governor. It certainly did not displace the relation of colonialism and coloniality in government corruption and the Fiscal Control Board. Yet it can be seen as hopeful protest. It requires the very transformation of the field of sense to grasp what it indexes, opposes, displaces. It requires the dislocation of the religious/conservative view that colludes with capital/the state to appear as a powerful act of protest. Crucially, it also requires displacing the reification of a culture of resistance now commodified in the mainstream's appropriation of reggaetón.[151] El perreo offended some, but it also interpolated others who do not experience the fate of Mano Dura, homophobia, transphobia.[152]

Despite its potential, hopeful protests cannot merely be a matter of challenging the scripted nature of opposition itself. They require material praxes that seize the power to bind beyond the field of epistemic, aesthetic, moral contestation. Puerto Rico's long-standing tradition of subverting private property is key, as we will see in the conclusion to the book. It resignifies space, place, and normative fields by challenging more than productivity. Material praxes that take back land challenge private property itself, recognizing it as central to capital/coloniality. They can even be understood as forms of reparation with the potential to unbind the world of capital/coloniality.

CONCLUSION DECOLONIALITY AS REPARATIONS

Decolonization is not a metaphor.
—EVE TUCK AND K. WAYNE YANG

Hay que organizar el pesimismo.
We must organize pessimism.
—RAFAEL BERNABE quoting WALTER BENJAMIN
quoting PIERRE NAVILLE

IN A COLUMN PUBLISHED IN *Claridad*, Rima Brusi takes stock of the role of the shipping container in times of austerity, including in the aftermath of Hurricane María.[1] Shipping container as school. Containers with rotten provisions. Lost containers. Improvised and insufficient containers as clinics. Containers full of the dead. Brusi invites us to link these with containers ubiquitous in Puerto Rico for some time. Shipping container as home for those living in poverty. Container as office for contractors. Containers that bring food and products that make up 85 percent of what is consumed in Puerto Rico. Brusi writes:

> In effect, it would seem that the modern history of our island can be told like this, container by container, that the containers are the trope that best represents some of the most tragic, indeed the starkest facets of our condition: the island-colony, the chronically forgotten island, the

poor island, the island of disaster, the island where children do not count neither do the dead.

Brusi begins her column by confessing that in moments of darkness she thinks of the containers. The containers take me to Christina Sharpe. In her book *In the Wake*, Sharpe ties the shipping container with the slave ship.[2] In "The Ship," the second chapter of her book, Sharpe offers a critical reading of the film *The Forgotten Space* by Allan Sekula and Noël Burch. Sekula and Burch present the ocean, the sea, as a key site of "globalization," arguing that there is no other place where neoliberalism expresses itself in its greatest disorientation, violence, and alienation. Sharpe points out that they ignore the origin of capital, which has always been global, in the trade of captured Africans. When these men say that shipping containers "are everywhere, mobile and anonymous: 'remote labor coffins,' which transport products manufactured by invisible workers on the other side of the world" without referring to the origin of this economic global system, they make invisible what Saidiya Hartman calls "the afterlife of slavery."[3]

In *Lose Your Mother*, Hartman writes:

If slavery persists as an issue in the political life of black America, it is not because of an antiquarian obsession with bygone days or the burden of a too-long memory, but because black lives are still imperiled and devalued by a racial calculus and a political arithmetic that were entrenched centuries ago. This is the afterlife of slavery—skewed life chances, limited access to health and education, premature death, incarceration, and impoverishment. I, too, am the afterlife of slavery.[4]

Hartman also speaks of the "afterlife of property." In "Venus in Two Acts," she describes this as "the detritus of lives with which we have yet to attend, a past that has yet to be done, and the ongoing state of emergency in which black life remains in peril."[5] Capital is not separable from slavery—and vice versa. While the inseparability of capital and slavery is crucial, the point is not to call attention to the fact that the origin of capital is violence. Rather, it is to track the continuation of the violence of slavery in contemporary modalities of racial violence.

Hartman traces the continuation of antiblack violence not in terms of effects or legacies, then. She aims to name its current actuality, effectivity, in institutions, norms, relations, sensibilities, and desires that live on in the present. Hartman and Sharpe emphasize that the past has not yet been done. The present *is* the past. We must turn the present *into* the past.

C.1 "Todo Se Pudre en el Vagón de la Colonial" (Everything rots in the colonial container/colonial containment), La Puerta. San Juan, Puerto Rico, November 20, 2018. Photo from La Puerta's Facebook page.

This requires more than writing the history of those who suffered the violence that founded the modern capitalist world in their singularity. To make memory, to turn the present into the past, is to attend to the lives that live modalities of this violence today. Attending requires dismantling the world it founded, rendering the effectivity of that past that is the present *inoperative*. It requires undoing the ways of binding—institutional, normative, perceptual, libidinal—that articulate this world, that reinstall that original violence in the present.

Ta-Nehisi Coates's remarks to the Judicial Committee of the House of Representatives on H.R. 40, which would create a commission for the study and development of proposals for reparations to the black community in the United States, make reference to the afterlife of slavery. Reparations would not only make memory. They are required to dismantle the present that updates, adapts, actualizes modalities of that original violence. It is crucial to put a figure on what is owed to black Americans, not just direct descendants of enslaved people. But reparations would require disarming antiblack violence and inequality by dismantling the political economy, legal regulations, social relations, and individual desires through which that past survives in the present. In short, reparations would have to contribute to the dismantling of this world here and now, to the dismantling of ourselves.

They would not be enough if they generate a monetary check that absolves the true debtor. "Decolonization which sets out to change the order of the world," as Fanon writes, "is clearly an agenda for total disorder."[6] "Decolonization," as Eve Tuck and K. Wayne Yang write, "is not a metaphor."[7]

It would be a mistake to assume that those who live or die in the colony are equally located in the race/gender/class hierarchy that is the afterlife of the installation of the capitalist world that began in the fifteenth century through enslavement, conquest, and colonialism—what Aníbal Quijano calls the "coloniality of power." We must track differences, intensities, privileges, precarities. We must track coloniality in the colony, not reduce one to the other. In Puerto Rico, the afterlife of the colonial condition sustains the colony, nourishes it. The past is the present in a double sense, then. The shipping containers index a logic of history that defies all linearity. The afterlife of the colony reinstalls the colony in altered material conditions—as we have seen throughout this book, through debt in the context of neoliberal financialized capitalism. In the case of Puerto Rico, one must dismantle both to turn the past into the past. Reparations, truth commissions, would be appropriate here. Locating ourselves in the Caribbean, thinking about reparations in reference to the Caribbean, would be crucial.[8]

Sharpe invites us to do what she calls "wake work"—to place ourselves in the vigil, in a state of wakefulness, in consciousness, in the track left on the water's surface (by a ship or a body in movement), in a region of disturbed flow.[9] These multiple meanings of the word *wake* orient the thought of "containment, regulation, punishment, capture, and captivity and the ways the manifold representations of blackness become the symbol, par excellence, for the less-than-human being condemned to death."[10] We cannot establish equivalence in historical experience, grief, vigil, consciousness. What purpose would a supposed equivalence serve? It would turn the specificity of experiences of capture invisible. It would turn their specific mode of operation and imagined forms of interruption impossible to grasp. The point is that Sharpe's invitation is important to the discussion of the case of Puerto Rico. One must locate oneself within the afterlife that is coloniality in order to turn the present into the past. This means thinking from the afterlife of slavery in Puerto Rico, linking it with its expression in the Caribbean, not only in the United States.

Brusi reminds us of the etymology of the word *vagón*—"container" in Spanish. It admits two roots: *vacuus* and *vagari*. The first implies emptiness, hollowness. It is present in nouns such as "laziness" (*vagancia*), "vacation" (*vacación*), and "vanity" (*vanidad*). The second is in words such as *wander* (*vagar* and *divagar*), *wanderer* (*vagabundo*). We have examples of "luminous" containers that suggest "creation" and "survival": container as mural, container as café. "But in my dark moments," Brusi writes, "I think that for those sad beings who decide our destinies, we are an island-container, empty of power or purpose but full of rotten food, of the dead and of unattended children, of nomads who do not move, of wandering beings [*seres errantes*] that are at the same time locked up [*a la vez encerrados*]."[11] These moments of darkness, of *pessimism*, I want to suggest, allow us to tell the modern history of our island, container by container, in order to *interrupt* it. Sharpe insists that wake work is a way of occupying the "I" of Hartman's "I, too, am the afterlife of slavery." Being not in mourning, then. Orienting oneself from the vigil, awake, conscious.

In this book, I have argued that debt is an apparatus of capture, one that functions as a form of coloniality. Debt captures land, coasts, body, time, the future itself. It actualizes a race/gender/class hierarchy by marking populations as culpable, hence, disposable. Debt is a product of a colonial history. It is materially indexed to the emergence, expansion, and mutations of capitalism. As a mode of coloniality, however, debt exceeds its origins, organizing material conditions in light of colonial/racial violence anew. It does so by updating forms of dispossession essential to the creation and capture of value in a capitalist economy. We must move from an account of financial debts to a reckoning with historical debts, however. In reckoning with past debts that are present as financial debts, we elucidate how financial debts update the work of race/gender/class and its modalities of violence. Reckoning requires practices that subvert the injunction to repay, the norm of productivity, and modes of intelligibility that reify propriety— all modalities of the racial norm of bourgeois whiteness at the center of modernity/coloniality. Reckoning, subversion, and refusal seek to interrupt the colonial condition by turning coloniality inoperative. They are political actions that require letting go of the assumption that debt is best approached through notions of financial, political, or moral cancellation or forgiveness. Moving from financial to historical debts does not represent a move away from matters of political economy. On the contrary. It centers material conditions that reinstall *or* interrupt the colonial/racial order.

Repayment, the injunction to pay, is a site of subversive interruption. Reckoning, subversion, refusal seek to interrupt the effectivity of debt by inverting culpability. Holding accountable, however, is not only a matter of signaling out individual political or economic agents responsible for public or private debt. It is neither only a matter of pointing out structures that make possible such forms of agency in the first place. It is a matter of dismantling such structures. This dismantling, this unbinding, must go all the way down to the collective and individual sensibility, perception, desire articulated by the race/gender norm. Turning coloniality inoperative, interrupting the reinstallation of the colony, requires the very transformation of sense. Protest that indexes the work of debt as updating a racial/gender order, as we have seen, attempts to dislocate perception, sensibility, and desire by interrupting the very framework of intelligibility. Historical reckoning and subversive interruption require more than epistemic or aesthetic intervention, however. They require more than juridico-political intervention. They entail political-economic disarticulation, unbinding. Decolonization requires seizing the power to bind that articulates existence in light of capitalism/coloniality. Decolonization gives way to decoloniality.

The topic of reparations requires book-length treatment. My aim in what follows is modest, hoping to generate questions for future work. Subversion, interruption, and refusal suggest a material praxis that seizes the power to bind. Exemplary here are practices that seek to turn inoperative the work of private property central to a capitalist economy and its racial order. These challenge modalities of dispossession but also articulate power in common. They seek to unbind in order to bind/bond anew. This material praxis can be seen as a form of reparation, shifting the latter from a juridical model to an exercise of power from within disempowerment. It *takes back what is owed*, subverting or rejecting the public/private distinction that subtends private property. The analytics of reparations go a long way for thinking decoloniality, yet they should not be seen as only affirming demands for financial compensation or discursive amelioration. Reparations should be seen as a site of historical reckoning that aims at political-economic unbinding. They have the capacity to unbind more than the bonds of financial debt itself while remaining directed at structures that reproduce the political economy distinctive of coloniality. Reparations—taking back what is owed—is a form of dismantling this world here and now.

The first section, Decoloniality, discusses Nelson Maldonado-Torres's distinction between decolonization and decoloniality. This discussion builds on my suggestion above that the coloniality of power should be understood in light of Hartman's notion of the afterlife of slavery/property and Sharpe's engagement with Hartman. It also considers Fanon's engagement with the question of reparations. The second section, Rescue/Occupation, explores cases of decolonial praxis in Puerto Rico. These challenge private property, seeking to build power in common by rescuing the common(s). They can be seen not only as modes of addressing the necropolitical operation of neoliberal coloniality. They also turn inoperative the reinstallation of the colony/coloniality through ongoing rounds of enclosure in the context of the debt crisis and in the aftermath of María. Key here is the work of Liliana Cotto-Morales, Érika Fontánez-Torres, Miriam Muñiz-Varela, and Marina Moscoso. Their work assesses Puerto Rico's long-standing praxis of "rescue"/"occupation" of land occupied through multiple rounds of colonial/ capitalist control. The last section, Organizing Pessimism, ends the book with a brief reflection on pessimism as the site of hope.

DECOLONIALITY

Thesis two of Maldonado-Torres's "Outline of Ten Theses on Coloniality and Decoloniality" distinguishes between decolonization and decoloniality to elaborate Fanon's understanding of decolonization as decoloniality.[12] As we have seen throughout this book, minimally, colonialism is a form of juridico-political subordination. Coloniality, by contrast, refers to a race/gender system of classification that exceeds colonialism as a juridico-political project. Colonialism and decolonization are "usually depicted as past realities," Maldonado-Torres writes.[13] They are not only located in the past. They are "locked in the past, located elsewhere, or confined to specific empirical dimensions."[14] Varieties of obfuscation of those who question the veracity or intensity or continuation of colonial violence are tied to claims of overcoming in space (progress has occurred here despite lacking there) and in time (forms of racial or gender violence are a thing of the past).[15]

In the case of Puerto Rico, we have seen, coloniality operates in the colony. The colony is reinstalled in altered material and historical conditions by the actualization of a racial order. Although one can say that coloniality is reproduced by the colonial condition, by the territorial status, it is important to stress the asymmetry at hand. The continuation of the colonial condition is possible by actualizations of race/gender/class. The productivity of colonialism and coloniality is a backward positing, then. The colony is posited—reinstalled—by its afterlife. The past *is* the present. Decoloniality seeks to turn the present that is the past into the past. It intervenes in the present, targeting the reproduction of a world to the measure of racial violence at every level. It does not seek to dismantle a colonial juridico-political project without also undoing modes of binding reality to that measure all the way down to the sensible. Decoloniality exceeds decolonization.

In chapter 4, I discussed the significance of sensibility for subversive interruption. In a recent essay, Maldonado-Torres stresses the aesthetic aspects of coloniality and decoloniality.[16] The significance of the sensible, he points out, is best captured in Fanon's concluding prayer in *Black Skin, White Masks*: "O my body, always make me a man who questions."[17] Coloniality constructs perception, sensibility itself—aesthesis, in the broadest sense of the term. It articulates desire, the somatic itself.[18] The construction of the world to the measure of colonial violence is the construction of an embodied orientation to that world, to others, to oneself. As we have seen throughout this book, not all colonized subjects are equally situated in the race/gender/class hierarchy that constructs an embodied orientation. The antiblack violence that structures such hierarchy in the case of Puerto Rico guides such bodily orientation. The misanthropic skepticism expressed in the ubiquitous violence of the everyday life of the colonized is a skeptical "attitude" but one oriented by the race/gender norm that we have seen is the center of modernity/coloniality: bourgeois whiteness, its expression in private property, it ethics/aesthetic of propriety, its modalities of authority, its practices of knowing. Decoloniality requires a change in attitude at the embodied level in order to effectively "turn away from the downturn" that coloniality represents. This turning away all the way down to the sensible, to the libidinal, for Maldonado-Torres, is a "metaphysical and material restoration of the human."[19]

Decoloniality exceeds the project of decolonization, especially if the latter draws from ideas of inclusion to a world posited in the measure of colonial/racial violence. Structures of recognition that purportedly restore humanity to the colonized are bound to the misanthropic skepticism that marked the colonized as disposable in the first place. In a widely debated passage, Fanon argues that "there is a zone of nonbeing, an extraordinarily sterile and arid region, an incline stripped bare of every essential from which a genuine new departure can emerge. In most cases, the black man cannot take advantage of this descent into a veritable hell."[20] Maldonado-Torres writes that "one's death as black" is the "precondition of entering the zone of being human."[21] The race/gender/class norm—bourgeois whiteness, its expression in property, productivity, propriety—drives an ongoing process that produces, as Celenis Rodríguez Moreno argues, "incomplete subjects/partially human" in failing to meet the norm's material/symbolic strictures.[22] Yet this "constitutive failure" is "the position from which one could actually risk that Fanonian 'real leap,'" as Axelle Karera writes.[23]

The modern colonial world is marked by "a constant denial of man, an avalanche of murders," Fanon writes in *The Wretched of the Earth*.[24] "From time to time [the black man] fights for liberty and justice, but it's always for a white liberty and a white justice, in other words, for values secreted by his masters," Fanon writes in *Black Skin, White Masks*.[25] Decoloniality involves abandoning the search for "recognition and validation in the modern/colonial world," as Maldonado-Torres argues.[26] It seeks to reconfigure the coordinates of power, knowing, sensing. It does so unbinding material reality thereby turning the work of the race/gender norm inoperative. The Fanonian real leap is the possibility of invention, of fundamentally "alter[ing] being," as Fanon argues.[27] "In the world I am heading for, I am endlessly creating myself," Fanon writes in *Black Skin, White Masks*. The real leap is a turning away from modernity/coloniality. It does not seek repair or reparation, as Karera argues. The norm of humanity itself is and continues to produce an ontological break, suggesting the possibility of an ontological break, albeit from it. Karera maintains that Fanon never retreats from the ambivalence that this predicament generates. It is from this ambivalence, I suggest, that a discussion of reparations beyond the juridical restorative paradigm can be approximated.

I want to center the political-economic aspects of decolonial praxis, stressing that they are crucial to unbinding *and* binding existence anew all the way down to the sensible. Fanon argues that the creation of a new humanity "cannot be attributed to a supernatural power."[28] The "'thing' colonized becomes a man through the very process of liberation." I want to shift from the language of liberation to praxes of unbinding the world of capital/coloniality, stressing that the Fanonian invention of a new "man" requires the creation of new material conditions. Decoloniality is necessarily an anti-capitalist praxis that seeks to undo the political economy that produces this racial order at every level. Such unbinding requires challenging not only the norms and institutions of capital, the forms of subjectivity and embodied experience that these necessitate. It requires material change that goes beyond efforts to redistribute wealth. Decoloniality does not seek amelioration. It turns coloniality inoperative, interrupting the norm of private property central to dispossession. Dislocating private property is a necessary though not sufficient condition of undoing the world of capital/coloniality.

In the case of Puerto Rico, unbinding takes the form of interruption, subversion, refusal, I have suggested. As a specifically material praxis, these challenge private property. Unbinding the world of capital/coloniality involves "rescuing" through "occupying" occupied land—the countryside, the coast, the city. The multiple rounds of colonial and capitalist occupation in Puerto Rico—from Spanish colonial rule beginning in the late fifteenth century to ongoing US colonial rule since the nineteenth century, from an agrarian to an industrial and postindustrial economy, from migration patterns to and from the United States but also the Caribbean—point to the complex terrain in which land rescue/occupation happens. Unbinding through a subversive praxis of occupying anew requires cross-referencing praxes such that binding life anew for one population is not at the cost of another navigating the no-place of life in the indebted colony, as Tuck and Yang's work urges us to do.[29] In their case, Tuck and Yang stress the need to track "incommensurable" decolonial praxes and face the "dangerous understanding of uncommonality that un-coalesces coalition politics."[30] The language and practice of "occupation" but also reparation, in the case of indigenous sovereignty, is deeply troubled when trading on and with stolen land and when exercising practices of settling that turn the settler colonial state "innocent."[31] In the case of Puerto Rico, Tuck and Yang's work helps specify that any material praxis must track the race/gender/class hierarchy liable to being reinstalled in its very contestation.

Decoloniality involves, then, material praxes of reckoning with histories of capture, dispossession, expulsion that continue to operate in the present neoliberal terrain. Before turning to the material praxis of land rescue/occupation in Puerto Rico, it is important to specify that this reckoning involves subverting culpability, as I have also argued in this book. Debt is a key site of reckoning because it indexes culpability. I have suggested that culpability is tied to disposability, since it updates the work of race/gender/class in altered material conditions. Debt functions by establishing who is debtor, who is creditor—who owes what to whom. Subverting the asymmetry debt institutes interrupts processes of racialization/gendering that are modalities of colonial violence in the neoliberal context. The promise and perils of demands for reparations are here instructive. They allow us to examine the strictures of such praxes. Given the breadth and complexity of this topic, I limit myself to examining Fanon's own treatment.[32] His assessment helps specify decoloniality as an anti-capitalist material praxis. Interventions in material conditions have the power to unbind the embodied and existential sites of coloniality in ways that cannot be matched by centering the existential aspects.

The complexity of Fanon's engagement with the question of reparations is insightful. In *Black Skin, White Masks*, he rejects reparations, arguing that it assumes a recoverable past. In *The Wretched of the Earth*, Fanon argues that reparations are the site of a "dual consciousness."[33] They express the awareness of the colonized that any such "aid" is their "due" but also the consciousness of "capitalist powers" that they must "pay up."[34] Fanon's critique of reparations is anchored in a rejection of the desire for a past to be recovered, one that in fact feeds structures of recognition that name humanity in its proximity to whiteness. Such desire binds ideas of repair and restoration to recognition within the strictures of bourgeois whiteness. His seeming affirmation of reparations underscores the subversive potential of historical-material reckoning. Although it is false to assume that these two analyses are separable, the latter seeks to materially unbind the world of colonial violence through an injunction to pay what is owed. It does not bind itself to a recoverable past, seeking to dismantle the past that is the present.

In the final chapter of *Black Skin, White Masks*, Fanon famously rejects reparations, arguing that the "density of history determines none of my acts."[35] "I, a man of color, insofar as I have the possibility of existing absolutely," Fanon argues, "have not the right to confine myself in a world of retroactive reparations."[36] "I am not a prisoner of history," Fanon stresses. "I must not look for the meaning of my destiny in that direction." This view of the past indexes a desire to recover an irrecoverable past, to repair an irreparable violence. Fanon's point, as Karera puts it, is that "there is no face behind the mask" to recover.[37] "What is called the black soul," as Fanon writes, "is a construction by white folk."[38] It is a projection of the racial norm—from language and desire to relation where there is no possibility of relation. In offering recognition of humanity, the racial norm shores itself up. Disalienation requires refusal to be defined by such construction or its terms for the sake of resolution.[39] Disalienation requires rejecting such reality as "definitive." Decolonization is a matter of invention for this reason.

Fanon describes the matter at hand in various ways. He says that the problem is the density of history, a matter of temporality, and a question of action.[40] They are all at play. However, I want to highlight the problem of action. Going beyond the density of history, rejecting recovery of an irrecoverable and irreparable past, makes possible "initiat[ing] my cycle of freedom."[41] It makes possible agency, though ambivalently. This is an agency caught in structures of dehumanization through the very idea of humanity.[42] In the chapter "The Black Man and Recognition," Fanon argues for the affirming *and* negating character of action. Action is a matter of affirmation: "Yes to life. Yes to love. Yes to generosity."[43] Yet it is also a matter of negation: "No to man's contempt. No to the indignity of man. To the exploitation of man. To the massacre of what is most human in man: freedom." The point is that affirmation and negation are coextensive "positings." "The I posits itself by opposing," writes Fanon.[44] Negation affirms the "values that make the world human." The negation of antiblack violence gives way to an affirmation—the invention of "humanity" beyond the strictures of bourgeois whiteness.

In the famous opening chapter of *The Wretched of the Earth*, "On Violence," Fanon argues that "what matters today, the issue which blocks the horizon, is the need for a redistribution of wealth."[45] Fanon radicalizes the notion of redistribution. "Colonialism and imperialism," he argues, "have not settled their debt to us once they have withdrawn their flag and their police force from our territories."[46] Colonialism has been reinstalled in economic "dependence."[47] Independence is tied to economic dependence, neutralizing decolonization, generating a terrain of action saturated by a conception of humanity bound to bourgeois whiteness. To be clear, capitalists have "behaved like real war criminals in the underdeveloped world" for centuries.[48] They have deployed outright violence, "deportation, massacres, forced labor, and slavery" as their methods of creation and capture of value.[49] Fanon addresses working conditions as well as the expansion of capital beyond work, in the dynamics of financial markets. In both cases, if material conditions are not modified, "it will take centuries to humanize this world."[50] The past is not a marker of an origin to be recovered, but of present material conditions to be dismantled.

"Europe is literally the creation of the Third World," Fanon writes.[51] "The riches which are choking [Europe] are those plundered from the underdeveloped peoples." They are the product of the "deportation of millions of slaves." The significance of reparations is introduced here. Far from "charity" or "aid," reparations express a "double consciousness." For the colonized, reparations are their "due." Reparations name what they are owed. For the colonizer, for "capitalist powers," reparations state that they must "pay up." Reparations index what they have taken but more importantly that it *has been taken*. Reparations are not to be seen as gratitude; neither are they a form of forgiveness of a bygone past.[52] They are not a matter of national restoration.[53] Reparations must "redistribute wealth"—end the "flight of capital," Fanon says.[54] Reparations should not seek the "development" of the "Third World," since the very idea of development posits a world in the image of Europe, the West, or simply "capitalist powers." Reparations articulate reality anew unbinding the world of capital. Redistribution is central to that unbinding, but it is here understood as a *taking back* beyond the image of capitalist modernity.

In the conclusion to *The Wretched of the Earth*, Fanon writes:

> The Third World is today facing Europe as one colossal mass whose project must be to try and solve the problems this Europe was incapable of finding the answers to. But what matters now is not a question of profitability, not a question of increased productivity, not a question of production rates. No, it is not a question of back to nature. It is the very basic question of not dragging man in directions which mutilate him, of not imposing on his brain tempos that rapidly obliterate and unhinge it. The notion of catching up must not be used as a pretext to brutalize man, to tear him from himself and his inner consciousness, to break him, to kill him.
>
> No, we do not want to catch up with anyone. But what we want is to walk in the company of man, every man, night and day, for all times.[55]

I seek to develop this point in relation to case of debt examined in this book. Demands for reparations are sites of historical reckoning when they involve the inversion of culpability, dismantling key norms that posit the modern capitalist colonial world anew. It is not the "Third World" that is underdeveloped. It has been "underdeveloped" through processes of dispossession. The "Third World" does not need to "catch up" economically but also politically, creating nation-states, institutions, and societies that draw from its norms and values.[56] It is not the "Third World" that is the debtor. The so-called Third World is the creditor. This inversion requires modes of reckoning that seek material rather than symbolic rectification. Financial compensation, redistribution of wealth, the institution of nation-states on the same terms merely reproduce capitalist/colonial power.

Fanon offers a view of decolonization that centers unbinding the world of capital, then. Faced with an irrecoverable past, faced with present modalities of violence that continue to turn that past into something that cannot be restored, decolonization aims to dismantle material conditions that reinstall the past in the present. It involves more than juridical-economic efforts. It requires turning inoperative the world of capital/coloniality, taking back the material organization of life itself. Reparations so understood can be sites of wakefulness, to recall Sharpe—consciousness of what is owed but also consciousness of the need to pay back. Decolonization/decoloniality entails disorder. Taking back and paying back without leaving the current order untouched is precisely what is at stake. Refusal to pay, subversion of repayment, and other forms of interruption that do not leave the current state of affairs untouched is precisely what is at stake. Disorder for the invention of a new life, a new sensibility.

RESCUE/OCCUPATION

It is instructive to consider the material praxis in Puerto Rico of taking back land (*toma de terrenos*), seeking to build power in common by rescuing the common(s).[57] Taking back land can be read as a form of reparation, since it subverts the injunction to repay. It inverts the positions of power the latter installs. More than merely demanding that the true debtor pay, it takes back what is owed. In Puerto Rico, taking back land through "rescue" (*rescate*) or "occupation" (*ocupación*), which may or may not include the subversion of financial instruments and juridical norms, challenges private property. This praxis seeks to interrupt ownership itself through refusal or appropriation. It responds to specific needs or aims—the need for housing due to economic downturn, displacement, gentrification; the need to interrupt ecological degradation and privatization; the need to generate work and livelihood. It indexes multiple colonizations/occupations that compose the history of the territory. By taking back land—the countryside, the coast, the city—many seek to posit our relation to land, water, energy, coasts, the body, power, the other anew.

In *Colonial Lives of Property*, Brenna Bhandar shows that ownership is grounded in the "capacity to appropriate" central to modern Western subjectivity, installing racial distinctions at the historical origin of the settler colonial project of modernity.[58] But she also traces the ongoing effectivity of conceptions of development, productivity, use; practices of mapping and measuring; and demands for title and title registration in and beyond indigenous communities. These are concrete sites of the unfolding of such a project. They sustain forms of displacement but also erasure, in fact, "elimination," that continue this founding violence in altered material conditions today.[59] For Bhandar, understanding the ongoing colonial operation of property is crucial to "resist contemporary forms of dispossession without replicating logics of appropriation and possessiveness that rely upon racial regimes for their sustenance."[60] Following Bhandar, taking back land has the potential to unbind the world of capital/coloniality, indeed bind relations anew. Yet it must avoid replicating logics of appropriation and possessiveness inextricable from the modern colonial project, albeit in a collectivist key. In the case of Puerto Rico, this praxis must avoid reinstalling a race/gender/

class hierarchy, its structuring race/gender norm, in the very subversion of private property.

Neoliberal cooptation but also the very coordinates of the field of opposition inevitably posited by neoliberalism generate complexity, degrees of complicity, to any taking back. Degrees of complicity do not neutralize subversive praxis, as we have seen throughout this book. One might track the complexities of this praxis considering the meanings and effects of its inversions of the public and the private.[61] In many cases, challenging private property runs through an affirmation of private property, as with the occupation of public land and infrastructure to fill the needs of individuals and communities. These practices can turn the public into the private, pressing against the state/law/capital's necropolitical operation, interrupting the erosion of material conditions especially for populations racialized as nonwhite. Yet they also run the risk of reifying the private, given the state's monopoly on the public. Others turn the private into the public, taking abandoned private property or subverting legal and financial norms that actualize it in order to generate "publics," communities, life in common. Yet they socialize governance or financial structures inevitably embedded in structures set by the state/law/capital. Taking back land is a complex praxis, then, yet it must be assessed in light of the forms of expulsion, displacement, and impoverishment in which they occur and to which they respond. Tracking the work of race/gender/class in the terrain in which they happen is thereby made possible.

The work of Cotto-Morales, Fontánez-Torres, Muñiz-Varela, and Moscoso is decisive here. While Cotto-Morales focuses on the impact of the long-standing land rescue movement for social movements in Puerto Rico, Fontánez-Torres discusses juridical theory and practice at the center of dispossession and its resistance. Muñiz-Varela, in turn, conceptualizes these interventions as modes of "interruption" that rather than seeking to restore the proper when rescuing land or subverting private property, build "infrastructures" for binding life anew. Variations of *autogestión* ("autonomous organizing or mutual aid") within economic downturn, hurricane disaster and recovery, and post #RickyRenuncia protests are important in this context. While these variations build power in common through alternative forms of organizing social power, their potential lies in reorganizing the reproduction of life itself despite the complexities mentioned above. Moscoso's discussion of new rounds of land "occupation" is insightful on this score.

In *Desalambrar*, Cotto-Morales documents the origins and effects of the land "rescue" movement in Puerto Rico.[62] The book recounts the taking back of land during two periods: from 1968 to 1972 and 1972 to 1976.[63] During these periods, approximately 186 communities, some 86,000 people, rescued lands.[64] Although, as we will see, this practice predates this period and continues to this day, it became ubiquitous in the context of Manos a la Obra's (Operation Bootstrap's) failure to eradicate unemployment, its increase rather than decrease of poverty, and the overall lack of housing that resulted from the state's development plan.[65] These communities "settled," established "informal housing," in the urban periphery.[66] *La toma de terrenos* was a "collective action, communitarian and immediate," Cotto-Morales writes, an "illegal mode of acquiring land."[67] It took the form of a spontaneous as well as organized mode of civil disobedience. La toma de terrenos appeared alongside a period of intensified student and worker activism, and employed a variety of strategies. Taking back land suffered different fates, ranging from government negotiation and donning of land titles to expulsion, forced evictions, and repression. *Lxs rescatadorxs* were criminalized, but they also found their aims subverted by wealthy groups who took coveted coastal land for recreational purposes.[68] Distinctions made in court, the media, and by law enforcement between "invaders" and "rescuers" ran along race/class lines.[69] For Cotto-Morales, land rescue constructed a new politics (*nueva forma de hacer política*).[70] New political actors emerged: impoverished populations facing a housing crisis.

Crucial here is the decision to understand their actions as land "rescue."[71] Cotto-Morales notes that some rescuers referenced Puerto Rico's original indigenous population, arguing that "invaders" are Spanish and especially US colonial powers.[72] Most significantly, the rescuers articulated moral-political positions against legal arguments concerning trespass and especially in the context of legal battles around property titles.[73] Rescuers/occupiers maintained that even if they had no legal right to the land, they had a moral right in view of their need for housing.[74] In discursively shifting the ground from legal to a moral-political argument yet pursuing a material praxis, lxs rescatadorxs linked private property, dispossession, and impoverishment. They took public land to fill private housing needs and they engaged in battles over property titles, to be sure. Yet, according to Fontánez-Torres, their praxis did not reify private property. Land rescue in this context raised questions beyond the validity of original property titles.[75] It questioned the very distribution of land, "indeed of space" itself, place itself. It questioned the allocation of resources, hence the relation among "bodies, non-human animals, ideas" and all that can be legally and economically coded in terms of use and development.

C.2 "We have a moral right to rescue our land" (Tenemos un derecho moral de rescatar nuestra tierra). Photo from *Desalambrando: The Documentary*, 2017.

In chapter 2, I discussed José Atiles-Osoria's proposal to "abandon the law," given its complicity with what he calls neoliberal colonialism. In contrast, Fontánez-Torres seeks to exploit the ambiguity distinctive of the law for subversive purposes. In a series of recent articles under the heading "La Propiedad (¿nuestra?) de cada día," Fontánez-Torres discusses legal cases and social movements that seek to "rescue the common" (*el rescate de lo común*).[76] They are published in a sequence that follows the reprint of a series of articles from 2006, published under the heading "La Defensa de lo público y lo común." The two sets of articles bring attention to the intensification of capture within the debt crisis, a pattern that continues with, for example, the newly implemented Opportunity Zones as well as the recently proposed zoning map that would reclassify land use.[77] Legal battles index a material praxis of resistance that aims to rescue the common by rescuing the commons. Fontánez-Torres examines struggles in Culebra, Vieques, Ocean Park, Isla Verde, Piñones, Luquillo, and the San Juan Bay against the privatization of the Land Maritime Zone (Zona Marítimo Terrestre).[78] These are battles over the enclosure of the "coast, the sea, the common," as the Zona Marítimo Terrestre is designated as public lands.[79] As Adriana Garriga-López notes, these are important sources of food and sustenance as well as sites of caretaking of natural resources for foragers and fishers.[80] Campamento Playas Pal' Pueblo is a related example, since it resisted a development project in Carolina for fourteen years.[81] The camp successfully blocked private development, though the result is complex given local government control of the zone. The point is that these battles interrupt the logic of enclosure, which dismantles "common well-being" by capturing "the common."[82] These forms of opposition build life in common by affirming the public nature of the coast.[83] Given the intensifying effects of climate change, the coast and waterways in general are key sites of unbinding and binding life anew.[84]

Fontánez-Torres's articles continue the work of *Ambigüedad y derecho: Ensayos de crítica jurídica*. In *Ambigüedad y derecho*, Fontanéz-Torres discusses paradoxes of juridification and representation, examining questions of property and environment in Puerto Rico. Tracing three moments in the history of Puerto Rico's economic development throughout the twentieth century, she argues that a critique of the law must "assume the challenge of reevaluating and resignifying dominant premises of justice, property rights, and environment."[85] She contrasts, for example, the first and the second moments by tracking reigning assumptions within legislation, an agrarian reform that sought but failed to address socioeconomic inequalities and a period of industrialization that affirmed a utilitarian logic. The first limited the power of US sugar corporations and redistributed land while the second articulated property ownership in light of the aims of industrialization and urbanization. The latter promoted environmental legislation that was "conservationist," forgoing an opportunity to dismantle social asymmetries by addressing matters of environmental justice, such as environmental racism.[86] Fontánez-Torres is most interested in cases where the law aids expropriation *as well as* resistance to dispossession. Economic and environmental justice intersect in cases where the law is subverted for the rearticulation of "social power."

A key example is the Caño Martín Peña Community Land Trust. This community was initially composed of displaced agricultural workers who moved to the city after Hurricane San Ciprian and in the context of the Great Depression. This community is composed of eight barrios (known collectively as the G-8), the ENLACE corporation, and the land trust.[87] It seeks to rehabilitate the area that comprises the G-8, which encompasses 26,000 families. The Caño is situated next to la Milla de Oro (the "Gold Mile"), Puerto Rico's financial district. The project was initially created to dredge the San José Lagoon in connection with the estuary of San Juan Bay, but it has resisted gentrification and other attempts at capture and displacement. El Caño is part of a long-standing history of taking and transforming mangrove land. While impoverished, displaced, racialized populations build up mangroves into communities, private and government interests attempt to expropriate these lands, given their now desirable location. The Vietnam community in Guaynabo is an example of the continuation of this process.[88] For Fontánez-Torres, what is distinctive of el Caño is the governance structure developed in light of the socialization of property itself, challenging the priority of economic interests over common well-being.[89] The project represents the rearticulation of social power through the subversion of ownership itself.

Muñiz-Varela deepens this analysis, arguing that el Caño represents a mode of "interruption" through the subversion of private property.[90] Such interruption, she suggests, makes possible the articulation of life beyond the aims of what I have called neoliberal coloniality. Like Fontánez-Torres, Muñiz-Varela maintains that the community rescues the common by rescuing the commons. The demand to dredge the canal becomes a site of historical reckoning. It targets the abandonment of the state coeval with the advance of economic interests. It does so by focusing on the environmental and health effects of a polluted waterway left unaddressed given the

C.3 Caño Martín Peña. Photo from Para la Naturaleza, originally from *El Nuevo día*, May 13, 2018.

affected population. Yet the demand also becomes a site of forms of social binding within the community around human needs and environmental degradation. These demands sustain practices of binding anew. In an interview with Miguel Rodríguez-Casellas and Juan Carlos Rivera-Ramos, Muñiz-Varela makes an even stronger case.[91] Through the corporation and the land trust, these communities resist movement itself. They interrupt displacement, dispossession. "In the midst of ruins," she says, "they are still standing, feet on the ground."[92] They have refused the "fate" of expulsion by subverting its very means: law, finance. They do not seek a return to something that is proper, reifying private property. Rather, she argues, el Caño is "generating infrastructure for what is to come."[93]

Praxes of taking back have multiplied in the context of the debt crisis, PROMESA, in the immediate aftermath of María, within hurricane recovery, and in the context of the #RickyRenuncia protests. Variations of autogestión are important in this context. Autogestión, one might say, seeks to build power at a distance from the state. In general, autogestión cannot be reduced to one tradition of thought or practice. Some reference the significance of anti-capitalist anarchist views of solidarity, horizontality, and participation, while others see taking as forms of fugitive freedom grounded in *cimarronaje*.[94] These are complex practices, since autogestión may fill the state's lacunae without interrupting its necropolitical operation, without

CONCLUSION

thematizing its subversive complicity with the neoliberal affirmation of the self as enterprise, without addressing the risk of reproducing race/gender/class hierarchies given the current economic juncture. Nevertheless, they have the potential to turn coloniality inoperative. Key here is the implicit or explicit confrontation with the state.

Yarimar Bonilla underscores that, already before María, numerous collapsed institutions had been "taken" by communities through Mutual Aid Centers (Centros de Apoyo Mutuo, CAM), neighborhood organizations, community kitchens, community schools, childcare centers, art galleries, and radio stations.[95] These are, as Bonilla puts it, the "silent coup" (*toma silenciosa de poder*) of autogestión. These *tomas de poder* multiply, are strengthened, and gain visibility in the aftermath of María. Given federal and local government inefficiency and corruption, communities organized around such basic needs as food, water, and energy. In the face of Puerto Rico's dependence on imports, given the food shortages in the immediate aftermath of María, praxes that seek to develop food sovereignty deepened long-standing subsistence farming and community kitchens.[96] Many homes remained without running water for months, making visible those who have lacked running water for decades and who thus already have generated alternative infrastructures to meet their needs.[97] Given the collapse of the electrical grid, energy sovereignty was consolidated as a key site of alternative infrastructures as well.

Puerto Rico's environmental justice movement is an important reference point.[98] The expulsion of the US Navy from Vieques in 2001 is a crucial success despite the challenges Vieques faces today.[99] A successful coalition buttressed a decades-long battle against the US Navy in the island-municipality of Vieques. Pollution left behind by la Marina, impoverishment, and forms of capture through real estate and tourist development discussed in previous chapters are among today's challenges. Most recently, the fight against toxic coal ash deposits in Tallaboa, Peñuelas, a predominantly black working-class community, has been central. These efforts have been headed by the women of Tallaboa. As they note, water, land, and air contamination are the continuing legacy of corporations that, since the mid and late twentieth century, took advantage of tax exemptions. Not only profits escaped.[100] A cycle of pollution and waste continues to impact communities racialized as nonwhite, especially black communities, in the territory disproportionately, as in the dumping of toxic coal ash produced by the AES corporation.[101]

Casa Pueblo in the town of Adjuntas is an example of efforts to build infrastructures for energy sovereignty. Its work has gained significance in the context of the hurricane and hurricane recovery. Casa Pueblo was at the forefront of the fight against the Gasoducto, a gas pipeline that would run the northern coast and cross from north to south through the Central Cordillera.[102] This project was developed in the energy crisis of 2010, declared by then-governor Luis Fortuño, as we saw in chapter 2. In 1996, Casa Pueblo proposed that the government designate an area as protected forest. As Gustavo García-López, Irina Velicu, and Giacomo D'Alisa explain, Casa Pueblo was thereby able to manage this area's conservation through forms of political horizontalism.[103] This made possible rearticulating modes of being in common, resignifying ways of conceiving anti-colonial praxis (redefining conceptions of "nationhood," for example) and sovereignty in reference to land and energy. Interrupting the interest of the state/capital in this case has been inseparable from ecological rearticulation of land in the hands of "the people." In the context of María and post-María, Casa Pueblo launched what they call an "energy insurrection," moving from renewable energy in many homes in this mountain range town to the entire town center.[104]

The emergence of *asambleas de pueblo*, town assemblies, in the context of #RickyRenuncia can be seen as an instance of autogestión.[105] The first asamblea was held in Ponce in mid-July.[106] By August 16, twenty-eight assemblies had convened.[107] Las asambleas sought direct participation in the construction of proposals, moving political organizing away from the government and the party.[108] They drew from the experience of the protests and the empowerment of their success in removing Rosselló but affirmed generating proposals rather than ongoing opposition. The asambleas addressed the elimination of the Fiscal Control Board, auditing the debt and government administration, declaring a state of emergency regarding gender violence, articulating a process of decolonization, and generating structures of sustainability. As Joselyn Vazquez reports, people time and again raised questions concerning "Who is owner of our lands, our beaches, forests, our homes," "Who takes away my home, who forces me to leave the country."[109] As Bonilla notes, recall, "assemblies are not imagined as [an] event but as communities. . . . They are emerging as new political constituencies."[110] Although it remains to be seen whether the asambleas will impact local governance, they aimed to build power in common by taking back political articulation.

Rather than stress the rearticulation of social power through governance structures, I want to highlight modalities of autogestión through taking back land. These modes of unbinding and binding life anew are a distinctively material praxis that specifically challenge private property. Some take back closed schools and abandoned infrastructure to meet the needs of a community.[111] Others occupy abandoned private property in urban spaces, some declared public nuisance while others are part of abandoned buildings that compose city blocks. Moscoso's work is key here. She explains that Puerto Rico is currently undergoing a new wave of land rescue/occupation.[112] We have seen some aspects of the first wave, which occurred throughout the early twentieth century, with the discussion of el Caño. We have seen some aspects of the second wave, which occurred in the second part of the twentieth century, with the discussion of land rescue/invasion. The third round of rescue/occupation responds to the current state of the territory as a "taken island" through the axiomatic of property in the mortgage and the apparatus of the capture of life through debt, to recall Muñiz-Varela's recent work discussed in chapter 2.

This third wave, Moscoso notes, has two general characteristics. First, it is "eminently urban," taking back urban space, claiming access to the city. Referencing the tradition of land rescue, Moscoso writes that "rather than *desalambrar*, the slogan could be *desbloquear*."[113] *Desalambrar* is to undo the wire that marks territory in mostly rural and coastal areas. *Desbloquear*, in contrast, is to remove concrete blocks that mark private property in urban spaces that have been declared a public nuisance.[114] This new round of land rescue/occupation, she explains, is not occurring at the periphery, but in the very center of an "unattended and decimated city." Recent occupations happen in "privately owned properties that remained abandoned in several of the most densely urbanized parts of the metropolitan area (such as Puerta de Tierra, Santurce, and Río Piedras) and traditional urban centers (Centros Urbanos Tradicionales, CUT) of some municipalities such as Caguas and Mayagüez."[115]

Second, the socioeconomic status and motivation of rescuers can be said to have been altered.[116] Rescuers/occupiers, Moscoso writes, "occupy in order to occupy themselves."[117] "Middle-class (including even upper-middle class)" individuals with "academic backgrounds" have become significant in this context. The need here is to generate occupation, livelihood, work. "[T]he desire to access a physical space," she continues, "has to do with the need to have a minimally adequate place to develop a professional, formative, productive activity, among others. Hence the willingness to invest long hours and physical effort in enabling an abandoned space (clean it, paint it, repair it, rebuild it, etc.)."[118] This is a complex phenomenon, then. It is a site of resistance to precarization and gentrification, to the operation of the axiomatic of property and the forms of expulsion it necessitates. But it also requires attention to its potential to update or shore up a race/class hierarchy, given immigrant communities, Dominican and Haitian, and impoverished communities that have practiced land occupation in urban centers for decades.

Moscoso notes that recent rescues/occupations of abandoned public property, such as schools closed in the context of austerity measures, may represent a fourth wave of occupations. She writes that "this is a much more recent phenomenon that, with hurricane María and given the speed (if not voracity) of the process of dispossession being executed, could be framed as another phase of occupation."[119] An example here is CAM (Centro de Apoyo Mutuo) Las Carolinas, which began as a community kitchen in the wake of María.[120] CAM Las Carolinas requested that the property title of the occupied abandoned school be transferred to the organization.[121] In both cases, rescuers/occupiers are responding to the "need for subsistence of some sectors of the population against a state that by action or inaction seems to forget that people live on this island." Rescue/occupation is a response to a necropolitical state, not merely an absent state. Moreover, in both cases, it seeks to bind life anew in building the common by meeting needs.

Moscoso discusses three cases of land rescue/occupation: ¡Aquí Vive Gente!, Casa Taft 169, and Urbe Apié. ¡Aquí Vive Gente! (People Live Here!) is the slogan adopted by residents of Puerta de Tierra, who occupied an abandoned lot that became the Puerta de Tierra Information Brigade Station. The station became a space for organizing against the construction of a boardwalk, which "redesigned, in keeping with the latest trends in international urban fashion, a section of the road that goes from (the also questionable) Paseo Caribe to (the no-less-questionable) 'house of laws' or Capitol." This is an attempt to "hyperurbanize" this section of San Juan with a bike path, commercial space, and art installations overlooking the caribbeanized Atlantic. This project turned the northern part of Puerta de Tierra visible, integrating it with the Capitol and Old San Juan, while deepening the "invisibility, insecurity, and contamination" of the southern part of the neighborhood. This community is still "active" in "a small space recovered from abandonment," Moscoso writes, "where the only bus stop, in the entire sector, designed with people in mind was installed, where people garden and where open-air cinema is free, among many other things."

Casa Taft 169, of which Moscoso is cofounder and project coordinator, began its work in 2013 by rescuing an abandoned property declared as public nuisance in the Machuchal sector of San Mateo de Cangrejos or, as it is known today, Santurce.[122] They were "under the wrong premise that the government, forced to protect the common good, would have some legal tool that a neighborhood organization could use to take charge of [property], transforming into a civic center/'off-the-grid'/*autogestionado*." The project targeted the state's management of properties declared a public nuisance through the campaign *Todos Somos Herederos* (We Are All Heirs). The result was Act 157 of 2016, which amended the inheritance chapter of Puerto Rico's 1930 Civil Code. The amendment allows the state to appropriate abandoned and nuisance properties without living owners or heirs. The state would assign, donate, sell, and rent these properties to community organizations like Casa Taft.[123] Fundamentally distinct from processes of expropriation or eviction, the amendment aimed to potentiate autogestión ("potenciar nuestras capacidades de autogestión") in the transformation of forgotten spaces by and for the community.

Urbe Apié is a community organization founded in 2015 in Caguas. Founded by and composed of members of the community, it has sought to restore social, cultural, and economic activity, specifically in Paseo Gautier Benítez. This city center contained over twenty abandoned buildings in addition to plazas, promenades, and streets. Urbe Apié rescued/occupied these spaces to generate cultural development that would in turn be the basis for economic development by and for the people living in the city of Caguas. The idea, they say, is to "work through the satisfaction of needs rather than work for the satisfaction of needs."[124] Through production of food, clothes, structures of support, such as childcare, but also art and queer performance spaces, they generate "support dynamics that do not exist in Puerto Rico today." In the context of María and hurricane recovery, these structures of support were able to mitigate the impact of the hurricane and the government's necropolitical management in its aftermath.

The possibilities in land rescue/occupation are significant, Moscoso highlights. "If we take into account that the inventory of properties that were partially or totally affected by Irma and María ranges from 250,000 to 270,000," Moscoso writes, "while, on the other hand, the 2015 census estimates at 326,435 'vacant' housing units, one might think that there is an extraordinary opportunity to rethink the problem of housing and land use in Puerto Rico." She adds, "it may be rash to say that this could happen in the near future, but the interest of forming a 'national network of recovered spaces' currently on the table could support the wider development of a recovery movement." *Ni gente sin casa, ni casa sin gente*, "Neither people

C.4 Huerto Feliz, Urbe Apié. Caguas, Puerto Rico. Photo from urbeapie.com, August 27, 2020.

without homes nor homes without people," one can read on the streets of Puerto Rico. Taking back land becomes a form of interrupting the work of coloniality, unbinding the strictures of the no-place of life in the indebted colony. It has the potential to bind anew by reconfiguring the social reproduction of life itself. *Todos somos herederos*, we are all heirs, then. I began this book with a poem by Raquel Salas Rivera precisely on this point. Debt functions as an apparatus of capture, as a form of coloniality, turning everything and everyone into an heir: something with which to pay back the debt of capital. In the hands of the rescuers/occupiers, that is precisely the point. We are the heirs, taking back what is owed.

ORGANIZING PESSIMISM

Despite the possibilities that land rescue/occupation and other modalities of taking back represent, I want to close with a reflection on pessimism.[125] Pessimism responds to the systemic nature of coloniality and thus the challenges of local intervention, interruption, turning inoperative. Pessimism, in other words, recognizes the challenges that decoloniality, as a project of invention that requires disorder, entails. Walter Benjamin's rejection of progress and affirmation of hope through an exploration of pessimism is helpful in this context. Key here, however, is not the affect of the pessimist. Rather, it is the turn away from images that capture, hence neutralize, decoloniality as a material praxis.[126]

In a critical encounter with surrealism in 1929, Benjamin distinguishes between the optimism of social-democratic progressivism and the "organization of pessimism" found in Pierre Naville's surrealism. The *gradus ad parnassum* of bourgeois resistance is optimism. It "promises" a future society in which "all act 'as if they were angels' and everyone has as much 'as if he were rich' and everyone lives 'as if he were free.'"[127] In contrast, Naville makes the organization of pessimism "the call of the hour." To organize pessimism, Benjamin suggests, is to "expel moral metaphor from politics." It is to "discover" the space of political action as "the one hundred percent image space."[128]

To organize pessimism is to labor from the concrete conditions that compose actuality. It is to bet on what is possible from the actual. The opposite of pessimism is not optimism, Rafael Bernabe wagers in a piece drawing from Benjamin on Naville.[129] It is hope. Optimism, like utopia, draws from abstraction. It bets lacking ground. It lacks not a reason (*Grund*), but contact with conditions here and now. It is therefore naïve. Pessimism, in contrast, draws from *catastrophe*. It knows that detritus left by a downturn— κατά (down) στροφή (turning)—are tasks.[130] To organize, to articulate, to establish complicities guided by such tasks is hopeful. Pessimism excises moral and political metaphors that turn us away from the tasks at hand. It clears the political space for the construction of new images that respond to the downturn that composes actuality. It orients responses to the specific dangers that the present exhibits.

Hay que organizar el pesimismo—we must organize pessimism. In quoting Benjamin quoting Naville, Bernabe seeks to distill the element of hope found in Benjamin's rejection of optimism. When there are few bases for optimism, "Hope can be nourished by pessimism." Bernabe ends his piece with a call "against decomposition." He recalls Lenin's observation that what is necessary is not always possible. Conditions might be ripe for change, yet political struggles might not be articulated in light of them. In such cases, pessimism can lead to decomposition, perhaps even "putrefaction." Precisely because decomposition is a real possibility, the organization of pessimism is the call of the hour. To seize the power to bind the world anew is to address the danger felt here and now. It is to turn the present that is the past into the past. This is not dialectical response to conditions at hand, but turning their strictures inoperative.

When Naville made the organization of pessimism the call of the hour, he aimed to affirm the clearing of the space of political action from moral images that capture political imagination. An affirmation of pessimism is a clearing of the image posited by capital/coloniality. In "On the Concept of History," Benjamin famously argues that "to articulate what is past does not mean to recognize 'how it really was.' It means to take control of a memory, as it flashes in a moment of danger."[131] To seize the power to bind, forgoing forgiveness, reconciliation, letting go until these are more than metaphors, is perhaps the most hopeful act in a moment of danger. This is not a moment of decision, or a mere critical stance, or a mode of thinking and witnessing that lacks action. It is a material praxis of undoing the productivity of the downturn itself, clearing the space to bind life anew.[132]

NOTES

INTRODUCTION

For the epigraph, see Raquel Salas Rivera, "coats are not exchanged for coats," *lo terciario/the tertiary* (Oakland, CA: Infinite Light, 2018), 20–21. A Spanish version of the poem is in this bilingual edition.

1 Sandra Rodríguez Cotto, an independent investigative journalist, released eleven pages of the thread on July 8. I discuss the protests in chap. 4.

2 See, e.g., Cristina P. Díaz, Jorge Lefevre, and Claudia Becerra, ed., *No. Impromptu: The Puerto Rico Review*, July 2019, http://www.thepuertoricoreview.com /rickyrenuncia.

3 See Kilómetro Cero's report: https://www.kilometroo.org/blog-desde-cero, and Rima Brusi, "Why Puerto Rico's Cops Ignore the Constitution at Night," *The Nation*, July 30, 2019, https://www.thenation.com/article/puerto-rico-police-abuse/.

4 Throughout, I use the gender inclusive "x" in Spanish, a practice ubiquitous among the queer community in Puerto Rico.

5   See Yarimar Bonilla's discussion of prefigurative politics in *Non-Sovereign Futures: French Caribbean Politics in the Wake of Disenchantment* (Chicago: University of Chicago Press, 2015).

6   See Yarimar Bonilla's post on Facebook: https://www.facebook.com/photo.php ?fbid=10156683956480888&set=pcb.10156683956550888&type=3&theater.

7   Yarimar Bonilla, "Puerto Rican Politics Will Never Be the Same," *Jacobin*, August 2, 2019, https://www.jacobinmag.com/2019/08/puerto-rico-ricardo -rossello-governor-unrest. On autogestión, see Adriana Garriga-López, "Puerto Rico: The Future in Question," *Shima* 13, no. 2 (2019). See also Beatriz Llenín-Figueroa, "The Maroons Are Deathless, We Are Deathless," *Radical History Review*, https://www.radicalhistoryreview.org/abusablepast/?p=3145.

8   As a Category 5 Hurricane, María devastated Dominica, making landfall as a Category 4 in Puerto Rico as a result.

9   Arelis R. Hernández and Brady Dennis, "Desperate Puerto Ricans Line Up for Water—At a Hazardous-Waste Site," *The Washington Post*, October 16, 2017, https://www.washingtonpost.com/news/energy-environment/wp/2017/10/16 /desperate-puerto-ricans-line-up-for-water-at-a-hazardous-waste-site/. See also Adriana Garriga-López, "Agua Dulce," in *Liquid Utility, e-flux architecture* 103 (2019).

10 See Leysa Caro González, "Más vulnerables las mujeres tras el paso de María," *El Nuevo día,* July 10, 2018, https://www.elnuevodia.com/noticias/locales/nota/ masvulnerableslasmujerestraselpasodemaria-2434047/.

11 See Víctor Rodríguez Velázquez, "Personas trans sufren el desastre de María desde la marginalización," *Centro de Periodismo Investigativo*, September 23, 2019, http://periodismoinvestigativo.com/2019/09/personas-trans-sufren-el -desastre-de-maria-desde-la-marginacion/.

12 Mara Pastor, "Ven la luz al final del camino," *Metro Puerto Rico*, August 15, 2018, https://www.metro.pr/pr/noticias/2018/08/15/ven-la-luz-al-final-del-camino .html.

13 See Ayuda Legal Puerto Rico: https://www.ayudalegalpuertorico.org/nuestros -proyectos/derecho-a-tu-casa/. See also, e.g., Wilma Maldonado Arrigoitía, "Las Comunidades están alertas ante los posibles intentos de expropiación," *El Nuevo día*, August 14, 2018, https://www.elnuevodia.com/noticias/locales/nota /lascomunidadesestanalertasantelosposiblesintentosdeexpropiacion-2441110/.

14 The Jones Act of 1920 restricts maritime commerce in US waters and between US ports by establishing that goods transported between these must be carried on ships built, flagged, and crewed by the United States. See chap. 2 for a discussion of the act.

15 In January 2020 a swarm of earthquakes with epicenters in the southwest of Puerto Rico disclosed the continuation of a necropolitical state: a crumbling infrastructure, failed distribution of aid and adequate shelter for children and the elderly, failure to inspect schools that would serve as shelters or house children on their return from the holidays. On January 18, 2020, citizens stormed a

warehouse in the southern town of Ponce found to be full of unused emergency supplies, some dating to the period just after Hurricane María. Thirteen such warehouses were identified and placed under government surveillance. See my dispatch for *Critical Times*, "Checklists: On Puerto Rico's SoVerano" 3, no. 2 (2020).

16 See Omaya Sosa Pascual, Ana Campoy, and Michael Weissenstein, "Los Muertos de María," *Centro de Periodismo Investigativo*, http://periodismoinvestigativo.com/2018/09/los-muertos-de-maria/.

17 Omaya Sosa Pascual and John Sutter, "Puerto Rico tuvo un brote de leptospirosis tras el Huracán María pero el gobierno no lo dice," *Centro de Periodismo Investigativo*, July 3, 2018, http://periodismoinvestigativo.com/2018/07/puerto-rico-tuvo-un-brote-de-leptospirosis-tras-el-huracan-maria-pero-el-gobierno-no-lo-dice/.

18 See Center for Puerto Rican Studies, Hunter College, March 2018: https://centropr.hunter.cuny.edu/sites/default/files/data_sheets/PostMaria-NewEstimates-3–15–18.pdf. That is, 4 percent of the population relocated. In October 2019, José Caraballo Cueto, director of the Centro de Información Censal, indicated that in 2018 149,000 people left the territory, representing 4.3 percent of the population. See "La Emigración registrada en 2018 en la isla fue la más alta desde 2006," *El Nuevo día*, October 4, 2019, https://www.elnuevodia.com/noticias/locales/nota/laemigracionregistradaen2018enlaislafu elamasaltadesde2006–2521683/.

19 See Yarimar Bonilla, "For Investors, Puerto Rico Is a Fantasy Blank Slate," *The Nation*, February 28, 2018, https://www.thenation.com/article/for-investors-puerto-rico-is-a-fantasy-blank-slate/.

20 See also Katy Steinmetz, "Governor Ricardo Rosselló: Puerto Rico Is a 'Geopolitical Black Hole,'" *Time*, May 9, 2018, //time.com/5271767/puerto-rico-governor-donald-trump-statehood-hurricane-maria/.

21 I am following Bonilla, "For Investors, Puerto Rico Is a Fantasy Blank Slate."

22 See chap. 2, where I discuss the political economy of Puerto Rico.

23 See Bonilla, "For Investors, Puerto Rico Is a Fantasy Blank Slate."

24 For an analysis of Hurricane María as exemplary of disaster capitalism, see Naomi Klein, *The Battle for Paradise: Puerto Rico Takes on the Disaster Capitalists* (Chicago: Haymarket Books, 2018), and *Aftershocks of Disaster: Puerto Rico before and after the Storm*, ed. Yarimar Bonilla and Marisol LeBrón (Chicago: Haymarket Books, 2019). See also Hilda Lloréns, "The Race of Disaster: Black Communities and the Crisis in Puerto Rico," *Black Perspectives*, April 17, 2019, https://www.aaihs.org/the-race-of-disaster-black-communities-and-the-crisis-in-puerto-rico/.

25 See Aníbal Quijano, "Colonialidad del poder y clasificación social," in *Festschrift for Immanuel Wallerstein, Journal of World Systems Research* 6, no. 2 (2000); all translations are my own. A general presentation of decolonial thought can be found in Nelson Maldonado-Torres, "The Decolonial Turn," in *New Approaches*

to *Latin American Studies: Culture and Power,* ed. Juan Poblete (London: Routledge, 2018). See also Santiago Castro Gómez and Ramón Grosfoguel, eds., *El Giro decolonial: Reflexiones para una diversidad epistémica más allá del capitalismo global* (Bogotá, Colombia: Siglo del Hombre Editores, 2007). For a general overview of decolonial feminism, see Breny Mendoza, "The Coloniality of Gender and Power: From Postcoloniality to Decoloniality," in *The Oxford Handbook of Feminist Theory,* ed. Lisa Disch and Mary Hawkesworth (Oxford: Oxford University Press, 2016). See especially Yuderkys Espinosa Miñoso and Karina Ochoa, eds., *Tejiendo de otro modo: Feminismo, epistemología y apuestas descoloniales en Abya Yala* (Bogotá: Editorial Universidad del Cauca, 2014); and Yuderkys Espinosa Miñoso, ed., *Feminismo descolonial: Nuevos aportes teóricos-metodológicos a más de una década* (Quito, Ecuador: Ediciones Abya-Yala, 2018).

26 See Saidiya Hartman, *Lose Your Mother: A Journey along the Atlantic Slave Route* (New York: Farrar, Straus and Giroux, 2017), and *Scenes of Subjection: Terror, Slavery, and Self-Making in Nineteenth Century America* (Oxford: Oxford University Press, 1994). See also Christina Sharpe, *In the Wake: On Blackness and Being* (Durham, NC: Duke University Press, 2016).

27 Ariadna Godreau-Aubert, *Las Propias: Apuntes para una pedagogía de las endeudadas* (Cabo Rojo, PR: Editora Educación Emergente, 2018), 68; all translations are my own.

28 See H.R. 5278, 114th Congress (2015–16).

29 See, e.g., Anthony Phillips, "Haiti, France, and the Independence Debt of 1825," Institute for Justice and Democracy in Haiti (2008); Simon Henochsberg, "Public Debt and Slavery: The Case of Haiti (1760–1915)" (PhD diss., Paris School of Economics, 2016); C. L. R. James, *The Black Jacobins: Toussaint L'Ouverture and the San Domingo Revolution* (New York: Random House, 1989); and Jérôme Duval, "Haiti: de la Colonización francesa a la esclavitud económica de la deuda," Comité para la Abolición de las Deudas Ilegítimas (CADTM), 26 de Septiembre de 2017, http://www.cadtm.org/Haiti-de-la-colonizacion-francesa. See my discussion in chap. 3.

30 Cf. Sandro Mezzadra and Bret Neilson, *The Politics of Operation: Excavating Contemporary Capitalism* (Durham, NC: Duke University Press, 2019). See Verónica Gago, *Neoliberalism from Below: Popular Pragmatics and Baroque Economies,* trans. Liz Mason-Deese (Durham, NC: Duke University Press, 2017).

31 For my use of "reproduction of life," see Tithi Battacharya, "How Not to Skip Class: The Social Reproduction of Labor and the Global Working Class," in *Social Reproduction Theory: Remapping Class, Recentering Oppression,* ed. Tithi Battacharya (New York: Pluto Press, 2017).

32 For a full account of my view of interruption with reference to Walter Benjamin, see my "Pasarse *Políticamente*—Interrupting Neoliberal Temporalities in Puerto Rico," *Collective Temporalities and the Construction of the Future,*

ed. María del Rosario Acosta and Gustavo Quintero, *Diacritics* 46, no. 2 (2018).

33 Frantz Fanon, *The Wretched of the Earth*, trans. Richard Philcox (New York: Grove Press, 1963), 2.

34 At various junctures in this book, I use and explore the language of "occupation" used and explored by those whose work I am engaging. I thematize the complexities of the language of occupation in the conclusion, when I examine land "rescue"/"occupation." There I work with Eve Tuck and K. Wayne Yang's "Decolonization Is Not a Metaphor," *Decolonization: Indigeneity, Education and Society* 1, no. 1 (2012). On the language of "occupy," see also Adam J. Barker, "Already Occupied: Indigenous Peoples, Settler Colonialism and the Occupy Movements in North America," *Social Movements Studies* 11 (2012).

35 Hartman, *Lose Your Mother*, 6.

36 Saidiya Hartman, "Venus in Two Acts," *Small Axe: A Caribbean Journal of Criticism* 26, no. 12/2 (2008), 13.

37 See especially Isar P. Godreau, *Scripts of Blackness: Race, Cultural Nationalism, and US Colonialism in Puerto Rico* (Urbana: University of Illinois Press, 2015); Ileana Rodriguez-Silva, *Silencing Race: Disentangling Blackness, Colonialism and National Identities in Puerto Rico* (London: Palgrave, 2012); and Hilda Lloréns, *Imaging the Great Puerto Rican Family: Framing Nation, Race, and Gender during the American Century* (Lanham, MD: Rowman and Littlefield, 2018).

38 See María Lugones, "Toward a Decolonial Feminism," *Hypatia* 25, no. 4 (2010).

39 Nelson Maldonado-Torres, "Outline of Ten Theses on Coloniality and Decoloniality," Foundation Frantz Fanon (2016) 11, https://fondation-frantzfanon.com /outline-of-ten-theses-on-coloniality-and-decoloniality/.

40 See Bonilla, *Non-Sovereign Futures*, for a discussion of the subversions of sovereignty. Relevant here as well is the politics of *jaibería*, which sought to subvert the colonial predicament in the 1990s, albeit by affirming statehood. See, e.g., Ramón Grosfoguel and Frances Negrón-Muntaner, eds. *Puerto Rican Jam: Essays on Culture and Politics* (Minneapolis: University of Minnesota Press, 1997); and Frances Negrón-Muntaner, ed., *None of the Above: Puerto Ricans in the Global Era* (New York: Palgrave, 2007). Cf. my "Boundary, Ambivalence, *Jaibería*, or, How to Appropriate Hegel," *Creolizing the Canon*, ed. Michael Monahan (Lanham, MD: Rowman and Littlefield, 2017).

41 This is la Colectiva's self-description. See https://www.facebook.com/Colectiva .Feminista.PR/. See their two core manifestos: *La Manifiesta*, 2017, https:// www.scribd.com/document/263057948/La-Manifiesta-Colectiva-Feminista -en-Construccion, and *Manifiesto Antirracista*, June 2, 2020, https://www .facebook.com/notes/colectiva-feminista-en-construcci%C3%B3n/manifiesto -antirracista-colectiva-feminista-en-construcci%C3%B3n/2968317379926640. In English, see *The Anti-Racist Manifesto*, in *Latino Rebels*, June 7, 2020, https:// www.latinorebels.com/2020/06/07/antiracistmanifesto/. See also my "Black

Feminist Tactics: On la Colectiva Feminista en Construcción's Politics without Guarantee," in *The Decolonial Geographies of Puerto Rico's 2019 Summer Protests: A Forum for Society and Space*, ed. Marisol LeBrón and Joaquín Villanueva (February 2020), where I discuss la Colectiva's black feminist, decolonial methodology and the actions through which it is developed at length.

42 Most recently, she works with "cuir" rather than "queer," especially with reference to Sayak Valencia's work. See Rodríguez-Centeno's "Antiproductivismo y (trans)feminismo en tiempos de trap y capitalismo gore: El Caso de Puerto Rico" (unpublished ms.); and Valencia's *Gore Capitalism*, trans. John Pluecker (Cambridge, MA: Semiotext(e), 2018).

CHAPTER ONE. NEOLIBERAL COLONIALITY

1 Ariadna Godreau-Aubert, "Aviso," in *Las Propias: Apuntes para una pedagogía de las endeudadas* (Cabo Rojo, PR: Editora Educación Emergente, 2018), 15; all translations are my own. The Spanish reads: "'Estar en deuda' es un estado material, politico, económico, social, afectivo. Significa tener y, al mismo tiempo, saberse desposeído de algo. Por lo mismo, deber es estar—temporal o permanentemente—en ninguna parte."

2 Godreau-Aubert, *Las Propias*, 67.

3 Godreau-Aubert, *Las Propias*, 15: "[I]nsistiré en la distancia entre prometer (deberse) y deber." See chapter 3.

4 A translation of "Nosotras que no nos debemos a nadie: Las Propias en tiempos de austeridad y deuda pública" as "We Women Who Don't Owe Anyone: Las Propias in Times of Austerity and Debt" by Tara Phillips is forthcoming in "On Debt, Blame, and Responsibility: Feminist Resistance in the Colony of Puerto Rico," ed. Rocío Zambrana, special section of *Critical Times*. All translations in this book, as noted above, are my own.

5 Godreau-Aubert, *Las Propias*, 68: "La colonia es lo que transcurre en 'repetidos actos de captura.'" Godreau-Aubert is quoting Ann Stoler, who writes: "A 'colony' criminalizes dissidence, disassembles and punishes those who refuse its terms, and suppresses contestatory and participatory politics. It produces and identifies enemies within and outside, eagerly invests in the hunt for those targeted as a threat, anxiously celebrates the ever false and short-lived security that follows the repeated rites of capture" (*Duress: Imperial Durabilities in Our Times* [Durham, NC: Duke University Press, 2016], 76).

6 Godreau-Aubert, *Las Propias*, 67.

7 Maurizio Lazzarato, "Neoliberalism, the Financial Crisis and the End of the Liberal State," *Theory, Culture and Society* 32, nos. 7–8 (2015): 67–68. He continues: "These subjective novelties reveal more clearly, and at a more fundamental level, the true nature of techniques of governmentality and of the relation between liberalism and capital than in the period when neoliberalism was emergent." See also Lazzarato, *Governing by Debt*, trans. Joshua

David Jordan (Cambridge, MA: MIT Press, 2015), 91, and *The Making of the Indebted Man*, trans. Joshua David Jordan (Cambridge, MA: MIT Press, 2012).

8 I discuss David Graeber's *Debt: The First 5,000 Years* (Brooklyn, NY: Melville House, 2011); Janet Roitman's *Fiscal Disobedience: An Anthropology of Fiscal Regulation in Central Africa* (Princeton, NJ: Princeton University Press, 2004); Richard Dienst, *The Bonds of Debt* (London: Verso, 2011); Fred Moten and Stefano Harney, *The Undercommons: Fugitive Planning and Black Study* (Wivenhoe, UK: Minor Compositions, 2013); and Saidiya Hartman, *Scenes of Subjection: Terror, Slavery, and Self-Making in Nineteenth Century America* (Oxford: Oxford University Press, 1994) in chapters that follow. In addition to the texts discussed below, see also, e.g., George Caffentzis, *Los Límites del capital: Deuda, moneda, y lucha de clases* (Buenos Aires: Fundación Rosa Luxemburgo and Tinta Limón, 2018); Susan Soederberg, *Debtfare States and the Poverty Industry* (London: Routledge, 2014); Éric Tousissant and Damien Millet, *Debt, The IMF, and the World Bank* (New York: Monthly Review Press, 2012); Miranda Joseph, *Debt to Society: Accounting for Life under Capitalism* (Minneapolis: Minnesota University Press, 2014); Étienne Balibar, "The Politics of Debt," *Postmodern Culture* 23, no. 2 (2013).

9 Specifically concerning the creation of tax havens in the Caribbean, see, e.g., Peter James Hudson, *Bankers and Empire: How Wall Street Colonized the Caribbean* (Chicago: University of Chicago Press, 2018); Tami Navarro, "'Offshore' Banking within the Nation: Economic Development in the United States Virgin Islands," *Global South* 4, no. 2 (2010). See also Clive Y. Thomas, *The Poor and the Powerless: Economic Policy and Change in the Caribbean* (London: Latin America Bureau, 1988). I discuss taxation in chapter 2.

10 See, especially, Aníbal Quijano, "Colonialidad del Poder y Clasificación Social," in *Festschrift for Immanuel Wallerstein, Journal of World Systems Research* 6, no. 2 (2000); all translations are my own.

11 Cf. Isabell Lorey, *State of Insecurity: Government of the Precarious* (London: Verso, 2015). For Lorey, "precarity" designates "the striation and distribution of precariousness in relations of inequality, the hierarchization of being with that accompanies the processes of othering." Her distinction develops further Judith Butler's conception of precariousness in *Frames of War* (London: Verso, 2009) and *Precarious Life* (London: Verso, 2004).

12 See, especially, Miriam Muñiz-Varela, "La Deuda: Axiomática de la propiedad y aparato de captura de la vida," in *Violencia y Deuda*, ed. Madeline Román, *Cruce*, November 11, 2019, https://issuu.com/revistacruce/docs/violencia_y _deuda_7_nov_2019; and "Taken Island" (unpublished ms.). I discuss Muñiz-Varela on this score extensively in chapter 2.

13 Nelson Maldonado-Torres, "The Coloniality of Being: Contributions to the De-velopment of a Concept," *Cultural Studies* 21, nos. 2–3 (2007), and "Outline of Ten Theses on Coloniality and Decoloniality," Foundation Frantz Fanon (2016),

https://fondation-frantzfanon.com/outline-of-ten-theses-on-coloniality-and
-decoloniality/.

14 Godreau-Aubert, *Las Propias*, 65.

15 Verónica Gago and Luci Cavallero, *Una Lectura feminista de la deuda* (Buenos Aires: Tinta Limón, 2019), 13; all translations are my own.

16 See chap. 2 for a discussion of necropolitical effects in relation to racialized masculinity, specifically black men and men racialized as nonwhite.

17 Accounts of neoliberalism are vast. In addition to Lazzarato, accounts that orient my reading include Miriam Muñiz-Varela, *Adiós a la economía* (San Juan: Ediciones Callejón, 2013); Verónica Gago, *Neoliberalism from Below: Popular Pragmatics and Baroque Economies*, trans. Liz Mason-Deese (Durham, NC: Duke University Press, 2017); David Harvey, *The New Imperialism* (Oxford: Oxford University Press, 2005); Sandro Mezzadra and Brett Neilson, *The Politics of Operations: Excavating Contemporary Capitalism* (Durham, NC: Duke University Press, 2019); Nancy Fraser, "Behind Marx's Hidden Abode," *New Left Review* 86 (2014); "Expropriation and Exploitation in Racialized Capitalism: A Reply to Michael Dawson," *Critical Historical Studies* 3, no. 1 (2016); "Legitimation Crisis," *Critical Historical Studies* 2, no. 2 (2015); Wendy Brown, *Undoing the Demos: Neoliberalism's Stealth Revolution* (Cambridge, MA: MIT Press, 2015); Melinda Cooper, *Family Values: Between Neoliberalism and the New Social Conservativism* (New York: Zone Books, 2017); Anita Chari, *A Political Economy of the Senses: Neoliberalism, Reification, Critique* (New York: Columbia University Press, 2015); Jean and John Comaroff, eds., *Millennial Capitalism and the Culture of Neoliberalism* (Durham, NC: Duke University Press, 2001); Pierre Dardot and Christian Laval, *The New Way of the World: On Neoliberal Society*, trans. Gregory Elliott (London: Verso, 2013), among others.

18 See Lazzarato, "Neoliberalism, the Financial Crisis and the End of the Liberal State."

19 Maurizio Lazzarato, "Debt, Neoliberalism and Crisis: Interview with Maurizio Lazzarato on the Indebted Condition," *Sociology* 48, no. 5 (2004), 1046. Cf. Colin Crouch's "Privatised Keynesianism: An Unacknowledged Policy Regime," *British Journal of Politics and International Relations* 11 (2009).

20 See also Roitman, *Fiscal Disobedience*, chap. 4.

21 See also accounts that stress the punitive aspect of precarity, such as Loïc Wacquant, *Punishing the Poor: The Neoliberal Government of Social Insecurity* (Durham, NC: Duke University Press, 2009); Joe Soss, Richard Fording, and Sanford Schram, *Disciplining the Poor: Neoliberal Paternalism and the Persistent Power of Race* (Chicago: University of Chicago Press, 2011); William Davies, "The New Neoliberalism," *New Left Review* 101 (2016); and Rafael Bernabe, "Neoliberalismo punitivo, melancolía financiera, y colonialism," *8ogrados*, April 7 2017, http://www.8ogrados.net/neoliberalismo-punitivo-melancolia-financiera-y
-colonialismo/. I discuss Marisol LeBrón's *Policing Life and Death: Race, Violence, and Resistance in Puerto Rico* (Oakland: University of California Press, 2019) in detail in chapter 2.

22 For discussions of personal responsibility, see, e.g., Lisa Duggan, *The Twilight of Equality?* (Boston: Beacon Press, 2012). See also Chari, *A Political Economy of the Senses*; and my "Paradoxes of Neoliberalism and the Tasks of Critical Theory," *Critical Horizons* 14, no. 1 (2013).

23 Lazzarato, "Debt, Neoliberalism, and Crisis," 1046.

24 Following Deleuze, Lazzarato argues that debt crises exploit the creditor-debtor relationship such that it should be understood as the fundamental social relationship in contemporary societies (Lazzarato, "Debt, Neoliberalism, and Crisis," 1045). See Gilles Deleuze, "Postscript on the Societies of Control," *October* 59 (1992). Cf. Graeber's *Debt*, which does not focus exclusively on debt within capitalism. See here as well Caffentzis, *Los Límites del capital*, especially his discussion of four types of class relations between debtor and creditor, 28–38. I will complicate this claim throughout.

25 Lazzarato, *The Making of the Indebted Man*, 94.

26 Lazzarato's example is student debt in the United States. See chapter 2 of *Governing by Debt*.

27 Lazzarato is here recalling Nietzsche's gloss on *Schuld* in the *Genealogy of Morals*. See *The Making of the Indebted Man*, esp. chap. 1.

28 See Lazzarato, "Neoliberalism, the Financial Crisis, and the End of the Liberal State," 68.

29 See Michel Foucault, *The Birth of Biopolitics: Lectures at the Collège de France 1978–1979*, trans. Graham Burchell (New York: Palgrave, 2008). See also Thomas Lemke, "Birth of Biopolitics: Michel Foucault and Lecture at the Collège de France on Neoliberal Governmentality," *Economy and Society* 30, no. 2 (2001).

30 Michel Foucault, "Questions of Method," in *The Foucault Effect: Studies in Governmentality*, ed. Colin Gordon and Peter Miller (Chicago: University of Chicago Press, 1991), 79.

31 See Michel Foucault, *Security, Territory, Population: Lectures at the Collège de France 1978–1979*, ed. Michel Senellart, trans. Graham Burchell (New York: Palgrave, 2009), 108.

32 Foucault, *Birth of Biopolitics*, 32.

33 Foucault, "Questions of Method," 79.

34 See Ulrich Bröckling, Susanne Krasmann, and Thomas Lemke's introduction to *Governmentality: Current Issues and Future Challenges* (London: Routledge, 2011). Most relevant to my purposes, see Verónica Gago's and Sayak Valencia's uses of Foucault on this score: *Neoliberalism from Below*, and *Gore Capitalism*, trans. John Pluecker (Cambridge, MA: Semiotext(e), 2018) respectively.

35 See here especially *Security, Territory, Population* and *The Birth of Biopolitics*.

36 See Foucault, *The Birth of Biopolitics*, first lecture. See also Lemke, "Birth of Biopolitics: Michel Foucault and Lecture at the Collège de France on Neoliberal Governmentality."

37 See Andrew Dilts, "From 'Entrepreneur of the Self' to 'Care of the Self': Neo-liberal Governmentality and Foucault's Ethics," *Foucault Studies* 12 (2011).

38 Lemke, "Birth of Biopolitics" 2.

39 Foucault, *Birth of Biopolitics*, 77.

40 See Foucault, *Birth of Biopolitics*, 30ff.

41 Cf. Chari, *A Political Economy of the Senses*, who argues that the neoliberal reconfiguration of the relationship between the economy and the state is obscured by the liberal commitments that neoliberalism retains.

42 See Chari, *A Political Economy of the Senses*, location 781.

43 Lazzarato, *Governing by Debt*, 215. On finance, see the introduction to Gretta Kripner, *Capitalizing on Crisis* (Cambridge, MA: Harvard University Press, 2011), for an overview of three competing interpretations of the rise of finance. Some accounts that inform my own include Giovanni Arrighi, *The Long Twentieth Century: Money, Power and the Origins of Our Times* (London: Verso, 2010); and Fernand Braudel, *Civilization and Capitalism, 15th–18th Century*, 3 vol. (New York: Harper and Row, 1981–84). See also Ian Baucom, *Specters of the Atlantic: Finance Capital, Slavery, and the Philosophy of History* (Durham, NC: Duke University Press, 2005). Cf. Immanuel Wallerstein, *The Modern World System*, esp. vol. 1, *Capitalist Agriculture and the Origins of the European World-Economy in the Sixteenth Century* (Berkeley: University of California Press, 2011). See as well Randy Martin, *The Financialization of Daily Life* (Philadelphia: Temple University Press, 2002); Cédric Durand, *Fictitious Capital: How Finance Is Appropriating Our Future* (London: Verso, 2017); Christian Marazzi, *The Violence of Financial Capitalism*, trans. Kristina Lebedeva and Jason Francis McGimsey (Cambridge, MA: Semiotext(e), 2011).

44 Marx, *Capital: A Critique of Political Economy*, vol. 3, trans. David Fernbach (London: Penguin, 1981), chap. 24, 516. See David Harvey, *Marx, Capital, and the Madness of Economic Reason* (Oxford: Oxford University Press, 2018); and Marx, *Grundrisse: Foundations of the Critique of Political Economy*, trans. Martin Nicolaus (London: Penguin, 1993), §§ 1 and 2. See also my "Abstraction and Critique in Marx's Capital," *Critique in German Philosophy*, ed. María del Rosario Acosta and Colin McQuillan (Albany: SUNY Press, forthcoming 2020).

45 Harvey, *Marx, Capital, and the Madness of Economic Reason*, 20. See also Rosa Luxemburg, *The Accumulation of Capital*, trans. Agnes Schwarzschild (London: Routledge, 2003), chap. 1, esp. 44–45. See as well Samir Amin, *Modern Imperialism, Monopoly Finance Capital, and Marx's Law of Value* (New York: Monthly Review, 2018). I am following Harvey closely here.

46 Marx, *Capital*, vol. 3, chap. 24, 515.

47 Marx, *Capital*, vol. 3.

48 See Michael Heinrich, *An Introduction to the Three Volumes of Karl Marx's Capital*, trans. Alexander Locascio (New York: Monthly Review Press, 2004), 156ff.

49 Lazzarato, *Governing by Debt*, 155, 156.

50 Lazzarato, *Governing by Debt*, 144.

51 Lazzarato, *Governing by Debt*, 154.

52 Lazzarato, *Governing by Debt*, 156.

53 Deleuze and Guattari define axioms as "operative statements that constitute the semiological form of Capital and that enter as component parts into assemblages of production, circulation and consumption" (quoted in Lazzarato, *Governing by Debt*, 148).

54 See Lazzarato, *Governing by Debt*, 141. Within finance capitalism, flows are configured in light of money, the "only 'code' compatible with capital" (Lazzarato, *Governing by Debt*, 157).

55 Lazzarato, *Governing by Debt*, 159.

56 Lazzarato, *Governing by Debt*, 139.

57 Lazzarato, *Governing by Debt*, 142.

58 Lazzarato, *Governing by Debt*, 147.

59 Lazzarato, *Governing by Debt*, 137; see also 144.

60 Lazzarato, *Governing by Debt*, 174.

61 See Lazzarato, *Governing by Debt*, 173.

62 To be sure, unpayable debt, also usury, as site of creation and extraction of wealth predates capitalist and neoliberal formations. See Graeber's *Debt* for a full discussion. See also Angela Mitropolous, *Contract and Contagion: From Biopolitics to Oikonomia* (Brooklyn, NY: Autonomedia, 2012). I discuss Mitropolous's work in chapter 3.

63 Lazzarato, *Governing by Debt*.

64 Lazzarato, *Governing by Debt*, 149.

65 Lazzarato, *Governing by Debt*, 160; see also 33: The technocratic management of the crisis is, Lazzarato concludes, "quintessentially political." Taxation is its "fundamental political instrument."

66 Lazzarato, *Governing by Debt*, 151.

67 Neoliberalism is thereby made perfectly compatible with a "maximum state," Lazzarato argues (Lazzarato, *Governing by Debt*). See also "Neoliberalism, the Financial Crisis, and the End of the Liberal State" and especially *Governing by Debt*, 102.

68 Lazzarato, *Governing by Debt*, 35.

69 Lazzarato, *Governing by Debt*, 35.

70 See Lazzarato, "The Political Consequences of the Debt Crisis," in *Una Proposición modesta: Puerto Rico a prueba/A Modest Proposal: Puerto Rico's Crucible*, initiative of Allora and Calzadilla, ed. Sara Nadal-Melisó (Barcelona: Fundació Antoni Tàpies, 2018), 33.

71 The "dividual" accounts for modes of subjection to the logic of self-valorizing money, ones that produce a subject that, at an unconscious level, "adapts in real time to the variations of the new circumstances of austerity and recession." Subjection here operates through the abstraction of information flows (Lazzarato, *Governing by Debt*, 210). The "dividual" provides an account of the different "interfaces" (from polling to profiles and other forms of "big data") between power and a population (Lazzarato, *Governing by Debt*, 197, 210).

72 Lazzarato, *Governing by Debt*, 164.

73 See Lazzarato, *The Making of the Indebted Man*, 94.

74 Foucault, *The Birth of Biopolitics*, 144.

75 Lazzarato, *The Making of the Indebted Man*, 46.

76 He also writes that debt "ward[s] off every potential 'deviation' in the behavior of the debtor that the future might hold" (Lazzarato, *The Making of the Indebted Man*, 45).

77 Lazzarato, *The Making of the Indebted Man*, 45.

78 Lazzarato, *Governing by Debt*, 248.

79 Arturo Escobar has shown that the apparatus of development and the ideas of poverty it produces are forms of coloniality that actualize the race/gender norm central to the modern colonial system. See his *Encountering Development: The Making and Unmaking of the Third World* (Princeton, NJ: Princeton University Press, 1995). See also Celenis Rodríguez Moreno, "Public Policies on Gender Equality: Technologies of Modern Colonial Gender," in *Decolonial Latin American, Caribbean and Latin Feminism: Contributions and Challenges*, ed. María Lugones, Yuderkys Espinosa-Miñoso, and Nelson Maldonado-Torres (Lanham, MD: Rowman and Littlefield, forthcoming).

80 See Muñiz-Varela, "Puerto Rico Post-936: ¿espejo del mundo y/o anomalía salvaje?" in *Adiós a la economía*, esp. 103ff. See also Gago and Cavallero, *Lectura feminista de la deuda*, 15, 60ff.

81 Gago and Cavallero, *Una Lectura feminista de la deuda*, 12.

82 Gago and Cavallero, *Una Lectura feminista de la deuda*, 12. See also Federica Gregoratto, "The Psychic Life of Debt-Guilt Regimes and Traditional Gender Identities: Nietzschean and Kleinian Perspectives" (unpublished ms.); and Tiziana Terranova, "Debt and Autonomy: Lazzarato and the Constituent Powers of the Social," *The New Reader 1* (2014), for analyses of Lazzarato's failure to consider gender.

83 Gago and Cavallero, *Una Lectura feminista de la deuda*, 12.

84 Gago and Cavallero, *Una Lectura feminista de la deuda*, 13ff.

85 Gago and Cavallero, *Una Lectura feminista de la deuda*, 15. This is close to their text; I am consolidating the cases they list.

86 Gago and Cavallero, *Una Lectura feminista de la deuda*, 16.

87 Gago and Cavallero, *Una Lectura feminista de la deuda*, 16.

88 Gago and Cavallero, *Una Lectura feminista de la deuda*, 13, esp. 42ff. Gago and Cavallero discuss race, though they do not center it.

89 Gago and Cavallero, *Una Lectura feminista de la deuda*, 11.

90 Gago, *Neoliberalism from Below*, 158.

91 Gago, *Neoliberalism from Below*, 157–58.

92 Gago, *Neoliberalism from Below*, 157.

93 See Gago and Cavallero, *Una Lectura feminista de la deuda*, 40ff.

94 Gago, *Neoliberalism from Below*, 164. See also the introduction to the book.

95 Gago, *Neoliberalism from Below*, 164.

96 Gago, *Neoliberalism from Below*, 14.

97 Verónica Gago, "What Are Popular Economies? Some Reflections from Argentina," *Radical Philosophy* 2, no. 2 (2018), 1. Gago is here drawing from René Zavaleta Mercado's notion of *sociedad abigarrada* and Silvia Rivera Cusicanqui's notion of *ch'ixi*. See René Zavaleta Mercado, *Lo Nacional-popular en Bolivia* (Mexico City: Siglo XXI, 1986); and Silvia Rivera Cusicanqui, *Ch'ixinacax utxiwa: Una reflexión sobre prácticas y discursos descolonizadores* (Buenos Aires: Tinta Limón, 2010). See also Bolívar Echeverría, *La Modernidad de lo barroco* (Mexico City: Ediciones ERA, 1998).

98 Gago, *Neoliberalism from Below*, 14.

99 Gago, *Neoliberalism from Below*, 15.

100 Cf. Lazzarato's *Governing by Debt* and Lazzarato and Éric Alliez, *Wars and Capital* (Cambridge, MA: Semiotext(e), 2016) for a divergent account of the geopolitics of debt.

101 See Fraser, "Behind Marx's Hidden Abode." Note the significance of Luxemburg's notion of *Landnahme* for Fraser, as for Gago and Cavallero. See *Una Lectura feminista de la deuda*, 40–45.

102 Marx, *Capital*, vol. 1, chap. 26, 874.

103 Marx, *Capital*, vol. 1, chap. 26, 874; emphasis mine.

104 Marx, *Capital*, vol. 1, chap. 31, 915.

105 Accounts that trace the relation between race and finance as well as finance and gender include: Moten and Harney, *The Undercommons*; Baucom, *Specters of the Atlantic*; Saidiya Hartman, *Scenes of Subjection*; *Race, Empire, and the Crisis of the Subprime*, ed. Paula Chakravarty and Denise Ferreira da Silva, special issue of *American Quarterly* 64, no. 3 (2012); Ferreira da Silva, "Unpayable Debt: Reading Scenes of Value against the Arrow of Time," *The Documenta 14 Reader*, ed. Quinn Latimer and Adam Szymczyk (Munich: Prestel Verlag, 2017); Zenia Kish and Justin Leroy, "Bonded Life: Technologies of Racial Finance from Slave Insurance to Philanthrocapital," *Cultural Studies* 29, nos. 5–6 (2015); Eric Williams's classic *Capitalism and Slavery* (Chapel Hill: University of North Carolina Press, 1944) and Cedric Robinson's *Black Marxism: The Making of the Black Radical Tradition* (Chapel Hill: University of North Carolina Press, 1983); Gwyn Campbell and Alessandro Stanziani, eds., *Debt and Slavery in the Mediterranean and Atlantic Worlds* (London: Routledge, 2013); Sven Beckert and Seth Rockman, eds., *Slavery's Capitalism* (Philadelphia: University of Pennsylvania Press, 2016); Michael Dawson, "Hidden in Plain Sight," *Critical Historical Studies* (2016); Agustín Laó Montes, "Neoliberalismo racial y políticas afrolatinoamericanas de cara a la crisis global," in *Afrodecendencias: Voces en resistencia*, ed. Rosa Campoalegre Septien (Buenos Aires: CLACSO, 2018); Jonathan Levy, *Freaks of Fortune: The Emerging World of Capitalism and Risk in America* (Cambridge, MA: Harvard University Press, 2012); Scott Reynolds Nelson, *A Nation of Deadbeats: An Uncommon History of America's Financial Disasters* (New York: Alfred A.

Knopf, 2012); Aida A. Hozić and Jacqui True, eds., *Scandalous Economics: Gender and the Politics of Financial Crises* (Oxford: Oxford University Press, 2016); Marieke De Goede, *Virtue, Fortuna, and Faith: A Genealogy of Finance* (Minneapolis: University of Minnesota Press, 2005), among others.

106 Marx, *Capital*, vol. 1, chap. 26, 874.

107 For a recent succinct overview of Marx on slavery, see John Bellamy Foster, Hannah Holleman, and Bret Clark, "Marx and Slavery," *Monthly Review* 70, no. 3 (2020).

108 Marx, *Capital*, vol. 1, chap. 31, 925.

109 Hartman, *Scenes of Subjection*, 21.

110 Hartman, *Scenes of Subjection*, 21. Hartman writes that the "relation between pleasure and the possession of slave property, in both the figurative and literal senses, can be explained in part by the fungibility of the slave—that is, the joy made possible by virtue of the replaceability and interchangeability endemic to the commodity—and by the extensive capacities of property—that is, the augmentation of the master subject through his embodiment in external objects and persons." Hartman adds that the fungibility of the commodity turns the captive body into an "abstract and empty vessel vulnerable to the projection of others' feelings, ideas, desires, and values."

111 Hartman, *Scenes of Subjection*, 21.

112 Hartman, *Scenes of Subjection*, 117.

113 Additional accounts that emphasize dispossession and expulsion include Miriam Muñiz-Varela, *Adiós a la economía*, which I discuss in chap. 2; David Harvey, *A Brief History of Neoliberalism* (Oxford: Oxford University Press, 2005); Saskia Sassen, "The Global City: Introducing A Concept," *Brown Journal of World Affairs* 11, no. 2 (2005), and *Expulsions: Brutality and Complexity in the Global Economy* (Cambridge, MA: Harvard University Press, 2014). See also Costas Lapavitsas, *Profiting without Producing: How Finance Exploits Us All* (London: Verso, 2014), and "Financialized Capitalism: Crisis and Financial Expropriation," Research on Money and Finance Discussion Papers, *Historical Materialism* 17 (2009). Cf. Naomi Klein, *The Shock Doctrine: The Rise of Disaster Capitalism* (New York: Picador, 2007).

114 One might distinguish alterity from otherness referring to differences between the conquest and the colonial period in relation to modalities of racial violence. The former outright violence and pillaging, the latter installing a system of labor, territory, and law that produces otherness through incorporation. See, for example, Tzvetan Todorov, *The Conquest of America: The Question of the Other*, trans. Richard Howard (New York: HarperCollins, 1984).

115 Aníbal Quijano, "El Fantasma del desarrollo en América Latina," *Revista Venezolana de economia y ciencias sociales* 6 (2000), 39; all translations are my own. Quijano understands neoliberalism as a specific "mutation" of the "global matrix of colonial power" (*patrón mundial de poder colonial*) in "América

Latina en la economía mundial," *Problemas del desarrollo* 24, no. 95 (1993). Cf. Santiago Castro Gómez's seminal essay "Foucault y la colonialidad del poder," *Tábula rasa* 6 (2009), for a competing account. Cf. also my "Normative Ambivalence and the Future of Critical Theory," in *Critical Theory and the Challenge of Praxis*, ed. Stefano Giachetti Ludovisi (London: Ashgate, 2015).

116 Quijano, "El Fantasma del desarrollo en América Latina," 39. See also Sylvia Wynter's key texts, "1492: A New World View," in *Race, Discourse, and the Origin of the Americas: A New World View*, ed. Sylvia Wynter, Vera Lawrence Hyatt, and Rex Nettleford (Washington, DC: Smithsonian Institution Press, 1995), and "Unsettling the Coloniality of Being/Power/Truth/Freedom: Towards the Human, After Man, Its Overrepresentation—An Argument," *CR: The New Centennial Review* 3, no. 3 (2003). Relevant here as well are Enrique Dussel, *The Invention of the Américas: The Eclipse of "the Other" and the Myth of Modernity*, trans. Michael D. Barber (New York: Continuum, 1995); and Ramón Grosfoguel, "Racismo/sexismo epistémico, universidades occidentalizadas y los cuatro genocidios/epistemicidios del largo siglo xvi," *Tábula rasa* 19 (2013).

117 See Quijano, "Colonialidad del poder y clasificación social." See my "Normative Ambivalence and the Future of Critical Theory" for a discussion of this concept.

118 Quijano, "Colonialidad del poder y clasificación social," 345. Quijano also writes that power "is a matter of the capacity of one group to obtain and find, to impose itself over others and articulate existence under its control, and indeed to reduce heterogeneous histories to one new social structure."

119 Quijano, "Colonialidad del poder y clasificación social," 342.

120 Quijano, "Colonialidad del poder y clasificación social," 344, 368.

121 Quijano, "Colonialidad del poder y clasificación social," 373.

122 Quijano, "Colonialidad del poder y clasificación social," 374.

123 María Lugones, "Heterosexualism and the Colonial/Modern Gender System," *Hypatia* 22, no. 1 (2007), and "Toward a Decolonial Feminism," *Hypatia* 25, no. 4 (2010). See also Celenis Rodríguez Moreno, "La Mujer y sus versiones oscuras," in *Feminismo descolonial: Nuevos aportes teóricos-metodológicos a más de una década*, ed. Yuderkys Espinosa Miñoso (Quito, Ecuador: Ediciones Abya-Yala, 2018). For an important critical engagement with Lugones, see Selamawit Terrefe, "The Pornotrope of Decolonial Feminism," *Critical Philosophy of Race* 8, nos. 1–2 (2020).

124 Celenis Rodríguez Moreno, "La Mujer y sus versiones oscuras." For an extended engagement with Rodríguez Moreno and her work on the mimetic formation of gender in the Caribbean with Yuderkys Espinosa Miñoso, see my "Subversiones caribeñas de la deuda," in *Eidos* 34 (2020) and my "Whither Theory? Debts to Caliban's 'Woman,'" forthcoming in *Diacritics*. See Rodríguez Moreno and Yuderkys Espinosa Miñoso, "Hacia la recuperación de una memoria de resistencia afrocaribeña a partir de los relatos de abuelas, madres e hijas de la comunidad Los Mercedes, República Dominicana," CLACSO (2020).

125 See Sojourner Truth, Hortense Spillers, and Sylvia Wynter for classic accounts of the production of the category of woman and its proximity to whiteness. See "Ain't I a Woman?" reprinted in *Words of Fire: An Anthology of African-American Feminist Thought* (New York: The New Press, 1995); Spiller's "Mama's Baby, Papa's Maybe: An American Grammar Book," *Diacritics* 17, no. 2 (1987); and Wynter, "Beyond Miranda's Meanings: Un/silencing the 'Demonic Ground' of Caliban's 'Woman,'" in *Out of the Kumbla: Caribbean Women and Literature,* ed. Carole Boyce Davies and Elaine Savory Fido (Trenton, NJ: Africa World Press, 1990).

126 Rodríguez Moreno, "La Mujer y sus versiones oscuras," 126.

127 Rita Segato, "Género y Colonialidad: Del Patriarcado comunitario de baja intensidad al patriarcado colonial moderno de alta intensidad," in *La Crítica de la colonialidad en ocho ensayos y una antropolgía por demanda* (Buenos Aires: Prometeo, 2013), 82. See also Segato, "Colonialidad y patriarcado moderno," in *La Guerra contra las mujeres* (Madrid: Traficantes de Sueños, 2016); all translations are my own.

128 Segato, "Género y Colonialidad: Del Patriarcado comunitario de baja intensidad al patriarcado colonial moderno de alta intensidad." Segato terms "pre-intervention" social relations *mundo-aldea* (world-village). This is not merely a distinction between precolonial and colonial social relations but also within contemporary nonmodern social relations that coexist within a postintervened colonial/modern world.

129 Segato, "Colonialidad y patriarcado moderno," *La Guerra contra las mujeres,* 118–19.

130 Segato, "Colonialidad y patriarcado moderno," *La Guerra contra las mujeres,* 54.

131 Segato, "Introduction," *La Guerra contra las mujeres,* 19, 20.

132 Segato, "Introduction," *La Guerra contra las mujeres,* 21.

133 Cf. Silvia Federici's *Caliban and the Witch: Women, the Body and Primitive Accumulation* (Brooklyn, NY: Autonomedia, 2004). Federici argues that primitive accumulation was not only the creation of exploitable workers. "It was also an accumulation of differences and divisions within the working class," she writes, "whereby hierarchies built upon gender, as well as 'race' and age, became constitutive of class rule and the formation of the proletariat" (*Caliban and the Witch,* 63–64). The feminization and devaluation of reproductive labor was central to the separation of commodity production from the reproduction of labor power. It was essential for the role men's waged labor played in capturing women's unwaged labor. The crucial point is that "women themselves became the commons, as their work was defined as a natural resource, laying outside of the sphere of market relations" (Federici, *Caliban and the Witch,* 97). Enclosing the time and space of women entailed seizing women's social power: seizing control over procreation, dismantling women's solidarity (discursively and spatially), demonizing knowledge and healing practices (and

the power they wielded over communities), and dismissing domestic labor as labor. See my "Whither Theory?" for a brief competing account.

134 See Rita Segato, *La Escritura en el cuerpo de las mujeres asesinadas en Ciudad Juárez: Territorio, soberanía y crímenes de segundo estado* (Buenos Aires: Tinta Limón, 2013), and *La Guerra contra las mujeres*. Cf. Alicia Gaspar de Alba and Georgina Guzmán, eds., *Making a Killing: Femicide, Free Trade, and La Frontera* (Austin: University of Texas Press, 2010); Rosa-Linda Fregoso and Cynthia Bejarano, eds., *Terrorizing Women: Feminicide in the Américas* (Durham, NC: Duke University Press, 2010); and Jill Radford and Diana Russell, eds., *Femicide: The Politics of Woman Killing* (New York: Twayne Publishers, 1992).

135 Lazzarato, *Governing by Debt*, 173. See Michel Foucault, "Society Must Be Defended": *Lectures at the Collège de France, 1975–1976*, ed. Mauro Bertani and Alessandro Fontana, trans. David Macey (New York: Picador, 2003), 240–41.

136 See Segato, *La Escritura en el cuerpo de las mujeres*.

137 See Achille Mbembe, "Necropolitics," *Public Culture* 15, no. 1 (2003).

138 See here Valencia, *Gore Capitalism*. See also Bobby Banerjee, "Necrocapitalism," *Organization Studies* 29, no. 12 (2008).

139 See Maldonado-Torres, "Outline of Ten Theses," 11.

140 Maldonado-Torres, "Outline of Ten Theses," 13.

141 Maldonado-Torres, "Outline of Ten Theses," 13.

142 See Wynter's "1491," 11. See also "Unsettling the Coloniality of Being/Power/ Truth/Freedom."

143 Enrique Dussel, "Meditaciones anti-cartesianas: Sobre el origen del anti-discurso filosófico de la modernidad," *Tabula rasa* 9 (2008).

144 Maldonado-Torres, "On the Coloniality of Being: Contributions to the Development of a Concept," *Cultural Studies* 21, no. 2–3 (2007): 256.

145 Maldonado-Torres, "On the Coloniality of Being," 255.

146 Maldonado-Torres, "On the Coloniality of Being," 248.

147 Maldonado-Torres, "Outline of Ten Theses," 12.

148 Maldonado-Torres, "Outline of Ten Theses," 17

149 Maldonado-Torres, "Outline of Ten Theses," 17.

150 Godreau-Aubert, *Las Propias*, 69: "la vida-endeudada es la continuación de la vida-colonial."

151 Godreau-Aubert, *Las Propias*, 67.

152 Godreau-Aubert, *Las Propias*, 54.

153 Godreau-Aubert, *Las Propias*, 57.

154 Godreau-Aubert, *Las Propias*, 15.

155 Godreau-Aubert, *Las Propias*, 54n35.

156 Godreau-Aubert, *Las Propias*, 54n35: "Una cuerpa es también una degenerada que ocupa o es ocupada por." Thanks to Tara Phillips and Ramsey McGlazer for discussions on how to render this term and the suggestion of a doublet.

157 Muñiz Varela also argues that especially women racialized as nonwhite are subject to "bioeconomic" management, hence seen as sites of Puerto Rico's "ghettoization"—its fall to "fourth world status" (*Adiós a la economía*, esp. 105). The bioeconomic management of women's bodies in the context of the neoliberalization of Puerto Rico's economy exceeds the well-documented experimentation in the context of the development of birth control. See, for example, Laura Briggs, *Reproducing Empire: Race, Sex, Science and US Imperialism in Puerto Rico* (Berkeley: University of California Press, 2002); and Annette Ramirez de Arellano, *Colonialism, Catholicism, and Contraception: A History of Birth Control in Puerto Rico* (Durham, NC: University of North Carolina Press, 2011).

158 Godreau-Aubert, *Las Propias*, 67.

159 Godreau-Aubert, *Las Propias*, 70.

160 See the United Nation's Guiding Principles of Foreign Debt and Human Rights submitted to the Human Rights Council in 2012 and endorsed by its resolution; https://www.ohchr.org/EN/Issues/Development/IEDebt/Pages/GuidingPrinciples.aspx.

161 Godreau-Aubert, *Las Propias*, 70–71. On average, poverty rates have remained steady at around 45.2 percent in Puerto Rico since 2010. In 2017, 72.3 percent of households headed by women with children under 18 were living in poverty. See "Un 43.5% de los puertorriqueños viven por debajo del nivel de pobreza," *Sin Comillas*, September 2, 2018, http://sincomillas.com/un-43-5-de-los-puertorriquenos-viven-por-debajo-del-nivel-de-pobreza/; and Luisa García Pelatti, "En 2017, 1.5 millones de puertorriqueños vivían por debajo del nivel de pobreza," *Sin Comillas*, March 3, 2019, http://sincomillas.com/en-2017-1-5-millones-de-puertorriquenos-vivian-por-debajo-del-nivel-de-pobreza/. The Centro de Periodismo Investigativo cites the 2015 US Transgender Survey, which included information about Puerto Rico. The survey reported that 43 percent of trans people, 45 percent of trans women, and 43 percent of nonbinary people were living below the poverty level. See Víctor Rodríguez Velázquez, "Personas trans sufren el desastre de María desde la marginalización," *Centro de Periodismo Investigativo*, September 23, 2019, http://periodismoinvestigativo.com/2019/09/personas-trans-sufren-el-desastre-de-maria-desde-la-marginacion/.

162 Statistics that track poverty along racial lines tend to lack. In 2018, 17 percent of the population in Puerto Rico identified as black. Among women, 12 percent identified as black; 46 percent of black women live below poverty level, with median income of $16,000. See Gloriann Sacha Antonetty and the editorial team of *Revista étnica*, "Ser una mujer negra en una pandemia y otras interseccionalidades," *Revista étnica*, April 12, 2020: https://www.revistaetnica.com/blogs/news/ser-una-mujer-negra-en-una-pandemia-y-otras-interseccionalidades. Colectivo Ilé and other antiracist collectives in Puerto Rico have done crucial work toward the 2020 Census. See https://colectivo-ile

.org/?page_id=8. In 2000, 80 percent of Puerto Ricans identified as white in the census, reflecting long-standing colonial discourses of racial mixing and racial "harmony" as well as US racial categories that do not map the histories of racialization in Puerto Rico. See Isar P. Godreau, *Scripts of Blackness: Race, Cultural Nationalism, and US Colonialism in Puerto Rico* (Urbana: University of Illinois Press, 2015); Ileana Rodriguez-Silva, *Silencing Race: Disentangling Blackness, Colonialism and National Identities in Puerto Rico* (London: Palgrave, 2012); Hilda Lloréns, *Imaging the Great Puerto Rican Family: Framing Nation, Race, and Gender during the American Century* (Lanham, MD: Rowman and Littlefield, 2018); and Agustín Laó-Montes, "Afro-Boricua Agency: Against the Myth of the Whitest of the Antilles," *ReVista* (2018).

163 Godreau-Aubert, *Las Propias*, 70. See also Max Haiven, *Cultures of Financialization: Fictitious Capital in Popular Culture and Everyday Life* (London: Palgrave, 2014), chap. 3, and with Cassie Thornton, "The Debts of the American Empire—Real and Imagined," *Roar* 3 (2016), where they remind us that Puerto Rico has the highest concentration of Walmart and Walgreens per square mile "anywhere in the world."

164 Godreau-Aubert, *Las Propias*, 70.

165 Godreau-Aubert, *Las Propias*, 70.

166 Despite accessing meager resources from a collapsing state, welfare recipients, especially women, are seen as taking advantage of federal "handouts." José Caraballo Cueto notes that there is an inverse relation between government spending on social programs and debt, showing that a "bloated" government and its "dependents" are not the cause of an unpayable debt, as is often stated. The percentage of the population that participated in the Supplemental Nutrition Program (Programa de Asistencia Nutricional, PAN), for example, was reduced from 58 percent in 1980 to 27 percent in 2006, the year the economic recession began. Government debt was reduced between 1977 and 1988 and increased afterward. He writes that it was after 2006 that PAN participation grew again. See José Caraballo Cueto, "Debunking 2 More Myths on Puerto Rico Economy," *The Hill*, July 21, 2017, http://thehill.com/blogs/pundits-blog/economy-budget/343118-debunking-2-more-myths-on-puerto-rico-economy. See also Linda Colón Reyes, *Sobrevivencia, pobreza y "mantengo": La Política asistencialista estadounidense en Puerto Rico: el PAN y el TANF* (San Juan: Ediciones Callejón, 2011). See Godreau-Aubert, "Los Chavos del PAN, la buena vida y nuestras pestes" and "Esta Tipa es una yal: El Chiste, la pobreza y la negritud sin retorno" in *Las Propias*.

167 Godreau-Aubert, *Las Propias*, 71.

168 Section 403 of PROMESA.

169 Godreau-Aubert, *Las Propias*, 71. For recent data on inequality in nutritional assistance among the US territories, see José Caraballo Cueto and Econometrika Corp, "The impact of disparities in SNAP and SSI on Puerto Rico's poverty and economic growth," https://media.noticel.com

/02com-noti-media-us-east-1/document_dev/2019/03/09/Estudio%
20sobre% 20disparidades% 20en% 20beneficios% 20del% 20PAN% 20y%
20SSI_1552160521539_37305880_ver1.0.pdf.

170 See Patricia Hill Collins, *Black Feminist Thought* (London: Routledge, 1990).

171 See also Kelvin Santiago-Valle, *Subject People and Colonial Discourses: Economic Transformation and Social Disorder in Puerto Rico 1898–1947* (Albany: SUNY Press, 2007); and Eileen Suárez Findlay, *Imposing Decency: The Politics of Sexuality and Race in Puerto Rico 1870–1920* (Durham, NC: Duke University Press, 2000).

172 Katsí Yarí Rodríguez-Velázquez, "Degradando a la 'yal': Racialización y violencia antinegra en Puerto Rico,"*Afro-Hispanic Review* 31, no. 7 (2018): 122.

173 Rodríguez-Velázquez, "Degradando a la 'yal,'" 122.

174 Zaire Dizney-Flores, *Locked In, Locked Out: Gated Communities in a Puerto Rican City* (Philadelphia: University of Pennsylvania Press, 2013).

175 See Dizney-Flores, *Locked In, Locked Out,* chap. 1. See also Godreau, *Scripts of Blackness*; and Rodriguez-Silva, *Silencing Race.* See as well Colectiva Feminista en Construcción, *Manifiesto Antirracista,* June 2, 2020, https://www.facebook
.com/notes/colectiva-feminista-en-construcci%C3%B3n/manifiesto-antirracista
-colectiva-feminista-en-construcci%C3%B3n/2968317379926640. An English translation of *The Anti-Racist Manifesto* was published by *Latino Rebels,* June 7, 2020, https://www.latinorebels.com/2020/06/07/antiracistmanifesto/. *Criollo* is not to be confused with creole or creolization. It is rather akin to *mestizaje* when in proximity to whiteness. See also Katherine Cepeda, "Ontología barrial negra y criolla de Puerto Rico," *8ogrados,* July 10, 2020, https://www.8ogrados
.net/ontologia-barrial-negra-y-criolla-de-puerto-rico/.

176 Colectiva Feminista en Construcción, *The Anti-Racist Manifesto.*

177 Zaire Dizney-Flores, "Criminalizing Communities of Poor, Dark Women in the Caribbean: The Fight against Crime through Puerto Rico's Public Housing," *Crime Prevention and Community Safety* 13, no. 1 (2011). See also Marisol LeBrón, "Mano Dura contra el Crimen and Premature Death in Puerto Rico," in *Policing the Planet: Why the Policing Crisis Led to Black Lives Matter,* ed. Jordan T. Camp and Christina Heatherton (London: Verso, 2016), and *Policing Life and Death.* See also Muñiz-Varela, *Adiós a la economía,* 103ff.

178 Dizney-Flores, "Criminalizing Communities of Poor, Dark Women in the Caribbean," 65. The spatial proximity of public housing and affluent neighborhoods was promoted by Luis Muñoz Marín in an effort to drive upward mobility. In reality, it not only reified cisheteronormativity, productivity, and a white bourgeois ethic/aesthetic. It spatially inscribed a distinction between populations in need of policing and those in need of security, as Marisol LeBrón emphasizes. I discuss this in detail in chap. 2.

179 Dizney-Flores, "Criminalizing Communities of Poor, Dark Women in the Caribbean," 65.

180 Godreau-Aubert, *Las Propias,* 105.

181 Godreau-Aubert, *Las Propias*, 105.

182 Godreau-Aubert, *Las Propias*, 104.

183 Rodríguez-Velázquez, "Degradando a la 'yal,'" 122.

184 See Colectiva Feminista en Construcción, "Plantón," November 14, 2018, https://www.facebook.com/Colectiva. Feminista. PR/photos/-plant% C3% B3n-feminista-contra-la-violencia-machistaen-lo-que-va-de-a% C3% B10-40-mujeres-ha/1925254470899608/. See also Vanesa Contreras Capó, "La Deuda y la violencia machista estructural," *8ogrados*, January 25, 2019, https://www .8ogrados.net/la-deuda-y-la-violencia-machista-estructural/; "El Ocho de marzo contra la deuda," *8ogrados*, March 1, 2019, https://www.8ogrados.net /el-8-de-marzo-contra-la-deuda/; and "Primavera feminista contra la deuda," *8ogrados*, April 5, 2019, https://www.8ogrados.net/primavera-feminista-contra -la-deuda/. A translation of "La Deuda y la violencia machista estructural" by Nicole Cecilia Delgado is forthcoming in "On Debt, Blame, and Responsibility: Feminist Resistance in the Colony of Puerto Rico," ed. Rocío Zambrana, special section of *Critical Times*.

185 See Joshua García Aponte, "El Incremento sexual contra las mujeres," Hoy en las Noticias, Departamento de Noticias, Radio Universidad de Puerto Rico, June 27, 2019, https://www.mixcloud.com/hoyenlasnoticias/en -incremento-las-agresiones-sexuales-contra-las-mujeres/? fbclid=IwAR0-q1_AOQYE9mhlOvP-xe9KYvDIErxtxdHOLk7oqnj8MwChCjYNt-qrdjM. García Aponte interviews Edda López Serrano, secretary of women's issues for Partido Independentista Puertorriqueño (Puerto Rican Independence Party). López Serrano underscores that sexual violence is a matter of "impunity" in Puerto Rico, since the laws and regulations against it exist. She ties impunity to a collapsing infrastructure and lack of resources.

186 García Aponte, "El Incremento sexual contra las mujeres."

187 See María Dolores Fernós, Marilucy González Báez, Yanira Reyes Gil, and Esther Vicente, eds., *Voces de mujeres: Estrategias de supervivencia y de fortalecimiento mutuo tras el paso de los Huracanes Irma y María* (San Juan: INTER-Mujeres, 2018).

188 See Claire Tighe and Lauren Gurley, "Official Reports of Violence against Women in Puerto Rico Unreliable after Hurricane María," *Centro de Periodismo Investigativo*, May 7, 2018, http://periodismoinvestigativo.com/2018 /05/datos-oficiales-de-violencia-contra-la-mujer-en-puerto-rico-no-son -confiables-despues-del-huracan-maria/. See also, e.g., Leysa Caro González, "Más vulnerables las mujeres tras el paso de María," *El Nuevo día*, July 10 2018, https://www.elnuevodia.com/noticias/locales/nota/masvulnerableslasmujer estraselpasodemaria-2434047/; and Jade Jackman, Rosalyn Warren, Marinés Montero, Antonio Ribeiro, Mark Pickles, and Mustafa Khalili, "Puerto Rico after María," *The Guardian*, April 30, 2018, https://www.theguardian.com /world/video/2018/apr/30/puerto-rico-after-hurricane-maria-were-american -too-why-dont-they-help.

189 See Rodríguez Velázquez, "Personas trans sufren el desastre de María desde la marginalización."

190 Colectiva Feminista en Construcción, "Orden Ejecutiva para aprobar un plan nacional en contra de la violencia machista," November 24, 2018, https://www.facebook.com/notes/colectiva-feminista-en-construcci% C3% B3n/orden-ejecutiva-para-aprobar-un-plan-nacional-en-contra-de-la-violencia-machista/1938470216244700/; and "Informe de la manifestación y la reunión con Johanne Vélez e Ileana Aymat," June 14, 2019,https://www .facebook.com/notes/colectiva-feminista-en-construcci%C3%B3n/informe -de-la-manifestaci%C3%B3n-y-la-reuni%C3%B3n-con-johanne-v%C3%A9lez -e-ileana-aymat-14-de-/2243215732436812/. In January 2021, *Revista étnica* reported that "2020 closed with a total of 60 direct and indirect femicides, of which 17 are considered intimate killings, 6 transfeminicides, and 26 cases that are being investigated or remain without information. . . . [B]ased on press reports, in 2020 there was an increase of 62% in the total number of femicides when comparing these figures with those of last year." *Étnica* reports that "23 of 57 missing women are evidently [*evidentemente*] black, which represents 40%." In September 2020, la Colectiva again convened protests. In January 2021, Governor Pedro Pierluisi declared a State of Emergency over gender violence. See Alejandra Rosa, Esther M. Andrade, Gloriann Sacha Antonetty Lebrón, and Raymond Alicano, "Estado de Emergencia en Puerto Rico: ¿Qué significa esto para las mujeres negras en todas sus diversidades?" *Revista étnica* (2021).

191 Eva Prados, "Violencia de género y auditoría de la deuda" (unpublished ms.). A translation of this text by Nicole Cecilia Delgado is forthcoming in "On Debt, Blame, and Responsibility: Feminist Resistance in the Colony of Puerto Rico," ed. Rocío Zambrana, special section of *Critical Times*. All translations in this book are my own.

192 Concerning the distinction between *feminicidio* and *femicidio*, see Segato, "Femigenocidio y feminicidio: Una Propuesta de tipificación," *Herramienta: Revista de debate y crítica marxista*, May 2011, https://herramienta.com.ar /articulo.php? id=1687.

193 Segato, *La Escritura en el cuerpo de las mujeres*, 8.

194 Verónica Gago, "La Pedagogía de la crueldad: Entrevista a Rita Segato," *Página12*, May 29, 2015, https://www.pagina12. com.ar/diario/suplementos /las12/13−9737−2015−05−29.html.

195 Segato, *La Escritura en el cuerpo de las mujeres*, 22.

196 Segato, *La Escritura en el cuerpo de las mujeres*, 23.

197 See Segato, *La Escritura en el cuerpo de las mujeres*, 55.

198 See here Valencia, *Gore Capitalism*.

199 Rita Segato, "Patriarcado: Del Borde al centro. Disciplinamiento, territori-alidad y crueldad en la fase apocalíptica del capital," in *La Guerra contra las mujeres*, 102.

200 Godreau-Aubert, *Las Propias*, 58.

201 Here Godreau-Aubert is quoting the Puerto Rican poet José María Lima and Guillermo Rebollo-Gil, *Decirla en pedacitos: Estrategias de cercanía* (Cabo Rojo, PR: Editora Educación Emergente, 2013). See Godreau-Aubert, *Las Propias*, 55.

202 Godreau-Aubert, *Las Propias*, 55n37.

203 She continues: "To live in austerity . . . is to subsist in small pieces, in small jumps, with stolen words and that never say what they should. Nevertheless, we cannot abandon the finding, movement, voice."

204 Godreau-Aubert, *Las Propias*, 69. See also "Gritarle al alcalde," in *Las Propias*. I discuss the case in chap. 3 in relation to an action by la Colectiva.

CHAPTER TWO. COLONIAL EXCEPTIONALITY

For the epigraphs, see https://www.facebook.com/seacabaronlaspromesas/. Jornada Se Acabaron las Promesas is a collective in opposition to PROMESA but also to all sectors that seek "to profit from a debt that is not of the people." Walter Benjamin, "On the Concept of History," in *Illuminations*, trans. Harry Zohn (New York: Harcourt Brace, 1968), Thesis VIII. Anayra Santory-Jorge, "Lo Prometido es deuda," in *Nada es igual: bocetos del país que nos acontece* (Cabo Rojo, PR: Editora Educación Emergente, 2018), 49.

1 James Dietz, *Historia económica de Puerto Rico* (San Juan: Huracán, 1989), 107–8.

2 In "Destruir un país es un asunto de hombres," *Actas del XI Coloquio Nacional sobre las Mujeres, Universidad de Puerto Rico, Recinto Universitario de Mayagüez: Feminismo, decolonialidad y otras intersecciones*, ed. Beatriz Llenín-Figueroa and Vanessa Vilches Norat (Cabo Rojo, PR: Editora Educación Emergente, 2019), Anayra Santory-Jorge makes a similar point. A translation of Santory-Jorge's text, "Destroying a Country Is a Man's Business," by Nicole Cecilia Delgado is forthcoming in "On Debt, Blame, and Responsibility: Feminist Resistance in the Colony of Puerto Rico," ed. Rocío Zambrana, special section of *Critical Times*. All translations in this book are my own. Miriam Muñiz Varela also stresses this moment of capture in "Taken Island" (unpublished ms.) and "La Deuda: Axiomática de la propiedad y aparato de captura de la vida," in *Violencia y Deuda*, ed. Madeline Román, *Cruce*, November 11. 2019, https://issuu.com/revistacruce/docs/violencia_y_deuda_7_nov_2019.

3 Puerto Rico, Guam, the Philippines, and Cuba were ceded to the United States. Cuba became a US protectorate. The Philippines was bought for $20 million.

4 José Atiles-Osoria, *Apuntes para abandonar el derecho: Estado de excepción colonial en Puerto Rico* (Cabo Rojo, PR: Editora Educación Emergente, 2016); all translations are my own. Cf. Ann Laura Stoler, "Degrees of Imperial Sovereignty," *Public Culture* 18, no. 1 (2006). Stoler argues that the creation of liminal spaces is distinctive of US imperialism, although she does not mention Puerto Rico. See here also *Agamben and Colonialism*, ed. Simone Bignall and Marcelo Svirsky (Edinburgh: Edinburgh University Press, 2012).

5 Cf. Aihwa Ong, *Neoliberalism as Exception: Mutations in Citizenship and Sovereignty* (Durham, NC: Duke University Press, 2006).

6 See Atiles-Osoria, *Apuntes*, 24.

7 See Atiles-Osoria, *Apuntes*, chap. 7.

8 Atiles-Osoria, *Apuntes*, 58.

9 Miriam Muñiz Varela, *Adiós a la economía* (San Juan: Ediciones Callejón, 2013); Santory-Jorge, "Destruir un país es un asunto de hombres." Santory builds on Rob Nixon's notion of catastrophe by attrition in *Slow Violence and the Environmentalism of the Poor* (Cambridge, MA: Harvard University Press, 2013). All translations of Muñiz-Varela and, as noted above, Santory-Jorge are my /own.

10 Lauren Berlant, *Cruel Optimism* (Durham, NC: Duke University Press, 2011). Cf. Veena Das, *Life and Words: Violence and the Descent into the Ordinary* (Berkeley: University of California Press, 2007); and Elizabeth Povinelli, *Economies of Abandonment: Social Belonging and Endurance in Late Liberalism* (Durham, NC: Duke University Press, 2011).

11 See Charles Venator-Santiago, "From the Insular Cases to Camp X-Ray: Agamben's State of Exception and the United States Territorial Law," *Studies in Law, Politics, and Society* 39 (2006). For an extended version of the argument, see Venator-Santiago's *Puerto Rico and the Origins of US Global Empire: The Disembodied Shade* (London: Routledge, 2015).

12 Marisol LeBrón, *Policing Life and Death: Race, Violence, and Resistance in Puerto Rico* (Oakland: University of California Press, 2019).

13 Giorgio Agamben, *State of Exception*, trans. Kevin Atell (Chicago: University of Chicago Press, 2005), 1.

14 Agamben, *State of Exception*, 39.

15 See Atiles-Osoria, *Apuntes*, 44.

16 Agamben, *State of Exception*, 23.

17 Venator-Santiago, "From the Insular Cases to Camp X-Ray," 16.

18 Atiles-Osoria, *Apuntes*, 43.

19 See *Downes v. Bidwell*, 182 U.S. 244 (1901). I discuss the Insular Cases below.

20 See Agamben, *State of Exception*. See also Atiles-Osoria, *Apuntes*, 53ff.

21 Atiles-Osoria argues that a genealogical approach imposes "linearity," generating crucial blind spots. See *Apuntes*, 65.

22 See Atiles-Osoria, *Apuntes*, 65–66.

23 Atiles-Osoria, *Apuntes*, 70.

24 Venator-Santiago, "From Insular Cases to Camp X-Ray," 19.

25 Venator-Santiago, *Puerto Rico and the Origins of U.S. Global Empire*, location 165.

26 I am here paraphrasing Venator-Santiago, "From Insular Cases to Camp X-Ray," 23. See also Atiles-Osoria, *Apuntes*, 81.

27 Venator-Santiago, *Puerto Rico and the Origins of U.S. Global Empire*, location 107–18.

28 Venator-Santiago, *Puerto Rico and the Origins of U.S. Global Empire*. I am following Venator-Santiago here and in the next paragraph.

29 Venator-Santiago, *Puerto Rico and the Origins of U.S. Global Empire*, location 117.

30 Venator-Santiago, "From Insular Cases to Camp X-Ray," 24. See here as well the essays collected in Frances Negrón-Muntaner, *Sovereign Acts: Contesting Colonialism across Indigenous Nations and Latinx America* (Tucson: University of Arizona Press, 2017).

31 Venator-Santiago, "From Insular Cases to Camp X-Ray," 30.

32 Venator-Santiago, "From Insular Cases to Camp X-Ray," 30.

33 Venator-Santiago, "From Insular Cases to Camp X-Ray," 26.

34 See Atiles-Osoria, *Apuntes*, 87, and Venator-Santiago, "From Insular Cases to Camp X-Ray," 29. For an exposition of centrality of the discourse of maturity, see Dardo Scavino, "Colonialidad del poder: Una Invención jurídica de la conquista" (unpublished ms.).

35 Venator-Santiago, "From Insular Cases to Camp X-Ray," 33.

36 Venator-Santiago, "From Insular Cases to Camp X-Ray," 34.

37 Venator-Santiago, "From Insular Cases to Camp X-Ray," 34.

38 Venator-Santiago, "From Insular Cases to Camp X-Ray," 34.

39 See Atiles-Osoria, *Apuntes*, 97–98. The islands were "represented as vessels or ships for legal purposes," Venator-Santiago writes, and the inhabitants labored in conditions "tantamount to slavery" ("From Insular Cases to Camp X-Ray," 35).

40 I am following Venator-Santiago, "From Insular Cases to Camp X-Ray," 39ff.

41 See Article IV, Section 3, Clause 2 of the United States Constitution, which states that "the Congress shall have power to dispose of and make all needful rules and regulations respecting the territory or other property belonging to the United States."

42 See especially Venator-Santiago's discussion of Brigadier General George W. Davis ("From Insular Cases to Camp X-Ray," 40). See also Dietz, *Historia*, 110.

43 In *Downes v. Bidwell* (1901), the territories' non-Anglo-Saxon populations were deemed "alien races."

44 Venator-Santiago, "From Insular Cases to Camp X-Ray," 119.

45 Venator-Santiago, "From Insular Cases to Camp X-Ray," 116, 168.

46 Dietz, *Historia*, 107.

47 Dietz, *Historia*, 109.

48 Most cases addressed questions pertaining to taxes and tariffs, territorial classification, boundaries between the foreign and the domestic, and matters of free movement. Some scholars restrict the Insular Cases to those seen during 1901, while others consider cases up to 1922, since they had a bearing on the question concerning whether the Constitution follows the flag. See Efrén Rivera Ramos, *The Legal Construction of Identity: The Juridical and Social Legacy of American Colonialism in Puerto Rico* (Washington, DC: American Psychological Association, 2011), and *American Colonialism in Puerto Rico: The Judiciary and Social Legacy* (Princeton, NJ: Markus Wiener,

2007); Bartholomew Sparrow, *The Insular Cases and the Emergence of the American Empire* (Lawrence: University of Kansas Press, 2006); *Reconsidering the Insular Cases: The Past and Present of American Empire*, ed. Gerard L. Neuman (Cambridge, MA: Harvard University Press, 2015); *Foreign in a Domestic Sense: Puerto Rico, American Expansion, and the Constitution*, ed. Christina Duffy Burnett, Burke Marshall, Gilbert M. Joseph, Emily S. Rosenberg (Durham, NC: Duke University Press, 2001); Juan Toruella, *The Supreme Court and Puerto Rico: The Doctrine of Separate and Unequal* (San Juan: Editorial de la Universidad de Puerto Rico, 1988); and César J. Ayala and Rafael Bernabe, *Puerto Rico in the American Century* (Chapel Hill: University of North Carolina Press, 2007).

49 Atiles-Osoria, *Apuntes*, 129, 140.

50 Atiles-Osoria, *Apuntes*, 128.

51 See *Downes v. Bidwell*.

52 See Gerald Neuman's *Introduction to Reconsidering the Insular Cases*, locations 127–39.

53 See Venator-Santiago, "From Insular Cases to Camp X-Ray," 18ff.

54 Atiles-Osoria, *Apuntes*, 23.

55 Atiles-Osoria, *Apuntes*, 117.

56 See Atiles-Osoria, *Apuntes*, 148.

57 See Charles Venator-Santiago and Edgardo Meléndez, "US Citizenship in Puerto Rico: One Hundred Years after the Jones Act," and Venator-Santiago, "Mapping the Contours of the History of the Extension of US Citizenship to Puerto Rico—1898 to the Present," in *Centro: Journal of the Center for Puerto Rican Studies* 29, no. 1 (2017). The issue assesses the Jones Act in its centenary year. It provides an account of economic and political interests beyond the First World War draft. Congress amended the Jones Act in 1927, 1934, and 1938 to correct inconsistencies created by collective naturalization in an unincorporated territory. See Venator-Santiago, "A Note on the Puerto Rican De-Naturalization Exception of 1948."

58 See Bernabe and Ayala, *Puerto Rico in the American Century*, 168ff. See Atiles-Osoria, *Apuntes*, 151.

59 The independence party (Partido Independentista Puertorriqueño, PIP) boycotted the referendum and the ratification, while the statehood party (Partido Nuevo Progresista, PNP) provided no clear indications on how to vote. See Bernabe and Ayala, *Puerto Rico in the American Century*, 188. Law 53, Ley de la Mordaza or Gag Law, which sought to suppress the independence movement, was in effect from 1948 to 1956. For a good summary, see Mario Cancel Sepúlveda, "La Constitución de 1952 y Estados Unidos," *8ogrados*, July 25, 2018, http://www.8ogrados.net/la-constitucion-de-1952-y-estados-unidos/.

60 Bernabe and Ayala, *Puerto Rico in the American Century*, 168.

61 See Bernabe and Ayala, *Puerto Rico in the American Century*, 171.

62 *United States v. Sanchez*, 992 F.2d 1143, 1151 (11th Cir. 1993), is one among a handful of decisions that established that Puerto Rico remained an unincorporated territory subordinate to Congress despite the creation of the ELA. See Atiles-Osoria, *Apuntes*, 164.

63 See here *None of the Above: Puerto Ricans in the Global Era*, ed. Frances Negrón-Muntaner (New York: Palgrave, 2007); *Puerto Rican Jam: Essays on Culture and Politics*, ed. Ramón Grosfoguel and Frances Negrón-Muntaner (Minneapolis: University of Minnesota Press, 1997); Carlos Pabón, *Nación postmortem: Ensayos sobre los tiempos de insoportable ambigüedad* (San Juan: Ediciones Callejón, 2002) and *Mínima política: Textos breves y fragmentos sobre la crisis contemporánea* (San Juan: La Secta de los Perros, 2015). See also Yarimar Bonilla, *Non-Sovereign Futures: French Caribbean Politics in the Wake of Disenchantment* (Chicago: University of Chicago Press, 2015), for a discussion of articulations of sovereignty in the Caribbean that go beyond the creation of a nation-state.

64 Rafael Bernabe, "Puerto Rico: Economic Reconstruction, Debt Cancellation, and Self-Determination," *International Socialist Review* 111 (winter 2018–19), https://isreview.org/issue/111/puerto-rico-economic-reconstruction-debt -cancellation-and-self-determination. See also his "Neoliberalism punitivo, melancolía financiera, y colonialism," *80grados*, April 7 2017, http://www .80grados.net/neoliberalismo-punitivo-melancolia-financiera-y-colonialismo /; "Detrás de la crisis de la deuda en Puerto Rico," Comité para la Abolición de las Deudas Ilegítimas (CADTM), July 30, 2015, http://www.cadtm.org/Detras -de-las-crisis-de-la-deuda; "Puerto Rico's New Era: A Crisis in Crisis Management," North American Congress on Latin America, https://nacla.org/article /puerto-rico% E2% 80% 99s-new-era-crisis-crisis-management. See also Dietz, *Historia*, and Muñiz Vaerla, *Adiós*, chap. 1.

65 See Bernabe, "Detrás de la crisis de la deuda" and "Puerto Rico: Economic Reconstruction, Debt Cancellation, and Self-Determination."

66 Bernabe, "Detrás de la crisis de la deuda" and "Puerto Rico: Economic Reconstruction, Debt Cancellation, and Self-Determination."

67 Bernabe, "Puerto Rico: Economic Reconstruction, Debt Cancellation, and Self-Determination."

68 Muñiz Varela, *Adiós*, 116. Note that Puerto Ricans have been incorporated into the US working class as one of its "discriminated and over-exploited sectors, along with African Americans and other Latinx populations" (Bernabe, "Puerto Rico Economic Reconstruction, Debt Cancellation, and Self-Determination"). See also Robert McGreevey, *Borderline Citizens: The United States, Puerto Rico, and the Politics of Colonial Migration* (Ithaca, NY: Cornell University Press, 2018).

69 See LeBrón, *Policing Life and Death*, 9.

70 See "New Mass Exodus of Puerto Ricans to the US," *El Nuevo día*, June 24, 2018, https://www.elnuevodia.com/english/english/nota/newmassexodusofpue rtoricanstotheus-2430651/.

71 See Center for Puerto Rican Studies, Hunter College, March 2018, https:// centropr.hunter.cuny.edu/sites/default/files/data_sheets/PostMaria -NewEstimates-3–15–18.pdf. See also United States Census Bureau data, https://www.census.gov/newsroom/pressreleases/2018/estimates-national -state.html). See as well Hilda Lloréns, "US Media Depictions of Climate Migrants: The Recent Case of the Puerto Rican 'Exodus,'" in *Aftershocks of Disaster: Puerto Rico before and after the Storm*, ed. Yarimar Bonilla and Marisol LeBrón (Chicago: Haymarket Books, 2019). See also Frances Negrón-Muntaner, "The Emptying Island—Puerto Rican Expulsion in Post-María," *E-misférica* 14 (2018).

72 Bernabe writes: "Puerto Rico's per capita income is a third of the US figure. It is half of the per capita income of the poorest state, Mississippi. The yearly median household income in the United States is $53,900. In Puerto Rico it is $19,000" ("Puerto Rico: Economic Reconstruction, Debt Cancellation, and Self-Determination"). As noted in chapter 1, black women earn on average $16,000. See Gloriann Sacha Antonetty and the editorial team of *Revista étnica*, "Ser una mujer negra en una pandemia y otras interseccionalidades," *Revista étnica*, April 12, 2020, https://www.revistaetnica.com/blogs/news/ser-una -mujer-negra-en-una-pandemia-y-otras-interseccionalidades. For a report on the conditions in the immediate aftermath of Hurricanes Irma and María, see "Justicia ambiental, desigualdad, y pobreza en Puerto Rico: Informe multisectorial sobre las violaciones de derechos económicos, sociales, y medioambientales tras el paso de los huracanes Irma y María en Puerto Rico," Instituto Caribeño de Derechos Humanos y Clínica Internacional de Derechos Humanos de la Facultad de Derecho de la Universidad Interamericana de Puerto Rico, December 7, 2017, https://noticiasmicrojuris.files.wordpress.com/2018/05/final -informe-cidh-audiencia-pr-dic-2017.pdf.

73 See also Muñiz-Varela, *Adiós*, 117.

74 See Bernabe, "Neoliberalism punitivo, melancolía financiera, y colonialism"; Diane Lourdes Dick, "US Tax Imperialism," *American University Law Review* 1 (2015); José I. Fusté, "The Repeating Island of Debt," *Radical History Review* 128 (2017); and Muñiz-Vaerla, "Puerto Rico Post-936," in *Adiós*.

75 Fusté, "The Repeating Island of Debt," 104.

76 See Muñiz-Varela, *Adiós*, 115.

77 Muñiz-Varela, *Adiós*, 115. I discuss Manos a la Obra in chapter 4.

78 Muñiz-Varela, *Adiós*, 68.

79 Cf. José Caraballo-Cueto and Juan Lara, "From Deindustrialization to Unsustainable Debt: The Case of Puerto Rico," *Journal of Globalization and Development* 8, no. 2 (2018). Caraballo-Cueto and Lara stress deindustrialization rather than tax exemption as the main reason for the accrual of an unpayable debt.

80 Cf. Rafael Bernabe, "Puerto Rico's New Era: A Crisis in Crisis Management," NACLA: *Report on the Americas* 40, no. 6 (2007). See Atiles-Osoria, *Apuntes*, 168. This is not to say that 2006 is the beginning of Puerto Rico's dependence on debt to balance its budget. Debt became central during the 1973–74 recession that resulted from OPEC's oil embargo and that greatly impacted the petrochemical industries in Puerto Rico. See Muñiz-Varela, *Adiós*.

81 The sales tax was initially 7 percent but was increased to 11.5 percent in 2015, the highest sales tax rate in the United States.

82 The colonial state of exception in Puerto Rico is a "double exceptionality," then. Cf. Ramón Grosfoguel, *Colonial Subjects: Puerto Ricans in a Global Perspective* (Berkeley: University of California Press, 2003), where he develops the notion of a double coloniality of power in Puerto Rico.

83 Atiles-Osoria, *Apuntes*, 172. To be sure, declarations of states of emergency were used to repress anti-colonial movements throughout the twentieth century. See José Atiles-Osoria, "The Criminalization of Anticolonial Struggle in Puerto Rico," in *Counter-Terrorism and State Political Violence: The "War on Terror" as Terror*, ed. Scott Poynting and David Whyte (London: Routledge, 2012), and "The Criminalization of Socio-Environmental Struggles in Puerto Rico," *Oñati Socio-Legal Series* 4, no. 1 (2012). Accounts of the history of political repression in Puerto Rico abound. See, e.g., Ivonne Acosta, *La Mordaza* (San Juan: Editorial Edil, 1987); and José Paralitici, *La Represión contra el independentismo puertorriqueño* (San Juan: Ediciones Gaviota, 2011).

84 Atiles-Osoria, *Apuntes*, 173. I discuss student resistance to these measures in chapter 4.

85 See Arturo Massol Deyá, *Amores que luchan* (San Juan: Ediciones Callejón, 2018), for an account of the victory of the environmentalist movement against the Gasoducto. See my discussion of Casa Pueblo in the conclusion to this book.

86 See, e.g., Mary William Walsh, "Puerto Rico Fights for Chapter 9 Bankruptcy in Supreme Court," *The New York Times*, March 22, 2016, https://www.nytimes.com/2016/03/23/business/dealbook/puerto-rico-fights-for-chapter-9-bankruptcy-in-supreme-court.html.

87 Atiles-Osoria, *Apuntes*, 177.

88 Atiles-Osoria, *Apuntes*, 178–79.

89 See Gloria Ruiz Kuilan, "Una Orden ejecutiva extiende estado de emergencia hasta fin de año," *El Nuevo día*, July 5, 2019, https://www.elnuevodia.com/noticias/locales/nota/unaordenejecutivaextiendeestadodeemergenciadepuertoricohastafindeano-2503731/.

90 Deborah Kobes documents how US fiscal emergency management has been used as "scapegoat," thereby advancing modes of capture. Key here is lack of clear definitions of "essential services" and citizen participation, which, in the cases of New York City, Washington, DC, and Detroit, intensified privatization, gentrification, and poverty. See her "Out of Control: Local Democracy Failures

and Fiscal Control Boards" (PhD diss., MIT, 2012). See also *Municipalities in Distress*, ed. Anne Acker, James E. Spiotto, and Laura E. Appleby (Chicago: Chapman and Cutler, 2012); Joel Cintrón Arbasetti and Carla Minet, "La Expansion silenciosa de las juntas de control fiscal en EEUU," *Centro de Periodismo Investigativo*, June 1, 2017, http://periodismoinvestigativo.com/2017/06/la -expansion-silenciosa-de-las-juntas-de-control-fiscal-en-ee-uu/; and Deepak Lamba-Nieves, "Presentación primer foro contra PROMESA" (unpublished ms.).

91 See Joel Cintrón Arbasetti, "Bajo la lupa dos integrantes de la Junta de Control Fiscal por su pasado en Banco Santander," *Centro de Periodismo Investigativo*, December 16, 2016, http://periodismoinvestigativo.com/2016/12/bajo-la -lupa-dos-integrantes-de-la-junta-de-control-fiscal-por-su-pasado-en-banco -santander/.

92 Frente Ciudadano para la Auditoría de la Deuda moved forward with a citizen audit, despite challenges accessing records. See http://www.auditoriayapr.org /. See here Joel Cintrón Arbasetti and Carla Minet, "Who Owns Puerto Rico's Debt, Exactly?," *In These Times*, October 17, 2017, http://inthesetimes.com /features/puerto_rico_debt_bond_holders_vulture_funds_named.html.

93 On August 7, 2018, e.g., Judge Swain ruled that rather than the government of Puerto Rico's budget for the fiscal year, the Fiscal Control Board's would be implemented. See Eva Lloréns Pérez, "Judge Swain Says PROMESA Provides Awkward Power-sharing Structure," *Caribbean Business*, August 7, 2018, http:// caribbeanbusiness.com/judge-swain-says-promesa-provides-awkward-power -sharing-structure/.

94 Luis J. Valentín Ortiz, "Puerto Rico's Fiscal Control Board: Parallel Government Full of Lawyers and Consultants," *Centro de Periodismo Investigativo*, August 1, 2018, http://periodismoinvestigativo.com/2018/08/puerto-ricos-fiscal-control -board-parallel-government-full-of-lawyers-and-consultants/.

95 An anti-colonial project in Puerto Rico must be undertaken at the "margins of law," "severing the nexus" with the legal structures that have produced the colony. On this basis, Atiles-Osoria provides a critique of what he calls the "hyperjuridification of the political" in Puerto Rico, where law is made into "the only space of political action." See *Apuntes*, 165–66, 187.

96 Cf. Érika Fontánez-Torres, *Ambigüedad y derecho: Ensayos de crítica jurídica* (Cabo Rojo, PR: Editora Educación Emergente, 2014), for an account of the subversion rather than abandonment of law. I discuss Fontánez-Torres's work in the conclusion to this book.

97 Muñiz-Varela draws from Quijano's notion throughout. See *Adiós*.

98 See also Miriam Muñiz-Varela, "Paradojas de la bioeconomía: Violencia y nuda vida," *Revista de ciencias sociales* 27 (2014). To be sure, in this text, Muñiz-Varela also highlights the forms of exceptionality that sustain the forms of dispossession she analyzes under the rubric of bioeconomy. Nevertheless, she emphasizes the socioeconomic rather than administrative aspects of exceptionality.

99 See Muñiz-Varela, "Paradojas de la bioeconomía: Violencia y nuda vida," 144–45.

100 Muñiz-Varela, "Paradojas de la bioeconomía: Violencia y nuda vida," 121.

101 Muñiz-Varela, *Adiós*, 24.

102 Muñiz-Varela, *Adiós*, 78.

103 Muñiz-Varela, *Adiós*, 78: "Un vector de muerte y una pulsión al terror se imponen hoy como parte de la especulación y el poder del capital."

104 One key site of the installation of the colonial condition through US intervention in Puerto Rico is the articulation of the latter's status as a site of experimentation—from birth control to the management of public debt in the territories through PROMESA. Muñiz-Verela argues that especially in the second half of the twentieth century, Puerto Rico has been a "postindustrial laboratory," continuing its status as "experimental island" (Muñiz-Varela, *Adiós*), 143. Cf. Melinda Cooper, *Life as Surplus: Biotechnology and Capitalism in the Neoliberal Era* (Seattle: University of Washington Press, 2008). Muñiz-Varela discusses Cooper's work. Tax exemption lands in Fordist and post-Fordist contexts first with the petrochemical industry then with pharmaceutical and agricultural industries that changed the character of labor and heightened the contraction of waged labor. See Muñiz-Varela's account of Monsanto in this context. Taking advantage of tax exemptions, Monsanto tests and grows GMO seeds in southern Puerto Rico.

105 Muñiz-Varela, *Adiós*, 136.

106 Miriam Muñiz-Varela, "La Deuda," 13: "Los tiempos hoy llamados pospolíticos, podrían entenderse o lo propongo así, como el del dominio de la bioeconomia, aquella que hace de la vida un valor dinerario, que va desde la farmaco/biotecnologia y tecnogenética a las distintas formas del endeudamiento. Aunque curiosamente y de manera paradojica coexiste y promueve formas de necroeconomía, que también vincula la deuda con la depredación, el empobrecimieto, la expropiación y el abandono de la vida. Puerto Rico exibe un expediente abultado de esas variadas formas de vida mercantilizada hasta en sus extremos de abandono y muerte."

107 Miriam Muñiz-Varela, "La Deuda," 13. See also Amado Martínez Lebrón, "El Banco Popular y la crisis colonial de Puerto Rico," *8ogrados*, September 5, 2017, https://www.8ogrados.net/banco-popular-y-la-crisis-colonial-de-puerto-rico/.

108 See Muñiz-Varela, *Adiós*, 41–65.

109 LeBrón, *Policing Life and Death*, 9. The informal economy ranges from "street-peddling, off-the-books construction work, unlicensed childcare, as well as . . . illicit organizations related to drugs, robbery, sex work, and gambling."

110 Muñiz-Varela, *Adiós*, 105.

111 Muñiz-Varela is here citing Elías Guitiérrez, "En la Trampa," *Cuadrenos de* PLERUS 2 (1997). See *Adiós*, 100–106.

112 Muñiz-Varela, *Adiós*, 109.

113 Muñiz-Varela, *Adiós*, 103, 104.

114 Muñiz-Varela, *Adiós*, 84ff. See also Edgardo Meléndez, *Sponsored Migration: The State and Puerto Rican Postwar Migration to the United States* (Columbus: Ohio State University Press, 2017).

115 Muñiz-Varela, *Adiós*, 110.

116 LeBrón, *Policing Life and Death*; Muñiz-Varela, *Adiós*, 96.

117 Muñiz-Varela, *Adiós*, 100–109.

118 Muñiz-Varela, *Adiós*, 104.

119 LeBrón, *Policing Life and Death*, 2. LeBrón here draws from Zaire Dinzey-Flores and José Fusté's work. See Dizney-Flores, *Locked In, Locked Out: Gated Communities in a Puerto Rican City* (Philadelphia: University of Pennsylvania Press, 2013); and Fusté, "Colonial Laboratories, Irreparable Subjects: The Experiment of '(b)ordering' San Juan's Public Housing Residents," *Social Identities* 16, no. 1 (2010).

120 LeBrón, *Policing Life and Death*, 32. See also José Villa Rodríguez, *Crimen y criminalidad en Puerto Rico: El Sujeto criminal* (San Juan: Ediciones SITUM, 2006).

121 LeBrón, *Policing Life and Death*, 33.

122 LeBrón, *Policing Life and Death*, 5.

123 LeBrón, *Policing Life and Death*, 3.

124 LeBrón, *Policing Life and Death*, 10; see Stuart Hall, *Policing the Crisis: Mugging, the State, and Law and Order* (London: Palgrave, 1978).

125 LeBrón, *Policing Life and Death*, 11.

126 LeBrón, *Policing Life and Death*, 4.

127 See "A Wave of Daytime Killings Has Puerto Rico on Edge," *The New York Times*, January 13, 2019, https://www.nytimes.com/2019/01/13/us/puerto-rico-crime-murders-violence.html.

128 LeBrón, *Policing Life and Death*, 44.

129 See LeBrón, *Policing Life and Death*, 46.

130 See LeBrón, *Policing Life and Death*, 76.

131 LeBrón, *Policing Life and Death*, 76–77.

132 LeBrón, *Policing Life and Death*, 76–77.

133 LeBrón, *Policing Life and Death*, 25.

134 LeBrón, *Policing Life and Death*, 47.

135 LeBrón, *Policing Life and Death*, 47.

136 LeBrón, *Policing Life and Death*, 42.

137 Muñiz-Varela, "Taken Island."

138 Muñiz-Varela, "La Deuda."

139 Muñiz-Varela, "La Deuda."

140 Muñiz-Varela, "La Deuda."

141 See Yarimar Bonilla and Marisol LeBrón, "Introduction," in *Aftershocks of Disaster: Puerto Rico before and after the Storm*, ed. Yarimar Bonilla and Marisol LeBrón (Chicago: Haymarket Books, 2019), 8–9.

142 Ayuda Legal Puerto Rico, "Hacia la recuperación justa: Fondos CDBG-DR y desplazamientos forzosos," May 16, 2019, https://www.ayudalegalpuertorico.org/2019/05/16/hacia-la-recuperacion-justa-fondos-cdbg-dr-y-desplazamientos-forzosos/.

143 Muñiz-Varela, "La Deuda," 14. COFINA's original objective was amended to include financing the operational expenses of government agencies.

144 See here Hilda Lloréns and Maritza Stanchich, "Water Is Life, but the Colony Is a Necropolis: Environmental Terrains of Struggle in Puerto Rico," *Cultural Dynamics* 31, no. 1–2 (2019).

145 Luis Valentin Ortiz, "Puerto Rico Announces Deal to Restructure Power Authority Debt," Reuters, May 3, 2019, https://www.reuters.com/article/us-usa-puertorico-prepa/puerto-rico-announces-deal-to-restructure-power-authority-debt-idUSKCN1SA026.

146 Santory-Jorge, "Destruir un país."

147 Nixon foregrounds the temporal character of slow violence and its challenge to a temporality of speed distinctive of neoliberal rationality. See *Slow Violence*.

148 Nixon, *Slow Violence*, 2.

149 Nixon, *Slow Violence*, 2.

150 Nixon, *Slow Violence*, 2.

151 Climate change is exemplary of this type of violence.

152 Berlant, *Cruel Optimism*, 7.

153 It frames, Berlant says, "extensive threats to survival" intensively, as the immediate domination over the "reproduction of life" (*Cruel Optimism*, 7).

154 Berlant, *Cruel Optimism*, 10.

155 "The extraordinary always turns out to be an amplification of something in the works," Berlant writes, "a labile boundary at best, not a slammed-door departure" (*Cruel Optimism*, 10).

156 Berlant, *Cruel Optimism*, 95.

157 Berlant, *Cruel Optimism*, 96.

158 Berlant, *Cruel Optimism*, 38.

159 Berlant, *Cruel Optimism*, 11. The current recession, Berlant argues, "congeals decades of class bifurcation, downward mobility, and environmental, political, and social brittleness that have increased progressively since the Reagan era. The intensification of these processes, which reshapes conventions of racial, gendered, sexual, economic, and nation-based subordination, has also increased the probability that structural contingency will create manifest crisis situations in ordinary existence for more kinds of people." I am stressing here the intensification of those conditions for racialized populations, however.

160 Berlant, *Cruel Optimism*, 96.

161 Berlant, *Cruel Optimism*, 98.

162 Berlant, *Cruel Optimism*, 100–101.

163 Berlant, *Cruel Optimism*, 101.

164 Berlant, *Cruel Optimism*, 101.

165 Berlant, *Cruel Optimism*, 102.

166 Berlant, *Cruel Optimism*, 100.

167 Berlant, *Cruel Optimism*, 99.

168 Berlant, *Cruel Optimism*, 99.

169 Berlant, *Cruel Optimism*, 115.

170 Santory-Jorge, "Destruir un país," 1.

171 See Gricel Surillo Luna, "From Peso to Dollar as the Official Currency," *Enciclopedia de Puerto Rico*, September 15, 2014, https://enciclopediapr.org/en/encyclopedia/from-peso-to-dollar-as-the-official-currency/.

172 Roberto Alejandro Rivera, "1899: Dos reflexiones," *8ogrados*, January 25, 2018, http://www.8ogrados.net/1899-dos-reflexiones/.

173 Santory-Jorge writes: "It is interesting to note that the resources that the United States government brought to Puerto Rico came from the army and from the humanitarian response organized by the mayors of cities with more than 150,000 inhabitants in the United States. There was no assignment of Congress" ("Destruir un país," 5).

174 See Natural Resources Defense Council, "Threats on Tap: Drinking Water Violations in Puerto Rico." Issue Paper No. 17-02-A, May 2017, quoted in Adriana Garriga-López, "Agua Dulce," in *Liquid Utility, e-flux architecture* 103 (2019).

175 Santory-Jorge, "Destruir un país," 1.

176 See, e.g., Jhoni Jackson, "La Colectiva Feminista en Construcción Is Helping Puerto Rico Recover from Hurricane Maria," *Teen Vogue*, October 27, 2017, https://www.teenvogue.com/story/la-colectiva-feminista-en-construccion-is-helping-puerto-rico-recover-from-hurricane-maria. I discuss this protest in my "Black Feminist Tactics: On la Colectiva Feminista en Construcción's Politics without Guarantee," in *The Decolonial Geographies of Puerto Rico's 2019 Summer Protests: A Forum for Society and Space*, ed. Marisol LeBrón and Joaquín Villanueva (February 2020).

177 Yarimar Bonilla, "The Wait of Disaster," in *Una Proposición modesta: Puerto Rico a prueba/A Modest Proposal: Puerto Rico's Crucible*, initiative of Allora and Calzadilla, ed. Sara Nadal-Melisó (Barcelona: Fundació Antoni Tàpies, 2018), and a longer version, "The Coloniality of Disaster: Race, Empire, and the Temporal Logics of Emergency in Puerto Rico, USA," *Political Geography* 78 (2020). Cf. Naomi Klein, *The Shock Doctrine* (New York: Random House, 2007) and *The Battle for Paradise: Puerto Rico Takes on the Disaster Capitalists* (Chicago: Haymarket Books, 2018).

178 Bonilla, "The Coloniality of Disaster," 2. She explores such rupture to think through how catastrophic events "impact our experience of time, progression, social action, and political possibility."

179 Bonilla, "The Wait of Disaster," 41.

180 Bonilla, "The Wait of Disaster," 42.

181 Bonilla, "The Wait of Disaster," 42.

182 Bonilla, "The Wait of Disaster," 42.

183 Bonilla, "The Coloniality of Disaster," 3.

184 Bonilla, "The Coloniality of Disaster," 4.

185 See Pedro Lebrón, "Matarse en la colonia es un asunto cotidiano," *8ogrados*, April 5, 2019, https://www.8ogrados.net/matarse-en-la-colonia-es-un-asunto-cotidiano/. Lebrón notes that in February 2019, a total of thirty-seven suicides had been reported. Sixteen suicides had been reported by the same date in 2018. At the time that Lebrón was writing, these numbers meant a suicide a day. Lebrón highlights the harm done when these deaths are considered effects of "mental illness," obfuscating the social, economic, and political reality of which they are expressions.

186 Saidiya Hartman, *Lose Your Mother: A Journey along the Atlantic Slave Route* (New York: Farrar, Straus and Giroux, 2017), 6.

187 Christina Sharpe, *In the Wake: On Blackness and Being* (Durham, NC: Duke University Press, 2016), 104.

188 Sharpe, *In the Wake*, 106: "In the United States, slavery is imagined as a singular event even as it changed over time and even as its duration expands into supposed emancipation and beyond. But slavery was not singular; it was, rather, a singularity—a weather event or phenomenon likely to occur around a particular time, or date, or set of circumstances. Emancipation did not make free Black life free; it continues to hold us in that singularity. The brutality was not singular; it was the singularity of antiblackness."

189 Sharpe, *In the Wake*, 106; Hartman, *Lose Your Mother*, 6.

190 The Fiscal Control Board's post-María austerity plan includes a policy to offshore a third of Puerto Rico's prison population (approximately 3,200 inmates), purportedly to save around $400 million over four years. See Joel Cintrón Arbasetti, "Departamento de Corrección adjudica contrato a CoreCivic para traslado de confinados a Estados Unidos," *Centro de Periodismo Investigativo*, August 7, 2018, http://periodismoinvestigativo.com/2018/08/departamento-de-correccion-adjudica-contrato-a-corecivic-para-traslado-de-confinados-a-estados-unidos/, and "This Is Human Trafficking: After María Puerto Rico to Move 3,200 Inmates to Arizona," *The Guardian*, August 7, 2018, https://www.theguardian.com/world/2018/aug/07/puerto-rico-prisons-inmates. Concerning the prison-industrial complex in Puerto Rico, see Luis A. Zambrana-González, "Privatización carcelaria por la cocina," *8ogrados*, May 18, 2018, http://www.8ogrados.net/privatizacion-carcelaria-por-la-cocina/, and "Punitivismo como negocio: Un Terrible presagio," *8ogrados*, December 9, 2016, http://www.8ogrados.net/punitivismo-como-negocio-un-terrible-presagio/.

191 El Vocero reports 550 deaths within prisons in the last decade. See Yaritza Rivera Clemente, "Unos 550 presos mueren en una década," *El Vocero*, October 1, 2019, https://www.elvocero.com/gobierno/unos-presos-mueren-en-una-d-cada/article_feoda6f4-e3f2-11e9-9de4-4f35f2266891. html.

192 See Angelina Marrero and Alexander Santiago's interviews in Víctor Rodríguez Velázquez, "Personas trans sufren el desastre de María desde la marginalización," *Centro de Periodismo Investigativo*, September 23, 2019, http://periodismoinvestigativo.com/2019/09/personas-trans-sufren-el-desastre-de-maria-desde-la-marginacion/.

193 Bonilla, "The Wait of Disaster," 47. Referring to Javier Auyero's work, Bonilla points out that bureaucratic waiting produces political subordination.

194 By 2019, 438 schools had been closed. I discuss the housing crisis in the conclusion to the book.

CHAPTER THREE. HISTORICAL RECKONING

1 C. L. R. James, *The Black Jacobins: Toussaint L'Ouverture and the San Domingo Revolution* (New York: Random House, 1989), ix–x; Jérôme Duval, "De la Colonización francesa a la esclavitud económica de la deuda," Comité para la Abolición de las Deudas Ilegítimas (CADTM), September 26, 2017, http://www.cadtm.org/Haiti-de-la-colonizacion-francesa. See also Anthony Phillips, "Haiti, France and the Independence Debt of 1825," Institute for Justice and Democracy in Haiti, 2008, https://caribbeansyllabus.wordpress.com/caribbean-syllabus/.

2 Anthony Phillips, "Haiti, France and the Independence Debt of 1825" (unpublished ms.), 2.

3 James, *The Black Jacobins*, ix.

4 Anthony Phillips, "Haiti, France and the Independence Debt of 1825," 2.

5 Anthony Phillips, "Haiti, France and the Independence Debt of 1825," 2.

6 James, *The Black Jacobins*, ix.

7 See Guillermo A. Baralt, *Esclavos Rebeldes: Conspiraciones y sublevaciones de esclavos en Puerto Rico (1795–1873)* (San Juan: Ediciones Huracán, 1981), esp. chap. 1, for a now classic account of the impact of the Haitian Revolution in Puerto Rico. See also Arturo Morales Carrión, "La revolución haitiana y el movimiento antiesclavista en Puerto Rico," *Boletín de la Academia Puertorriqueña de la Historia* 8, no. 30 (1983); Antonio Pinto, "Negro sobre blanco: La conspiración esclava de 1812 en PR," *Caribbean Studies* 40, no. 1 (2012); Jose Luis Belmonte Postigo, "Esclavitud y status social en Santo Domingo y Puerto Rico durante la diáspora de la Revolución Haitiana," in *Formas de Liberdade: Gratidâo, condicionalidade e incertezas no mundo escravista nas Américas*, ed. Jonis Freire and María Verónica Secreto (Río de Janeiro: Mauad, 2018).

8 See Hilary Beckles, *Britain's Black Debt: Reparations for Caribbean Slavery and Native Genocide* (Kingston, Jamaica: University of the West Indies Press, 2013), location 4587–88.

9 See Phillips, "Haiti, France and the Independence Debt of 1825."

10 The French government acknowledged the payment of 90 million francs in 1893. Haiti paid the associated interest of the debt in 1947. Debt was again accrued by the Duvalier government, some of which was waived in 2010 by the IMF in the wake of the devastating earthquake that occurred that year.

11 Duval, "De la Colonización francesa a la esclavitud económica de la deuda."

12 Naomi Klein, "Haiti: A Creditor, Not a Debtor," *The Nation*, February 11, 2010, https://www.thenation.com/article/haiti-creditor-not-debtor/.

13 Camille Chalmers, "Deudocracia y nuevo colonialismo: Europa, América Latina y el Caribe," December 4, 2018, https://aldia.microjuris.com/2018/12/03 /microjuris-transmitira-panel-deudocracia-y-el-nuevo-colonialismo-europa -america-y-el-caribe/.

14 See Shariana Ferrer-Núñez from Colectiva Feminista en Construcción, "Nosotras contra la deuda," in El Panal, April 9, 2019, https://www.facebook.com /Colectiva. Feminista. PR/videos/323512275032312/.

15 Ariadna Godreau-Aubert, *Las Propias: Apuntes para una pedagogía de las endeudadas* (Cabo Rojo, PR: Editora Educación Emergente, 2018), 68; all translations are my own.

16 Godreau-Aubert, *Las Propias*, 69.

17 See Maurizio Lazzarato, *The Making of the Indebted Man*, trans. Joshua David Jordan (Cambridge, MA: MIT Press, 2012), and *Governing by Debt*, trans. Joshua David Jordan (Cambridge, MA: MIT Press, 2015).

18 Godreau-Aubert, *Las Propias*, 15.

19 In addition, Richard Dienst, *The Bonds of Debt* (London: Verso, 2011); Federica Gregoratto, "Debt, Power, and the Normativity of Interdependence: Current Debates and the Young Marx," in *Hegel, Marx and Contemporary World*, ed. K. Boveiri, E. Chaput, and A. Theurillat-Cloutier (Cambridge: Cambridge Scholars Publishing, 2016); Angela Mitropolous, *Contract and Contagion: From Biopolitics to Oikonomia* (New York: Autonomedia, 2012), and with Melinda Cooper, "In Praise of Usura," *Mute* 2 (2009); Janet Roitman, *Fiscal Disobedience: An Anthropology of Fiscal Regulation in Central Africa* (Princeton, NJ: Princeton University Press, 2004); and Fred Moten and Stefano Harney, *The Undercommons: Fugitive Planning and Black Study* (Wivenhoe, UK: Minor Compositions, 2011), whose work I discuss in this chapter; see Randy Martin, "What Difference Do Derivatives Make? From the Technical to the Political Conjuncture," *Culture Unbound* 6 (2014), and "A Precarious Dance: A Derivative Sociality," *TDR: The Drama Review* 56, no. 4 (2012); Max Haiven, *Cultures of Financialization: Fictitious Capital in Popular Culture and Everyday Life* (London: Palgrave, 2014), and Denise Ferreira da Silva, "Unpayable Debt," in *The Documenta 14 Reader*, ed. Quinn Latimer and Adam Szymczyk (Munich: Prestel Publishing, 2017).

20 See David Graeber, *Debt: The First 5,000 Years* (Hoboken, NJ: Melville, 2011), 120ff. This is Jason Read's gloss. See his "I Owe You an Explanation: Graeber

and Marx on Origin Stories," *Unemployed Negativity*, September 21, 2011, http://www.unemployednegativity.com/2011/09/i-owe-you-explanation -graeber-and-marx.html.

21 Dienst, *Bonds of Debt*, 150.
22 See, e.g., Elettra Stimilli, *The Debt of the Living*, trans. Arianna Bove (Albany: SUNY Press, 2017), for a recent account of some of these themes.
23 For an overview of variations on these themes, see Gustav Peebles, "The Anthropology of Credit and Debt," *Annual Review of Anthropology* 39 (2010).
24 Ariadna Godreau-Aubert, "Nosotras que no noes debemos a nadie: Las Propias en tiempos de austeridad y deuda pública," XI Coloquio Nacional sobre las Mujeres, Universidad de Puerto Rico, Recinto Universitario de Mayagüez (2017), Q&A.
25 Godreau-Aubert, "Nosotras."
26 Graeber, *Debt*, 94.
27 Graeber, *Debt*, 96.
28 It is not the individual, then, but the disposition that is equal. See Graeber, *Debt*, 100.
29 Graeber, *Debt*, 95.
30 This form of interaction "tends toward" equivalence. See Graeber, *Debt*, 103.
31 Graeber, *Debt*, 103.
32 Graeber, *Debt*, 103.
33 Graeber, *Debt*, 109.
34 Graeber, *Debt*, 120ff.
35 Graeber, *Debt*, 120.
36 Graeber, *Debt*, 120.
37 Graeber, *Debt*, 121.
38 Graeber, *Debt*, 122.
39 Graeber, *Debt*, 391.
40 Graeber, *Debt*, 386.
41 Graeber, *Debt*, 386.
42 Gregoratto, "Debt, Power, and the Normativity of Interdependence," 220. There are roughly three perspectives, she argues, from which to undertake a critique of debt: a historical-anthropological, a political-economic, and an account of subjectivation. Graeber's work exemplifies the first perspective, Costas Lapavistas's the second, Maurizio Lazzarato's the third. See Maurizio Lazzarato, *Governing by Debt*, trans. Joshua David Jordan (Cambridge, MA: MIT Press, 2015), and *The Making of the Indebted Man*, trans. Joshua David Jordan (Cambridge, MA: MIT Press, 2012); and Costas Lapavitsas, *Profiting without Producing: How Finance Exploits Us All* (London: Verso, 2014).
43 Gregoratto, "Debt, Power, and the Normativity of Interdependence," 220.
44 Gregoratto, "Debt, Power, and the Normativity of Interdependence," 223.
45 Gregoratto, "Debt, Power, and the Normativity of Interdependence," 226. Debt, Gregoratto argues, "has another, specular face, that of the lending man" (224).

46 See Friedrich Nietzsche, *On the Genealogy of Morals* in *On the Genealogy of Morals* and *Ecce Homo*, trans. Walter Kaufmann and RJ Hollingdale (New York: Vintage, 1989), 62–63.

47 See Marx, "Estranged Labor," *Paris Manuscripts*, in *Collected Works*, vol. 3: *Marx and Engels: 1843–1844* (New York: International Publishers, 1975), 270ff.

48 Marx, "Comments on James Mill," in *Collected Works*, vol. 3, 212.

49 Marx, "Comments," 214.

50 Marx, "Comments," 214.

51 Marx, "Comments," 215.

52 Marx, "Comments," 214.

53 Marx, "Comments," 215.

54 Marx, "Comments," 215–16.

55 Marx, "Comments," 216.

56 Marx, "Comments," 216.

57 Marx, "Comments," 216.

58 Marx, "Comments," 216.

59 Marx, "Comments," 216.

60 Gregoratto, "Debt, Power, and the Normativity of Interdependence," 228.

61 Marx, "Comments," 225, 227.

62 Marx, "Comments," 227, 228.

63 Gregoratto, "Debt, Power, and the Normativity of Interdependence," 235.

64 Gregoratto, "Debt, Power, and the Normativity of Interdependence," 228.

65 Gregoratto, "Debt, Power, and the Normativity of Interdependence," 233.

66 Gregoratto, "Debt, Power, and the Normativity of Interdependence," 233.

67 Gregoratto, "Debt, Power, and the Normativity of Interdependence," 235.

68 Gregoratto, "Debt, Power, and the Normativity of Interdependence," 235.

69 This is key for articulating practices of resistance, though they must also respond to systemic factors such as "laws regulating economic transaction, prevailing political and military powers, etc." (Gregoratto, "Debt, Power, and the Normativity of Interdependence," 236).

70 Gregoratto, "Debt, Power, and the Normativity of Interdependence," 227. For an extended criticism of the normative paradigm in Critical Theory, see my "Paradoxes of Neoliberalism and the Tasks of Critical Theory," *Critical Horizons: A Journal of Philosophy and Social Theory* 14, no. 1 (2013).

71 Gregoratto, "Debt, Power, and the Normativity of Interdependence," 231.

72 See Mitropoulos, "Mutuum Mutare," in *Contract and Contagion*, 209.

73 Mitropoulos, "Legal, Tender," in *Contract and Contagion*, 95. Cf. Saidiya Hartman's *Scenes of Subjection: Terror, Slavery, and Self-Making in Nineteenth-Century America* (Oxford: Oxford University Press, 1997), which explores forms of subjection through the contract in the context of emancipation.

74 Cf. Roitman, *Fiscal Disobedience*.

75 Dienst, *Bonds of Debt*, 47.

76 Dienst, *Bonds of Debt*, 47n7.

77 Dienst, *Bonds of Debt*, 149.

78 Dienst, *Bonds of Debt*, 12.

79 Dienst, *Bonds of Debt*, 149.

80 Marx, *Capital: A Critique of Political Economy*, vol. 1, trans. Ben Fowkes (London: Penguin, 1976), chap. 26, 874.

81 Dienst, *Bonds of Debt*, 147.

82 Dienst, *Bonds of Debt*, 147.

83 Dienst points out Marx's apparent belief in the sacrificial origins of debt, establishing the primordial violence that sustains the money form. Like the ancient debtor, the worker is punished before the law, "dismembered" for a failure to pay (Dienst, *Bonds of Debt*, 147).

84 Such an originary accumulation is "renewed at every turn" (Dienst, *Bonds of Debt*, 150).

85 Dienst, *Bonds of Debt*, 150. See chap. 5 of Hartman's *Scenes of Subjection*.

86 Dienst, *Bonds of Debt*, 150.

87 See my discussion of the relation between wage work and unwaged labor in chap. 1.

88 Marx, *Capital*, vol. 1, chap. 25, 781ff.

89 Dienst, *Bonds of Debt*, 150.

90 Marx, *Capital*, vol. 1, chap. 25, 782.

91 Marx, *Capital*, vol. 1, chap. 25, 784.

92 See Marx, *Capital*, vol. 1, chap. 25, 792.

93 Marx, *Capital*, vol. 1, chap. 25, 792. See also John Bellamy Foster and Fred Magdoff, "Disposable Workers: Today's Reserve Army of Labor," *Monthly Review* 55, no. 11 (2004).

94 Marx, *Capital*, vol. 1, chap. 25, 789.

95 Marx, *Capital*, vol. 1, chap. 25, 789.

96 Marx, *Capital*, vol. 1, chap. 25, 794ff.

97 I am here paraphrasing Silvia Federici's gloss on these famous passages. See *Caliban and the Witch: Women, the Body, and Primitive Accumulation* (New York: Autonomedia, 2004), chap. 2.

98 Marx, *Capital*, vol. 1, chap. 25, 797.

99 Dienst, *Bonds of Debt*, 150.

100 Dienst, *Bonds of Debt*, 150.

101 Dienst, *Bonds of Debt*, 150.

102 See Dienst, *Bonds of Debt*, 150.

103 Dienst, *Bonds of Debt*, 151.

104 Dienst, *Bonds of Debt*, 147.

105 Marx, *Capital: A Critique of Political Economy*, vol. 3, trans. David Fernbach (London: Penguin, 1981), chap. 27, 572.

106 Dienst, *Bonds of Debt*, 153.

107 Dienst, *Bonds of Debt*, 153.

108 See Haiven, *Cultures of Financialization,* and Cédric Durand, *Fictitious Capital: How Finance Is Appropriating Our Future,* trans. David Broder (London: Penguin, 2017).

109 Dienst suggests, far more incisively, that "the moment of hope can be glimpsed neither in the debt that inaugurates the story nor in the tale that it obligates each of us to read, but rather it is to be found in the prospect of return, where history is reopened by extinguishing the story that led us there" (*Bonds of Debt,* 153).

110 Dienst, *Bonds of Debt,* 153; emphasis mine.

111 Dienst, *Bonds of Debt,* 147.

112 Mitropoulos, "Legal, Tender," 71.

113 Mitropoulos, "Legal, Tender," 77.

114 Mitropoulos, "Mutuum, Mutare," in *Contract and Contagion,* 209.

115 Mitropoulos, "Legal, Tender," 91.

116 Mitropoulos, "Legal, Tender," 76.

117 Mitropoulos, "Debt Servitude, Service Work, Oikos," *sometim3s,* December 5, 2013, http://sometim3s.com/2013/12/05/.

118 Mitropoulos, "Debt Servitude, Service Work, Oikos."

119 Mitropoulos, "Debt Servitude, Service Work, Oikos."

120 Mitropoulos, "Debt Servitude, Service Work, Oikos."

121 Mitropoulos, "Mutuum, Mutare," 230.

122 Mitropoulos, "Mutuum, Mutare," 230.

123 Cf. Roitman, *Fiscal Disobedience.*

124 The question is whether debt will be allowed to be "constitutive," as Godreau-Aubert puts it, or whether it will be subverted. Godreau-Aubert, "Nosotras que no nos debemos a nadie," XI Coloquio Nacional Sobre las Mujeres, Q&A.

125 Cf. Miranda Joseph, *Debt to Society: Accounting for Life under Capitalism* (Minneapolis: University of Minnesota Press, 2014).

126 Moten and Harney, *The Undercommons.*

127 Moten and Harney, *The Undercommons,* 63.

128 Moten and Harney, *The Undercommons,* 61.

129 Godreau-Aubert, "Nosotras que no nos debemos a nadie," in *Las Propias.*

130 Godreau-Aubert, *Las Propias,* 15: "Insistiré en la distancia entre prometer (deberse) y deber."

131 See Alejandra Azuero-Quijano, "Criminal Enterprise, Forensics and the Reproduction of Corporate Power as Crime in Colombia," dissertation proposal, Department of Anthropology, University of Chicago. See also her *Conviction by Design: Remaking Criminal Responsibility at the Nuremberg Trials* (SJD diss., Harvard Law School, 2013).

132 See Janet Roitman, *Fiscal Disobedience* (Princeton, NJ: Princeton University Press, 2005), chap. 4.

133 Roitman, *Fiscal Disobedience*, 97.

134 Roitman, *Fiscal Disobedience*, 98.

135 Roitman, *Fiscal Disobedience*, 98; emphasis mine.

136 See Armando J. S. Pintado, "Pausa para la auditoría," *Centro de Periodismo Investigativo*, March 24, 2017, http://www.80grados.net/pausa-para-la-auditoria. See also Luis J. Valentín Ortiz, "Rosselló deroga comisión de auditoría de la deuda," *Caribbean Business*, April 19, 2017, https://cb.pr/rossello-firma-ley-que-deroga-comision-para-auditar-la-deuda/.

137 The Constitution sets a 15 percent limit to the state budget for purposes of servicing the debt. See Katefrans Flores, "Razones por las que no se audita la deuda pública," *El Nuevo día*, April 19, 2017, http://www.indicepr.com/noticias/2017/04/19/news/69703/razones-por-las-que-no-se-audita-la-deuda-publica/. See also Joanisabel Gonzalez, "Mitad de la deuda podría ser inconstitucional," *El Nuevo día*, June 2, 2016, https://www.elnuevodia.com/negocios/economia/nota/mitaddeladeudapodriaserinconstitucional-2205945. See here as well Eva Prados, "Violencia de género y auditoría de la deuda" (unpublished ms). As noted in chap. 1, a translation of this text by Nicole Cecilia Delgado is forthcoming in "On Debt, Blame, and Responsibility: Feminist Resistance in the Colony of Puerto Rico," ed. Rocío Zambrana, special section of *Critical Times*. All translations in this book are my own.

138 See "Constituida la comisión ciudadana para la auditoría integral del crédito público," June 6, 2017, https://www.facebook.com/FrenteCiudadanoAuditoria DeLaDeuda/photos/a.1804786283110736/1918075851781778/?type=3. See also VAMOSPR, which was the initial multisectoral group to demand a citizen debt audit. See Pierre Gotiniaux, "La Auditorá en curso ya revela una deuda ampliamente ilegal," Comité para la Abolición de las Deudas Ilegítimas (CADTM), July 5, 2016, http://www.cadtm.org/Puerto-Rico-La-auditoria-en-curso.

139 See Auditoría Ya, http://www.auditoriaya.org/.

140 José Nicolás Medinas Fuentes, "Tres teorías sobre la deuda pública," *El Nuevo día*, February 20, 2018, https://www.elnuevodia.com/opinion/columnas/tresteoriassobreladeudapublica-columna-2400424/.

141 Prados, "Violencia de género y auditoría de la deuda."

142 Prados, "Violencia de género y auditoría de la deuda."

143 Prados, "Violencia de género y auditoría de la deuda," 3.

144 See Sarah Molinari, "The Public Reckoning: Anti-debt Futures After #RickyRenuncia," in *The Decolonial Geographies of Puerto Rico's 2019 Summer Protests: A Forum for Society and Space*, ed. Marisol LeBrón and Joaquín Villanueva (February 2020).

145 See my "Checklists: On Puerto Rico's SoVerano," *Critical Times* 3, no. 2 (2020).

146 See, e.g., Rafael Bernabe and Manuel Rodríguez Banchs, "La Política de la anti-política," *80grados*, July 26, 2019, https://www.80grados.net/la-politica-de-la-anti-politica/.

147 For recent discussions of this history, see, e.g., José Atiles Osoria, *Jugando con el derecho: Movimientos anticoloniales puertorriqueños y la fuerza de la ley* (Cabo Rojo, PR: Editora Educación Emergente, 2019); Arturo Massol Deya, *Amores que luchan: Relato de la victoria contra el gasoducto en tiempos de crisis energética* (San Juan: Ediciones Callejón, 2018); and Liliana Cotto-Morales, *Desalambrar: Orígenes de los rescates de terreno en Puerto Rico y su pertenencia en los movimientos sociales contemporáneos* (San Juan: Editorial Tal Cual, 2006).

148 See my "Black Feminist Tactics: On la Colectiva Feminista en Construcción's Politics without Guarantee," in *The Decolonial Geographies of Puerto Rico's 2019 Summer Protests: A Forum for Society and Space*, ed. Marisol LeBrón and Joaquín Villanueva (February 2020).

149 Shariana Ferrer-Núñez's confrontation with O'Neill at a restaurant in Santurce can be seen as an *escrache*. Escrache is a form of direct action first used by HIJOS (Daughters and Sons for Identity and Justice against Forgetting and Silence) in postdictatorship Argentina. It named those responsible for the torture, killing, and disappearance of thousands but also who benefited from amnesty laws. I would argue that escrache differs from "cancel culture" in its genealogy but also form, as it seeks to interrupt impunity, do the work of memory, and pursue reparations once formal processes have failed and especially in relation to those in positions of power. See Susana Kaiser, "Escraches: Demonstrations, Communication and Political Memory in Post-dictatorial Argentina," *Media, Culture, and Society* 24, no.4 (2002).

150 O'Neill was also involved in displacing the Vietnam community in Guaynabo for a waterfront development. See Dalila Rodríguez Saavedra, "Vietnam, Puerto Rico: Lucha por los terrenos," *8ogrados*, July 20, 2018, https://www.8ogrados.net/vietnam-puerto-rico-lucha-por-los-terrenos/. See also Gabriel Miranda's 2017 documentary *Vietnam, Puerto Rico*.

151 See Héctor Ramos, "Feministas arrestan y encarcelan a Héctor O'Neill," *NotiUno 630*, https://www.notiuno.com/noticias/fotos-feministas-arrestan-y-encarcelan-a-h-ctor-o-neill/article_a61af18b-57eb-51db-a703-f5ec98640f2b.html.

152 I thank Shariana Ferrer-Núñez for sharing reflections on details of the performance.

153 See Colectiva Feminista en Construcción, *La Manifiesta*, 2017, https://www.scribd.com/document/263057948/La-Manifiesta-Colectiva-Feminista-en-Construccion, and *Manifiesto Antirracista*, June 2, 2020, https://www.facebook.com/notes/colectiva-feminista-en-construcci%C3%B3n/manifiesto-antirracista-colectiva-feminista-en-construcci%C3%B3n/2968317379926640; in English, *The Anti-Racist Manifesto*, *Latino Rebels*, June 7, 2020, https://www.latinorebels.com/2020/06/07/antiracistmanifesto/.

154 On the prison-industrial complex in Puerto Rico, see Luis A. Zambrana-González, "Privatización carcelaria por la cocina," *8ogrados*, May 18, 2018,

http://www.8ogrados.net/privatizacion-carcelaria-por-la-cocina/, and "Punitivismo como negocio: Un Terrible presagio," *8ogrados*, December 9, 2016,
http://www.8ogrados.net/punitivismo-como-negocio-un-terrible-presagio
/. In addition to Marisol LeBrón's *Policing Life and Death: Race, Violence,
and Resistance in Puerto Rico* (Oakland: University of California Press, 2019),
discussed in previous chapters, see Fernando Picó, *El Día menos pensado: Historia de los presidiarios en Puerto Rico, 1793–1993* (San Juan: Huracán, 1994).

155 See Ramos, "Feministas arrestan y encarcelan a Héctor O'Neill."

156 These are Ferrer-Núñez's clarifications. I am grateful for our conversations
about this performance and its relation to carceral feminism.

157 See, e.g., Vanesa Contreras, "El 8 de Marzo contra la deuda," *8ogrados*,
March 1, 2019, https://www.8ogrados.net/el-8-de-marzo-contra-la-deuda/.

158 See press release: "Colectiva Feminista en Construcción realiza embargo
feminista a la banca por su rol en la crisis de vivienda que vive el país," https://
www.facebook.com/Colectiva.Feminista.PR/posts/2088021774622876.

159 Ayuda Legal Puerto Rico, "Hacia la recuperación justa: Fondos CDBG-DR y
desplazamientos forzosos," May 16, 2019, https://www.ayudalegalpuertorico
.org/2019/05/16/hacia-la-recuperacion-justa-fondos-cdbg-dr-y
-desplazamientos-forzosos/.

160 "Piden declarar una emergencia por ejecuciones hipotecarias," *Sin Comillas*
(May 15, 2019), http://sincomillas.com/piden-declarar-una-emergencia-por
-ejecuciones-hipotecarias/.

161 Ayuda Legal Puerto Rico, "Hacia la recuperación justa: Fondos CDBG-DR y
desplazamientos forzosos."

162 Miguel Rodríguez-Casellas, "El 'Adiós' de Miriam Muñiz-Varela," *8ogrados*,
November 29, 2013, http://www.8ogrados.net/eladiosdemiriam-muniz-varela
/. *Cuponeros* refers to *cupones* or food stamps.

163 Roitman, *Fiscal Disobedience*, 98.

164 Roitman, *Fiscal Disobedience*, 98.

165 Roitman, *Fiscal Disobedience*, 94.

166 Roitman, *Fiscal Disobedience*, 98. In the Cameroonian context, Roitman
argues, these practices function as a "limiting truth and just representation of
social relations" that, while criminalized, also appear as the acts of the "unseiz-
able, the unstoppable thief."

CHAPTER FOUR. SUBVERSIVE INTERRUPTION

For the epigraphs, see Guillermo Rebollo-Gil, *Última llamada* (Carolina, PR:
Ediciones UNE, 2017); all translations are my own. Miguel Rodríguez Casellas,
"De lo Superfluo," *8ogrados*, February 28, 2014. https://www.8ogrados.net/de
-lo-superfluo/; all translations are my own.

1 Ariadna Godreau-Aubert, "Protestar contra la Junta: derecho e incomodidad,"
in *Las Propias: Apuntes para una pedagogía de las endeudadas* (Cabo Rojo, PR:

Editora Educación Emergente, 2018), 142; emphasis mine; all translations are my own. See also Godreau-Aubert, "Protesta peligrosa y democracia en riesgo: Disentir en el marco de la representatividad," *Revista jurídica de la Universidad de Puerto Rico* (2012).

2 Godreau-Aubert, "Protestar contra la Junta."

3 Rebollo-Gil, *Última llamada*, 90.

4 Rebollo-Gil, *Última llamada*, 90.

5 Rebollo-Gil, *Última llamada*, 90.

6 My thanks to Raquel Salas Rivera, Yarimar Bonilla, Marisol LeBrón, Ronald Mendoza de Jesús, and Nicole Cecilia Delgado for thoughts on how to render this term in English.

7 For an overview of the strike, see the essays collected in *Public Education: Crisis and Dialogue at the University of Puerto Rico*, special issue of *Sargasso* 1 (2011–12).

8 César Pérez-Lizasuain, *Rebelión, no-derecho y poder estudiantil: La Huelga de 2010 en la Universidad de Puerto Rico* (Cabo Rojo, PR: Editora Educación Emergente, 2018), 61ff. In addition to the discussion of José Atiles-Osoria and Rafael Bernabe's work in chap. 2, see here Atiles-Osoria, "Neoliberalism, Law, and Strikes: Law as an Instrument of Repression at the University of Puerto Rico 2010–2011," *Latin American Perspectives* 2013; Rima Brusi, "The University of Puerto Rico: A Testing Ground for the Neoliberal State," *NACLA Report on the Americas* 44, no. 2 (2011), and "A New Violent Order at the University of Puerto Rico," *Graduate Journal of Social Science* (2011).

9 See Marisol LeBrón, *Policing Life and Death: Race, Violence, and Resistance in Puerto Rico* (Oakland: University of California Press, 2019), 146. See also César Pérez-Lizasuain, *Rebelión, no-derecho y poder estudiantil: La Huelga de 2010 en la Universidad de Puerto Rico* (Cabo Rojo, PR: Editora Educacion Emergente, 2018), chap 2.

10 Brusi, "A New Violent Order," 43.

11 See, e.g., LeBrón, *Policing Life and Death*, 147.

12 E.g., Fortuño appointed former FBI director José Figueroa Sancha as police superintendent in January 2009. Figueroa Sancha immediately declared his commitment to "zero tolerance" (*mano dura*). See Brusi, "The University of Puerto Rico," 8.

13 LeBrón, *Policing Life and Death*, 149.

14 Marx, *Capital: A Critique of Political Economy*, vol. 1, trans. Ben Fowkes (London: Penguin, 1976), appendix, 1007.

15 Marx, *Capital*, vol. 1, appendix, 1014.

16 Marx, *Capital*, vol. 1, appendix, 1013.

17 Pérez-Lizasuain, *Rebelión*, 26.

18 LeBrón, *Policing Life and Death*, chap. 5.

19 Pérez-Lizasuain, *Rebelión*, 36.

20 Pérez-Lizasuain, *Rebelión*, 42.

21 Pérez-Lizasuain, *Rebelión*, 51.

22 Pérez-Lizasuain, *Rebelión*, 50.

23 See Iván Chaar López, "Student Strikes in Puerto Rico: A Rupture for the Common?" (unpublished ms.), and his entries in *Multitud enred(ada)*, multitudenredada.com.

24 In this context, students conducted a six-hour shutdown of the Expreso las Américas. Already within the nonviolent general strike, students faced police brutality. See Brusi, "A New Violent Order"; and José Atiles-Osoria, "Neoliberalism, Law, and Strikes: Law as an Instrument of Repression at the University of Puerto Rico 2010–2011," *Latin American Perspectives* 40, no. 5 (2013).

25 The eleventh campus was the Recinto de Ciencias Médicas, which did not shut down due to the time-sensitive nature of its investigations, as LeBrón notes. See *Policing Life and Death*, 149.

26 See Atiles-Osoria, "Neoliberalism, Law, and Strikes."

27 See Brusi, "A New Violent Order," 45.

28 See Brusi, "A New Violent Order," 47–48.

29 Atiles-Osoria writes: "The Supreme Court ruled in *University of Puerto Rico vs. Laborde et al.* (CT-2010–008) on December 13, 2010, that students had no right to strike. The main argument for this was the 'contractual nature' of students' relationship with the institution. The court claimed that the students had 'purchased' a service contract, which made them 'consumers of education' and therefore not entitled to strike as workers were" ("Neoliberalism, Law, and Strikes," 7).

30 Brusi, "The University of Puerto Rico," 10: "This critique reached its highest point in March when Ana Guadalupe, the Río Piedras chancellor, was assaulted by an angry mob of protesters. The government and its supporters immediately condemned the incident."

31 Brusi, "The University of Puerto Rico," 10.

32 See Vanesa Contreras-Capó, "¡Huelga!" *8ogrados*, March 31, 2017, http://www.8ogrados.net/huelga-2/.

33 The demands can be found in "UPR aprueba huelga sistemática," *Metro Puerto Rico*, April 5, 2017, https://www.metro.pr/pr/noticias/2017/04/05/upr-aprueba-huelga-sistemica.html.

34 See Héctor Meléndez, "La Huelga y sus significados," *8ogrados*, May 19, 2017, http://www.8ogrados.net/la-huelga-y-sus-significados/.

35 The penal code was amended in May 2017, deepening the criminalization of protests, as especially seen during the May 1 national strike. See, e.g., "'Estrategia de intimidación' las enmiendas al Código Penal," *Diálogo*, May 18, 2017, http://dialogoupr.com/estrategia-de-intimidacion-las-enmiendas-al-codigo-penal/.

36 Rebollo-Gil, *Última llamada*, 94.

37 Rebollo-Gil, *Última llamada*, 94.

38 Cf. Melisa Rosario, "Public Pedagogy in the Creative Strike: Destabilizing Boundaries and Re-imagining Resistance in the University of Puerto Rico," *Curriculum Inquiry* (2015); and Iván Chaar López, "Huelga creativa," *Multitud*

enred(ada), June 17, 2010, http://www.multitudenredada.com/2010/06/huelga
-creativa-victoria-pa-la-historia.html.

39 Rebollo-Gil, *Última llamada*, 94.

40 *Pelú*, literally "hairy," is a reference to purportedly unkempt social justice fight-
ers during college years. This is, of course, racializing language.

41 Rebollo-Gil, *Última llamada*, 89. Vanesa Contreras-Capó's term *coloniality of
struggle* (*la colonialidad de la lucha*) is appropriate here. See "La Colonialidad
de la lucha," *Ahora la turba*, September 5, 2019, https://ahoralaturba.net/2019
/09/05/colonialidad-de-la-lucha/.

42 Rebollo-Gil, *Última llamada*, 101.

43 Rebollo-Gil, *Última llamada*, 96. Chaar López himself does not use this language.

44 LeBrón, *Policing Life and Death*, 155.

45 See Marisol Lebrón, "Policing Solidarity: State Violence, Blackness and the
University of Puerto Rico Strikes," *Souls* 17, no. 1–2 (2015), 119ff. See also the
version published in *Policing Life and Death*, chap. 5. See Giovanni Roberto,
"De Cuando el barrio entró a la UPR," in *Public Education: Crisis and Dialogue
at the University of Puerto Rico*, special issue of *Sargasso* 1 (2011–12). Relevant
here as well is Lebrón's "Carpeteo Redux: Surveillance and Subversion
against the Puerto Rican Student Movement," *Radical History Review* 128
(2017).

46 LeBrón, "Policing Solidarity," 119.

47 See Roberto, "De Cuando el barrio entró a la UPR." His speech is available here:
https://www.youtube.com/watch?v=xXzpbYB7Ndo. Roberto's reflections on
race/class tensions within the student movement are crucial.

48 See LeBrón, *Policing Life and Death*, 163.

49 LeBrón, *Policing Life and Death*, 159.

50 LeBrón, *Policing Life and Death*, 159.

51 LeBrón, *Policing Life and Death*, 173.

52 Rebollo-Gil, *Última llamada*, 101.

53 See Rebollo-Gil, *Última llamada*, 101.

54 Rebollo-Gil, *Última llamada*, 101.

55 Rebollo-Gil, *Última llamada*, 101.

56 Rebollo-Gil, *Última llamada*, 113. "Killjoy" is Sara Ahmed's term.

57 Rebollo-Gil, *Última llamada*, 115.

58 Rebollo-Gil, *Última llamada*, 115. Here, Rebollo-Gil is building on Bernat Tort,
"Democracia, irracionalidad y violencia," *8ogrados*, January 15, 2011, http://www
.8ogrados.net/democracia-irracionalidad-y-violencia/.

59 Rebollo-Gil, *Última llamada*, 117; my emphasis.

60 Rebollo-Gil, *Última llamada*, 115.

61 Rebollo-Gil, *Última llamada*, 116.

62 Rebollo-Gil, *Última llamada*, 116.

63 See Nirmal Puwar, *Space Invaders: Race, Gender, and Bodies Out of Place* (New
York: Berg, 2004).

64 Rebollo-Gil, *Última llamada*, 118.

65 See Rebollo-Gil, *Última llamada*, 118: "SENOR GOBERNADOR LO PEOR K A
ECHO ES JO . . . KON EL DINERODEL PUEBLO NO SIGA ASIENDO BRUTALI-
DADES K LE PUEDE KOSTAR LA VIDA"; "USTED ANDA EN UN 300C Y YO
EN . . . BIEN KA . . . NO SIGNIFIK K NO SEA APRUEBA DE BALA NOSEA
PUREKO SAKO D AKI PA METER AKA"; "Mañana marcha a la 1 pm . . . Mi reinte-
gro O SEKUESTRO AL K . . . GIBERNADOR Y K VENGA KIEN KIERA AREGLARME
POR LO DICHO SE VA AMORIR ATT YO."

66 Rebollo-Gil, *Última llamada*, 121.

67 Rebollo-Gil, *Última llamada*, 123.

68 Rebollo-Gil, *Última llamada*, 123.

69 Rebollo-Gil, *Última llamada*, 123; my emphasis.

70 Rebollo-Gil, *Última llamada*, 124.

71 Rebollo-Gil, *Última llamada*, 124.

72 Rebollo-Gil, *Última llamada*, 125.

73 Rebollo-Gil, *Última llamada*, 126.

74 Rebollo-Gil, *Última llamada*, 131.

75 Rebollo-Gil, *Última llamada*, 132.

76 Rebollo-Gil, *Última llamada*, 132.

77 In his recent *Writing Puerto Rico: Our Decolonial Moment* (London: Palgrave,
2018), locations 1369–71, Rebollo-Gil characterizes these as "decolonial moments," arguing that these are "fleeting occurrences that are likely to be missed
insomuch as they are spearheaded by subjects, who by virtue of their class,
race, and/or gender are relegated to the background of our socio-political
landscape."

78 Rodríguez-Casellas, "De lo Superfluo."

79 See Banco Popular's website: http://echarpalante.com/.

80 Rodríguez-Casellas, "Echarpalantismo," *8ogrados*, October 25, 2013, https://
www.8ogrados.net/echarpalantismo/; all translations are my own.

81 Rodríguez-Casellas, "Echarpalantismo."

82 Rodríguez-Casellas, "Echarpalantismo." There is a long history of positing
Puerto Rican personality in terms of laziness due to its colonial and geographic
determination. The classic texts are René Marqués, *El Puertorriqueño dócil*
(San Juan: Editorial Cultural, 2014); and Antonio Pedreira, *Insularismo: Ensayo
de interpretación puertorriqueña* (San Juan: Ediciones Edil, 1968). The classic
text that counters this discourse, especially in terms of its hispanophilia and its
racial composition, is José Luis González, "El País de cuatro pisos," in *El País
de cuatro pisos y otros ensayos* (San Juan: Huracán, 1980). For a recent exploration of this theme, see Rubén Nazario Velasco, *La historia de los derrotados:
americanización y romantismo en Puerto Rico, 1898–1917* (San Juan: Ediciones
Laberinto, 2019). See also Beatriz Llenín Figueroa's work in this context, specifically *Puerto islas: Crónicas, crisis, amor* (Cabo Rojo, PR: Editora Educación
Emergente, 2018).

83 See Amado Martínez Lebrón, "El Banco Popular y la crisis colonial de Puerto Rico," *8ogrados*, September 5, 2017, https://www.8ogrados.net/banco-popular-y-la-crisis-colonial-de-puerto-rico/.

84 Rodríguez-Casellas, an architect and public intellectual, is interested in "the role that planning played in Puerto Rico in the invention of a political culture of the government."

85 "Forward-facing amnesia" is Raquel Salas Rivera's suggestion.

86 See Jeremy Walker and Melinda Cooper, "Genealogies of Resilience: From Systems Ecology to the Political Economy of Crisis Adaptation," *Security Dialogue* 42, no. 2 (2011); and James Scott, *Domination and the Arts of Resistance: Hidden Transcripts* (New Haven, CT: Yale University Press, 1990).

87 Yarimar Bonilla, "The Coloniality of Disaster: Race, Empire, and the Temporal Logics of Emergency in Puerto Rico, USA," *Political Geography* 78 (2020), 2.

88 For an alternative account, see Frances Negrón-Muntaner, "The Emptying Island—Puerto Rican Expulsion in Post-María," *E-misférica* 14 (2018). Negrón-Muntaner argues that #YoNoMeQuito is a form of refusal. I come back to practices of refusal in the conclusion to the book.

89 Mabel Rodriguez-Centeno, ".Vagancia queer?" *8ogrados*, April 11, 2014, https://www.8ogrados.net/vagancia-queer/; all translations are my own.

90 Judith [Jack] Halberstam, *The Queer Art of Failure* (Durham, NC: Duke University Press, 2011).

91 Halberstam, *The Queer Art of Failure*, 88.

92 Halberstam is drawing from Saidiya Hartman's use of James Scott's notion to discuss maroon tactics.

93 Halberstam, *The Queer Art of Failure*, 89.

94 Halberstam, *The Queer Art of Failure*, 89.

95 José Esteban Muñoz, *Disidentifications: Queers of Color and the Performance of Politics* (Minneapolis: University of Minnesota Press, 2011). Muñoz, whom Rodríguez-Centeno also cites, calls disidentification "a strategy that works on and against dominant ideology" that "negotiates strategies of resistance within the flux of discourse and power" (19).

96 Mabel Rodríguez-Centeno, "Las Perezas insulares," *8ogrados*, November 18, 2011, https://www.8ogrados.net/las-perezas-insulares/; all translations are my own. See also her "Sobre 'echaparlantismos' y perezas. Apuntes para mirarlas gracias reales de 1815 desde las desgracias fiscales del 2015," *Revista Umbral* 12 (2016).

97 Luis A. Figueroa, *Sugar, Slavery, and Freedom in Nineteenth-Century Puerto Rico* (Chapel Hill: The University of North Carolina Press, 2005), 73ff. See Ileana Rodriguez-Silva, *Silencing Race: Disentangling Blackness, Colonialism and National Identities in Puerto Rico* (London: Palgrave, 2012), chap. 1. See also Gervasio Luis García, "Economía y Trabajo en el Puerto Rico del Siglo XIX," *Historia Mexicana* 38, no. 4 (1989).

98 Figueroa, *Sugar, Slavery, and Freedom in Nineteenth-Century Puerto Rico*, 166.

99 James Dietz, *Historia económica de Puerto Rico* (San Juan: Huracán, 1989), 45. See Fernando Picó, *Libertad y servidumbre en el Puerto Rico del Siglo XIX (los jornaleros utuadeños en vísperas del auge del café)* (San Juan: Huracán, 1983), *Al filo del poder: Subalternos y dominantes en Puerto Rico 1739-1910* (San Juan: Editorial de la Universidad de Puerto Rico, 1993), and *Los irrespetuosos* (San Juan: Huracán, 2000) for the many ways jornaleros avoided the libreta system. See also Figueroa, *Sugar, Slavery, and Freedom in Nineteenth-Century Puerto Rico*, 142ff.

100 See Figueroa, *Sugar, Slavery, and Freedom in Nineteenth-Century Puerto Rico* and cf. Saidiya Hartman's discussion of idleness in chap. 5 of *Scenes of Subjection: Terror, Slavery, and Self-Making in Nineteenth-Century America* (Oxford: Oxford University Press, 1994).

101 Mabel Rodríguez-Centeno, "Antiproductivismo y (trans)feminismo en tiempos de trap y capitalismo gore: El Caso de Puerto Rico" (unpublished ms.).

102 Rodríguez-Centeno, "Antiproductivismo y (trans)feminismo en tiempos de trap y capitalismo gore: El Caso de Puerto Rico."

103 Rodríguez-Centeno, "Perezas insulares."

104 Rodríguez-Centeno, "¿Vagancia queer?"

105 Rodríguez-Centeno, "¿Vagancia queer?"

106 Rodríguez-Centeno, "¿Vagancia queer?"

107 Even in the biblical mandate, her expiation is not work, Rodríguez-Centeno notes. See "¿Vagancia queer?"

108 Rodríguez-Centeno, "¿Vagancia queer?"

109 For an extended discussion of racialization through music in Puerto Rico, see Bárbara I. Abadía-Rexach, *Musicalizando la raza: La racialización en Puerto Rico a través de la música* (San Juan: Ediciones Puerto, 2012).

110 Rodríguez-Centeno, "¿Vagancia queer?" Rodríguez-Centeno also writes: "But if in addition to having to work to sustain some masculinity, you must do so in the territory-body heir of slavery, the mandate is inescapable because the infamy of non-work emasculates. Hence the need for derision, insult, and mockery as substitutes for the condemnatory punishments of the laws against the laziness of other times" ("Antiproductivismo y (trans)feminismo en tiempos de trap y capitalismo gore: El Caso de Puerto Rico").

111 Rodríguez-Centeno, "¿Vagancia queer?"

112 Rodríguez-Centeno, "¿Vagancia queer?"

113 Vanessa Colón-Almenas, Carla Minet, Laura Candelas, Laura Moscoso, and Joel Cintrón Arbasetti, "934 Días en La Fortaleza," *Centro de Periodismo Investigativo*, July 25, 2019, http://periodismoinvestigativo.com/2019/07/934-dias-en-la-fortaleza/.

114 See Carla Minet and Luis J. Valentín Ortiz, "The 889 Pages of the Telegram Chat between Rosselló Nevares and His Closest Aides," *Centro de Periodismo Investigativo*, July 13, 2019, http://periodismoinvestigativo.com/2019/07/the

-889-pages-of-the-telegram-chat-between-rossello-nevares-and-his-closest
-aides/.

115 See Omaya Sosa Pascual, Ana Campoy, and Michael Weissenstein, "Los
Muertos de María," *Centro de Periodismo Investigativo*, September 14, 2018,
http://periodismoinvestigativo.com/2018/09/los-muertos-de-maria/.

116 See "Highlights of Rosselló's Chat," comp. and trans. by Raquel Salas Rivera,
No. Impromptu: The Puerto Rico Review, issue ed. Cristina P. Díaz, Jorge
Lefevre, and Claudia Becerra, July 2019, http://www.thepuertoricoreview.com
/rickyrenuncia. The cockfights refer to a 2018 ban on the practice.

117 See, e.g., Rafael Bernabe and Manuel Rodríguez Banchs, "La Política de la
anti-política," *8ogrados*, July 26, 2019, https://www.8ogrados.net/la-politica-de
-la-anti-politica/.

118 This is so even when they ceased work for 180 days, given political instability.

119 For a sustained discussion, see my "Checklists: On Puerto Rico's SoVerano,"
Critical Times 3, no. 2 (2020)."

120 Yara Maite Colón-Rodríguez and Luz Marie Rodríguez-López, "(O)ponerse
donde sea: Escenarios combativos de la indignación," *8ogrados*, August 26,
2019, https://www.8ogrados.net/oponerse-donde-sea-escenarios-combativos
-de-la-indignacion/.

121 Calle del Cristo was changed to Calle del Corrupto, Calle de la Fortaleza to
Calle de la Resistencia on the actual streets and in Google Maps. The motorized caravan was convened by Rey Charlie, who gathered around 3,000 supporters in motorbikes in several housing projects and neighborhoods starting
from the Cantera sector in San Juan. See *No. Impromptu: The Puerto Rico
Review*.

122 On *patx*, see Lawrence La Fountain, "Queer ducks, Puerto Rican Patos, and
Jewish-American Feygelekh: Birds and the Cultural Representation of Homosexuality," *Centro: Journal of the Center for Puerto Rican Studies* 19, no. 1
(2007).

123 Joel Cintrón Arbasetti, "La Guerilla sonora," in *No. Impromptu: The Puerto
Rico Review*.

124 Cintrón Arbasetti, "La Guerilla sonora": "El ruido de las cacerolas marca el
punto de tensión a la vez que rompe el silencio del orden suburbano. Las
sirenas y la explosión de las granadas de gases lacrimógenos es el único ruido
que se permite la fuerza policial que ejecuta el monopolio de la violencia.
Un sonido aéreo fugaz que se ahoga pronto ante el rugir de las motoras. Rey
Charlie y su caballería motorizada hacen su entrada subiendo por la Norza-
garay, bajan por la calle del Cristo. La multitud estalla en gritos, hay fuegos
artificiales. El rúm Rúm prá Prá del motor que se vuelca contra el orden que lo
concibió como signo del progreso."

125 Cintrón Arbasetti, "La Guerilla sonora."

126 Cintrón Arbasetti, "La Guerilla sonora": "La protesta 'se expande, entra, hiere
y se adhiere.'"

127 See Charo Henríquez, "Cantar, bucear, perrear y rezar: Las Protestas creativas en Puerto Rico," *The New York Times*, July 26, 2019, https://www.nytimes.com /es/2019/07/26/protestas-creativas-puerto-rico/.

128 The last "a" in "junta" contained the anarchist symbol.

129 See my "Checklists."

130 See Rima Brusi, "Why Puerto Rico's Cops Ignore the Constitution at Night," *The Nation*, July 30, 2019, https://www.thenation.com/article/puerto-rico -police-abuse/.

131 See Kilómetro Cero's report, https://www.kilometro0.org/blog-desde-cero. See also Evan Hill and Ainara Tiefenthäler, "Did Puerto Rican Police Go Too Far during Protests? What the Video Shows," *The New York Times*, July 27, 2019, https://www.nytimes.com/2019/07/27/us/puerto-rico-violence-protests .html.

132 For a recent account, see José Atiles-Osoria, *Jugando con el derecho: Movimientos anticoloniales puertorriqueños y la fuerza de la ley* (Cabo Rojo, PR: Editora Educación Emergente, 2019).

133 I am here following Jorell A. Meléndez-Badillo, "Commemorating May Day in Puerto Rico," NACLA *Report on the Americas* 51, no. 3 (2019).

134 Ileán Pérez, "Poner el cuerpo," *No. Impromptu: The Puerto Rico Review*. See also Edrimael Delgado-Reyes, "Perreo combativo frente a la Catedral: Una Perspectiva cuir," *Todas PR*, July 28, 2019, https://www.todaspr.com/perreo -combativo-frente-a-la-catedral-una-perspectiva-cuir/.

135 Raw footage can be found here: https://www.youtube.com/watch?v=Gx -GotxXEdA. See also Karla Claudio Betancourt's *Perreo Combativo*: https:// vimeo.com/350139441.

136 "Arzobispo repudia perreo frente a la Catedral de San Juan," *Primera hora*, July 25, 2019, https://www.primerahora.com/noticias/puerto-rico/nota/arzobi sporepudiaperreofrentealacatedraldesanjuan-1354760/.

137 Petra R. Rivera-Rideau, *Remixing Reggaetón: The Cultural Politics of Race in Puerto Rico* (Durham, NC: Duke University Press, 2015), location 1345.

138 See Eileen Suárez Findlay, *Imposing Decency: The Politics of Sexuality and Race in Puerto Rico 1870–1920* (Durham, NC: Duke University Press, 2000).

139 Mayra Santos Febres, "Geografía en decibeles: Utopías pancaribeñas y el territorio del rap," *Revista de crítica literaria latinoamericana* 23, no. 45 (1997); *Reggaetón*, ed. Raquel Z. Rivera, Wayne Marshall, and Deborah Pacini Hernandez (Durham, NC: Duke University Press, 2009).

140 Raquel Z. Rivera, "Policing Morality, Mano Dura Style: The Case of Underground and Reggae in Puerto Rico in the Mid 1990s," in *Reggaetón*, location 1735.

141 Rivera, "Policing Morality."

142 Rivera, "Policing Morality, Mano Dura Style," location 1551–52. See Santos Febres, "Geografía en decibeles," and LeBrón, *Policing Life and Death*. See also

Mayra Santos Febres, "Puerto Rican Underground," *Centro* 8, no. 1–2 (1996); and Raquel Z. Rivera, "Rap in Puerto Rico: Reflections from the Margins," in *Globalization and Survival in the Black Diaspora: The New Urban Challenge* (Albany: SUNY Press, 1997).

143 Rivera, "Policing Morality, Mano Dura Style," location 1632–33.

144 Yoryie Irrizarry, "Paro Nacional, perreo, y Antonio Pantojas," *8ogrados*, August 16, 2019, https://www.8ogrados.net/paro-nacional-perreo-y-antonio -pantojas/.

145 See House Bill 2068 related to Religious Liberty and to Senate Bill 1254 related to Conversion Therapies. See also Bill PS 950. Aborto Libre Puerto Rico and other long-standing organizations, including Proyecto Matria, Taller Salud, CLADEM—Puerto Rico, Caucus de la Mujer del Movimiento Socialista de Trabajadores (MST), Centro de la Mujer Dominicana, Casa Protegida Julia de Burgos, have resisted these efforts (https://www.facebook.com/Aborto-Libre -Puerto-Rico-1782867918476628 and https://8demarzopr.wordpress.com).

146 See here Ramón Rivera-Servera's notion of "racialized queerness." For Rivera-Servera, a "black Caribbean aesthetics" "enable[s] erotic agency" in the context of reggaetón. El perreo intenso in the footsteps of the cathedral might be considered as a racialized queerness that indexes a history of antiblack violence. See Rivera-Servera, "Reggaetón's Crossings: Black Aesthetics, Latina Nightlife, and Queer Choreography," in *No Tea, No Shade: New Writings in Black Queer Studies*, ed. E. Patrick Johnson (Durham, NC: Duke University Press, 2016).

147 See Josué Caamaño-Dones, "Palabras malsonantes, impías, y blasfemias hereticales en Puerto Rico: El Proceso inquisitorial contra el Gobernador Don Diego de Aguilera y Gamboa, 1654–1664," *Op. Cit. Revista del Centro de Investigaciones Históricas* 18 (2007–8). Yolanda Arroyo Pizarro called attention to this writing on social media. See also Jalil Sued Badillo and Angel López Cantos, *Puerto Rico Negro* (San Juan: Editorial Cultural, 1986).

148 Lawrence La Fountain, "Gay Shame, Latina- and Latino-Style: A Critique of White Queer Performativity," *Gay Latino Studies: A Critical Reader*, ed. Michael Hames-García and Ernesto Javier Martínez (Durham, NC: Duke University Press, 2011).

149 Graffiti also subverted a famous quote by Albizu Campos, "Cuando la tiranía es ley, la revolución es orden" (When tyranny is law, revolution is order) into "Cuando la tiranía es ley, el perreo es orden" (When tyranny is law, perreo is order).

150 Irrizarry, "Paro Nacional, perreo, y Antonio Pantojas."

151 For a recent overview of the current debate within mainstream media, see Hermes Ayala, "El racismo en el reggaetón y el blanqueamiento del género," *El Calce*, June 20, 2020, https://elcalce.com/contexto/racismo-reggaeton -blanqueamiento-del-genero/.

152 See here Rivera-Servera, "Reggaetón's Crossings," 107.

For the epigraphs, see Eve Tuck and K. Wayne Yang, "Decolonization Is Not a Metaphor," *Decolonization: Indigeneity, Education and Society* 1, no. 1 (2012); Rafael Bernabe, "Manifiesto de la esperanza sin optimismo en Puerto Rico," *80grados,* November 24, 2017, http://www.80grados.net/manifiesto-de-la-esperanza-sin-optimismo-en-puerto-rico/; all translations are my own.

1 Rima Brusi, "Vagones," *Claridad,* June 26, 2019, https://www.claridadpuertorico.com/vagones/; all translations are my own.

2 Christina Sharpe, *In the Wake: On Blackness and Being* (Durham, NC: Duke University Press, 2016).

3 Sharpe, *In the Wake,* 29.

4 Saidiya Hartman, *Lose Your Mother: A Journey along the Atlantic Slave Route* (New York: Farrar, Straus and Giroux, 2017), 6.

5 Saidiya Hartman, "Venus in Two Acts," *Small Axe* 26, no. 12/2 (2008), 13.

6 Frantz Fanon, *The Wretched of the Earth,* trans. Richard Philcox (New York: Grove Press, 1963), 2.

7 Tuck and Yang argue that decolonization is not a matter of ameliorating present conditions across a range of experiences, practices, and institutions. It "specifically requires the repatriation of Indigenous life and land" ("Decolonization Is Not a Metaphor," 22).

8 See the Caribbean Community's (CARICOM) Reparations Commission, specifically its Ten Point Plan, https://www.caricom.org/caricom-ten-point-plan-for-reparatory-justice/. See also Hilary Beckles, *Britain's Black Debt: Reparations for Caribbean Slavery and Native Genocide* (Kingston, Jamaica: University of the West Indies Press, 2013); Ralph Gonsalves, *The Case for Caribbean Reparatory Justice* (Kingston, Jamaica: Strategy Forum, 2014); Alfred Brophy, "The Case for Reparations for Slavery in the Caribbean," *Slavery and Abolition* 35, no. 1 (2014); and José Atiles-Osoria, "Colonial State Terror in Puerto Rico: A Research Agenda," *State Crime Journal* 5, no. 2 (2018). See also Yomaira Figueroa-Vázquez's *Decolonizing Diasporas: Radical Mappings of Afro-Atlantic Literature* (Evanston, IL: Northwestern University Press, 2020), which contains an important treatment of the topic of reparations. The book was published as this book was in production.

9 Sharpe, *In the Wake,* 3.

10 Sharpe, *In the Wake,* 21.

11 Brusi, "Vagones": "Pero en mis momentos de oscuridad pienso que para esos seres sombríos que deciden nuestros destinos, somos una isla-vagón, vacía de poder o propósito pero llena de comida podrida, de muertos y niños desatendidos, de nómadas que no se mueven de sitio, de seres errantes y a la vez encerrados."

12 Nelson Maldonado-Torres, "Outline of Ten Theses on Coloniality and Decoloniality," Foundation Franz Fanon (2016): https://fondation-frantzfanon.com/outline-of-ten-theses-on-coloniality-and-decoloniality/.

13 Maldonado-Torres, "Outline of Ten Theses," 10.

14 Maldonado-Torres, "Outline of Ten Theses," 10.

15 See Maldonado-Torres's discussion of evasion and bad faith of responses to decolonization in Thesis 1.

16 See Nelson Maldonado-Torres, "On Metaphysical Catastrophe, Post-Continental Thought, and the Decolonial Turn," in *Relational Undercurrents: Contemporary Art of the Caribbean Archipelago*, ed. Tatiana Flores and Michelle A. Stephens (Los Angeles: Museum of Latin American Art, 2017).

17 Frantz Fanon, *Black Skin, White Masks*, trans. Richard Philcox (New York: Grove Press, 1967), 206.

18 For my use of *somatic* here, see Nirmal Puwar, *Space Invaders: Race, Gender, and Bodies Out of Place* (London: Bloomsbury, 2004).

19 Maldonado-Torres, "Outline of Ten Theses," 22, 23. See also Nelson Maldonado-Torres, "Afterword: Critique and Decoloniality in the Face of Crisis, Disaster, and Catastrophe," in *Aftershocks of Disaster: Puerto Rico before and after the Storm*, ed. Yarimar Bonilla and Marisol LeBrón (Chicago: Haymarket Books, 2019), esp. 338–40.

20 Fanon, *Black Skin, White Masks*, xii.

21 Maldonado-Torres, "Outline of Ten Theses," 14.

22 See Celenis Rodríguez Moreno, "La Mujer y sus versiones oscuras," in *Feminismo descolonial: Nuevos aportes teórico-metodológicos a más de una década*, ed. Yuderkys Espinosa Miñoso (Quito, Ecuador: Ediciones Abya-Yala, 2018): "Esta 'mujer' producida por los dispositivos diferenciadores y homogeneizadores de un estado y una sociedad que se organiza sobre la base de un discurso colonial racista y clasista solo logra cumplir parcialmente con las condiciones simbólicas y materiales necesarias para la encarnación del sujeto mujer original" [This "woman" produced by the differentiating and homogenizing devices of a state and a society that is organized on the basis of a racist and classist colonial discourse only partially fulfills the symbolic and material conditions necessary for the embodiment of the original woman subject; translation mine].

23 Axelle Karera, "Frantz Fanon and the Future of Critical Phenomenology in an Anti-Black World" (unpublished ms.). See here David Marriott's *Whither Fanon? Studies in the Blackness of Being* (Stanford, CA: Stanford University Press, 2018). Karera's position is far from Maldonado-Torres's, to be sure, in not affirming a Levinasian resolution to the constitutive violence Fanon tracks. Her reading guides my own in this respect.

24 Fanon, *The Wretched of the Earth*, 236.

25 Fanon, *Black Skin, White Masks*, 195. See also *The Wretched of the Earth*, 236.

26 Maldonado-Torres, "Outline of Ten Theses," 22.

27 Fanon, *The Wretched of the Earth*, 2. Fanon adds that decolonization "transforms the spectator crushed to a nonessential state into a privileged actor."

28 Fanon, *The Wretched of the Earth*, 2.

29 See Tuck and Yang, "Decolonization Is Not a Metaphor." See also Glen
    Coulthard, *Red Skin, White Masks: Rejecting the Colonial Politics of Recognition*
    (Minneapolis: University of Minnesota Press, 2014).

30 Tuck and Yang, "Decolonization Is Not a Metaphor," 35.

31 Particularly relevant here is their discussion of "occupy." See Tuck and Yang,
    "Decolonization Is Not a Metaphor," 23ff.

32 Cf. Chris Buck, "Sartre, Fanon, and the Case for Slavery Reparations," *Sartre
    Studies International* 10, no. 2 (2004); and Françoise Vergès, "'I Am Not the
    Slave of Slavery': The Politics of Reparation in (French) Postslavery Com-
    munities," in *Frantz Fanon: Critical Perspectives*, ed. Anthony C. Alessandrini
    (London: Routledge, 1999).

33 Fanon, *The Wretched of the Earth*, 59.

34 Fanon, *The Wretched of the Earth*, 59.

35 Fanon, *Black Skin, White Masks*, 205.

36 Fanon, *Black Skin, White Masks*, 205.

37 Karera, "Frantz Fanon and the Future of Critical Phenomenology in an Anti-
    Black World."

38 Fanon, *Black Skin, White Masks*, xviii.

39 Fanon, *Black Skin, White Masks*, xviii.

40 Fanon, *Black Skin, White Masks*, 201, 204, 205. The epigraph to "The Black Man
    and Recognition" is from Marx's *Eighteenth Brumaire*, which captures all three
    dimensions.

41 Fanon, *Black Skin, White Masks*, 205.

42 See Anita Chari, "Exceeding Recognition," *Sartre Studies International* 10, no. 2
    (2004).

43 Fanon, *Black Skin, White Masks*, 197.

44 Fanon is here quoting Fichte.

45 Fanon, *The Wretched of the Earth*, 55.

46 Fanon, *The Wretched of the Earth*, 57.

47 See Fanon, *The Wretched of the Earth*, 55.

48 Fanon, *The Wretched of the Earth*, 57.

49 Fanon, *The Wretched of the Earth*, 57.

50 Fanon, *The Wretched of the Earth*, 57.

51 Fanon, *The Wretched of the Earth*, 57.

52 Fanon, *The Wretched of the Earth*, 59.

53 Fanon, *The Wretched of the Earth*, 58: "Moral reparation for national inde-
    pendence does not fool us and it doesn't feed us. The wealth of the imperialist
    nations is also our wealth."

54 Fanon, *The Wretched of the Earth*, 59.

55 Fanon, *The Wretched of the Earth*, 238.

56 Fanon, *The Wretched of the Earth*, 239: "So comrades, let us not pay tribute to
    Europe by creating states, institutions, and societies that draw their inspiration
    from it." See also Walter Rodney, *How Europe Underdeveloped Africa* (London:

Verso, 2018), and Arturo Escobar, *Encountering Development: The Making and Unmaking of the Third World* (Princeton, NJ: Princeton University Press, 1995).

57 On the common(s), see Raquel Gutiérrez Aguilar, *Horizonte Comunitario-popular: Antagonismo y producción de lo común en América Latina* (Madrid: Traficante de Sueños, 2017); the essays collected in *Cuidado, Comunidad, y común: Extracciones, apropiaciones y sostenimiento de la vida*, ed. Cristina Vega Solís, Raquel Martínez Buján, and Myriam Paredes Chauca (Madrid: Traficante de Sueños, 2018); and George Caffentzis and Silvia Federici, "Commons against and beyond Capitalism," *Community Development Journal* 49, no. 1 (2014).

58 Brenna Bhandar, *The Colonial Lives of Property: Law, Land, and Racial Regimes of Ownership* (Durham, NC: Duke University Press, 2018).

59 See Bhandar, *The Colonial Lives of Property*, 95.

60 Bhandar, *The Colonial Lives of Property*, 18.

61 My thanks to Marina Moscoso for conversations about this point. See her "¡Aquí Vive Gente! O Sobre la lucha por el lugar," *8ogrados*, June 8, 2018, https://www.8ogrados.net/aqui-vive-gente-o-sobre-la-lucha-por-el-lugar/. Tracking the inversions of public and private, on my reading, structures her text.

62 Liliana Cotto-Morales, *Desalambrar: Orígenes de los rescates de terreno en Puerto Rico y su pertenencia en los movimientos sociales contemporáneos* (San Juan: Editorial Tal Cual, 2006); all translations are my own. See also Juan Llanes-Santos, *Desafiando al poder: Las Invasiones de terrenos en Puerto Rico, 1967–1972* (San Juan: Huracán, 2001); and Eduardo Bonilla-Silva, "Squatters, Politics, and State Responses: The Political Economy of Squatters in Puerto Rico, 1900–1992" (PhD diss., University of Wisconsin, Madison, 1993).

63 Moscoso sketches the examples I discuss here and below in terms of "waves" of land "occupation," as we will see. See "¡Aquí Vive Gente!"

64 See Érika Fontánez-Torres, "Frente al vacío, a rescatar el futuro," *8ogrados*, September 17, 2017, http://www.8ogrados.net/frente-al-vacio-a-rescatar-el-futuro/.

65 See Cotto-Morales, *Desalambrar*, 30–32. Cotto-Morales writes: "Poverty and unemployment, although reduced, had not been completely eliminated by industrialization or emigration. The income of about 70% of the families in the island remained below the poverty level. With regard to housing, some of the factors that neutralized the favorable effects of the increase in income were: the capture, by private industry, of popular housing areas for commercial use; the loss of housing units due to natural causes and the suppression, carried out by the state, of working class *barrios* and *arrabales*, all as part of urban renewal in order to build roads and other public works" (29).

66 Moscoso, "¡Aquí Vive Gente!"

67 Liliana Cotto-Morales, *Desalambrar*, 10.

68 See Cotto-Morales, *Desalambrar*, esp. chap. 2. See also Rima Brusi, "Deluxe Squatters in Puerto Rico: The Case of La Parguera's Casetas," *Centro: Journal of the Center for Puerto Rican Studies* 20, no. 2 (2008).

69 See Cotto-Morales, *Desalambrar*; and Brusi, "Deluxe Squatters."

70 Cotto-Morales, *Desalambrar*, 125. See also *Desalambrando*, a 2016 documentary based on the book and directed by Pedro Ángel Rivera.

71 The independence movement aided this discursive decision. See Cotto-Morales, *Desalambrar*, 10.

72 See Cotto-Morales, *Desalambrar* and the documentary *Desalambrando*.

73 This is a crucial topic today in post-María recovery efforts blocked by lack of titles and heightened by the housing crisis already unfolding, as we have seen in chaps. 1–3 above.

74 Cotto-Morales, *Desalambrar*, 38.

75 See Fontánez-Torres, "Frente al vacío, a rescatar el futuro." See also her *Casa, suelo, y título: Vivienda e informalidad en Puerto Rico* (San Juan: Ediciones Laberinto, 2020), which was published as I was reviewing proofs of this book.

76 Érika Fontánez-Torres, "La Defense de lo público y lo común," pts. 1, 2, and 3, in *8ogrados*, May 18, 25, June 8, 2018, https://www.8ogrados.net/la-defensa-de-lo -publico-y-lo-comun/. Also, "La Propiedad (¿nuestra?) de cada día," pts. 1 and 2, *8ogrados*, July 20 and August 3, 2018, http://www.8ogrados.net/author/erika -fontanez-torres/.

77 See chap. 2. For a good overview and critical account of the proposed maps, including a discussion of its relation to the issue of opportunity zones, see Martha Quiñonez, "El Plan perverso del nuero mapa de calificación de suelos," *Claridad*, October 16, 2019, https://www.claridadpuertorico.com/el-plan -perverso-el-nuevo-mapa-de-calificacion-de-suelos/.

78 As Rima Brusi explains, the 1880 Ley de Puertos establishes the Zona Marítimo Terrestre (ZMT). This zone includes the "waters' edge and those portions of land touched by the sea up to the high tide mark," as she puts it. "In 1917," she writes, "the ZMT was declared to be part of the public domain, belonging not to the state (who according to this law must act as an enforcer and guardian of the law) but to the Puerto Rican people. . . . The state is represented in this guardianship role by agencies such as the Department of Natural Resources (Law 23, 1972 . . .), created in 1972 to ensure the conservation and protection of the ZMT, and the Puerto Rican Planning Board, that has, as part of its duties, the revision, approval, and monitoring of projects performed in natural reserves." ("Deluxe Squatters," 74).

79 Brusi, "Deluxe Squatters."

80 See Adriana Garriga-López, "Agua dulce," in *Liquid Utility*, e-flux architecture 103 (2019).

81 For an extended analysis of Playas Pal' Pueblo and its relation to the victorious fight against the US Naval Training Range in Vieques, see Melissa Rosado, "Inhabiting the Aporias of Empire: Protest Politics in Contemporary Puerto Rico," in *Ethnographies of Empire*, ed. Carole McGranahan and John F. Collins (Durham, NC: Duke University Press, 2018).

82 Fontánez-Torres, "La Defensa de lo público y lo común," pt. 1, 2.

83 Fontánez-Torres, "La Propiedad (¿nuestra?) de cada día," pt. 2, 10.

84 See Garriga-López, "Agua dulce."

85 Érika Fontánez-Torres *Ambigüedad y derecho: Ensayos de crítica jurídica* (Cabo Rojo, PR: Editora Educación Emergente, 2014), 15.

86 See here Catalina de Onís, "'Es una lucha doble': Articulating Environmental Nationalism in Puerto Rico," in *Racial Ecologies*, ed. Kim Hester-Williams and Leilani Nishime (Seattle: University of Washington Press, 2018). See also José Atiles-Osoria, "Environmental Colonialism, Criminalization and Resistance: Puerto Rican Mobilizations for Environmental Justice in the 21st Century," RCCS *Annual Review* 6 (2014).

87 I am following here Miriam Muñiz-Varela, "Paradojas de la bioeconomía: Violencia y nuda vida," *Revista de ciencias sociales* 27 (2014): 37–38.

88 See also Gabriel Miranda's 2017 documentary *Vietnam, Puerto Rico*.

89 See "Caño Martín Peña: Land Ownership and Politics Collide in Puerto Rico," Harvard Kennedy School of Government Case Program, https://case.hks.harvard .edu/cano-martin-pena-land-ownership-and-politics-collide-in-puerto-rico/. See the community's website: http://cano3punto7.org/nuevo/index.html.

90 See Muñiz-Varela, "Paradojas de la bioeconomía" and her interview with *Puerto crítico*, episode 96, https://www.youtube.com/watch?v=O8g22-onBV8.

91 See Muñiz-Varela's interview with *Puerto crítico*.

92 Muñiz-Varela, interview with *Puerto crítico*. Cf. Frances Negrón-Muntaner, "The Emptying Island—Puerto Rican Expulsion in Post-María," *E-misférica* 14 (2018). While Negrón-Muntaner argues that this is a strategy of refusal in resistance to movement, yet equals it to #YoNoMeQuito, Muñiz-Varela affirms the creation of infrastructures that bind the sensible without individualizing displacement as a matter of choice. To be sure, Negrón-Muntaner also links migration patterns to forms of resistance, indeed as forms of fugitive freedom. Nevertheless, the difference between her account and Muñiz-Varela's stands.

93 Muñiz-Varela, interview with *Puerto crítico*.

94 See here Jorell A. Meléndez-Badillo, "Commemorating May Day in Puerto Rico," NACLA *Report on the Americas* 51, no. 3 (2019); Pedro Lebrón Ortiz, "Contra el blanqueamiento del cimarronaje," *8ogrados*, March 1, 2019, https:// www.8ogrados.net/contra-el-blanqueamiento-del-cimarronaje/; and, esp., Garriga-López, "Agua dulce." See Hilda Lloréns, "The Race of Disaster: Black Communities and the Crisis in Puerto Rico," *Black Perspectives*, April 17, 2019, https://www.aaihs.org/the-race-of-disaster-black-communities-and-the-crisis -in-puerto-rico/.

95 See Yarimar Bonilla, "Fantasías del colapso," *El Nuevo día*, July 3, 2019, https:// www.elnuevodia.com/opinion/columnas/fantasiasdelcolapso-columna-2503096/. See Red de Apoyo Mutuo de Puerto Rico: https://redapoyomutuo.com/.

96 See here Giovanni Roberto, "Community Kitchens: An Emerging Movement," and Sarah Molinari, "Authenticating Loss and Contesting Recovery: FEMA and the Politics of Colonial Disaster Management," in *Aftershocks of Disaster*.

See also *Voces de mujeres: Estrategias de supervivencia y de fortalecimiento mutuo tras el paso de los Huracanes Irma y María*, ed. María Dolores Fernós, Marilucy González Báez, Yanira Reyes Gil, and Esther Vicente (San Juan: INTER-Mujeres, 2018). Thanks to Sarah Molinari for the latter source. See as well *Voices from Puerto Rico Post-Hurricane María*, ed. Iris Morales (New York: Red Sugarcane Press, 2019).

97 Garriga-López, "Agua dulce."

98 See Carmen Concepción, "The Origins of Modern Environmental Activism in Puerto Rico in the 1960s," *International Journal of Urban and Regional Research* 19, no. 1 (1995).

99 See Hilda Lloréns and Maritza Stanchich, "Water Is Life, but the Colony Is a Necropolis: Environmental Terrains of Struggle in Puerto Rico," *Cultural Dynamics* 31, no. 1–2 (2019). See also Katherine McCaffrey and Sherrie Baver, "'Ni una bomba mas': Reframing the Vieques Struggle," in *Beyond Sun and Sand: Caribbean Environmentalisms*, ed. S. L. Baver and B. D. Lynch (New Brunswick, NJ: Rutgers University Press. 2006).

100 See Centro de Periodismo Investigativo's series, "Bomba de tiempo: Las Cenizas de carbón," September 26, 2019, http://periodismoinvestigativo.com/series /bomba-de-tiempo-las-cenizas-de-carbon/; and Sandra Guzmán, "Meet the Women Leading Puerto Rico's Feminist Revolution," *Shondaland*, August 9, 2019, https://www.shondaland.com/live/a28653844/puerto-rico-protests -feminist-revolution/.

101 See, esp., Hilda Lloréns, Ruth Santiago, and Catalina de Onís, *"¡Ustedes tienen que limpiar las cenizas e irse de Puerto Rico para siempre!": La lucha por la justicia ambiental, climática y energética como trasfondo del verano de Revolución Boricua 2019* (Cabo Rojo, PR: Editora Educación Emergente, 2020); and Hilda Lloréns, "Puerto Rico's Coal-Ash Material Publics and the Summer 2019 Boricua Uprising," in *The Decolonial Geographies of Puerto Rico's 2019 Summer Protests: A Forum for Society and Space*, ed. Marisol LeBrón and Joaquín Villanueva (February 2020). See also Lloréns and Stanchich, "Water Is Life, But the Colony Is a Necropolis." See as well Catalina de Onís, "Energy Colonialism Powers the Ongoing Unnatural Disaster in Puerto Rico," *Frontiers in Communication* 3, no. 2 (2018).

102 See Arturo Massol-Deyá, *Amores que luchan: Relato de la victoria contra el gasoducto en tiempos de crisis energética* (San Juan: Ediciones Callejón, 2018).

103 As Gustavo García López, Irina Velicu, and Giacomo D'Alisa explain, Casa Pueblo's interventions draw from the principle of autogestión, which they gloss, quoting Arturo Massol-Deya, as breaking "the bonds of dependency and political manipulation" developing "independent voice and initiatives." See Gustavo A. García López, Irina Velicu, and Giacomo D'Alisa, "Performing Counter-Hegemonic Common(s) Senses: Rearticulating Democracy, Community and Forests in Puerto Rico," *Capitalism Nature Socialism* (2017). See also Catalina M. de Onís, "Fueling and Delinking from Energy Coloniality in

Puerto Rico," *Journal of Applied Communication Research* (2018); and Lloréns and Stanchich "Water Is Life, but the Colony Is a Necropolis."

104 See Arturo Massol-Deyá, "The Energy Uprising: A Community-Driven Search for Sustainability and Sovereignty in Puerto Rico," in *Aftershocks of Disaster*.

105 Jacqueline Villarrubia-Mendoza and Roberto Vélez-Vélez, "Puerto Rican People's Assemblies Shift from Protest to Proposal," *Jacobin*, August 24, 2019, https://www.jacobinmag.com/2019/08/puerto-rico-ricardo-rossello-peoples -assemblies.

106 Benjamín Torres Gotay, "Ciudadanos se reúnen en asambleas de pueblo y reclaman nueva gobernanza," *El Nuevo día*, August 17, 2019, https://www .elnuevodia.com/noticias/locales/nota/ciudadanossereunenenasambleasdepu ebloyreclamannuevagobernanza-2512354/.

107 See Asambleas de Pueblo's Facebook page: https://www.facebook.com /AsambleasDePueblo/.

108 *De la Protesta a la propuesta* [From protest to proposal] and *El Pueblo es el que manda* [The people govern] were common slogans.

109 See Dialogando con Benny, Radio Isla, September 22, 2019, www.radioisla.tv.

110 See Yarimar Bonilla's post on Facebook on August 9, 2019: https:// www.facebook.com/photo.php?fbid=10156683956480888&set=pcb .10156683956550888&type=3&theater.

111 See Ankur Singh, "Puerto Ricans Transform Closed Schools into Commu- nity Centers," *Truthout*, May 12, 2019, https://truthout.org/articles/puerto -ricans-transform-closed-schools-into-community-centers/. See also Diana Zeyneb Alhindawi, "The Disappearing Schools of Puerto Rico," *The New York Times*, September 12, 2019, https://www.nytimes.com/interactive/2019/09/12 /magazine/puerto-rico-schools-hurricane-maria.html.

112 Moscoso, "¡Aquí vive gente!"

113 Moscoso, "¡Aquí vive gente!"

114 Moscoso, "¡Aquí vive gente!"

115 Moscoso, "¡Aquí vive gente!"

116 See Moscoso, "¡Aquí vive gente!"

117 Moscoso, "¡Aquí vive gente!"

118 Moscoso, "¡Aquí vive gente!"

119 Moscoso, "¡Aquí vive gente!"

120 See Molinari, "Authenticating Loss and Contesting Recovery," in *Aftershocks of Disaster*.

121 See Javier Colón Dávila, "Piden que se apruebe resolución para transferir una escuela de Caguas a CAM," *El Nuevo día*, October 16, 2019, https://www .elnuevodia.com/noticias/politica/nota/pidenqueseaprueberesolucionparatran sferirunaescueladecaguasacam-2523798/.

122 Casa Taft 169 today is a nonprofit organization. On the complexities of recovering the very name *Machuchal*, see Moscoso's 2015 interview with *Puerto crítico*, episode 112, https://www.8ogrados.net/puerto-critico-con

-marina-moscoso/. She recounts that to resist census-driven reduction of the zone itself, the nineteenth-century designation of the area as "*Machuchal* was adopted." *Machuchal* is literally "group of machos," in the sense of men, she explains. However, it indexed the first settlement of maroons as well, indicating a race/class distinction between those who lived in the Condado area and those who lived in San Mateo de Cangrejos. Machuchal is the site of a new round of gentrification, especially after María, centered around la Calle Loíza. See also Fernando Picó, *Santurce y las voces de su gente* (San Juan: Huracán, 2014).

123 See Marina Moscoso and Luis Gallardo, "Casa Taft 169: Groundbreaking Grassroots Solutions in Puerto Rico," *Artplace America*, May 10, 2017, https://www.artplaceamerica.org/blog/casa-taft-169-groundbreaking -grassroots-solutions-puerto-rico. See also https://www.facebook.com/ todossomosherederos.

124 See Urbe Apié's website: https://www.urbeapie.com/.

125 On hope and disappointment, see Yarimar Bonilla, *Non-Sovereign Futures: French Caribbean Politics in the Wake of Disenchantment* (Chicago: University of Chicago Press, 2015), esp. chap. 6.

126 See here Quijano's discussion of the colonization of the imagination in "Coloniality and Modernity/Rationality," reprinted in *Cultural Studies* 21, no. 2–3 (2007). See my "Distopía y contramemoria descolonial y afropesimista: reflexiones en torno a Yuderkys Espinosa Miñoso y Saidiya Hartman," forthcoming in *Utopie et dystopie dans l'imagination politique*, ed. Obed Frausto and Angélica Montes Montoya, for a further reflection on the capture of the imagination.

127 Walter Benjamin, *Selected Writings, vol. 2, Part 1: 1927–1930*, trans. Rodney Livingston (Cambridge, MA: Harvard University Press, 1999), 216.

128 Benjamin, *Selected Writings, vol. 2, Part 1: 1927–1930*, 217.

129 Bernabe, "Manifiesto de la esperanza sin optimismo."

130 As Frances Negrón-Muntaner argues, "Understanding of the current juncture as a 'catastrophe' or a turning point may resignify the 'emptying island' as an opportunity to enact an end to colonial-capitalist modernity through different forms of governance, non-growth approaches to resource production, and new forms of habitation" ("The Emptying Island—Puerto Rican Expulsion in Post-María." See also Maldonado-Torres, "Afterword: Critique and Decoloniality in the Face of Crisis, Disaster, and Catastrophe."

131 Walter Benjamin, "On the Concept of History," in *Illuminations*, trans. Harry Zohn (New York: Harcourt Brace, 1968), Thesis VI.

132 See la Colectiva Feminista en Construcción's notes on radical hope in its presentation at the Frantz Fanon Foundation Annual Conference, December 2019, https://fondation-frantzfanon.com/fanon-hope-and-the-day-after -4th-rencontres-of-the-frantz-fanon-foundation/.

BIBLIOGRAPHY

Abadía-Rexach, Bárbara I. *Musicalizando la raza: La racialización en Puerto Rico a través de la música*. San Juan: Ediciones Puerto, 2012.

Acker, Anne, James E. Spiotto, and Laura E. Appleby, eds. *Municipalities in Distress*. Chicago: Chapman and Cutler, 2012.

Acosta, Ivonne. *La Mordaza*. San Juan: Editorial Edil, 1981.

Agamben, Giorgio. *State of Exception*. Translated by Kevin Atell. Chicago: University of Chicago Press, 2005.

Alhindawi, Diana Zeyneb. "The Disappearing Schools of Puerto Rico." *The New York Times*, September 12, 2019. https://www.nytimes.com/interactive/2019/09/12/magazine/puerto-rico-schools-hurricane-maria.html.

Alliez, Éric. *Wars and Capital*. Cambridge, MA: Semiotext(e), 2016.

Amin, Samir. *Modern Imperialism, Monopoly Finance Capital, and Marx's Law of Value*. New York: Monthly Review Press, 2018.

Antonetty, Gloriann Sacha, and the editorial team of *Revista étnica*. "Ser una mujer negra en una pandemia y otras interseccionalidades." *Revista étnica*, April 12,

2020. https://www.revistaetnica.com/blogs/news/ser-una-mujer-negra-en
-una-pandemia-y-otras-interseccionalidades.

Arrighi, Giovanni. *The Long Twentieth Century: Money, Power and the Origins of Our Times*. London: Verso, 2010.

"Arzobispo repudia perreo frente a la Catedral de San Juan." *Primera Hora*, July 25, 2019. https://www.primerahora.com/noticias/puerto-rico/nota/arzobisporep
udiaperreofrentealacatedraldesanjuan-1354760/.

Asambleas de pueblo. https://www.facebook.com/AsambleasDePueblo/.

Atiles-Osoria, José. *Apuntes para abandonar el derecho: Estado de excepción colonial en Puerto Rico*. Cabo Rojo, PR: Editora Educación Emergente, 2016.

Atiles-Osoria, José. "Colonial State Terror in Puerto Rico: A Research Agenda." *State Crime Journal* 5, no. 2 (2018).

Atiles-Osoria, José. "The Criminalization of Anticolonial Struggle in Puerto Rico." In *Counter-Terrorism and State Political Violence: The 'War on Terror' as Terror*, edited by Scott Poynting and David Whyte. London: Routledge, 2012.

Atiles-Osoria, José. "The Criminalization of Socio-Environmental Struggles in Puerto Rico." *Oñati Socio-Legal Series* 4, no. 1 (2012).

Atiles-Osoria, José. "Environmental Colonialism, Criminalization and Resistance: Puerto Rican Mobilizations for Environmental Justice in the 21st Century." *RCCS Annual Review* 6 (2013).

Atiles-Osoria, José. *Jugando con el derecho: Movimientos anticoloniales puertorriqueños y la fuerza de la ley*. Cabo Rojo, PR: Editora Educación Emergente, 2019.

Atiles-Osoria, José. "Neoliberalism, Law, and Strikes: Law as an Instrument of Repression at the University of Puerto Rico 2010–2011." *Latin American Perspectives* 40, no. 5 (2013).

Ayala, César J., and Rafael Bernabe. *Puerto Rico in the American Century: A History since 1898*. Chapel Hill: University of North Carolina Press, 2007.

Ayala, Hermes. "El racismo en el reggaetón y el blanqueamiento del género," *El Calce*, June 20, 2020. https://elcalce.com/contexto/racismo-reggaeton
-blanqueamiento-del-genero/.

Ayuda Legal Puerto Rico. https://www.ayudalegalpuertorico.org/nuestros
-proyectos/derecho-a-tu-casa/.

Ayuda Legal Puerto Rico. "Hacia la recuperación justa: Fondos cdbg-dr y desplazamientos forzosos," May 16, 2019. https://www.ayudalegalpuertorico.org/2019/05
/16/hacia-la-recuperacion-justa-fondos-cdbg-dr-y-desplazamientos-forzosos.

Azuero-Quijano, Alejandra. "Conviction by Design: Remaking Criminal Responsibility at the Nuremberg Trials." SJD diss., Harvard Law School, 2013.

Azuero-Quijano, Alejandra. "Criminal Enterprise, Forensics and the Reproduction of Corporate Power as Crime in Colombia." Dissertation proposal, Department of Anthropology, University of Chicago, 2018.

Balibar, Etienne. "The Politics of Debt." *Postmodern Culture* 23, no. 2 (2013).

Bannerjee, Bobby. "Necrocapitalism." *Organization Studies* 29, no. 12 (2008).

Baralt, Guillermo A. *Esclavos Rebeldes: Conspiraciones y sublevaciones de esclavos en Puerto Rico (1795–1873)*. San Juan: Ediciones Huracán, 1981.

Barker, Adam J. "Already Occupied: Indigenous Peoples, Settler Colonialism and the Occupy Movements in North America." *Social Movement Studies* 11 (2012).

Baucom, Ian. *Specters of the Atlantic: Finance Capital, Slavery, and the Philosophy of History*. Durham, NC: Duke University Press, 2005.

Beckert, Sven, and Seth Rockman, eds. *Slavery's Capitalism*. Philadelphia: University of Pennsylvania Press, 2016.

Beckles, Hilary. *Britain's Black Debt: Reparations for Caribbean Slavery and Native Genocide*. Kingston, Jamaica: University of the West Indies Press, 2013.

Belmonte Postigo, Jose Luis. "Esclavitud y status social en Santo Domingo y Puerto Rico durante la diáspora de la Revolución Haitiana." In *Formas de Liberdade. Gratidâo, condicionalidade e incertezas no mundo escravista nas Américas*, ed. Jonis Freire and María Verónica Secreto. Río de Janeiro: Mauad, 2018.

Benjamin, Walter. "On the Concept of History." Edited and with an introduction by Hannah Arendt. Translated by Harry Zohn. In *Illuminations*. New York: Harcourt Brace, 1968.

Benjamin, Walter. *Selected Writings, Volume 2, Part 1: 1927–1930*. Translated by Rodney Livingston. Cambridge, MA: Harvard University Press, 1999.

Berlant, Lauren. *Cruel Optimism*. Durham, NC: Duke University Press, 2011.

Bernabe, Rafael. "Detrás de la crisis de la deuda en Puerto Rico." Comité para la Abolición de las Deudas Ilegítimas, July 30, 2015. http://www.cadtm.org /Detras-de-las-crisis-de-la-deuda.

Bernabe, Rafael. "Manifiesto de la esperanza sin optimismo en Puerto Rico." *8ogrados*, November 24, 2017. http://www.8ogrados.net/manifiesto-de-la -esperanza-sin-optimismo-en-puerto-rico/.

Bernabe, Rafael. "Neoliberalism punitivo, melancolía financiera, y colonialism." *8ogrados*, April 7, 2017. http://www.8ogrados.net/neoliberalismo-punitivo -melancolia-financiera-y-colonialismo/.

Bernabe, Rafael. "Puerto Rico: Economic Reconstruction, Debt Cancellation, and Self-Determination." *International Socialist Review* 111 (winter 2018–19). https://isreview.org/issue/111/puerto-rico-economic-reconstruction-debt -cancellation-and-self-determination.

Bernabe, Rafael. "Puerto Rico's New Era: A Crisis in Crisis Management." *NACLA: Report on the Americas* 40, no. 6 (2007).

Bernabe, Rafael, and Manuel Rodríguez Banchs. "La Política de la anti-política." *8ogrados*, July 26, 2019. https://www.8ogrados.net/la-politica-de-la-anti-politica/.

Bhandar, Brenna. *The Colonial Lives of Property: Law, Land, and Racial Regimes of Ownership*. Durham, NC: Duke University Press, 2018.

Bhattacharya, Tithi. "How Not to Skip Class: The Social Reproduction of Labor and the Global Working Class." In *Social Reproduction Theory: Remapping Class, Recentering Oppression*, edited by Tithi Bhattacharya. New York: Pluto Press, 2017.

Bignall, Simone, and Marcelo Svirsky, eds. *Agamben and Colonialism*. Edinburgh: Edinburgh University Press, 2012.

"Bomba de Tiempo: Las Cenizas de carbón." *Centro de Periodismo Investigativo*, April 10, 2018. http://periodismoinvestigativo.com/series/bomba-de-tiempo -las-cenizas-de-carbon/.

Bonilla, Yarimar. Facebook Post on Asambleas de Pueblo, August 9, 2019. https://www.facebook.com/photo.php?fbid=10156683956480888&set=pcb .10156683956550888&type=3&theater.

Bonilla, Yarimar. "Fantasías del colapso." *El Nuevo día*, July 3, 2019. https://www .elnuevodia.com/opinion/columnas/fantasiasdelcolapso-columna-2503096/.

Bonilla, Yarimar. "For Investors, Puerto Rico Is a Fantasy Blank Slate." *The Nation*, February 28, 2018. https://www.thenation.com/article/for-investors-puerto -rico-is-a-fantasy-blank-slate/.

Bonilla, Yarimar. *Non-Sovereign Futures: French Caribbean Politics in the Wake of Disenchantment*. Chicago: University of Chicago Press, 2015.

Bonilla, Yarimar. "Puerto Rican Politics Will Never Be the Same." *Jacobin*, August 2, 2019. https://www.jacobinmag.com/2019/08/puerto-rico-ricardo-rossello -governor-unrest.

Bonilla, Yarimar. "The Wait of Disaster." In *Una Proposición modesta: Puerto Rico a prueba/a Modest Proposal: Puerto Rico's Crucible*, edited by Sara Nadal-Melisó. Barcelona: Fundació Antoni Tàpies, 2018.

Bonilla, Yarimar, and Marisol LeBrón, eds. *Aftershocks of Disaster: Puerto Rico before and after the Storm*. Chicago: Haymarket Books, 2019.

Bonilla-Silva, Eduardo. "Squatters, Politics, and State Responses: The Political Economy of Squatters in Puerto Rico 1900–1992." Ph.D. diss., University of Wisconsin-Madison, 1993.

Briggs, Laura. *Reproducing Empire: Race, Sex, Science and US Imperialism in Puerto Rico*. Berkeley: University of California Press, 2002.

Bröckling, Ulrich, Susanne Krasmann, and Thomas Lemke, eds. *Governmentality: Current Issues and Future Challenges*. London: Routledge, 2011.

Brophy, Alfred. "The Case for Reparations for Slavery in the Caribbean." *Slavery and Abolition* 35, no. 1 (2014).

Brown, Wendy. *Undoing the Demos: Neoliberalism's Stealth Revolution*. New York: Zone Books, 2015.

Brusi, Rima. "Deluxe Squatters in Puerto Rico: The Case of La Parguera's Casetas." *Centro: Journal of the Center for Puerto Rican Studies* 20, no. 2 (2008).

Brusi, Rima. "A New Violent Order at the University of Puerto Rico." *Graduate Journal of Social Science* 8, vol. 1 (2011).

Brusi, Rima. "The University of Puerto Rico: A Testing Ground for the Neoliberal State." *NACLA: Report on the Americas* 44, no. 2 (2011).

Brusi, Rima. "Vagones." *Claridad*, June 26, 2019. https://www.claridadpuertorico .com/vagones/.

Brusi, Rima. "Why Puerto Rico's Cops Ignore the Constitution at Night." *The Nation*, July 30, 2019. https://www.thenation.com/article/puerto-rico-police -abuse/.

Buck, Chris. "Sartre, Fanon, and the Case for Slavery Reparations." *Sartre Studies International* 10, no. 2 (2004).

Burnett, Christina Duffy, Burke Marshall, Gilbert M. Joseph, and Emily S. Rosenberg, eds. *Foreign in a Domestic Sense: Puerto Rico, American Expansion, and the Constitution*. Durham, NC: Duke University Press, 2001.

Butler, Judith. *Frames of War*. London: Verso, 2009.

Butler, Judith. *Precarious Life*. London: Verso, 2004.

Caamaño-Dones, Josué. "Palabras malsonantes, impías, y blasfemias hereticales en Puerto Rico: El Proceso inquisitorial contra el Gobernador Don Diego de Aguilera y Gamboa, 1654–1664." *Op. Cit. Revista del Centro de Investigaciones Históricas* 18 (2007–8).

Caffentzis, George. *Los Límites del capital: Deuda, moneda, y lucha de clases*. Buenos Aires: Fundación Rosa Luxemburgo and Tinta Limón, 2018.

Caffentzis, George, and Silvia Federici. "Commons against and beyond Capitalism." *Community Development Journal* 49, no. 1 (2014).

Campbell, Gwyn, and Alessandro Stanziani, eds. *Debt and Slavery in the Mediterranean and Atlantic Worlds*. London: Routledge, 2013.

Cancel Sepúlveda, Mario. "La Constitución de 1952 y Estados Unidos." *8ogrados*, July 25, 2018. http://www.8ogrados.net/la-constitucion-de-1952-y-estados -unidos/.

Caraballo Cueto, José. "Debunking 2 More Myths on Puerto Rico Economy." *The Hill*, July 21, 2017. http://thehill.com/blogs/pundits-blog/economy-budget /343118-debunking-2-more-myths-on-puerto-rico-economy.

Caraballo Cueto, José. "La Emigración registrada en 2018 en la Isla Fue la más alta desde 2006." *El Nuevo día*, October 4, 2019. https://www.elnuevodia.com /noticias/locales/nota/laemigracionregistradaen2018enlaislafuelamasaltadesd e2006-2521683/.

Caraballo Cueto, José. "The Impact of Disparities in SNAP and SSI on Puerto Rico's Poverty and Economic Growth." *Econometrika*, February 2019. https://www .researchgate.net/publication/340610699_The_impact_of_disparities_in _SNAP_and_SSI_on_Puerto_Rico's_poverty_and_economic_growth.

Caraballo Cueto, José, and Juan Lara. "From Deindustrialization to Unsustainable Debt: The Case of Puerto Rico." *Journal of Globalization and Development* 8, no. 2 (2018).

Caro González, Leysa. "Más vulnerables las mujeres tras el paso de María." *El Nuevo día*, July 10, 2018. https://www.elnuevodia.com/noticias/locales/nota/ masvulnerableslasmujerestraselpasodemaria-2434047/.

Castro-Gómez, Santiago. "Foucault y la colonialidad del poder." *Tábula rasa* 6 (2009).

Castro-Gómez, Santiago, and Ramón Grosfoguel, eds. *El Giro decolonial: Reflexiones para una diversidad epistémica más allá del capitalismo global*. Bogotá, Colombia: Siglo del Hombre Editores, 2007.

Cepeda, Katherine. "Ontología barrial negra y criolla de Puerto Rico." *80grados*, July 10, 2020. https://www.80grados.net/ontologia-barrial-negra-y-criolla-de-puerto-rico/.

Chaar López, Iván. "Huelga creativa." *Multitud enredada*. http://www.multitudenredada.com/2010/06/huelga-creativa-victoria-pa-la-historia.html.

Chaar López, Iván. "Student Strikes in Puerto Rico: A Rupture for the Common?" (unpublished ms.). Accessed July 2019.

Chakravarty, Paula, and Denise Ferreira da Silva, eds. *Race, Empire, and the Crisis of the Subprime*. Baltimore: Johns Hopkins University Press, 2013.

Chalmers, Camille. "Deudocracia y nuevo colonialismo: Europa, América Latina y el Caribe," December 4, 2018. https://aldia.microjuris.com/2018/12/03/microjuris-transmitira-panel-deudocracia-y-el-nuevo-colonialismo-europa-america-y-el-caribe/.

Chari, Anita. "Exceeding Recognition." *Sartre Studies International* 10, no. 2 (2004).

Chari, Anita. *A Political Economy of the Senses: Neoliberalism, Reification, Critique*. New York: Columbia University Press, 2015.

Cintrón Arbasetti, Joel. "Bajo la lupa dos integrantes de la junta de control fiscal por su pasado en Banco Santander." *Centro de Periodismo Investigativo*, December 16, 2016. http://periodismoinvestigativo.com/2016/12/bajo-la-lupa-dos-integrantes-de-la-junta-de-control-fiscal-por-su-pasado-en-banco-santander/.

Cintrón Arbasetti, Joel. "Departamento de corrección adjudica contrato a corecivic para traslado de confinados a Estados Unidos." *Centro de Periodismo Investigativo*, August 7, 2018. http://periodismoinvestigativo.com/2018/08/departamento-de-correccion-adjudica-contrato-a-corecivic-para-traslado-de-confinados-a-estados-unidos/.

Cintrón Arbasetti, Joel. "La Guerrilla sonora que derrocó a Rosselló, o la protesta como tumulto sónico." In *Puerto Rico Review: No. Impromptu*, edited by Cristina P. Díaz, Jorge Lefevre, and Claudia Becerra (2019). http://www.thepuertoricoreview.com/rickyrenuncia.

Cintrón Arbasetti, Joel, and Carla Minet. "La Expansion silenciosa de las juntas de control fiscal en EE.UU." *Centro de Periodismo Investigativo*, June 1, 2017. http://periodismoinvestigativo.com/2017/06/la-expansion-silenciosa-de-las-juntas-de-control-fiscal-en-ee-uu/.

Cintrón Arbasetti, Joel, and Carla Minet. "Who Owns Puerto Rico's Debt, Exactly?" *These Times*, October 17, 2017. http://inthesetimes.com/features/puerto_rico_debt_bond_holders_vulture_funds_named.html.

Colectiva Feminista en Construcción. "The Anti-racist Manifesto, Latino Rebels." June 7, 2020. https://www.latinorebels.com/2020/06/07/antiracistmanifesto/.

Colectiva Feminista en Construcción. "Colectiva Feminista en Construcción realiza embargo feminista a la banca por su rol en la crisis de vivienda que vive el País." March 8, 2019. https://www.facebook.com/Colectiva.Feminista.PR/posts/2088021774622876.

Colectiva Feminista en Construcción. "Fanon, Hope, and the Day After." December 12, 2019. https://fondation-frantzfanon.com/fanon-hope-and-the-day-after-4th-rencontres-of-the-frantz-fanon-foundation/.

Colectiva Feminista en Construcción. "Informe de la manifestación y la reunión con Johanne Vélez e Ileana Aymat." June 14, 2019. https://www.facebook.com/notes/colectiva-feminista-en-construcci% C3% B3n/informe-de-la-manifestaci% C3% B3n-y-la-reuni% C3% B3n-con-johanne-v% C3% A91ez-e-ileana-aymat-14-de-/2243215732436812/.

Colectiva Feminista en Construcción, *La Manifiesta*. 2017. https://www.scribd.com/document/263057948/La-Manifiesta-Colectiva-Feminista-en-Construccion.

Colectiva Feminista en Construcción. "Manifiesto Antirracista." June 2, 2020. https://www.facebook.com/notes/colectiva-feminista-en-construcci%C3%B3n/manifiesto-antirracista-colectiva-feminista-en-construcci%C3%B3n/2968317379926640.

Colectiva Feminista en Construcción. "Para Aprobar un plan nacional en contra de la violencia machista." November 24, 2018. https://www.facebook.com/notes/colectiva-feminista-en-construcci% C3% B3n/orden-ejecutiva-para-aprobar-un-plan-nacional-en-contra-de-la-violencia-machista/1938470216244700/.

Colectiva Feminista en Construcción. "Plantón." November 24, 2018. https://www.facebook.com/Colectiva. Feminista. PR/photos/-plant% C3% B3n-feminista-contra-la-violencia-machistaen-lo-que-va-de-a% C3% B10-40-mujeres-ha/1925254470899608/.

Collins, Patricia Hill. *Black Feminist Thought*. London: Routledge, 1990.

Colón-Almenas, Vanessa, Carla Minet, Laura Candelas, Laura Moscoso, and Joel Cintrón Arbasetti. "934 Días en la Fortaleza." *Centro de Periodismo Investigativo*, July 25, 2019. http://periodismoinvestigativo.com/2019/07/934-dias-en-la-fortaleza/.

Colón Dávila, Javier. "Piden que se apruebe resolución para transferir una escuela de caguas a cam." *El Nuevo día*, October 16, 2019. https://www.elnuevodia.com/noticias/politica/nota/pidenqueseapruebresolucionparatransferirunaescueladecaguasacam-2523798/.

Colón Reyes, Linda. *Sobrevivencia, pobreza y "mantengo": La Política asistencialista estadounidense en Puerto Rico: El Pan y el tanf*. San Juan: Ediciones Callejón, 2011.

Colón-Rodríguez, Yara Maite, and Luz Marie Rodríguez-López. "(O)ponerse donde sea: Escenarios combativos de la indignación." *8ogrados*, August 26, 2019. https://www.8ogrados.net/oponerse-donde-sea-escenarios-combativos-de-la-indignacion/.

Comaroff, Jean, and John Comaroff. "Millennial Capitalism: First Thoughts on a Second Coming." *Public Culture* 12, no. 29 (2000).

Comaroff, Jean, and John Comaroff, eds. *Millennial Capitalism and the Culture of Neoliberalism*. Durham, NC: Duke University Press, 2001.

Concepción, Carmen. "The Origins of Modern Environmental Activism in Puerto Rico in the 1960s." *International Journal of Urban and Regional Research* 19, no. 1 (1995).

Contreras Capó, Vanesa. "El Ocho de Marzo contra La deuda." *8ogrados*, March 1, 2019. https://www.8ogrados.net/el-8-de-marzo-contra-la-deuda.

Contreras Capó, Vanesa. "La Colonialidad de la lucha." *Ahora la turba*, September 5, 2019. https://ahoralaturba.net/2019/09/05/colonialidad-de-la-lucha/.

Contreras Capó, Vanesa. "La Deuda y la violencia machista estructural." *8ogrados*, January 25, 2019. https://www.8ogrados.net/la-deuda-y-la-violencia-machista -estructural.

Contreras Capó, Vanesa. "La Deuda y la violencia machista estructural." Translated by Nicole Cecilia Delgado. In "On Debt, Blame, and Responsibility: Feminist Resistance in the Colony of Puerto Rico," edited by Rocío Zambrana, special section of *Critical Times: Interventions in Global Critical Theory*, forthcoming.

Contreras Capó, Vanesa. "¡Huelga!" *8ogrados*, March 31, 2017. http://www.8ogrados .net/huelga-2/.

Contreras Capó, Vanesa. "Primavera feminista contra la deuda." *8ogrados*, April 5, 2019. https://www.8ogrados.net/primavera-feminista-contra-la-deuda/.

Cooper, Melinda. *Family Values: Between Neoliberalism and the New Social Conservatism*. Brooklyn, NY: Zone Books, 2017.

Cooper, Melinda. *Life as Surplus: Biotechnology and Capitalism in the Neoliberal Era*. Seattle: University of Washington Press, 2008.

Cortés Chico, Ricardo. "New Mass Exodus of Puerto Ricans to the US." *El Nuevo día*, June 25, 2018. https://www.elnuevodia.com/english/english/nota/newma ssexodusofpuertoricanstotheus-2430651/.

Cotto-Morales, Liliana. *Desalambrar: Orígenes de los rescates de terreno en Puerto Rico y su pertenencia en los movimientos sociales contemporáneos*. San Juan: Editorial Tal Cual, 2006.

Coulthard, Glen. *Red Skin, White Masks: Rejecting the Colonial Politics of Recognition*. Minneapolis: University of Minnesota Press, 2014.

Crouch, Colin. "Privatised Keynesianism: An Unacknowledged Policy Regime." *British Journal of Politics and International Relations* 11 (2009).

Dardot, Pierre, and Christian Laval. *The New Way of the World: On Neoliberal Society*. Translated by Gregory Elliott. London: Verso, 2013.

Das, Veena. *Life and Words: Violence and the Descent into the Ordinary*. Berkeley: University of California Press, 2007.

Davies, William. "The New Neoliberalism." *New Left Review* 101 (2016).

Dawson, Michael. "Hidden in Plain Sight: A Note on Legitimation Crises and the Racial Order." *Critical Historical Studies* 3, no. 1 (2016).

Deleuze, Gilles. "Postscript on the Societies of Control." *October* 59 (1992).

Delgado-Reyes, Edrimael. "Perreo combativo frente a la catedral: Una Perspectiva cuir." *Todas PR*, July 28, 2019. https://www.todaspr.com/perreo-combativo -frente-a-la-catedral-una-perspectiva-cuir/.

De Onís, Catalina. "Energy Colonialism Powers the Ongoing Unnatural Disaster in Puerto Rico." *Frontiers in Communication* 3, no. 2 (2018).

De Onís, Catalina. "'Es una lucha doble': Articulating Environmental National- ism in Puerto Rico." In *Racial Ecologies*, edited by Kim Hester-Williams and Leilani Nishime. Seattle: University of Washington Press, 2018.

De Onís, Catalina. "Fueling and Delinking from Energy Coloniality in Puerto Rico." *Journal of Applied Communication Research* (2018).

"Deuda pública, política fiscal, y pobreza en Puerto Rico." Clínica Internacional de Derechos Humanos de la Facultad de Derecho de la Universidad Interameri- cana de Puerto Rico and Instituto Caribeño de Derechos Humanos (2016). http://periodismoinvestigativo.com/wp-content/uploads/2016/04/FINAL -Informe-Audiencia-Pu% CC% 81blica-PR-4-DE-ABRIL-2016.pdf.

Díaz, Cristina P., Jorge Lefevre, and Claudia Becerra, eds. *No. Impromptu: The Puerto Rico Review* (2019). http://www.thepuertoricoreview.com /rickyrenuncia.

Dick, Diane Lourdes. "US Tax Imperialism." 65 *American University Law Review* 1 (2015).

Dienst, Richard. *The Bonds of Debt*. London: Verso, 2011.

Dietz, James. *Historia económica de Puerto Rico*. San Juan: Huracán, 1989.

Dilts, Andrew. "From 'Entrepreneur of the Self' to 'Care of the Self': Neo-Liberal Governmentality and Foucault's Ethics." *Foucault Studies* 12 (2011).

Dizney-Flores, Zaire. "Criminalizing Communities of Poor, Dark Women in the Caribbean: The Fight against Crime through Puerto Rico's Public Housing." *Crime Prevention and Community Safety* 13, no. 1 (2011).

Dizney-Flores, Zaire. *Locked in, Locked Out: Gated Communities in a Puerto Rican City*. Philadelphia: University of Pennsylvania Press, 2013.

Downes v. Bidwell, 182 U.S. 244 (1901).

Duggan, Lisa. *The Twilight of Equality?* Boston: Beacon Press, 2012.

Durand, Cédric. *Fictitious Capital: How Finance Is Appropriating Our Future*. Translated by David Broder. London: Verso, 2017.

Dussel, Enrique. *The Invention of the Américas: The Eclipse of "the Other" and the Myth of Modernity*. Translated by Michael Barber. New York: Continuum, 1995.

Dussel, Enrique. "Meditaciones anti-cartesianas: Sobre el origen del anti-discurso filosófico de la modernidad." *Tábula rasa* 9 (2008).

Duval, Jérôme. "De la Colonización francesa a la esclavitud económica de la deuda." Comité para la Abolición de las Deudas Ilegítimas, September 26, 2017. http://www.cadtm.org/Haiti-de-la-colonizacion-francesa.

Echeverría, Bolívar. *La Modernidad de lo barroco*. Mexico City: Ediciones ERA, 1998.

Encarnación, José. "'Estrategia de intimidación' Las Enmiendas al Código Penal." *Diálogo*, May 18, 2017. http://dialogoupr.com/estrategia-de-intimidacion-las -enmiendas-al-codigo-penal/.

Escobar, Arturo. *Encountering Development: The Making and Unmaking of the Third World*. Princeton, NJ: Princeton University Press, 1995.

Fanon, Frantz. *Black Skin, White Masks*. Translated by Richard Philcox. New York: Grove Press, 1967.

Fanon, Frantz. *The Wretched of the Earth*. Translated by Richard Philcox. New York: Grove Press, 1963.

Federici, Silvia. *Caliban and the Witch: Women, the Body and Primitive Accumulation*. Brooklyn, NY: Autonomedia, 2004.

Fernós, María Dolores, Marilucy González Báez, Yanira Reyes Gil, and Esther Vicente, eds. *Voces de mujeres: Estrategias de supervivencia y de fortalecimiento mutuo tras el paso de los Huracanes Irma y María*. San Juan: INTER-Mujeres, 2018.

Ferreira da Silva, Denise. "Unpayable Debt: Reading Scenes of Value against the Arrow of Time." In *The Documenta 14 Reader*, edited by Quinn Latimer and Adam Szymczyk. Munich: Prestel Verlag, 2017.

Figueroa, Luis A. *Sugar, Slavery, and Freedom in Nineteenth-Century Puerto Rico*. Chapel Hill: University of North Carolina Press, 2005.

Figueroa-Vázquez, Yomaira. *Decolonizing Diasporas: Radical Mappings of Afro-Atlantic Literature*. Evanston, IL: Northwestern University Press, 2020.

Findlay, Eileen Suárez. *Imposing Decency: The Politics of Sexuality and Race in Puerto Rico 1870–1920*. Durham, NC: Duke University Press, 2000.

Flores, Katefrans. "Razones por las que no se audita la deuda pública." *El Nuevo día*, April 19, 2017. http://www.indicepr.com/noticias/2017/04/19/news/69703 /razones-por-las-que-no-se-audita-la-deuda-publica/.

Fontánez-Torres, Érika. *Ambigüedad y derecho: Ensayos de crítica jurídica*. Cabo Rojo, PR: Editora Educación Emergente, 2014.

Fontánez-Torres, Érika. *Casa, suelo, y título: Vivienda e informalidad en Puerto Rico*. San Juan: Ediciones Laberinto, 2020.

Fontánez-Torres, Érika. "Frente al vacío, a rescatar el futuro." *8ogrados*, September 17, 2017. http://www.8ogrados.net/frente-al-vacio-a-rescatar-el-futuro/.

Fontánez-Torres, Érika. "La Defensa de lo público y lo común (Parte I)." *8ogrados*, May 18, 2018. https://www.8ogrados.net/la-defensa-de-lo-publico-y-lo-comun/.

Fontánez-Torres, Érika. "La Defensa de lo público y lo común (Parte II)." *8ogrados*, May 25, 2018. https://www.8ogrados.net/la-defensa-de-lo-publico-y-lo -comun-parte-ii/.

Fontánez-Torres, Érika. "La Defensa de lo público y lo común (Parte III)." *8ogrados*, June 8, 2018. https://www.8ogrados.net/la-defensa-de-lo-publico-y-lo-comun -parte-iii/.

Fontánez-Torres, Érika. "La Propiedad (¿nuestra?) de cada día (Parte I)." *8ogrados*, July 20, 2018. https://www.8ogrados.net/la-propiedad-nuestra-de-cada-dia -parte-i/.

Fontánez-Torres, Érika. "La Propiedad (¿nuestra?) de cada día (Parte II)." *8ogrados*, August 3, 2018. https://www.8ogrados.net/la-propiedad-nuestra-de-cada-dia -parte-ii/.

Foster, John Bellamy, Hannah Holleman, and Bret Clark. "Marx and Slavery." *Monthly Review* 70, no. 3 (2020).

Foster, John Bellamy, and Fred Magdoff. "Disposable Workers: Today's Reserve Army of Labor." *Monthly Review* 55, no. 11 (2004).

Foucault, Michel. *The Birth of Biopolitics: Lectures at the Collège de France 1978– 1979*. Translated by Graham Burchell. New York: Palgrave, 2008.

Foucault, Michel. "Questions of Method." In *The Foucault Effect: Studies in Govern- mentality*, edited by Colin Gordon and Peter Miller. Chicago: University of Chicago Press, 1991.

Foucault, Michel. *Security, Territory, Population: Lectures at the Collège de France 1977–1978*. Translated by Graham Burchell. Edited by Michel Senellart. New York: Palgrave, 2009.

Foucault, Michel. *"Society Must Be Defended": Lectures at the Collège de France, 1975–1976*. Translated by David Macey. Edited by Mauro Bertani and Ales- sandro Fontana. New York: Picador, 2003.

Fraser, Nancy. "Behind Marx's Hidden Abode." *New Left Review*, no. 86 (2014).

Fraser, Nancy. "Expropriation and Exploitation in Racialized Capitalism: A Reply to Michael Dawson." *Critical Historical Studies* 3, no. 1 (2016).

Fraser, Nancy. *Fortunes of Feminism*. London: Verso, 2013.

Fraser, Nancy. "Legitimation Crisis." *Critical Historical Studies* 2, no. 2 (2015).

Fregoso, Rose-Linda, and Cynthia Bejarano, eds. *Terrorizing Women: Feminicide in the Américas*. Durham, NC: Duke University Press, 2010.

Frente Ciudadano por la Auditoría de la Deuda. "Constituida La comisión ciu- dadana para la auditoría integral del crédito público," June 6, 2017. https:// www.facebook.com/FrenteCiudadanoAuditoriaDeLaDeuda/photos/a .1804786283110736/1918075851781778/?type=3.

Fusté, José I. "Colonial Laboratories, Irreparable Subjects: The Experiment of '(B) ordering' San Juan's Public Housing Residents." *Social Identities* 16, no. 1 (2010).

Fusté, José I. "The Repeating Island of Debt." *Radical History Review* 128 (2017).

Gago, Verónica. "La Pedagogía de la crueldad: Entrevista a Rita Segato." *Página12*, May 29, 2015. https://www.pagina12. com.ar/diario/suplementos/las12 /13–9737–2015–05–29.html.

Gago, Verónica. *Neoliberalism from Below: Popular Pragmatics and Baroque Economies*. Translated by Liz Mason-Deese. Durham, NC: Duke University Press, 2017.

Gago, Verónica. "What Are Popular Economies? Some Reflections from Argentina." *Radical Philosophy* 2, no. 2 (2018).

Gago, Verónica, and Luci Cavallero. *Una Lectura feminista de la deuda*. Buenos Aires: Tinta Limón, 2019.

García, Gervasio Luis. "Economía y trabajo en el Puerto Rico del siglo XIX," *Historia Mexicana* 38, no. 4 (1989).

García López, Gustavo A., Irina Velicu, and Giacomo D'Alisa. "Performing Counter-Hegemonic Common(s) Senses: Rearticulating Democracy, Community and Forests in Puerto Rico." *Capitalism Nature Socialism* 3 (2017).

Garriga-López, Adriana. "Agua dulce." *e-flux architecture* 103 (2019).

Garriga-López, Adriana. "Puerto Rico: The Future in Question." *Shima* 13, no. 2 (2019).

Gaspar de Alba, Alicia, and Georgina Guzmán, eds. *Making a Killing: Femicide, Free Trade, and La Frontera.* Austin: University of Texas Press, 2010.

Godreau, Isar P. *Scripts of Blackness: Race, Cultural Nationalism, and US Colonialism in Puerto Rico.* Urbana: University of Illinois Press, 2015.

Godreau-Aubert, Ariadna. *Las Propias: Apuntes para una pedagogía de las endeudadas.* Cabo Rojo, PR: Editora Educación Emergente, 2018.

Godreau-Aubert, Ariadna. "Protesta peligrosa y democracia en riesgo: Disentir en el marco de la representatividad." *Revista jurídica de la Universidad de Puerto Rico* 1 (2012).

Godreau-Aubert, Ariadna. "We Women Who Don't Owe Anyone: Las Propias in Times of Austerity and Debt." Translated by Tara Phillips. In "On Debt, Blame, and Responsibility: Feminist Resistance in the Colony of Puerto Rico," edited by Rocío Zambrana, special section of *Critical Times: Interventions in Global Critical Theory*, forthcoming.

Goede, Marieke de. *Virtue, Fortuna, and Faith: A Genealogy of Finance.* Minneapolis: University of Minnesota Press, 2005.

Gonsalves, Ralph. *The Case for Caribbean Reparatory Justice.* Kingston, Jamaica: Strategy Forum, 2014.

Gonzalez, Joanisabel. "Mitad de la deuda podría ser inconstitucional." *El Nuevo día*, June 2, 2016. https://www.elnuevodia.com/negocios/economia/nota/mitaddel adeudapodriaserinconstitucional-2205945.

González, José Luis. "El País de cuatro pisos." In *El País de cuatro pisos y otros ensayos.* San Juan: Huracán, 1980.

Gotiniaux, Pierre. "La Auditorá en curso ya revela una deuda ampliamente ilegal." Comité para la Abolición de las Deudas Ilegítimas, July 5, 2016. http://www.cadtm.org/Puerto-Rico-La-auditoria-en-curso.

Graeber, David. *Debt: The First 5,000 Years.* Hoboken, NJ: Melville House, 2011.

Gregoratto, Federica. "Debt, Power, and the Normativity of Interdependence: Current Debates and the Young Marx." In *Hegel, Marx and the Contemporary World*, edited by Kaveh Boiveiri, Emmanuel Chaput, and Arnaud Theurillat-Cloutier. Cambridge: Cambridge Scholars Publishing, 2016.

Gregoratto, Federica. "The Psychic Life of Debt-Guilt Regimes and Traditional Gender Identities: Nietzschean and Kleinian Perspectives" (unpublished ms.).

Grosfoguel, Ramón. *Colonial Subjects: Puerto Ricans in a Global Perspective.* Berkeley: University of California Press, 2003.

Grosfoguel, Ramón. "Racismo/sexismo epistémico, universidades occidentalizadas y los cuatro genocidios/epistemicidios del largo siglo XVI." *Tábula rasa* 19 (2013).

Grosfoguel, Ramón, and Frances Negrón-Muntaner, eds. *Puerto Rican Jam: Essays on Culture and Politics*. Minneapolis: University of Minnesota Press, 1997.

Gutiérrez, Elías. "En la Trampa." *Cuadrenos de PLERUS* 2 (1997).

Gutiérrez Aguilar, Raquel. *Horizonte Comunitario-popular: Antagonismo y producción de lo común en América Latina*. Madrid: Traficante de Sueños, 2017.

Guzmán, Sandra. "Meet the Women Leading Puerto Rico's Feminist Revolution." *Shondaland*, August 9, 2019. https://www.shondaland.com/live/a28653844 /puerto-rico-protests-feminist-revolution/.

Haiven, Max. *Cultures of Financialization: Fictitious Capital in Popular Culture and Everyday Life*. London: Palgrave, 2014.

Haiven, Max, and Cassie Thornton. "The Debts of the American Empire—Real and Imagined." *Roar* 3 (2016).

Halberstam, Judith [Jack]. *The Queer Art of Failure*. Durham, NC: Duke University Press, 2011.

Hall, Stuart. *Policing the Crisis: Mugging, the State, and Law and Order*. London: Palgrave, 1978.

Hartman, Saidiya. *Lose Your Mother: A Journey along the Atlantic Slave Route*. New York: Farrar, Straus and Giroux, 2007.

Hartman, Saidiya. *Scenes of Subjection: Terror, Slavery, and Self-Making in Nineteenth Century America*. Oxford: Oxford University Press, 1997.

Hartman, Saidiya. "Venus in Two Acts." *Small Axe* 12, no. 2 (2008).

Harvard Kennedy School of Government Case Program. "Caño Martín Peña: Land Ownership and Politics Collide in Puerto Rico." https://case.hks.harvard.edu /cano-martin-pena-land-ownership-and-politics-collide-in-puerto-rico/.

Harvey, David. *A Brief History of Neoliberalism*. Oxford: Oxford University Press, 2005.

Harvey, David. *Marx, Capital, and the Madness of Economic Reason*. Oxford: Oxford University Press, 2018.

Harvey, David. *The New Imperialism*. Oxford: Oxford University Press, 2005.

Heinrich, Michael. *An Introduction to the Three Volumes of Karl Marx's Capital*. Translated by Alexander Locascio. New York: Monthly Review Press, 2004.

Henochsberg, Simon. "Public Debt and Slavery: The Case of Haiti (1760–1915)." MA thesis, Paris School of Economics, 2016.

Henríquez, Charo. "Cantar, bucear, perrear y rezar: Las Protestas creativas en Puerto Rico." *The New York Times*, July 26, 2019. https://www.nytimes.com/es /2019/07/26/protestas-creativas-puerto-rico/.

Hernández, Arelis R., and Brady Dennis. "Desperate Puerto Ricans Line up for Water—at a Hazardous-Waste Site." *The Washington Post*, October 16, 2017. https://www.washingtonpost.com/news/energy-environment/wp/2017/10/16 /desperate-puerto-ricans-line-up-for-water-at-a-hazardous-waste-site/.

Hill, Evan, and Ainara Tiefenthäler. "Did Puerto Rican Police Go Too Far during Protests? What the Video Shows." *The New York Times*, July 27, 2019. https://www.nytimes.com/2019/07/27/us/puerto-rico-violence-protests.html.

Hozić, Aida, and Jacqui True, eds. *Scandalous Economics: Gender and the Politics of Financial Crises*. Oxford: Oxford University Press, 2016.

Hudson, Peter James. *Bankers and Empire: How Wall Street Colonized the Caribbean*. Chicago: The University of Chicago Press, 2018.

Irrizarry, Yoryie. "Paro nacional, perreo, y Antonio Pantojas." *80grados*, August 16, 2019. https://www.80grados.net/paro-nacional-perreo-y-antonio-pantojas/.

Jackman, Jade, Rosalyn Warren, Marinés Montero, Antonio Ribeiro, Mark Pickles, and Mustafa Khalili. "Puerto Rico after Maria." *The Guardian*, April 30, 2018. https://www.theguardian.com/world/video/2018/apr/30/puerto-rico-after-hurricane-maria-were-american-too-why-dont-they-help.

Jackson, Jhoni. "La Colectiva Feminista en Construcción Is Helping Puerto Rico Recover from Hurricane Maria." *Teen Vogue*, October 27, 2017. https://www.teenvogue.com/story/la-colectiva-feminista-en-construccion-is-helping-puerto-rico-recover-from-hurricane-maria.

James, C. L. R. *The Black Jacobins: Toussaint L'Ouverture and the San Domingo Revolution*. New York: Random House, 1989.

Joseph, Miranda. *Debt to Society: Accounting for Life under Capitalism*. Minneapolis: University of Minnesota Press, 2014.

"Justicia ambiental, desigualdad, y pobreza en Puerto Rico: Informe multisectorial sobre las violaciones de derechos económicos, sociales, y medioambientales tras el paso de los Huracanes Irma y María en Puerto Rico." Instituto Caribeño de Derechos Humanos and Clínica Internacional de Derechos Humanos de la Facultad de Derecho de la Universidad Interamericana de Puerto Rico, December 7, 2017. https://noticiasmicrojuris.files.wordpress.com/2018/05/final-informe-cidh-audiencia-pr-dic-2017.pdf.

Kaiser, Susana. "Escraches: Demonstrations, Communication and Political Memory in Post-dictatorial Argentina." *Media, Culture, and Society* 24, no. 4 (2002).

Karera, Axelle. "Frantz Fanon and the Future of Critical Phenomenology in an Anti-Black World" (unpublished ms.). Accessed November 2019.

Kilómetro Cero. "Desde cero." https://www.kilometroo.org/blog-desde-cero.

Kish, Zenia, and Justin Leroy. "Bonded Life: Technologies of Racial Finance from Slave Insurance to Philanthrocapital." *Cultural Studies* 29, no. 5–6 (2015).

Klein, Naomi. *The Battle for Paradise: Puerto Rico Takes on the Disaster Capitalists*. Chicago: Haymarket Books, 2018.

Klein, Naomi. "Haiti: A Creditor, Not a Debtor." *The Nation*, February 11, 2010. https://www.thenation.com/article/haiti-creditor-not-debtor/.

Klein, Naomi. *The Shock Doctrine: The Rise of Disaster Capitalism*. New York: Picador, 2007.

Kobes, Deborah. "Out of Control: Local Democracy Failures and Fiscal Control Boards." PhD diss., MIT, 2012.

Kripner, Gretta. *Capitalizing on Crisis*. Cambridge, MA: Harvard University Press, 2011.

La Fountain, Lawrence. "Gay Shame, Latina-and Latino-Style: A Critique of White Queer Performativity." In *Gay Latino Studies: A Critical Reader*, edited by Michael Hames-García and Ernesto Javier Martínez. Durham, NC: Duke University Press, 2011.

La Fountain, Lawrence. "Queer Ducks, Puerto Rican Patos, and Jewish-American Feygelekh: Birds and the Cultural Representation of Homosexuality." *Centro: Journal of the Center for Puerto Rican Studies* 19, no. 1 (2007).

Lamba-Nieves, Deepak. "Presentación primer foro contra PROMESA" (unpublished ms.). Accessed September 2016.

Laó Montes, Agustín. "Afro-Boricua Agency: Against the Myth of the Whitest of the Antilles." *ReVista*, 2018.

Laó Montes, Agustín. "Neoliberalismo racial y políticas afrolatinoamericanas de cara a la crisis global." In *Afrodecendencias: Voces en resistencia*, edited by Rosa Campoalegre Septien. Buenos Aires: CLASCO, 2018.

Lapavitsas, Costas. "Financialized Capitalism: Crisis and Financial Expropriation." Research on Money and Finance Discussion Papers. *Historical Materialism* 17 (2009): 114–48.

Lapavitsas, Costas. *Profiting without Producing: How Finance Exploits Us All*. London: Verso, 2014.

Laughland, Oliver. "'This Is Human Trafficking': After María Puerto Rico to Move 3,200 Inmates to Arizona." *The Guardian*, August 7, 2018. https://www.theguardian.com/world/2018/aug/07/puerto-rico-prisons-inmates.

Lazzarato, Maurizio. "Debt, Neoliberalism and Crisis: Interview with Maurizio Lazzarato on the Indebted Condition." *Sociology* 48, no. 4 (2004).

Lazzarato, Maurizio. *Governing by Debt*. Translated by Joshua David Jordan. Cambridge, MA: MIT Press, 2015.

Lazzarato, Maurizio. *The Making of the Indebted Man*. Translated by Joshua David Jordan. Cambridge, MA: MIT Press, 2012.

Lazzarato, Maurizio. "Neoliberalism, the Financial Crisis and the End of the Liberal State." *Theory, Culture and Society* 32, no. 7–8 (2015).

Lazzarato, Maurizio. "The Political Consequences of the Debt Crisis." In *Una Proposición modesta: Puerto Rico a prueba/a Modest Proposal: Puerto Rico's Crucible*, edited by Sara Nadal-Melisó. Barcelona: Fundació Antoni Tàpies, 2018.

LeBrón, Marisol. "Carpeteo Redux: Surveillance and Subversion against the Puerto Rican Student Movement." *Radical History Review* 128 (2017).

LeBrón, Marisol. "Mano Dura contra el Crimen and Premature Death in Puerto Rico." In *Policing the Planet: Why the Policing Crisis Led to Black Lives Matter*, edited by Jordan T. Camp and Christina Heatherton. London: Verso, 2016.

LeBrón, Marisol. *Policing Life and Death: Race, Violence, and Resistance in Puerto Rico* (Oakland: University of California Press, 2019).

LeBrón, Marisol. "Policing Solidarity: State Violence, Blackness and the University of Puerto Rico Strikes." *Souls* 17, no. 1–2 (2015).

Lebrón Ortiz, Pedro. "Contra el blanqueamiento del cimarronaje." *8ogrados*, March 1, 2019. https://www.8ogrados.net/contra-el-blanqueamiento-del -cimarronaje/.

Lebrón, Pedro. "Matarse en la colonia es un asunto cotidiano." *8ogrados*, April 5, 2019. https://www.8ogrados.net/matarse-en-la-colonia-es-un-asunto-cotidiano/.

Lemke, Thomas. "Birth of Biopolitics: Michel Foucault and Lecture at the Collège de France on Neoliberal Governmentality." *Economy and Society* 30, no. 2 (2001).

Levy, Jonathan. *Freaks of Fortune: The Emerging World of Capitalism and Risk in America*. Cambridge, MA: Harvard University Press, 2012.

Llanes-Santos, Juan. *Desafiando al poder: Las Invasiones de terrenos en Puerto Rico, 1967–1972*. San Juan: Huracán, 2001.

Llenín Figueroa, Beatriz. "The Maroons Are Deathless, We Are Deathless." *Radical History Review*, July 20, 2019. https://www.radicalhistoryreview.org /abusablepast/?p=3145.

Llenín Figueroa, Beatriz. *Puerto islas: Crónicas, crisis, amor*. San Juan: Editora Educación Emergente, 2018.

Lloréns, Hilda. *Imaging the Great Puerto Rican Family: Framing Nation, Race, and Gender during the American Century*. Lanham, MD: Rowman and Littlefield, 2018.

Lloréns, Hilda. "Puerto Rico's Coal-Ash Material Publics and the Summer 2019 Boricua Uprising." In *The Decolonial Geographies of Puerto Rico's 2019 Summer Protests: A Forum for Society and Space*, edited by Marisol LeBrón and Joaquín Villanueva (February 2020).

Lloréns, Hilda. "The Race of Disaster: Black Communities and the Crisis in Puerto Rico." *Black Perspectives*, April 17, 2019. https://www.aaihs.org/the-race-of -disaster-black-communities-and-the-crisis-in-puerto-rico.

Lloréns, Hilda, Ruth Santiago, and Catalina de Onís. *"¡Ustedes tienen que limpiar las cenizas e irse de Puerto Rico para siempre!": La lucha por la justicia ambiental, climática y energética como trasfondo del verano de Revolución Boricua 2019*. Cabo Rojo, PR: Editora Educación Emergente, 2020.

Lloréns, Hilda, and Maritza Stanchich. "Water Is Life, but the Colony Is a Necropolis: Environmental Terrains of Struggle in Puerto Rico." *Cultural Dynamics* 31, no. 1–2 (2019).

Lloréns Pérez, Eva. "Judge Swain Says PROMESA Provides Awkward Power-Sharing Structure." *Caribbean Business*, August 7, 2018. http://caribbeanbusiness.com /judge-swain-says-promesa-provides-awkward-power-sharing-structure/.

López Serrano, Edda. "El Incremento sexual contra las mujeres." Interview Joshua García Aponte. Hoy en las Noticias, Departamento de Noticias, Radio Universidad de Puerto Rico, July 27, 2019. https://www.mixcloud .com/hoyenlasnoticias/en-incremento-las-agresiones-sexuales-contra-las -mujeres/.

Lorey, Isabell. *State of Insecurity: Government of the Precarious*. London: Verso, 2015.

Lugones, María. "Heterosexualism and the Colonial Modern/Gender System." *Hypatia* 22, no. 1 (2007).

Lugones, María. "Toward a Decolonial Feminism." *Hypatia* 25, no. 4 (2010).

Luxemburg, Rosa. *The Accumulation of Capital*. Translated by Agnes Schwarzschild. London: Routledge, 2003.

Maldonado Arrigoitía, Wilma. "Las Comunidades están alertas ante los posibles intentos de expropiación." *El Nuevo día*, August 14, 2018. https://www .elnuevodia.com/noticias/locales/nota/lascomunidadesestanalertasantelospos iblesintentosdeexpropiacion-2441110/.

Maldonado-Torres, Nelson. "Afterword: Critique and Decoloniality in the Face of Crisis, Disaster, and Catastrophe." In *Aftershocks of Disaster: Puerto Rico before and after the Storm*, edited by Yarimar Bonilla and Marisol LeBrón.

Maldonado-Torres, Nelson. "The Decolonial Turn." In *New Approaches to Latin American Studies: Culture and Power*, edited by Juan Poblete. London: Routledge, 2018.

Maldonado-Torres, Nelson. "On Metaphysical Catastrophe, Post-Continental Thought, and the Decolonial Turn." In *Relational Undercurrents: Contemporary Art of the Caribbean Archipelago*, edited by Tatiana Flores and Michelle A. Stephens. Los Angeles: Museum of Latin American Art, 2017.

Maldonado-Torres, Nelson. "On the Coloniality of Being: Contributions to the Development of a Concept." *Cultural Studies* 21, no. 2–3 (2007).

Maldonado-Torres, Nelson. "Outline of Ten Theses on Coloniality and Decoloniality." Foundation Frantz Fanon, 2016. https://fondation-frantzfanon.com /outline-of-ten-theses-on-coloniality-and-decoloniality/.

Marazzi, Christian. *The Violence of Financial Capitalism*. Translated by Kristina Lebedeva and Jason Francis McGimsey. Cambridge, MA: Semiotext(e), 2011.

Marqués, René. *El Puertorriqueño dócil*. San Juan: Editorial Cultural, 2014.

Marriott, David. *Whither Fanon? Studies in the Blackness of Being*. Stanford, CA: Stanford University Press, 2018.

Martin, Randy. *The Financialization of Daily Life*. Philadelphia: Temple University Press, 2002.

Martin, Randy. "A Precarious Dance: A Derivative Sociality." *TDR: The Drama Review* 56, no. 4 (2012).

Martin, Randy. "What Difference Do Derivatives Make? From the Technical to the Political Conjuncture." *Culture Unbound* 6 (2014).

Martínez Lebrón, Amado. "El Banco Popular y la crisis colonial de Puerto Rico." *8ogrados*, September 5, 2017. https://www.8ogrados.net/banco-popular-y-la -crisis-colonial-de-puerto-rico/.

Marx, Karl. "Alienated Labor." In *Karl Marx and Frederick Engels, Collected Works*, vol. 3: *Marx and Engels: 1843–1844*. New York: International Publishers, 1975.

Marx, Karl. *Capital: A Critique of Political Economy*. Vol. 1. Translated by Ben Fowkes. London: Penguin, 1976.

Marx, Karl. *Capital: A Critique of Political Economy*. Vol. 3. Translated by David Fernbach. London: Penguin, 1981.

Marx, Karl. "Comments on James Mill." In *Karl Marx and Frederick Engels, Collected Works*, vol. 3: *Marx and Engels: 1843–1844*. New York: International Publishers, 1975.

Marx, Karl. *Grundrisse: Foundations of the Critique of Political Economy*. Translated by Martin Nicolaus. London: Penguin, 1993.

Massol Deyá, Arturo. *Amores que luchan: Relato de la victoria contra el gasoducto en tiempos de crisis energética*. San Juan: Ediciones Callejón, 2018.

Mbembe, Achille. *Critique of Black Reason*. Translated by Laurent Dubois. Durham, NC: Duke University Press, 2017.

Mbembe, Achille. "Necropolitics." *Public Culture* 15, no. 1 (2003).

McCaffrey, Katherine, and Sherrie Baver. "'Ni Una Bomba Mas': Reframing the Vieques Struggle." In *Beyond Sun and Sand: Caribbean Environmentalisms*, edited by S. L. Baver and B. D. Lynch. New Brunswick, NJ: Rutgers University Press, 2006.

McGreevey, Robert. *Borderline Citizens: The United States, Puerto Rico, and the Politics of Colonial Migration*. Ithaca, NY: Cornell University Press, 2018.

Medinas Fuentes, José Nicolás. "Tres teorías sobre la deuda pública." *El Nuevo día*, February 20, 2018. https://www.elnuevodia.com/opinion/columnas /tresteoriassobreladeudapublica-columna-2400424/.

Meléndez, Edgardo. *Sponsored Migration: The State and Puerto Rican Postwar Migration to the United States*. Columbus: Ohio State University Press, 2017.

Meléndez, Héctor. "La Huelga y sus significados." *8ogrados*, May 19, 2017. http:// www.8ogrados.net/la-huelga-y-sus-significados/.

Meléndez, Lyanne. "Upr aprueba huelga sistemática." *Metro Puerto Rico*, April 5, 2017. https://www.metro.pr/pr/noticias/2017/04/05/upr-aprueba-huelga -sistemica.html.

Meléndez-Badillo, Jorell A. "Commemorating May Day in Puerto Rico." *NACLA Report on the Americas* 51, no. 3 (2019).

Mendoza, Breny. "The Coloniality of Gender and Power: From Postcoloniality to Decoloniality." In *The Oxford Handbook of Feminist Theory*, edited by Lisa Disch and Mary Hawkesworth. Oxford: Oxford University Press, 2016.

Mendoza, Breny. "Epistemología del Sur, la colonialidad de género y los feminis- mos latinoamericanos." In *Tejiendo de otro modo: Feminismo, epistemología y apuestas descoloniales en abya yala*, edited by Yuderkys Espinosa Miñoso and Karina Ochoa. Bogotá, Colombia: Editorial Universidad del Cauca, 2014.

Mezzadra, Sandro, and Bret Neilson. *The Politics of Operation: Excavating Con- temporary Capitalism*. Durham, NC: Duke University Press, 2019.

Minet, Carla, and Luis J. Valentín Ortiz. "The 889 Pages of the Telegram Chat between Rosselló Nevares and His Closest Aides." *Centro de Periodismo Investigativo*,

July 13, 2019. http://periodismoinvestigativo.com/2019/07/the-889-pages-of
-the-telegram-chat-between-rossello-nevares-and-his-closest-aides/.

Miranda, Gabriel, dir. *Vietnam, Puerto Rico*. 2017.

Mitropolous, Angela. *Contract and Contagion: From Biopolitics to Oikonomia*.
Brooklyn, NY: Autonomedia, 2012.

Mitropolous, Angela. "Debt Servitude, Service Work, Oikos." *sometim3s*, December 5, 2013. http://sometim3s.com/2013/12/05/.

Mitropolous, Angela, and Melinda Cooper. "In Praise of Usura." *Mute* 2 (2009).

Molinari, Sarah. "Authenticating Loss and Contesting Recovery: FEMA and the Politics of Colonial Disaster Management." In *Aftershocks of Disaster: Puerto Rico before and after the Storm*, edited by Yarimar Bonilla and Marisol LeBrón.

Molinari, Sarah. "The Public Reckoning: Anti-Debt Futures after #Rickyrenuncia." *Society and Space, The Decolonial Geographies of Puerto Rico's 2019 Summer Protests: A Forum* (February 2020).

Morales, Iris, ed. *Voices from Puerto Rico Post-Hurricane María*. New York: Red Sugarcane Press, 2019.

Morales Carrión, Arturo. "La revolución haitiana y el movimiento antiesclavista en Puerto Rico." *Boletín de la Academia Puertorriqueña de la Historia* 8, no. 30 (1983).

Moscoso, Marina. "¡Aquí vive gente! O Sobre la lucha por el lugar." *8ogrados*, June 8, 2018. https://www.8ogrados.net/aqui-vive-gente-o-sobre-la-lucha-por-el-lugar/.

Moscoso, Marina. "Puerto crítico con Marina Moscoso." *8ogrados*, September 25, 2015. https://www.8ogrados.net/puerto-critico-con-marina-moscoso/.

Moscoso, Marina, and Luis Gallardo. "Casa Taft 169: Groundbreaking Grassroots Solutions in Puerto Rico." *Artplace America*, May 10, 2017. https://www
.artplaceamerica.org/blog/casa-taft-169-groundbreaking-grassroots-solutions
-puerto-rico.

Moten, Fred, and Stefano Harney. *The Undercommons: Fugitive Planning and Black Study*. Wivenhoe, UK: Minor Compositions, 2013.

Muñiz-Varela, Miriam. *Adiós a la economía*. San Juan: Ediciones Callejón, 2013.

Muñiz-Varela, Miriam. "Episode 96." May 6, 2015. *Puerto crítico*. https://www
.youtube.com/watch?v=O8g22-onBV8.

Muñiz-Varela, Miriam. "La Deuda: Axiomática de la propiedad y aparato de captura de la vida." In *Violencia y Deuda, Cruce*, edited by Madeline Román (November 2019).

Muñiz-Varela, Miriam. "Paradojas de la bioeconomía: Violencia y nuda vida." *Revista de ciencias sociales* 27 (2014).

Muñiz-Varela, Miriam. "Taken Island" (unpublished ms.). Accessed June 7, 2019.

Muñoz, José Esteban. *Disidentifications: Queers of Color and the Performance of Politics*. Minneapolis: University of Minnesota Press, 2011.

Natural Resources Defense Council, "Threats on Tap: Drinking Water Violations in Puerto Rico." NRDC Issue Paper No. 17-02-A, May 2017.

Navarro, Tami. "'Offshore' Banking within the Nation: Economic Development in the United States Virgin Islands." *The Global South* 4, no. 2 (2010).

Nazario Velasco, Rubén. *La historia de los derrotados: americanización y romantismo en Puerto Rico, 1898–1917*. San Juan: Ediciones Laberinto, 2019.

Negrón-Muntaner, Frances. "The Emptying Island—Puerto Rican Expulsion in Post-María." *e-misférica* 14 (2018).

Negrón-Muntaner, Frances, ed. *None of the Above: Puerto Ricans in the Global Era*. New York: Palgrave, 2007.

Negrón-Muntaner, Frances, ed. *Sovereign Acts: Contesting Colonialism across Indigenous Nations and Latinx America*. Tucson: University of Arizona Press, 2017.

Nelson, Scott Reynolds. *A Nation of Deadbeats: An Uncommon History of America's Financial Disasters*. New York: Alfred A. Knopf, 2012.

Neuman, Gerard L., ed. *Reconsidering the Insular Cases: The Past and Present of American Empire*. Cambridge, MA: Harvard University Press, 2015.

"New Estimates: 135,000+ Post-Maria Puerto Ricans Relocated to Stateside." Centro: Center for Puerto Rican Studies, Hunter College, March 2018. https://centropr.hunter.cuny.edu/sites/default/files/data_sheets/PostMaria -NewEstimates-3-15-18.pdf.

Nietzsche, Friedrich. *On the Genealogy of Morals* in *On the Genealogy of Morals and Ecce Homo*. Translated by Walter Kaufmann and R. J. Hollingdale. New York: Vintage, 1989.

Nixon, Rob. *Slow Violence and the Environmentalism of the Poor*. Cambridge, MA: Harvard University Press, 2013.

Ong, Aihwa. *Neoliberalism as Exception: Mutations in Citizenship and Sovereignty*. Durham, NC: Duke University Press, 2006.

Pabón, Carlos. *Mínima política: Textos breves y fragmentos sobre la crisis contemporánea*. San Juan: La Secta de los Perros, 2015.

Pabón, Carlos. *Nación postmortem: Ensayos sobre los tiempos de insoportable ambigüedad*. San Juan: Ediciones Callejón, 2002.

Paralitici, José. *La Represión contra el independentismo puertorriqueño*. San Juan: Ediciones Gaviota, 2011.

Pastor, Mara. "Ven la luz al final del camino." *Metro Puerto Rico*, August 15, 2018. https://www.metro.pr/pr/noticias/2018/08/15/ven-la-luz-al-final-del-camino .html.

Pedreira, Antonio. *Insularismo: Ensayo de interpretación puertorriqueña*. San Juan: Ediciones Edil, 1968.

Peebles, Gustav. "The Anthropology of Credit and Debt." *Annual Review of Anthropology* 39 (October 2010).

Pérez-Lizasuain, César. *Rebelión, no-derecho y poder estudiantil: La Huelga de 2010 en la Universidad De Puerto Rico*. Cabo Rojo, PR: Editora Educación Emergente, 2018.

Phillips, Anthony. "Haiti, France, and the Independence Debt of 1825." Boston: Institute for Justice and Democracy in Haiti, 2008.

Picó, Fernando. *Al filo del poder: Subalternos y dominantes en Puerto Rico 1739–1910*. San Juan: Editorial de la Universidad de Puerto Rico, 1993.

Picó, Fernando. *El Día menos pensado: Historia de los presidiarios en Puerto Rico, 1793–1993*. San Juan: Huracán, 1994.

Picó, Fernando. *Libertad y servidumbre en el Puerto Rico del Siglo XIX (los jornaleros utuadeños en vísperas del auge del café)*. San Juan: Huracán, 1983.

Picó, Fernando. *Los irrespetuosos*. San Juan: Huracán, 2000.

Picó, Fernando. *Santurce y las voces de su gente*. San Juan: Huracán, 2014.

Pintado, Armando J. S. "Pausa para la auditoría." *8ogrados*, March 24, 2017. http://www.8ogrados.net/pausa-para-la-auditoria.

Pinto, Antonio. "Negro sobre blanco: La conspiración esclava de 1812 en PR," *Caribbean Studies* 40, no. 1 (2012).

Povinelli, Elizabeth. *Economies of Abandonment: Social Belonging and Endurance in Late Liberalism*. Durham, NC: Duke University Press, 2011.

Prados, Eva. "Gender Violence and Debt Auditing." Translated by Nicole Cecilia Delgado. "On Debt, Blame, and Responsibility: Feminist Resistance in the Colony of Puerto Rico," edited by Rocío Zambrana, special section of *Critical Times: Interventions in Global Critical Theory*, forthcoming.

Prados, Eva. "Violencia de género y auditoría de la deuda," edited by Rocío Zambrana, special section of *Critical Times: Interventions in Global Critical Theory*, forthcoming.

"Public Education: Crisis and Dialogue at the University of Puerto Rico." Special issue of *Sargasso* 1 (2011–12).

Puwar, Nirmal. *Space Invaders: Race, Gender, and Bodies Out of Place*. New York: Berg, 2004.

Quijano, Aníbal. "América Latina en la economía mundial." *Problemas del desarrollo* 24, no. 95 (1993).

Quijano, Aníbal. "Colonialidad del poder y clasificación social." *Journal of World-Systems Research* 6, no. 2 (2000).

Quijano, Aníbal. "Coloniality and Modernity/Rationality." *Cultural Studies* 21, no. 2 (2007).

Quijano, Aníbal. "El Fantasma del desarrollo en América Latina." *Revista Venezolano de economia y ciencias sociales* 6 (2000).

Quijano, Aníbal. "Notas sobre los problemas de la investigación social en América Latina." *Revista de sociología* 6, no. 7 (1990).

Quiñonez, Martha. "El Plan perverso del nuero mapa de calificación de suelos." *Claridad*, October 16, 2019. https://www.claridadpuertorico.com/el-plan-perverso-el-nuevo-mapa-de-calificacion-de-suelos/.

Ramirez de Arellano, Annette. *Colonialism, Catholicism, and Contraception: A History of Birth Control in Puerto Rico*. Durham, NC: University of North Carolina Press, 2011.

Ramos, Héctor. "Feministas arrestan y encarcelan a Héctor O'Neill." *NotiUno 630*. https://www.notiuno.com/noticias/fotos-feministas-arrestan-y-encarcelan-a -h-ctor-o-neill/article_a61af18b-57eb-51db-a703-f5ec98640f2b.html.

Read, Jason, "I Owe You an Explanation: Graeber and Marx on Origin Stories." *Unemployed Negativity*, September 21, 2011. http://www.unemployednegativity .com/2011/09/i-owe-you-explanation-graeber-and-marx.html.

Rebollo Gil, Guillermo. *Decirla en pedacitos: Estrategias de cercanía*. Cabo Rojo, PR: Editora Educación Emergente, 2013.

Rebollo Gil, Guillermo. *Última llamada*. Carolina, PR: Ediciones UNE, 2017.

Rebollo Gil, Guillermo. *Writing Puerto Rico: Our Decolonial Moment*. London: Palgrave, 2018.

Rivera, Raquel Z. "Policing Morality, Mano Dura Style: The Case of Underground and Reggae in Puerto Rico in the Mid 1990s." In *Reggaetón*, edited by Raquel Z. Rivera, Wayne Marshall, and Deborah Pacini Hernandez. Durham, NC: Duke University Press, 2009.

Rivera, Raquel Z. "Rap in Puerto Rico: Reflections from the Margins." In *Globalization and Survival in the Black Diaspora: The New Urban Challenge*, edited by Charles Green. Albany: SUNY Press, 1997.

Rivera, Raquel Z., Wayne Marshall, and Deborah Pacini Hernandez, eds. *Reggaetón*. Durham, NC: Duke University Press, 2009.

Rivera Clemente, Yaritza. "Unos 550 presos mueren en una década." *El Vocero*, October 1, 2019. https://www.elvocero.com/gobierno/unos-presos-mueren-en -una-d-cada/article_feoda6f4-e3f2-11e9-9de4-4f35f2266891.html.

Rivera Ramos, Efrén. *American Colonialism in Puerto Rico: The Judiciary and Social Legacy*. Princeton, NJ: Markus Wiener, 2007.

Rivera Ramos, Efrén. *The Legal Construction of Identity: The Juridical and Social Legacy of American Colonialism in Puerto Rico*. Washington, DC: American Psychological Association, 2011.

Rivera-Rideau, Petra R. *Remixing Reggaetón: The Cultural Politics of Race in Puerto Rico*. Durham, NC: Duke University Press, 2015.

Rivera-Servera, Ramón. "Reggaetón's Crossings: Black Aesthetics, Latina Nightlife, and Queer Choreography." In *No Tea, No Shade: New Writings in Black Queer Studies*, edited by E. Patrick Johnson. Durham, NC: Duke University Press, 2016.

Roberto, Giovanni. "Community Kitchens: An Emerging Movement." In *Aftershocks of Disaster: Puerto Rico before and after the Storm*, edited by Yarimar Bonilla and Marisol LeBrón.

Roberto, Giovanni. "De Cuando el barrio entró a la UPR." In *Public Education: Crisis and Dialogue at the University of Puerto Rico*, special issue of *Sargasso* 1 (2011–12).

Robison, Cedric. *Black Marxism: The Making of the Black Radical Tradition*. Chapel Hill: University of North Carolina Press, 1983.

Rodney, Walter. *How Europe Underdeveloped Africa*. London: Verso, 2018.

Rodríguez-Casellas, Miguel. "De lo Superfluo." *8ogrados*, February 28, 2014. https://www.8ogrados.net/de-lo-superfluo/.

Rodríguez-Casellas, Miguel. "Echarpalantismo." *8ogrados*, October 25, 2013. https://www.8ogrados.net/echarpalantismo/.

Rodríguez-Casellas, Miguel. "El 'Adiós' de Miriam Muñiz-Varela." *8ogrados*, November 29, 2013. http://www.8ogrados.net/eladiosdemiriam-muniz-varela/.

Rodríguez-Centeno, Mabel. "Antiproductivismo y (trans)feminismo en tiempos de trap y capitalismo gore: El Caso de Puerto Rico" (unpublished ms.). Accessed August 8, 2019.

Rodríguez-Centeno, Mabel. "Las Perezas insulares." *8ogrados*, November 18, 2011. https://www.8ogrados.net/las-perezas-insulares/.

Rodríguez-Centeno, Mabel. "Sobre 'echaparlantismos' y perezas. Apuntes para mirarlas gracias reales de 1815 desde las desgracias fiscales del 2015," *Revista Umbral* 12 (2016).

Rodríguez-Centeno, Mabel. "¿Vagancia queer?" *8ogrados*, April 11, 2014. https://www.8ogrados.net/vagancia-queer/.

Rodríguez Moreno, Celenis. "La Mujer y sus versiones oscuras." In *Feminismo descolonial: Nuevos aportes teóricos-metodológicos a más de una década*, edited by Yuderkys Espinosa Miñoso. Quito, Ecuador: Ediciones Abya-Yala, 2018.

Rodríguez Moreno, Celenis. "Public Policies on Gender Equality: Technologies of Modern Colonial Gender." In *Decolonial Latin American, Caribbean and Latin Feminism: Contributions and Challenges*, edited by María Lugones, Yuderkys Espinosa Miñoso, and Nelson Maldonado-Torres. Lanham, MD: Rowman and Littlefield, forthcoming.

Rodríguez Moreno, Celenis, and Yuderkys Espinosa Miñoso. "Hacia la recuperación de una memoria de resistencia afrocaribeña a partir de los relatos de abuelas, madres e hijas de la comunidad Los Mercedes, República Dominicana." CLACSO (2020).

Rodríguez Saavedra, Dalila. "Vietnam, Puerto Rico: Lucha por los terrenos." *8ogrados*, September 26, 2019. https://www.8ogrados.net/vietnam-puerto-rico-lucha-por-los-terrenos/.

Rodriguez-Silva, Ileana. *Silencing Race: Disentangling Blackness, Colonialism and National Identities in Puerto Rico*. London: Palgrave, 2012.

Rodríguez-Velázquez, Katsí Yarí. "Degradando a la 'yal': Racialización y violencia antinegra en Puerto Rico." *Afro-Hispanic Review* 31, no. 7 (2018).

Rodríguez Velázquez, Víctor. "Personas trans sufren el desastre de María desde la marginalización." *Centro de Periodismo Investigativo*, September 23, 2019. http://periodismoinvestigativo.com/2019/09/personas-trans-sufren-el-desastre-de-maria-desde-la-marginacion/.

Roitman, Janet. *Fiscal Disobedience: An Anthropology of Fiscal Regulation in Central Africa*. Princeton, NJ: Princeton University Press, 2004.

Rosa, Alejandra, and Frances Robles. "A Wave of Daytime Killings Has Puerto Rico on Edge." *The New York Times*, January 13, 2019. https://www.nytimes.com /2019/01/13/us/puerto-rico-crime-murders-violence.html.

Rosado, Melissa. "Inhabiting the Aporias of Empire: Protest Politics in Contemporary Puerto Rico." In *Ethnographies of Empire*, edited by Carole McGranahan and John F. Collins. Durham, NC: Duke University Press, 2018.

Rosario, Melissa. "Public Pedagogy in the Creative Strike: Destabilizing Boundaries and Re-Imagining Resistance in the University of Puerto Rico." *Curriculum Inquiry* 45, no. 1 (2015).

Ruiz Kuilan, Gloria. "Una Orden ejecutiva extiende estado de emergencia hasta fin de año." *El Nuevo día*, July 5, 2019. https://www.elnuevodia.com/noticias /locales/nota/unaordenejecutivaextiendeestadodeemergenciadepuertoricoha stafindeano-2503731/.

Russell, Diana, and Jill Radford, eds. *Femicide: The Politics of Woman Killing*. New York: Twayne Publishers, 1992.

Salas Rivera, Raquel. "Highlights of Rosselló's Chat: Compiled and Translated by Raquel Salas Rivera." In *Puerto Rico Review: No. Impromptu*, edited by Cristina P. Díaz, Jorge Lefevre, and Claudia Becerra (2019). http://www .thepuertoricoreview.com/rickyrenuncia.

Salas Rivera, Raquel. *lo terciario / the tertiary*. Oakland, CA: Infinite Light, 2018.

Santiago-Valle, Kelvin. *Subject People and Colonial Discourses: Economic Transformation and Social Disorder in Puerto Rico 1898–1947*. Albany: SUNY Press, 2007.

Santos Febres, Mayra. "Geografía en decibeles: Utopías pancaribeñas y el territorio del rap." *Revista de crítica literaria latinoamericana* 23, no. 45 (1997).

Santos Febres, Mayra. "Puerto Rican Underground." *Centro: Journal of the Center for Puerto Rican Studies* 8, no. 1–2 (1996).

Santory-Jorge, Anayra. "Destroying a Country Is a Man's Business." Translated by Nicole Cecilia Delgado. In "On Debt, Blame, and Responsibility: Feminist Resistance in the Colony of Puerto Rico," edited by Rocío Zambrana, special section of *Critical Times: Interventions in Global Critical Theory*, forthcoming.

Santory-Jorge, Anayra. "Destruir un país es un asunto de hombres." *Actas del XI Coloquio Nacional sobre las Mujeres, Universidad de Puerto Rico, Recinto Universitario de Mayagüez: Feminismo, decolonialidad y otras intersecciones*, edited by Beatriz Llenín-Figueroa and Vanessa Vilches Norat. Cabo Rojo, PR: Editora Educación Emergente, 2019.

Santory-Jorge, Anayra. "Lo Prometido es deuda." In *Nada es igual: bocetos del país que nos acontece*. Cabo Rojo, PR: Editora Educación Emergente, 2018.

Sassen, Saskia. *Expulsions: Brutality and Complexity in the Global Economy*. Cambridge, MA: Harvard University Press, 2014.

Sassen, Saskia. "The Global City: Introducing a Concept." *Brown Journal of World Affairs* 11, no. 2 (2005).

Scavino, Dardo. "Colonialidad del poder: Una Invención jurídica de la conquista" (unpublished ms.). Accessed May 2018.

Scott, James. *Domination and the Arts of Resistance: Hidden Transcripts*. New Haven, CT: Yale University Press, 1990.

Segato, Rita. *La Crítica de la colonialidad en ocho ensayos*. Buenos Aires: Prometeo, 2013.

Segato, Rita. *La Escritura en el cuerpo de las mujeres asesinadas en Ciudad Juárez: Territorio, soberanía y crímenes de segundo estado*. Buenos Aires: Tinta Limón, 2013.

Segato, Rita. "Femigenocidio y feminicidio: Una Propuesta de tipificación." *Herramienta: Revista de debate y crítica marxista* (2011). https://herramienta.com.ar/articulo.php?id=1687.

Segato, Rita. *La Guerra contra las mujeres*. Madrid: Traficantes de Sueños, 2016.

"September 22, 2019." *Dialogando con Benny*. Radio Isla. www.radioisla.tv.

Sharpe, Christina. *In the Wake: On Blackness and Being*. Durham, NC: Duke University Press, 2016.

Singh, Ankur. "Puerto Ricans Transform Closed Schools into Community Centers." *Truthout*, May 12, 2019. https://truthout.org/articles/puerto-ricans-transform-closed-schools-into-community-centers/.

Soederberg, Susanne. *Debtfare States and the Poverty Industry: Money, Discipline and the Surplus Population*. London: Routledge, 2014.

Sosa Pascual, Omaya, Ana Campoy, and Michael Weissenstein. "Los Muertos de María." *Centro de Periodismo Investigativo*, September 28, 2019. http://periodismoinvestigativo.com/2018/09/los-muertos-de-maria/.

Sosa Pascual, Omaya, and John Sutter. "Puerto Rico tuvo un brote de leptospirosis tras el Huracán María pero el gobierno no lo dice." *Centro de Periodismo Investigativo*, July 3, 2018. http://periodismoinvestigativo.com/2018/07/puerto-rico-tuvo-un-brote-de-leptospirosis-tras-el-huracan-maria-pero-el-gobierno-no-lo-dice/.

Soss, Joe, Richard Fording, and Sanford Schram. *Disciplining the Poor: Neoliberal Paternalism and the Persistent Power of Race*. Chicago: University of Chicago Press, 2011.

Sparrow, Bartholomew. *The Insular Cases and the Emergence of the American Empire*. Lawrence: University of Kansas Press, 2006.

Spillers, Hortense. "Mama's Baby, Papa's Maybe: An American Grammar Book." *Diacritics* 17, no. 2 (1987).

Steinmetz, Katy. "Governor Ricardo Rosselló: Puerto Rico Is a 'Geopolitical Black Hole.'" *Time*, May 9, 2018. http://time.com/5271767/puerto-rico-governor-donald-trump-statehood-hurricane-maria/.

Stimilli, Elettra. *The Debt of the Living*. Albany: SUNY Press, 2017.

Stoler, Ann Laura. "Degress of Imperial Sovereignty." *Public Culture* 18, no. 1 (2006).

Stoler, Ann Laura. *Duress: Imperial Durabilities in Our Times*. Durham, NC: Duke University Press, 2016.

Sued Badillo, Jalil, and Angel López Cantos. *Puerto Rico Negro*. San Juan: Editorial Cultural, 1986.

Surillo Luna, Gricel. "From Peso to Dollar as the Official Currency." In *Enciclopedia de Puerto Rico*, September 15, 2014. https://enciclopediapr.org/en /encyclopedia/from-peso-to-dollar-as-the-official-currency/.

Terranova, Tiziana. "Debt and Autonomy: Lazzarato and the Constituent Powers of the Social." *The New Reader* 1 (2014).

Terrefe, Selamawit. "The Pornotrope of Decolonial Feminism." *Critical Philosophy of Race* 8, nos. 1–2 (2020).

Tighe, Claire, and Lauren Gurley. "Official Reports of Violence against Women in Puerto Rico Unreliable after Hurricane Maria." *Centro de Periodismo Investigativo*, May 7, 2018. http://periodismoinvestigativo.com/2018/05/datos -oficiales-de-violencia-contra-la-mujer-en-puerto-rico-no-son-confiables -despues-del-huracan-maria/.

Todorov, Tzvetan. *The Conquest of America: The Question of the Other*. New York: HarperCollins, 1984.

Torres Gotay, Benjamín. "Ciudadanos se reúnen en asambleas de pueblo y reclaman nueva gobernanza." *El Nuevo día*, August 17, 2019. https://www.elnuevodia .com/noticias/locales/nota/ciudadanossereunenenasambleasdepuebloyrecla mannuevagobernanza-2512354/.

Tort, Bernat. "Democracia, irracionalidad y violencia." *8ogrados*, January 15, 2011. http://www.8ogrados.net/democracia-irracionalidad-y-violencia/.

Toruella, Juan. *The Supreme Court and Puerto Rico: The Doctrine of Separate and Unequal*. San Juan: Editorial de la Universidad de Puerto Rico, 1988.

Tousissant, Éric, and Damien Millet. *Debt, the IMF, and the World Bank*. New York: Monthly Review Press, 2012.

Truth, Sojourner. "Ain't I a Woman?" In *Words of Fire: An Anthology of African-American Feminist Thought*, edited by Beverly Guy-Sheftall. New York: The New Press, 1995.

Tuck, Eve, and K. Wayne Yang. "Decolonization Is Not a Metaphor." *Decolonization: Indigeneity, Education and Society* 1, no. 1 (2012).

United States v. Sanchez, 992 F.2d 1143, 1151 (11th Cir. 1993).

Valencia, Sayak. *Gore Capitalism*. Translated by John Pluecker. Cambridge, MA: Semiotext(e), 2018.

Valentín Ortiz, Luis J. "Puerto Rico Announces Deal to Restructure Power Authority Debt." Reuters, May 3, 2019. https://www.reuters.com/articleus -usa-puertorico-prepa/puerto-rico-announces-deal-to-restructure-power -authority-debt-idUSKCN1SA026.

Valentín Ortiz, Luis J. "Puerto Rico's Fiscal Control Board: Parallel Government Full of Lawyers and Consultants." *Centro de Periodismo Investigativo*, August 1, 2018. http://periodismoinvestigativo.com/2018/08/puerto-ricos-fiscal-control -board-parallel-government-full-of-lawyers-and-consultants/.

Valentín Ortiz, Luis J. "Rosselló deroga comisión de auditoría de la deuda." *Caribbean Business*, April 9, 2017. https://cb.pr/rossello-firma-ley-que-deroga -comision-para-auditar-la-deuda/.

Vega Solís, Cristina, Raquel Martínez Buján, and Myriam Paredes Chauca, eds. *Cuidado, Comunidad, y común: Extracciones, apropiaciones y sostenimiento de la vida*. Madrid: Traficante de Sueños, 2018.

Venator-Santiago, Charles. "From the Insular Cases to Camp X-Ray: Agamben's State of Exception and the United States Territorial Law." *Studies in Law, Politics, and Society* 39 (2006).

Venator-Santiago, Charles. "Mapping the Contours of the History of the Extension of US Citizenship to Puerto Rico—1898 to the Present." *Centro: Journal of the Center for Puerto Rican Studies* 29, no. 1 (2017).

Venator-Santiago, Charles. "A Note on the Puerto Rican De-Naturalization Exception of 1948." *Centro: Journal of the Center for Puerto Rican Studies* 29, no. 1 (2017).

Venator-Santiago, Charles. *Puerto Rico and the Origins of US Global Empire: The Disembodied Shade*. London: Routledge, 2015.

Vergès, Françoise. "'I Am Not the Slave of Slavery': The Politics of Reparation in (French) Postslavery Communities." In *Frantz Fanon: Critical Perspectives*, edited by Anthony C. Alessandrini. London: Routledge, 1999.

Villa Rodríguez, José. *Crimen y criminalidad en Puerto Rico: El Sujeto criminal*. San Juan: Ediciones SITUM, 2006.

Villarrubia-Mendoza, Jacqueline, and Roberto Vélez-Vélez. "Puerto Rican People's Assemblies Shift from Protest to Proposal." *Jacobin*, August 24, 2019. https://www.jacobinmag.com/2019/08/puerto-rico-ricardo-rossello-peoples -assemblies.

Wacquant, Loïc. *Punishing the Poor: The Neoliberal Government of Social Insecurity*. Durham, NC: Duke University Press, 2009.

Walker, Jeremy, and Melinda Cooper. "Genealogies of Resilience: From Systems Ecology to the Political Economy of Crisis Adaptation." *Security Dialogue* 42, no. 2 (2011).

Wallerstein, Immanuel. *The Modern World System*, volume 1: *Capitalist Agriculture and the Origins of the European World-Economy in the Sixteenth Century*. Berkeley: University of California Press, 2011.

Walsh, Mary William. "Puerto Rico Fights for Chapter 9 Bankruptcy in Supreme Court." *The New York Times*, March 22, 2016. https://www.nytimes.com/2016 /03/23/business/dealbook/puerto-rico-fights-for-chapter-9-bankruptcy-in -supreme-court.html.

Williams, Eric. *Capitalism and Slavery*. Chapel Hill: University of North Carolina Press, 1944.

Wynter, Sylvia. "Beyond Miranda's Meanings: Un/Silencing the 'Demonic Ground' of Caliban's 'Woman.'" In *Out of the Kumbla: Caribbean Women and Literature*, edited by Carole Boyce Davies and Elaine Savory Fido. Trenton, NJ: Africa World Press, 1990.

Wynter, Sylvia. "1492: A New World View." In *Race, Discourse, and the Origin of the Americas: A New World View*, edited by Sylvia Wynter, Vera Lawrence Hyatt, and Rex Nettleford. Washington, DC: Smithsonian Institution Press, 1995.

Wynter, Sylvia. "Unsettling the Coloniality of Being/Power/Truth/Freedom: Towards the Human, after Man, Its Overrepresentation—an Argument." *CR: The New Centennial Review* 3, no. 3 (2003).

Zambrana, Rocío. "Abstraction and Critique in Marx's Capital." In *Critique in German Philosophy*, edited by María del Rosario Acosta and Colin McQuillian. Albany: SUNY Press, forthcoming.

Zambrana, Rocío. "Black Feminist Tactics: On la Colectiva Feminista en Construcción's Politics without Guarantee." In *The Decolonial Geographies of Puerto Rico's 2019 Summer Protests: A Forum for Society and Space* (February 2020).

Zambrana, Rocío. "Boundary, Ambivalence, Jaibería, or, How to Appropriate Hegel." In *Creolizing the Canon*, edited by Michael Monahan. Lanham, MD: Rowman and Littlefield, 2017.

Zambrana, Rocío. "Checklists: On Puerto Rico's SoVerano." *Critical Times: Interventions in Global Critical Theory*, 3, no. 2 (2020).

Zambrana, Rocío. "Deudas coloniales/Colonial Debts," In *Una Proposición modesta: Puerto Rico a prueba/A Modest Proposal: Puerto Rico's Crucible*, an initiative of Allora and Calzadilla, edited by Sara Nadal-Melisó. Barcelona: Fundació Antoni Tàpies, 2018.

Zambrana, Rocío. "Distopía y contramemoria descolonial y afropesimista: reflexiones en torno a Yuderkys Espinosa Miñoso y Saidiya Hartman." In *Utopie et dystopie dans l'imagination politique*, edited by Obed Frausto and Angélica Montes Montoya, forthcoming.

Zambrana, Rocío. "Paradoxes of Neoliberalism and the Tasks of Critical Theory Today." *Critical Horizons: A Journal of Philosophy and Social Theory* 14, no. 1 (2013).

Zambrana, Rocío. "Pasarse Políticamente—Interrupting Neoliberal Temporalities in Puerto Rico." In *Collective Temporalities and the Construction of the Future*, edited by María del Rosario Acosta and Gustavo Quintero. *Diacritics* 46, no. 2 (2018).

Zambrana-González, Luis A. "Privatización carcelaria por la cocina." *8ogrados*, May 18, 2018. http://www.8ogrados.net/privatizacion-carcelaria-por-la -cocina/.

Zambrana-González, Luis A. "Punitivismo como negocio: Un Terrible presagio." *8ogrados*, December 9, 2016. http://www.8ogrados.net/punitivismo-como -negocio-un-terrible-presagio/.

Zavaleta Mercado, René. *Lo Nacional-Popular en Bolivia*. Mexico City: Siglo XXI, 1986.

INDEX

Page numbers followed by *f* indicate illustrations.

credit, 25; debt and, 31, 93–100; Dienst on, 96–97; Marx on, 28, 91–92, 96; Mitropoulos on, 98–99

creditor-debtor relation, 10–12, 15–16, 29–32; asymmetries in, 84–92; Godreau-Aubert on, 86; Lazzarato on, 175n24; Marx on, 90–92

criminal justice system, 66, 105, 110, 209n154

criollo, 48–49, 186n177

culpability, 30–31, 43; debt as, 84, 90, 148; markers of, 15; poverty and, 121

debt, 86, 99, 164, 204n42; cartography of, 23, 24, 44–45, 51; as coloniality, 10–12, 23, 40, 143; credit and, 31, 93–100; critical theory of, 89–90; definitions of, 21, 86, 87, 99; disposability and, 41, 43–44; feminist reading of, 32–35; guilt and, 84, 90, 148; imaginary of, 46–48, 47f; moralization of, 101–2; scholarship on, 173n8, 175n24; "unpayable," 45

debt crises, 30, 125; Lazzarato on, 22–25, 84, 175n24

decoloniality, 19, 145–52; decolonization versus, 144–46, 151–52; definitions of, 14–15; as reparations, 16, 139–66. See also coloniality

decolonization, 12, 14, 142; Maldonado-Torres on, 144–46; Rebollo-Gil on, 213n77; Tuck on, 142, 148, 219n7

degenerada (degenerate/degendered), 44–45, 184n158

Deleuze, Gilles, 24–30, 177n53, 178n71

desalambrar, 153–54, 155f, 161

Descartes, René, 42

deterritorialization, 29–30. See also reterritorialization

Dienst, Richard, 85, 93–99, 206n109

Dietz, James, 53, 59

Dinzey-Flores, Zaire, 48–49, 68

disaster capitalism, 9, 169n24, 180n113

disposability: debt and, 41, 43–44; logic of, 79–81; visibility and, 45–49, 79–80

domestic violence, 7, 42–43, 125, 130–31; femicide and, 33, 40, 45, 49–51; impunity and, 51, 187n187; incidence of, 49–50. See also sexual violence

Dominica, 168n8

Downes v. Bidwell (1901), 59

Dred Scott decision (1857), 58

Droz, Nina, 134

Dussel, Enrique, 42

earthquakes (2020), 168n15

Echar Pa'lante campaign, 122–24, 126, 128

echarpalantismo (forward-facing resilience), 18, 112, 123–28

Ecuador, 104

ELA. See Estado Libre Asociado

Embargo Feminista (2019), 86, 105–9, 108f

emergency. See state of emergency

emigration. See migration

enclosure, 19, 35, 37, 145, 156; of bodies, 85–86, 94–95

Energy Affairs Administration, 63

entramado de entendidos (framework of sense), 111, 115, 119

environmental movement, 63, 195n85; alliances with, 115–17; deposit of toxic coal ash in Peñuelas and, 107, 159

Escobar, Arturo, 178n79

escrache, 208n149

Estado Libre Asociado (ELA), 61; creation of, 10, 23, 60; "obituary" of, 11f

Eurocentrism, 37–38, 56

exceptionality, 73–74, 112–13; colonial, 54–71. See also state of emergency

failure: unpayable debt, 15, 205n83; personal responsibility, 25, 31, 45; political power, 18, 111; strike, 112, 116, 117, 119. See also Halberstam, Jack; neoliberalism; Rebollo-Gil, Guillermo; Rodriguez-Centeno, Mabel

"indebted man," 22, 23, 25, 30–31, 45
"indebted woman," 21–25, 44, 51
Insular Cases (1901–22), 54, 57, 59,
    191n48
International Monetary Fund (IMF),
    63, 83, 202n10
interruption, 12; subversive, 86–87,
    93, 96, 110–12. *See also* refusal
Irrizarry, Yoryie, 137

James, C. L. R., 82
Jim Crow laws, 58
Jones Act: of 1917, 54, 60, 62, 192n57;
    of 1920, 7, 54, 60, 168n14
Jornada Se Acabaron las Promesas,
    53, 82, 104, 132, 135*f*
jornaleros (day workers), 127, 131
la Junta. *See* Fiscal Control Board

Karera, Axelle, 146, 147, 149
Keleher, Julia, 130
Keynesian state, 25
Kilómetro Cero, 167n3
Klein, Naomi, 83, 169n24
Kobes, Deborah, 195n90

La Fountain, Lawrence, 137
labor, 35–36; reserve army of, 95; use
    value of, 114; vagrancy laws and, 127
land rescue/occupation. See *rescate*
Law 97 (2015), 102–3
Law 600 (1950), 54, 60
"laziness," 44, 66–67, 95, 142–43.
    See also culpability; *vagancia queer*
Lazzarato, Maurizio, 10, 16; on debt,
    22–25, 84, 175n24; on governmen-
    tality, 24–28; Gregoratto and, 90;
    on "indebted man," 23, 25, 30–31;
    on taxation, 30
LeBrón, Marisol, 17, 113; on policing,
    70, 114, 117–18; on punitive gover-
    nance, 55, 67–68
Lebrón, Pedro, 200n185
leptospirosis, 7
LGBTQ community, 136–37; alliances
    of, 115; police raids on, 136; protests

by, 6, 112–30, 134–38, 136*f*, 218n45;
    transphobia against, 50, 79, 130–31,
    133, 138
libreta de jornal, 127, 131
López-Serrano, Edda, 50, 187n187
Lorey, Isabell, 173n11
Lugones, María, 13–14, 38–40
Luxemburg, Rosa, 179nn100–101

machista violence, 32–33, 51,
    187nn186–87. *See also* femicide
Machuchal, 163, 227n122
Maldonado-Torres, Nelson, 17; on
    coloniality, 13–14, 42–43; on decolo-
    niality, 144–46; on "metaphysical ca-
    tastrophe," 13–17, 24, 41–42, 227n130
Mano Dura contra el Crimen, 68–70,
    69*f*, 118, 136–38, 211n12
Manos a la Obra (Operation Boot-
    strap), 62, 123, 154
Marronage. See *cimarronaje*
Marshall Trilogy (1823–32), 58
Martin, Ricky, 131
Marx, Karl, 28, 35, 113–14; on alien-
    ated labor, 90; on credit, 28, 91–92,
    96; on debt, 17–18, 85–99; on
    slavery, 35–38
Mbembe, Achille, 41
Medina-Fuentes, José Nicolás, 103
migration: Dominican, 50, 162;
    Haitian, 162; Puerto Rican, 62, 125,
    126, 169n18
Mills, James, 89–92
Mitropoulos, Angela, 93, 98–99
Monsanto, 197n104
mortgage crisis (2008), 72
Moscoso, Marina, 19, 145, 161–63
Moten, Fred, 100
Muñiz-Varela, Miriam, 17, 19, 80;
    on "bioeconomic management,"
    184n159; on Caño Martín Peña,
    157–58; on coloniality of power,
    65–67; on economy of catastrophe,
    54–55, 65, 70–71, 75, 81; on Internal
    Revenue Code, 62; on necroecon-
    omy, 153; on rescue/occupation, 145

race, 18, 49, 126–29, 153; finance and, 179n105; LeBrón on, 70; Lugones on, 13–14, 38–40; Quijano on, 37–39; Rodríguez-Centeno on, 215n109; spatial production of, 118
rationality, neoliberal, 51, 63, 75, 79–81, 93, 100–101
Rebollo-Gil, Guillermo, 18, 130, 188n203; *entramado de entendidos*, 111, 119; on *pasarse políticamente*, 111, 116–17; on student strikes, 112–21, 132
reckoning, 99–109
refusal, 14, 40, 45; as interruption, 31, 143, 147, 152; laziness, 128; to pay, 15, 101, 102, 151; power of, 111; productivity, 112; as protest, 111, 122; Rodriguez-Velazquez on, 49; as a tactic, 12, 18, 44, 52, 122, 126, 214n88; to work, 31, 46, 129. See also *pasarse politicamente*; *vagancia queer*
reggaetón, 136–38, 218n145
Reglamento Especial de Jornaleros, 127
reparations, 219n8; decoloniality as, 16, 139–66; Fanon on, 19, 148–51; Sharpe on, 151
rescate (rescue), 19, 152–64, 155*f*, 171n34
reterritorialization, 29–30; coloniality of power and, 36–37, 43, 142; necropolitical effects of, 45–46
Rivera, Raquel Z., 136
Rivera-Ramos, Juan Carlos, 158
Rivera-Rideau, Petra, 136
Rivera-Servera, Ramón, 218n145
Roberto, Giovanni, 117, 212n45, 212n47
Rodríguez-Casellas, Miguel, 107–10, 122, 158; on *echarpalantismo*, 18, 112, 123–25; on Pedro Rosselló, 126
Rodríguez-Centeno, Mabel, 18, 126–29
Rodríguez Cotto, Sandra, 130
Rodríguez-López, Luz Marie, 131–32

Rodríguez Moreno, Celenis, 39, 146
Rodríguez-Velázquez, Katsí Yarí, 48, 49
Roitman, Janet, 102, 108–9, 210n166
Rosselló, Pedro, 68–69, 126, 137
Rosselló, Ricardo "Ricky": colonial political economy and, 8–9; Hurricane María and, 130–31; protests against, 3–7, 4–6*f*, 50, 104, 130, 133–34; resignation of, 3, 135, 158

Salas Rivera, Raquel, 1–2, 130–31, 164
Santory-Jorge, Anayra, 17, 53; on "catastrophe by attrition," 17, 54–55, 73–75, 189n9; on risk, 77
Santos Febres, Mayra, 136
Schmitt, Carl, 55–56
Scott, James, 126
Segato, Rita, 16, 128, 131; on coloniality of gender, 24, 39–40; on "expressive violence," 50–51; on femicide, 40
self-management, 7, 27, 125–26, 153, 158–64
sexual violence, 32–33, 38–43, 49–52, 125, 130–31, 187nn186–87
Sharpe, Christina, 17, 55, 71, 78–79, 140, 201n188; on afterlife of slavery, 79, 140; Hartman and, 78–79; on wake work, 142, 143
sinvergüencería (shamelessness), 137, 138
slavery, 82, 150; afterlife of, 13, 78–79, 140, 143; *cimarronaje*/marronage and, 58, 158, 214n91, 227n122; economy of, 36–37, 140–41; Hartman on afterlife of slavery, 13, 78–79, 140, 143; Marx on, 35–38; Rodríguez-Centeno on, 215n109; Sharpe on, 79, 140
sovereignty, 74; Atiles-Osoria on, 56, 60–61; neoliberal subjectivity and, 34; subversions of, 171n40
Spanish-American War (1898), 54, 57–58
Spillers, Hortense, 182n125